U.S. TRADE

FOCUS ON EDUCATION, HEALTHCARE, LEGAL, AND INFRASTRUCTURE SERVICES

TRADE ISSUES, POLICIES AND LAWS

Additional books in this series can be found on Nova's website
under the Series tab.

Additional e-books in this series can be found on Nova's website
under the e-book tab.

TRADE ISSUES, POLICIES AND LAWS

U.S. TRADE

FOCUS ON EDUCATION, HEALTHCARE, LEGAL, AND INFRASTRUCTURE SERVICES

CARINA VINCENT
EDITOR

nova
publishers
New York

NOTICE TO THE READER

The Publisher has taken reasonable care in the preparation of this book, but makes no expressed or implied warranty of any kind and assumes no responsibility for any errors or omissions. No liability is assumed for incidental or consequential damages in connection with or arising out of information contained in this book. The Publisher shall not be liable for any special, consequential, or exemplary damages resulting, in whole or in part, from the readers' use of, or reliance upon, this material. Any parts of this book based on government reports are so indicated and copyright is claimed for those parts to the extent applicable to compilations of such works.

Independent verification should be sought for any data, advice or recommendations contained in this book. In addition, no responsibility is assumed by the publisher for any injury and/or damage to persons or property arising from any methods, products, instructions, ideas or otherwise contained in this publication.

This publication is designed to provide accurate and authoritative information with regard to the subject matter covered herein. It is sold with the clear understanding that the Publisher is not engaged in rendering legal or any other professional services. If legal or any other expert assistance is required, the services of a competent person should be sought. FROM A DECLARATION OF PARTICIPANTS JOINTLY ADOPTED BY A COMMITTEE OF THE AMERICAN BAR ASSOCIATION AND A COMMITTEE OF PUBLISHERS.

Additional color graphics may be available in the e-book version of this book.

Library of Congress Cataloging-in-Publication Data

ISBN: 978-1-63117-423-0

Published by Nova Science Publishers, Inc. † New York

CONTENTS

PREFACE

This book discusses developments in the United States' exports and imports of professional services, with a focus on education, healthcare, and legal services. The United States continues to be a world leader in professional services, which generated a cross-border trade surplus of nearly $50 billion in 2011. The expansion of professional services trade in recent years has been driven by a number of factors. Globalization, including businesses setting up operations in foreign markets, has created trade opportunities for diverse professional services providers, such as legal and management consulting professionals. This book focuses on United States trend reports from 2012 and 2013.

Chapter 1 - *Recent Trends in U.S. Services Trade: 2013 Annual Report* discusses developments in the United States' exports and imports of professional services, with a focus on education, healthcare, and legal services. The United States continues to be a world leader in professional services, which generated a cross-border trade surplus of nearly $50 billion in 2011. The contribution of U.S. professional services to U.S. GDP was $2.2 trillion in 2011, which accounted for nearly 20 percent of U.S. GDP. Employment in most of these industries increased in 2011 and, as a group, professional services were the leading source of U.S. private sector employment. All three of the professional services industries covered in this report are global leaders, yet they face strong competitive pressures at home and abroad. The U.S. market for higher education is mature and relatively saturated, with universities seeking alternative revenue sources due to tight budgets. The U.S. healthcare industry is integrating technology to meet growing demand, cut costs, and improve patient outcomes. Legal services providers are facing increased competition from nontraditional suppliers, technology-driven commoditization of legal services, and increased use of in-house counsel. Although all three industries are expected to maintain their leadership positions in the near to medium term, these competitive pressures should continue to present substantial challenges.

Chapter 2 - *Recent Trends in U.S. Services Trade: 2012 Annual Report* focuses on exports and imports of infrastructure services, including banking, insurance, logistics, retail, securities, and telecommunications services. These services are essential inputs to firms in virtually every economic sector. The largest infrastructure service firms are located in developed countries and offer their services globally through cross-border trade and affiliate transactions. Economic growth in developing and emerging countries continues to create new opportunities for expansion and investment by infrastructure service firms, though many countries maintain regulations and policies that pose challenges for stakeholders in services trade.

Infrastructure service industries have shown signs of recovery following the recent financial crisis and ensuing economic downturn. Employment in infrastructure services continued to decline slightly in 2010, but wages, productivity, and value added grew strongly. While the United States had a small cross-border trade deficit in infrastructure services, it maintained a large trade surplus in affiliate sales, which accounted for the majority of infrastructure services trade.

In: U.S. Trade
Editor: Carina Vincent

ISBN: 978-1-63117-423-0
© 2014 Nova Science Publishers, Inc.

Chapter 1

RECENT TRENDS IN U.S. SERVICES: 2013 ANNUAL REPORT[*]

Joann Peterson, Cynthia Payne, Eric Forden, Samantha Pham, Tamar Khachaturian and Isaac Wohl

ABSTRACT

Recent Trends in U.S. Services Trade: 2013 Annual Report discusses developments in the United States' exports and imports of professional services, with a focus on education, healthcare, and legal services. The United States continues to be a world leader in professional services, which generated a cross-border trade surplus of nearly $50 billion in 2011. The contribution of U.S. professional services to U.S. GDP was $2.2 trillion in 2011, which accounted for nearly 20 percent of U.S. GDP. Employment in most of these industries increased in 2011 and, as a group, professional services were the leading source of U.S. private sector employment. All three of the professional services industries covered in this report are global leaders, yet they face strong competitive pressures at home and abroad. The U.S. market for higher education is mature and relatively saturated, with universities seeking alternative revenue sources due to tight budgets. The U.S. healthcare industry is integrating technology to meet growing demand, cut costs, and improve patient outcomes. Legal services providers are facing increased competition from nontraditional suppliers, technology-driven commoditization of legal services, and increased use of in-house counsel. Although all three industries are expected to maintain their leadership positions in the near to medium term, these competitive pressures should continue to present substantial challenges.

ACRONYMS AND ABBREVIATIONS

ABA	American Bar Association
ARRA	American Recovery and Reinvestment Act

---

[*] This is an edited, reformatted and augmented version of U.S. International Trade Commission Publication, No. 4412, dated July 2013.

BEA	Bureau of Economic Analysis
CAGR	compound annual growth rate
EHR	electronic health records
EIU	Economist Intelligence Unit
EU	European Union
FTE	full-time equivalent
GATS	General Agreement on Trade in Services
GDP	gross domestic product
IT	information technology
J.D.	Juris Doctor
LLM	Master of Laws
MOOC	massive open online course
NAICU	National Association of Independent Colleges and Universities
NHS	National Health Service
NTD	neglected tropical disease
OECD	Organisation for Economic Co-operation and Development
PPACA	Patient Protection and Affordable Care Act
U-M	University of Michigan
UN	United Nations
UNCTAD	United Nations Conference on Trade and Development
UPMC	University of Pittsburgh Medical Center
USDOC	U.S. Department of Commerce
USITC	U.S. International Trade Commission
WHO	World Health Organization
WTO	World Trade Organization

EXECUTIVE SUMMARY

The United States is the world's largest services market and was the world's largest cross-border exporter and importer of services in 2011.[1] Global trade in services continued to recover and expand from the 2008–09 recession, with U.S. exports and imports both increasing rapidly (figure ES.1).

This report, part of an annual series prepared by the U.S. International Trade Commission (Commission or USITC), provides an overview of U.S. trade in services. This year's report primarily focuses on recent developments in certain professional services: education, healthcare, and legal services.[2] These industries are essential to modern economies; they build human capital, promote human development and well-being, and help businesses navigate the legal and regulatory environment. Professional service providers like lawyers, accountants, healthcare workers, and educators are among the most highly educated and highly skilled workers in the global economy. The United States remained a world leader in professional services, generating a cross-border trade surplus in these industries of nearly $50 billion in 2011.

The expansion of professional services trade in recent years has been driven by a number of factors. Globalization, including businesses setting up operations in foreign markets, has created trade opportunities for diverse professional services providers, such as legal and management consulting professionals. The relatively weak domestic economy has stimulated growth in professional services trade, as U.S. legal, management consulting, and engineering firms are expanding by opening offices in fast-growing foreign markets, particularly in the Asia-Pacific region. Continued progress in digital technologies and the increase in global access to broadband Internet also allow increased trade in professional services—for example, through telemedicine and online education.

Key Findings

Total U.S. Trade in Services

The United States Was the Leading Global Services Supplier in 2010–11

In 2011, services contributed $9.1 trillion (79 percent) to U.S. private sector gross domestic product (GDP) and accounted for 84 million private sector employees (82 percent of the total). In 2011, U.S. services exports were $587 billion, or 14 percent of global cross-border exports, while imports were $393 billion, or 10 percent of global imports. Travel services and passenger fares accounted for the largest share of U.S. services trade by value in 2011, representing 26 percent of exports and 28 percent of imports. Professional services were the second-largest traded service category, accounting for 21 percent and 19 percent of total services exports and imports, respectively.

U.S. Cross-Border Trade in Services Continued to Expand in 2011

The U.S. cross-border trade surplus in services reached $194 billion in 2011, increasing by 14 percent from 2010. U.S. exports showed continued strength following the 2008–09 recession and grew by 9 percent in 2011, compared to a 7 percent compound annual growth rate during 2006–10. A number of services industries recorded strong export growth in 2011, including construction services (67 percent growth); architectural, engineering, and other technical services (31 percent); and passenger fares (18 percent).

Affiliates' Services Transactions Rebounded in 2010

Sales by foreign affiliates of U.S. firms, the leading channel by which many U.S. services are provided to foreign markets, increased by 6 percent to $1.1 trillion in 2010. Distribution services (including wholesale and retail trade) led affiliate sales, accounting for $354 million or 30 percent of total sales. Professional services accounted for $96 billion or 8 percent of the total. Leading U.S. markets for affiliate sales were the United Kingdom, Canada, Japan, and Ireland. Purchases from U.S. affiliates of foreign firms were $696 billion in 2010, an increase of 4 percent over 2009 as the U.S. domestic economy recovered from the 2008–09 recession. The United Kingdom was the leading supplier of such services (15 percent), and over 55 percent of these services were purchased from affiliates of EU-based firms.

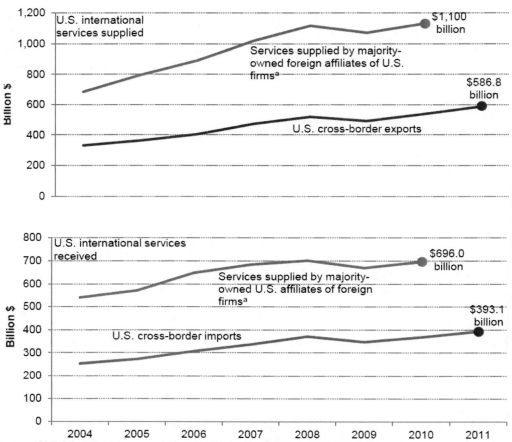

Source: USDOC, BEA, *Survey of Current Business*, October 2012, 15–58.
Note: Data prior to 2004 were calculated differently and are therefore not included in this figure.
[a] Data are available only through 2010.

Figure ES.1. The United States posted large increases in cross-border and affiliate trade in recent years.

Professional Services

Cross-Border Exports of Professional Services Accounted for the Majority of U.S. Trade in Professional Services during 2010–11

Professional services accounted for 21 percent of total U.S. cross-border exports in 2011 and 19 percent of cross-border imports. The United States exported $124 billion and imported $75 billion of such services, resulting in a $49 billion surplus in 2011. Leading professional services exports by share were management and consulting services (26 percent), research and development and testing services (19 percent), and education services (18 percent). The United Kingdom and Switzerland were the top markets for U.S. professional services exports in 2011.

In contrast to many services industries, sales by foreign affiliates of U.S. professional services firms were smaller than cross-border exports of professional services in 2010. Such sales totaled $96 billion in 2010 and were relatively concentrated, with three industries accounting for 60 percent of the total: architectural, engineering, and other technical services

(26 percent); management, scientific, and technical consulting services (20 percent); and accounting, auditing, and bookkeeping services (13 percent). Services purchased from U.S. affiliates of foreign firms totaled $44 billion and were concentrated in advertising and related services, which accounted for $28 billion—nearly two-thirds of total purchases.

Professional Services' Value Added, Employment, and Wages All Grew in 2011

The contribution of U.S. professional services to U.S. GDP was $2.2 trillion in 2011, accounting for 24 percent of total services GDP. The output of professional services grew by 3 percent in 2011, outpacing growth in the private sector (2 percent) and in all other major services categories except electronic services (6 percent). Among the professional services industries themselves, however, output growth varied: output rose for miscellaneous professional, scientific, and technical services (6.5 percent) and health care and social assistance (1.8 percent) in 2011, while it declined for legal services (−1.7 percent) and management of companies and enterprises (−0.5 percent).

Professional services employed 26 million full-time equivalent (FTE) employees in 2011, or 26 percent of total U.S. private sector employment. Employment in these services increased by 2 percent in 2011, and all sectors added employees during the year except for legal services, which shrank by 400,000 FTEs. Healthcare and social assistance led all professional services, with over 15 million FTEs, or 58 percent of the total (figure ES.2). Annual salaries in professional services, measured in wages per FTE, grew in all subsectors in 2011, and were led by legal services ($88,949) and miscellaneous professional, scientific, and technical services ($79,218).

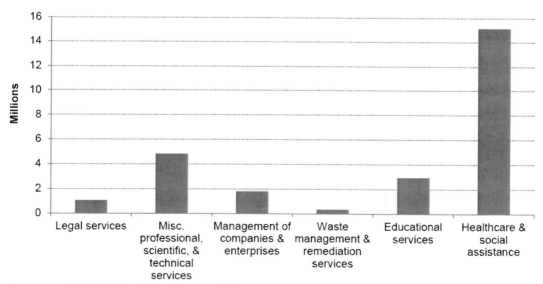

Source: USDOC, BEA, "Full-Time Equivalent Employees by Industry," interactive tables, September 17, 2012.

Figure ES.2. Employment in healthcare services led all professional services in 2011.

Professional Services Trade Faces a Variety of Entry and Operational Barriers

Barriers to professional services trade in some cases are the byproduct of a country's focus on protecting and developing its domestic workforce. Such barriers can include economic needs tests, whereby foreign providers are allowed to enter only if domestic firms or individuals cannot supply such services, and quotas limiting the number of foreign providers. Restrictions on commercial establishment (the form a new business may take) can also impede professional services, such as requirements that foreign firms operate as joint ventures with domestic firms or that a certain number of staff or managerial positions be filled by citizens or permanent residents. Government and private sector certification and licensing requirements can also restrict professional services trade; such requirements are often intended to protect consumers, but they can be unclear and unequal across countries.

Many U.S. Professional Services Firms Expect Demand Abroad to Increase Faster Than Domestic Demand

While the U.S. economy has recovered in recent years, demand growth in developing countries is likely to continue to exceed demand growth in the United States. For this reason, many large U.S. professional services providers will likely continue to expand overseas by establishing new offices, merging with foreign companies, and recruiting foreign consumers. For example, budgetary constraints may continue to put pressure on U.S. public education funding, prompting universities in the United States to seek more foreign students, who are likelier to pay full-cost tuition. Healthcare spending in developed countries may grow more slowly as consumers bear rising shares of healthcare costs, but demand is expected to grow rapidly in Asia, where populations are becoming both wealthier and older. In the legal services industry, price competition and pressure from nontraditional providers will likely require consolidation in the U.S. industry, motivating firms to follow their clients into high-growth markets abroad.

Education Services

The United States Is the Global Leader in Education Services; However Revenue Growth Is Expected to Be Modest over the Next Five Years

U.S. education services, limited in this study to services in higher education, accounted for nearly one-quarter of the $903 billion global education services industry in 2011, roughly twice the size of the second-largest market, China (12 percent of global revenues). In 2011, international education services revenues increased by 5 percent, reflecting growth in many developing countries. In the United States and other developed countries, education is a mature industry and growth in these markets is below the global average. By contrast, in developing markets such as China, university capacity is rapidly expanding to accommodate rising education demand. Relatively modest revenue growth, tighter budgets, and weakness in the U.S. economy are expected to lead U.S. universities to continue to seek additional revenue sources by working to attract out-of-state and foreign students, who tend to pay higher tuition.

Growth in U.S. Cross-Border Exports of Education Services Reflected Higher Numbers of Foreign Students As Well As Tuition Increases in 2011

The U.S. trade surplus in education services grew by 9 percent in 2011 to $17 billion. U.S. exports of these services (i.e., foreign students' education expenditures in the United

States) grew by 8 percent to $23 billion during the year, as the number of foreign students grew by 6 percent to 764,495 students. Asian countries were the top markets for U.S. education services, including China ($5 billion), India ($3 billion), and the Republic of Korea ($2 billion). Roughly 274,000 U.S. students studied abroad in 2011, causing U.S. imports to increase by 7 percent to $6 billion. Leading destinations for U.S. students were the United Kingdom ($1 billion), Italy ($540 million), and Spain ($498 million).

Healthcare Services

Global Healthcare Expenditures Grew Steadily, Buoyed by Public Expenditures during 2006–10, and Global Expenditures Will Likely Continue to Grow Moderately in the Near Term

The United States posted a trade surplus in healthcare services, which totaled $1.9 billion in 2011. In contrast, services supplied by foreign-owned U.S. affiliates significantly exceed services supplied by foreign affiliates of U.S. firms, largely due to opportunities available in the U.S. market. Motivated partly by rising healthcare costs, the United States passed major healthcare reform legislation overhauling the financing and delivery of these services. Global spending on healthcare expanded at a compound annual growth rate of 8 percent during 2006–10 to $6.6 trillion, over 10 percent of global GDP. Public expenditures fueled the increase in global healthcare spending during the period, as private expenditures slowed in the United States (which is by far the world's largest healthcare market) and many European countries. Globally, healthcare spending is forecast to grow moderately in the near future, given that slow growth in developed countries will temper sharper spending increases in fast-growing developing countries. The healthcare industry is increasingly adopting information technology such as telemedicine and electronic records management to reduce healthcare costs and improve outcomes. Additionally, healthcare consumerism, whereby patients take a more active role in their healthcare decisions and expenditures, also may contribute to improved health outcomes and slow the growth in costs.

The United States Continued to Post a Trade Surplus in Healthcare Services in 2011 As Cross-Border Healthcare Investment Grew

Trading largely with its regional partners Canada and Mexico, the United States posted cross-border exports of healthcare services worth $3 billion in 2011, while imports were $1.1 billion, generating a surplus of $1.9 billion. At the same time, as the world's largest and most profitable market, the United States was the leading destination for healthcare investment. Healthcare services purchased from U.S. affiliates of foreign firms exceeded sales by foreign affiliates of U.S. firms by a substantial margin. Certain U.S. healthcare firms are looking overseas to expand, and are providing increasing volumes of services in foreign markets. Most U.S. healthcare firms invest directly in existing facilities and form joint ventures. In certain markets such as India, China, and South America, burdensome regulations and the lack of existing facilities may be limiting foreign participation.

Legal Services

Facing a Declining Domestic Market, the U.S. Legal Services Industry Is Restructuring, with Revenue and Profits Expected to Grow Moderately in the Near Term

The market for U.S. legal services shrank by 7 percent in 2011, continuing a trend of declining revenues since the 2008–09 recession. By contrast, the EU market grew by 4 percent and markets in the Asia-Pacific region grew by 5 percent in 2011. Despite falling revenues, the United States remained the world's largest legal services market, accounting for 39 percent of the global total, though this figure is down from 43 percent before the recession. U.S. law firms are likely to continue to face diverse challenges, including lower-cost alternatives and nontraditional providers, technology-driven commoditization of legal services, the growing popularity of alternative fee arrangements, and the increased use of in-house counsel. In response, law firms are expected to continue the trend of downsizing and holding partners to higher productivity standards; some are de-equitizing equity partners (partners who own a share of the firm's profits) or reducing their number.

Despite Weakness in the U.S. Legal Services Market, the U.S. Trade Surplus in These Services Increased in 2011

The U.S. trade surplus in legal services expanded to $5.7 billion in 2011, up 4 percent from 2010. U.S. export growth (4 percent) was significantly lower than import growth (16 percent), reflecting recovery of the U.S. legal services market from the economic downturn. U.S. exports of legal services were relatively concentrated, with the United Kingdom and Japan accounting for nearly one-third of the industry's exports in 2011. Sales by foreign affiliates of U.S. law firms increased by nearly 60 percent in 2009 to $5.0 billion before declining in 2010 to $4.9 billion (still vastly exceeding the $111 million in purchases from U.S. affiliates of foreign law firms). Europe accounted for nearly three-quarters of such sales, with the United Kingdom representing 34 percent of the European total. Japan was the leading non-European market, purchasing 7 percent of exports through affiliates.

Recent USITC Roundtable Discussion

The Commission hosted its sixth annual services roundtable on November 13, 2012, with USITC Chairman Irving A. Williamson presiding and Commissioners Meredith Broadbent and Shara L. Aranoff moderating. Participants from industry, government, and academia discussed the need for appropriate regulations that allow economies to reap the gains of services liberalization, including the need for different liberalization sequences for countries with different levels of economic development. Participants also debated the prospects for services trade agreements, both for broad and comprehensive liberalization agreements (such as the World Trade Organization International Services Agreement currently being promoted by many countries including the United States) and for smaller bilateral and plurilateral agreements among like-minded trade partners. Finally, panelists considered the need for a new trade liberalization framework that integrates goods and services, as trade is typically conducted by firms that provide both. A full summary of the roundtable's discussion is provided in section 6.

SECTION 1. INTRODUCTION

The U.S. economy is dominated by services, which account for nearly 80 percent of U.S. gross domestic product (GDP) and employment, and the United States leads the world in exports of services. This annual report examines U.S. services trade, both in the aggregate and in selected industries; identifies important U.S. trading partners; and analyzes global market conditions in professional services industries, which represent one-quarter of the United States' services GDP. This year's report focuses on the following professional services: education, healthcare, and legal services.[3]

Data and Organization

The U.S. International Trade Commission (Commission or USITC) draws much of the services trade data used throughout this report from the Bureau of Economic Analysis (BEA) at the U.S. Department of Commerce (USDOC). The BEA collects services trade data through a number of surveys, which under most conditions require respondents with more than $2 million in exports or $1 million in imports to furnish details about their international services transactions. The BEA estimates trade flow data using these survey data.[4] For this report, the Commission has supplemented the BEA data with information from other sources, including individual firms, trade associations, industry and academic journals and reports, international organizations, and other government agencies.

This section examines the U.S. services sector, global services trade, and U.S. services trade. It looks at both cross-border trade in services from 2006 through 2011 and affiliate firms' sales of services from 2006 through 2010,[5] comparing the trade picture in recent years with previous trends. Section 2 examines trends affecting professional service industries and discusses the contribution of these industries to economic output, employment, labor productivity, and trade. Sections 3 through 5 discuss the education, healthcare, and legal service industries. These sections give an overview of global competitiveness, supply and demand factors, and recent trends in cross-border trade and/or affiliate transactions for each industry. Section 6 summarizes the information and views presented at the sixth annual USITC services trade roundtable, hosted by the Commission in November 2012. Appendix A provides a snapshot of recent services research conducted by Commission staff.

The U.S. Services Sector

Service industries account for an overwhelming majority of U.S. production and employment. In 2011, industries producing private services accounted for 79 percent (or $9.1 trillion) of total real GDP of U.S. private industry and 82 percent (or 84 million) of U.S. private industry full-time employees, compared to 21 percent and 18 percent, respectively, for the goods-producing sector. Recent trends in the U.S. services sector have mirrored overall trends in the U.S. economy, as average annual increases in services sector GDP, employment, and wages were within 1 percent of the annual growth rates registered for the United States as a whole from 2006 through 2011.[6]

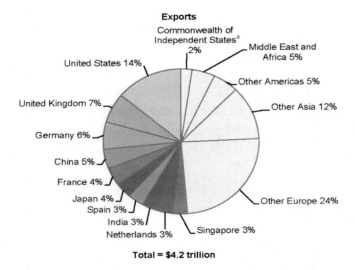

Total = $4.2 trillion

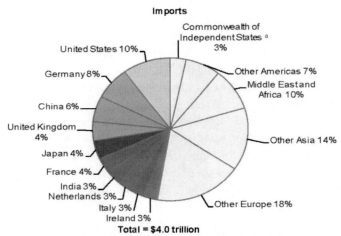

Total = $4.0 trillion

Source: WTO, International Trade Statistics 2012, 2012, tables A8 and A9.

Note: Excludes public-sector transactions. Geographic regions are shaded yellow. Figures m ay not total 100 percent due to rounding.

[a] The WTO includes the following countries under Commonwealth of Independent States : Armenia, Azerbaijan, Belarus, Georgia, Kazakhstan, Kyrgyz Republic, Moldova, Russia, Tajikistan, Ukraine, and Uzbekistan.

Figure 1.1. Global services: The United States led the world in cross-border exports and imports of services in 2011.

Global Services Trade

The United States is highly competitive in the global services market. As the world's top exporter of services, the United States accounted for $580.9 billion, or 14 percent, of global cross-border commercial services exports in 2011 (figure 1.1).[7] Other top single- country exporters included the United Kingdom and Germany, which accounted for 7 percent and 6 percent, respectively. Although most of the world's top 10 services exporters in 2011 were developed countries, China was the 4th-largest services exporter, and India ranked 8th. Overall, the top 10 exporting countries accounted for 51 percent of global cross-border services exports in 2011.[8]

The United States was also the world's largest services importer in 2011, with $395.3 billion, or 10 percent, of global commercial services imports. In that year, Germany was the second-largest importer, accounting for 8 percent of such imports, and the top 10 importing countries together accounted for 47 percent of global commercial services imports. China was the third-largest importer of commercial services in 2011, and India was the seventh largest.

The World Trade Organization (WTO) reports that the U.S. services trade surplus in 2011 ($185.6 billion) was the world's highest, followed by that of the United Kingdom ($103.3 billion). China and Saudi Arabia had the world's largest services trade deficits, with imports exceeding exports by $54.1 billion and $43.8 billion, respectively.[9]

U.S. Trade in Services

BOX 1.1. SERVICES TRADE UNDER THE GENERAL AGREEMENT ON TRADE IN SERVICES

The GATS identifies four modes of supply through which services are traded:

Mode 1 is cross-border supply. In this mode, a service is supplied by an individual or firm in one country to an individual or firm in another (i.e., the service crosses national borders). An example would be a digital file of a final architectural design emailed to a foreign client. WTO data for this mode of supply do not completely overlap with BEA's data for cross-border trade (see discussion below).

Mode 2 is consumption abroad. In this mode, an individual from one country travels to another country and consumes a service in that country. An example would be foreign nationals visiting the United States for medical care.

Mode 3 is commercial presence. In this mode, a firm based in one country establishes an affiliate in another country and supplies services from that locally established affiliate. An example would be a U.S.-based law firm providing legal services to citizens of a foreign country from its affiliated office located in that country.

Mode 4 is the temporary presence of natural persons. In this mode, an individual service supplier from one country travels to another country on a short-term basis to supply a service there—for example, as a consultant, contract employee, or intracompany transferee at an affiliate in the host country.[a] An example would be U.S.-based engineers traveling to a foreign country to assist local staff on a construction project.

Cross-border trade and affiliate transactions data reported by the BEA do not correspond exactly to the channels of service delivery reflected in the GATS of the WTO.[b] The BEA notes that mode 1 and mode 2 transactions, as well as some mode 4 transactions, generally are grouped together in its data on cross-border trade, while mode 3 transactions are included, with some exceptions, in affiliate transactions data.

[a] USDOC, BEA, *Survey of Current Business*, October 2009, 40–43, tables 1 and 2.
[b] For more information on the four modes of supply under the GATS, see WTO, "Chapter 1: Basic Purpose and Concepts," n.d. (accessed April 7, 2009).

The BEA annually publishes data on both cross-border trade and affiliate transactions in services, which together account for a substantial portion of the services provided through all four "modes of supply" specified in the General Agreement on Trade in Services (GATS) (box 1.1). The BEA publishes these data at the highest level of detail that its surveys allow. The agency also publishes quarterly cross-border trade data in highly aggregated form.

"Cross-border trade" occurs when suppliers in one country sell services to consumers in another country, with people, information, or money crossing national boundaries in the process. Such transactions appear as imports and exports in a country's balance of payments. Firms also provide services to foreign consumers through affiliates established in host (i.e., foreign) countries; the income generated through "affiliate transactions" appears as direct investment income in the balance of payments.

The channel of delivery used by service providers depends primarily on the nature of the service. For example, retail services are usually supplied through affiliates located close to consumers. Conversely, education, healthcare, and legal services are predominantly traded across borders, as students and medical patients consume services abroad and attorneys travel abroad to consult with clients. Affiliate transactions are the principal means of providing services to overseas customers, accounting for nearly 68 percent of overall U.S. services trade in 2010 (box 1.2).

Box 1.2. The Rise of Affiliate Transactions

Since 1986, when the U.S. Department of Commerce began collecting statistics on U.S. services trade, the relative importance of cross-border trade and affiliate transactions has shifted significantly.[a] In each of the 10 years from 1986 through 1995, U.S. cross-border exports of services exceeded sales by majority-owned foreign affiliates of U.S. firms. Since 1996, however, sales by U.S. firms' foreign affiliates have exceeded exports of cross-border services. In 2010, services supplied by U.S. firms' affiliates abroad ($1.1 trillion) were more than double the value of U.S. cross-border exports of services ($537.7 billion). Similarly, services supplied to U.S. citizens by foreign-owned affiliates have exceeded cross-border services imports since 1989. In 2010, the value of services supplied to U.S. citizens by the U.S. affiliates of foreign companies ($696.0 billion) was nearly twice the value of U.S. services imports ($368.0 billion).[b]

The growing predominance of affiliate transactions largely reflects the global spread of service firms, facilitated by liberalization—the removal or lessening of barriers to trade—in investment and services. Liberalization first occurred in developed countries and has occurred more recently in a growing number of low- and middle-income countries.

[a] USDOC, BEA, *Survey of Current Business*, October 2006.
[b] USDOC, BEA, *Survey of Current Business*, October 2012, 15.

Cross-border Trade, 2011

U.S. exports of private sector services totaled $586.8 billion in 2011, while U.S. imports totaled $393.1 billion, resulting in a $193.8 billion trade surplus (figure 1.2).[10] Professional services[11] accounted for 21 percent of exports and 19 percent of imports (figure 1.3). Travel services and passenger fares accounted for the largest share of U.S. services trade in 2011, representing 26 percent of U.S. exports and 28 percent of U.S. imports.[12]

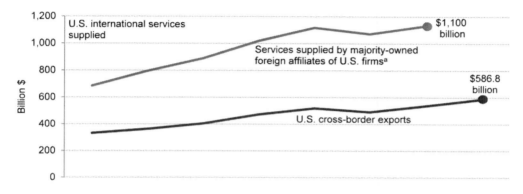

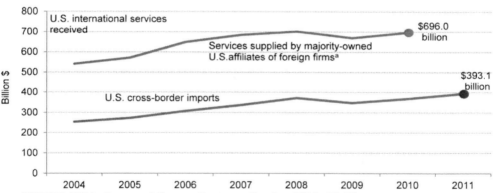

Source: USDOC, BEA, *Survey of Current Business*, October 2012, 15–58.

Note: Data for the period prior to 2004 were calculated differently and are therefore not included in this figure.

[a] Data are available through 2010 only.

Figure 1.2. Affiliate transactions continue to predominate as means of trading services.

In 2011, U.S. cross-border services exports increased by 9 percent from the previous year, exceeding their compound annual growth rate of 7 percent during 2006–10.[13] This increase was spread across service industries, led by construction services (67 percent); architectural, engineering, and other technical services (31 percent); industrial processes (19 percent); and passenger fares (18 percent). At the same time, the value of U.S. services imports grew by 7 percent in 2011. Import growth was particularly high for architectural, engineering, and other technical services (37 percent); advertising services (32 percent); installation, maintenance, and repair of equipment (22 percent); audiovisual services (22 percent); and research and development and testing services (18 percent).

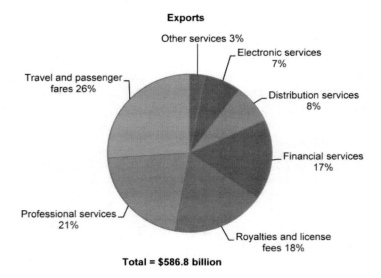

Exports

Other services 3%

Electronic services 7%

Travel and passenger fares 26%

Distribution services 8%

Financial services 17%

Professional services 21%

Royalties and license fees 18%

Total = $586.8 billion

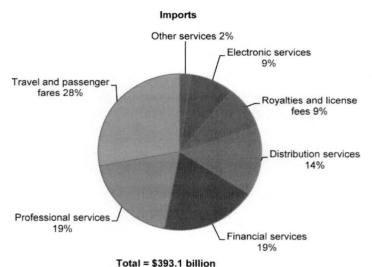

Imports

Other services 2%

Electronic services 9%

Travel and passenger fares 28%

Royalties and license fees 9%

Distribution services 14%

Professional services 19%

Financial services 19%

Total = $393.1 billion

Source: USDOC, BEA, *Survey of Current Business*, October 2012, 34–35.

Figure 1.3. U.S. services: Travel and passenger fares accounted for the largest share of U.S. cross-border trade in 2011.

As in previous years, the majority of U.S. service industries registered cross-border trade surpluses in 2011. Royalties and license fees for sales of intellectual property achieved the largest surplus in 2011 ($72.0 billion), followed by financial services ($57.8 billion), travel services ($37.5 billion), industrial processes ($21.3 billion), and education services ($16.8 billion). Service industries with cross-border trade deficits in 2011 included insurance services ($41.1 billion); transportation services ($11.6 billion); computer and data processing services ($12.5 billion); and accounting, auditing, and bookkeeping services ($1.4 billion). Deficits were recorded for a variety of reasons. The deficit in insurance services principally reflects U.S. primary insurers' payments to European and Bermudian reinsurers[14] in return for their assuming a portion of large risks. The deficit in transportation services (i.e., freight transport and port fees) largely reflects the U.S. deficit in manufactured goods trade and the way in which U.S. imports of freight transportation services are measured. For example, Chinese shipments of manufactured goods to the United States typically exceed U.S. shipments of goods to China, and payments to Chinese or other foreign shippers for transporting U.S. merchandise imports are recorded by the BEA as U.S. imports of transportation services. Lastly, the deficit in computer and data processing services largely reflects U.S. firms outsourcing many of these services to foreign providers.

A small number of developed countries account for a substantial share of U.S. cross-border services trade. Canada, the United Kingdom, and Japan collectively received 26 percent of total U.S. cross-border services exports in 2011. During the same year, the United Kingdom (11 percent), Bermuda and Canada (7 percent each), and Japan (6 percent) supplied the largest single-country shares of U.S. services imports. Separately, in 2011, the European Union (EU) accounted for 32 percent of U.S. services exports and 35 percent of U.S. imports.

Cross-border Trade, 2012

Preliminary data for 2012 suggest that the United States' services exports, services imports, and surplus in services trade all continued to grow that year. Annual services exports in 2012 exceeded those in 2011 by 4 percent or $24.3 billion (table 1.1). Annual services imports in 2012 exceeded those in 2011 by about 3 percent, or $10.9 billion.

Annual services trade posted a surplus of $207.1 billion in 2012, or $14 billion more than in 2011.

Affiliate Transactions

In 2010, services supplied by U.S.-owned foreign affiliates[15] increased by 6 percent to $1.1 trillion.[16] Professional services accounted for 8 percent[17] of services supplied by U.S.-owned foreign affiliates in 2010 (figure 1.4).[18] Sales of non-professional services were led by distribution services, including wholesale trade, which accounted for approximately 30 percent of total services supplied by U.S.-owned foreign affiliates. The largest foreign purchasers of services from U.S.-owned affiliates were the United Kingdom (17 percent), Canada (10 percent), Japan (6 percent), and Ireland (5 percent).

The EU accounted for 44 percent of total services supplied by U.S.-owned affiliates in 2010.[19]

The value of services purchased from foreign-owned affiliates in the United States increased by 4 percent in 2010 to $696.0 billion, as the U.S. economy improved. This increase was larger than the 2 percent annual growth for the period from 2006 through 2009. Professional services purchased from foreign-owned U.S. affiliates accounted for 6 percent of total services supplied by such affiliates in 2010.[20] Distribution services accounted for 29 percent of purchases and were the largest type of non-professional services supplied by foreign-owned affiliates in the United States. By country, the United Kingdom accounted for the biggest share of services purchased from foreign-owned affiliates in 2010 (15 percent), followed by Germany and Japan (14 percent each). Canada and France rounded out the top five with 10 percent each. Overall, 55 percent of services purchased in the United States from foreign-owned affiliates were from affiliates of EU-based parent firms.

Services supplied by foreign affiliates of U.S. firms[a]

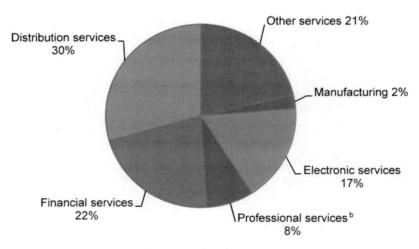

Other services 21%

Distribution services
30%

Manufacturing 2%

Electronic services
17%

Financial services
22%

Professional services[b]
8%

Total = $1,130.5 billion

Purchases from U.S. affiliates of foreign firms[c]

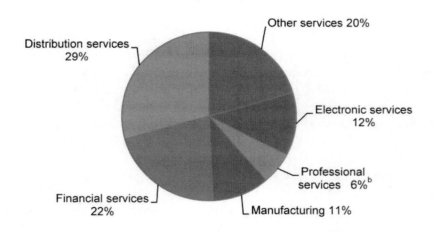

Other services 20%

Distribution services
29%

Electronic services
12%

Professional
services 6%[b]

Financial services
22%

Manufacturing 11%

Total = $696.0 billion

Source: USDOC, BEA, *Survey of Current Business*, October 2012, 56, 58, tables 8.2 and 10.2.

Note: Trade data excluded public sector transactions. Figures may not total 100 percent due to rounding.

[a] Services supplied by majority-owned affiliates of U.S. parent firms.

[b] Data are underreported by the BEA to avoid disclosing confidential company information.

[c] Services supplied by majority-owned U.S. affiliates of foreign parent firms.

Figure 1.4. U.S. services: Distribution services accounted for the largest share of U.S. affiliate transactions in 2010.

Table 1.1. U.S. private services exports and imports to the world, by category, 2011–12

Service industry	2011	2012	% change, 2011–12
Exports	Million $		
Travel	116,115	128,555	10.7
Passenger fares	36,631	39,521	7.9
Freight	21,730	21,896	0.8
Port services	21,334	21,397	0.3
Royalties and license fees	120,836	121,810	0.8
Education	22,726	24,096	6.0
Financial services	74,055	71,247	−3.8
Insurance services	15,477	17,110	10.6
Telecommunications	12,650	13,620	7.7
Business, professional, and technical services	134,416	140,916	4.8
Other	10,870	10,988	1.1
Total	586,839	611,156	4.1
Imports	Million $		
Travel	78,651	83,651	6.4
Passenger fares	31,109	34,443	10.7
Freight	40,337	41,773	3.6
Port services	14,374	13,396	−6.8
Royalties and license fees	36,620	40,037	9.3
Education	5,888	6,210	5.5
Financial services	16,207	16,076	−0.8
Insurance services	56,619	53,419	−5.7
Telecommunications	7,690	7,391	−3.9
Business, professional, and technical services	104,773	106,796	1.9
Other	797	814	2.1
Total	393,065	404,007	2.8

Source: USDOC, BEA, U.S. International Transactions Accounts Data, March 14, 2012, table 3a.
Note: Data for 2012 are preliminary.

SECTION 2. PROFESSIONAL SERVICES

Overview

Despite their small share of total services trade, professional services are an important feature of the global economy: they are responsible for establishing the financial, legal, and regulatory framework in which business takes place and for providing services that are critical to human development and well-being, such as education and healthcare.[21] Reflecting the important work they do, professional service providers such as accountants, lawyers, physicians, and educators are among the most highly educated and highly skilled workers in the global economy. Most professional services are subject to registration, certification, and licensing requirements; these requirements are often intended to ensure that only qualified personnel provide such services, but they may also act as trade barriers for foreign service providers when they are overly complex, opaque, or burdensome in nature. Notwithstanding some hurdles, trade in these services is growing rapidly, spurred by increased international demand for them and enabled by advances in the use of information technology.[22]

How Professional Services Are Traded

Professional services may be traded in each of the four modes defined under the GATS (box 1.1). Certain professional services are less likely to involve cross-border transactions because providing them requires either face-to-face contact (e.g., physical examinations and classroom instruction) or commercial presence in the target country for practical or regulatory reasons.[23] In instances where a service results in a deliverable that can be sent to the consumer—such as an architectural plan or a legal brief—mode 1 (cross-border supply) is feasible, and commonly involves the transmission of materials over the Internet.[24] Professional services may be supplied through mode 2 when a resident of one country temporarily travels to another country to consume a service. One example of this type of transaction would be a student from China traveling to the United States to receive his or her college education. Mode 3 trade, commercial presence, is a prevalent form of trade in professional services. This form of trade takes place when a large professional services provider, such as the U.S. law firm Baker & McKenzie or the U.S. accounting firm KPMG, sets up an affiliated company abroad to serve local clients.

Many times, professional services trade through commercial presence entails mode 4 trade, defined as the movement of natural persons. Under mode 4, for example, managers or technical personnel who are employed at a company's headquarters in the home market are sent to do short-term work at one of the firm's overseas affiliates.[25] Mode 4 trade may also take place when a foreign national enters the United States for a limited time to provide services in the U.S. domestic market—for example, when a healthcare aide from the Philippines immigrates temporarily to the United States to provide home healthcare in this country.[26]

Barriers to Trade in Professional Services

Both entry and operational barriers impede trade in professional services, and in particular affect supply through modes 3 and 4. These barriers are typically byproducts of a country's domestic policy objectives at the national, state, or provincial level—such as the protection and development of its indigenous workforce—and they often take the form of complex and opaque regulations concerning the supply of professional services by foreign providers.[27] Examples of some of the most onerous and restrictive barriers on foreign services providers include economic needs tests (which seek to verify that a certain service cannot be supplied by a domestic firm or individual as a condition for granting temporary entry and stay of foreign service providers) and quotas on the number of foreign providers that may enter the domestic market. Other significant barriers on professional services trade include mode 3 restrictions on setting up a foreign affiliate (requiring, for instance, that a foreign firm supply services through a joint venture with a domestic entity) and requirements that managerial staff be either citizens or permanent residents of the foreign country in which they seek to provide services.[28]

Government certification and licensing requirements may also limit the activity of professional services providers in foreign markets. Such requirements are often intended to protect consumers against the ill effects of information asymmetries when choosing a service provider by ensuring that only qualified individuals supply such services—and, in many cases, they are complemented by industry efforts to self-regulate.[29] However, where these requirements are unclear and unequal across countries, they deter trade in professional services.[30] Many countries are working to make their regulations more transparent, and some groups of countries that are trading partners have negotiated agreements to harmonize and mutually recognize professional service standards. Nonetheless, such requirements remain a challenge for many international service providers.[31]

Globalization and Fragmentation

Despite barriers to trade in professional services, such trade remains robust. Growth in professional services trade has largely been driven by two trends: the globalization of commerce, and the fragmentation of services. An example of the first trend would be the decision of a U.S. manufacturing firm to locate its operations abroad, which may create a new cross-border demand for legal services. The second trend, services fragmentation, results from the practice of separating non-core functions within a professional service and outsourcing those functions to third-party providers, who are frequently based overseas.[32] For instance, a U.S. healthcare firm may choose to outsource medical transcription services (e.g., in which a physician's voice recordings on patient care are transcribed into text) to a provider located in India, even as the firm continues to supply core services (e.g., primary medical care) at home.[33] This geographic dispersion of professional service activities is likely to influence the distribution of services trade in the foreseeable future and will have implications for trade policy.

U.S. Trade in Professional Services

In 2011, professional services accounted for 21 percent of total U.S. cross-border services exports (GATS mode 1) (see box 1.1) and 19 percent of U.S. cross-border services imports.[34] The United States posted a cross-border trade surplus in professional services of $49.0 billion in 2011, with exports of $124.0 billion and imports of $75.0 billion. Between 2006 and 2010, the U.S. trade surplus in professional services grew at a compound annual rate of 12 percent,[35] driven by the growth in U.S. trade surpluses in management and consulting (38 percent) and in the installation, maintenance, and repair of equipment (24 percent).

Among the principal professional services subsectors, the trade situation varied substantially in 2011. In that year, management and consulting represented roughly a quarter of U.S. sector exports ($32.2 billion) (figure 2.1). Other leading subsector exports were those in research and development (R&D) and testing ($23.4 billion or 19 percent), education ($22.7 billion or 18 percent), and installation, maintenance, and repair of equipment ($13.8 billion or 11 percent).[36] In 2011, the United Kingdom and Switzerland were the leading markets for U.S. management consulting exports and for R&D and testing exports, respectively. During the same year, the United Kingdom was the largest source for U.S. imports of both of these types of services.[37]

U.S.-owned foreign affiliates (i.e., U.S.-owned companies located abroad) supplied $96.5 billion of professional services in 2010.[38] Architectural, engineering, and other technical services posted the largest share, accounting for 27 percent ($26 billion) of the total. Management, scientific and technical consulting represented 20 percent ($19 billion) of services provided by U.S. affiliates abroad, and accounting, auditing, and bookkeeping represented 13 percent ($12 billion), rounding out the top three (figure 2.2).

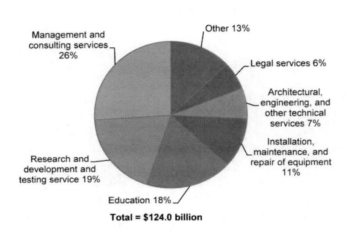

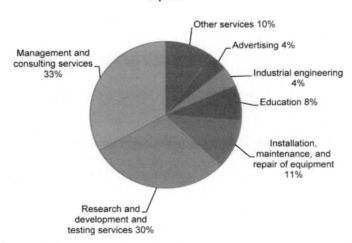

Source: USDOC, BEA, *Survey of Current Business*, October, 2012, 34–35, table 1.
Note: Trade data exclude public-sector transactions.

Figure 2.1. U.S. professional services: Management and consulting services accounted for the largest share of U.S. cross-border exports and imports of professional services in 2011.

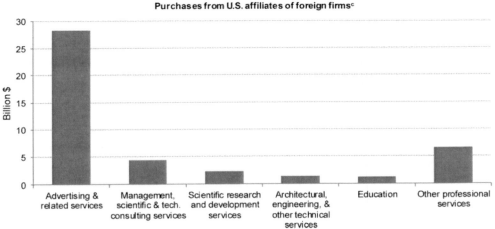

Source: USDOC, BEA, *Survey of Current Business*, October 2012, 56, 58, tables 9.2 and 10.2.

Note: Trade data excluded public sector transactions. Figures may not total 100 percent due to rounding.

[a] Services supplied by majority-owned affiliates of U.S. parent firms. Data are underreported by the BEA to avoid disclosuring individual company information.

[b] Other professional services includes scientific research and development services and education ($4 billion each), health care and social assistance ($3 billion), specialized design services ($2 billion), and all other professional services ($10 billion).

[c] Services supplied by majority-owned U.S. affiliates of foreign parent firms.

Figure 2.2. Architectural and engineering services accounted for the largest share of professional services supplied by foreign affiliates of U.S. firms in 2010.

By contrast, the value of services purchased from foreign-owned U.S. affiliates (i.e., foreign-owned companies located in the United States) was $44.4 billion in 2010.[39] Advertising and related services accounted for the largest share (64 percent) of professional services purchased from foreign-owned U.S. affiliates at $28 billion.

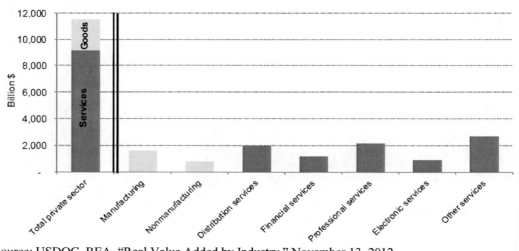

Source: USDOC, BEA, "Real Value Added by Industry," November 13, 2012.
[a] Real value added by industry using 2005 chained dollars.

Figure 2.3. Services accounted for the largest share of U.S. private-sector GDP in 2011.a

Gross Domestic Product, Employment, Labor Productivity, and Salaries in Professional Services

The contribution of U.S. professional services to U.S. GDP in 2011 was $2.2 trillion, which represented 24 percent of the U.S. gross domestic product (GDP) in services (figure 2.3).[40] Among professional service industries, miscellaneous professional, scientific, and technical services (6.5 percent) and health care and social assistance (1.8 percent) had the fastest growth in 2011. By contrast, during the same year, legal services and management of companies and enterprises posted output declines of −1.7 percent and −0.5 percent, respectively.

Employment in professional services accounted for a significant share of total private sector employment in 2011. In that year, the number of full-time equivalent (FTE) employees in professional services stood at 26 million, or 26 percent of total U.S. private sector employment. Health care and social assistance represented more than half (58 percent) of professional services employment at 15.2 million workers (figure 2.4).

Miscellaneous professional, scientific, and technical services (18 percent) and educational services (11 percent) were the second- and third-largest sectors in professional services in terms of employment. Among all service sectors, only employment in professional services (1.5 percent) and electronic services (0.5 percent) rose during 2006–10. The largest decline in services employment during the period was in financial services (−2.2 percent) and distribution services (−1.9 percent).

In 2011, labor productivity in professional services (measured as output in dollars per FTE) grew by 0.9 percent. During that year, professional services were the least productive U.S. sector, with an average output per worker of $82,549. However, labor productivity varied substantially among professional service industries: average output per worker ranged from $43,712 in education services to $145,345 in legal services (figure 2.5). From 2006 to 2010, productivity in the professional services sector remained nearly unchanged at −0.2

percent. However, productivity grew by 0.9 percent in 2011, second only to growth in electronic services (10.5 percent).

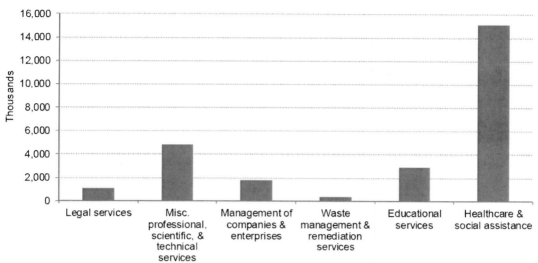

Source: USDOC, BEA, "Full-Time Equivalent Employees by Industry," interactive tables, September 17, 2012.

Figure 2.4. Healthcare and social assistance had the largest number of U.S. FTEs in the professional services sector in 2011.

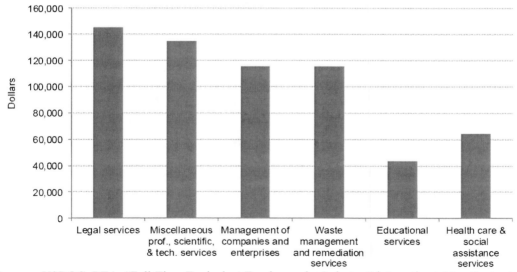

Sources: USDOC, BEA, "Full-Time Equivalent Employees by Industry," interactive tables, September 17, 2012; and USDOC, "Real Value Added by Industry," November 13, 2012.

Figure 2.5. Legal services had the highest labor productivity among all U.S. professional service sectors in 2011.

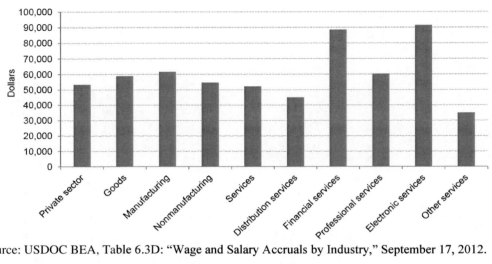

Source: USDOC BEA, Table 6.3D: "Wage and Salary Accruals by Industry," September 17, 2012.

Figure 2.6. Wages per FTE in the private sector were the highest for electronic services in 2011.

Professional service workers earned an average wage of $60,368 in 2011, which exceeded the private sector average ($53,463) but trailed wages in electronic services ($91,432), financial services ($88,557) and goods manufacturing ($61,680) (figure 2.6). Average wages varied substantially within the sector. For example, average annual wages in educational services were $42,405, compared to $110,115 for management of companies and enterprises. During 2006–10, annual wage growth in professional services was 2.7 percent, which was in line with the 2.6 percent growth rate for private sector services as a whole. In 2011, average wages for professional services rose by 2.8 percent, the fifth-largest increase after electronic and financial services (4.4 percent each), nonmanufacturing goods (3.4 percent), and manufactured goods (2.8 percent).[41]

SECTION 3. EDUCATION SERVICES

SUMMARY

The global market for education services, measured by revenues at colleges and universities, grew by approximately 5 percent in 2011; the United States was the largest country market, followed by China, Japan, Germany, and France. Education is a mature industry, with instruction taking place primarily on physical campuses, although online instruction is growing in popularity. Worldwide, the largest market segment is students aged 18–22 years, although students aged 22–30 years and over 30 years represent growing shares of the market. The industry's concentration is low due to the sheer number and diversity of institutions worldwide, as well as the tendency of colleges and universities to focus on home-market students. The main factors affecting demand for university education are population growth and demographics, secondary-school completion rates, household income, tuition levels, employer needs, economic conditions, and socioeconomic factors.

The supply of education services, as measured by the number of available student slots, is growing in many developing countries, but tends to be static in developed countries. Competition among universities is shaped by a wide variety of factors, ranging from an institution's academic reputation to its campus facilities. Budget cuts and rising tuition levels have driven many universities to cover budget shortfalls by actively recruiting foreign students. Over the past decade, mainland China has become the world's largest source of foreign students. Over the past couple of years, some elite universities have started to experiment with massive open online courses, i.e., free classes streamed over the Internet via specialty websites.

Introduction

Education services include formal academic instruction at primary, secondary, and tertiary (higher education) institutions, as well as instructional services offered by libraries and vocational, correspondence, language, and special education schools. This section focuses on instruction at universities and colleges (hereafter referred to as universities) by students studying abroad, because such university-level students represent the bulk of international trade in education services and because university studies are the only education services for which data on cross-border trade are reported. Cross-border trade is the primary means of providing education services to foreign markets. Such trade occurs when a student from one country travels to another country for university-level study; it consists of expenditures by students and their dependents, if any, for tuition, fees, and living expenses. As an example, expenditures incurred by a Chinese student studying in the United States are considered U.S. exports of education services, whereas expenditures incurred by a U.S. student studying in China are considered U.S. imports.

Market Conditions in Global Education Services

In 2011, the global market for education services, measured by revenues earned by colleges and universities, grew by approximately 5 percent to $902.8 billion.[42] The United States was the largest country market in the global education services industry, accounting for 23 percent of total global revenues. Other large markets included China (12 percent), Japan (9 percent), Germany (6 percent), France (4 percent), Brazil (4 percent), the United Kingdom (4 percent), and Italy (3 percent). All other countries each accounted for less than 3 percent of the global market in 2011. Worldwide, more than 17 million people worked in roughly 79,000 colleges and universities in 2011.[43]

Due to the long existence of many universities[44] as well as high start-up costs and market saturation in many countries, education services is a mature industry whose annual revenue growth rates approximate the overall rate of population growth. The primary service offered by universities is educational instruction, involving a specified course of study (in a wide variety of fields) that is certified by an academic degree upon completion.[45] Instruction takes place primarily on university campuses, although online instruction and hybrid programs are growing in popularity. Many universities also provide lodging, food, recreation, and transportation services to enrolled students. Some universities also earn sales revenues, licensing fees, royalties, and other forms of income by operating hospitals, publishing houses, specialized research facilities.

The market for education services is typically segmented by student age. In most countries, the largest single market is students aged 18 to 22 years. Having completed secondary education, students in this age group often enroll in universities to improve long-term job prospects and for family/social/cultural reasons. The second market segment, students aged 22 to 30 years, draws late high school graduates, individuals returning to complete a college degree, and students seeking a professional, graduate, or doctoral degree. Students 30 and older constitute a small but growing market segment for many universities. Often part-time students, people in the over-30 segment, typically return to school to advance their careers or to master new skills for a career change.[46]

The global education services industry displays a very low level of industry concentration, with even the largest university systems, such as the University of California system, accounting for only a tiny share of global industry revenues in 2010.[47]

This fragmentation stems largely from the fact that most universities earn almost all of their revenues in their home-country markets. It also results from the sheer number and diversity of universities in the global industry, which comprises more than 80,000 institutions in more than a hundred countries.

Demand and Supply Factors

The main factors affecting demand for university-level education include population growth and demographics, secondary education completion rates, household income, tuition levels, employer needs, economic conditions, and socioeconomic factors. The growth and age distribution of the population has a direct impact on the demand, with increasing demand likely in countries with growing populations and/or a growing share of the 18–30 age group. A related trend involves rising secondary education completion rates, which often correlate with increased demand for education services as more students meet universities' basic eligibility requirements. Tuition levels and household income, which together determine the affordability of higher education, also tend to impact demand, with lower tuition levels and higher household incomes widening access to colleges and universities. Demand also rises when companies require applicants to have specialized skill sets and/or a higher level of general education. Job and income gains associated with periods of economic growth tend to increase demand as well, whereas slowing growth tends to decrease demand, although countercyclical enrollment patterns tend to moderate the impact of economic conditions.[48] Finally, positive personal, family, and societal perceptions of the value of higher education—to satisfy social needs and/or improve employment opportunities—also tend to increase demand for education services.[49]

The supply of education services, as measured by the number of available student slots, tends to be actively controlled by universities based upon institution-specific objectives. In the United States, for example, many universities, particularly high-prestige universities, often maintain a constant number of slots, which decreases acceptance rates[50] (a key measure of status) as the number of applicants rises. By contrast, the number of university seats in some countries, particularly developing countries like China, is expanding to accommodate the soaring demand for educated workers induced by rapid economic growth.

For the most part, competition between universities takes place at the national level, with most universities catering predominantly to home-country students, although a growing number of universities actively recruit foreign students. One of the most important distinguishing factors among universities is an institution's reputation. This is often based on a subjective assessment of factors, including placement in various rankings, name recognition, perception of academic selectivity and quality,[51] students' postgraduation prospects, and even a university's history and heritage. To compete for students, universities, particularly in the United States, have also redesigned curricula, upgraded academic facilities, installed state-of-the-art communications networks, and even bolstered campus amenities, including expansive landscaping, high-end dormitory facilities, and gourmet dining options.[52] Universities also compete for students, especially highly qualified students, by offering various types of financial aid, including scholarships, tuition grants or waivers, stipends, low-interest loans, and on-campus employment opportunities. Other inducements may include top-quality professors; winning sports teams; a wide range of courses and academic programs, including study- abroad programs; and the existence of strategic alliances with both domestic and foreign universities.[53]

Elite Universities Experiment with Massive Open Online Courses

Recently, massive open online courses (MOOCs) have emerged as one of the most notable trends in higher education. MOOCs are free university-level classes offered via streaming video. First emerging in 2009 and 2010, websites like Academic Earth and Open Culture offered videos of professors teaching classes ranging from Corporate Finance to The History of the Roman Empire. Although viewers were unable to earn credit—and video quality and class selection were often poor—these early sites attracted attention because they featured top-level academic instruction at some of the world's leading universities, including Harvard University, the Massachusetts Institute of Technology (MIT), and Stanford University.[54] After a relatively slow start, MOOCs received a surge of attention in 2012 after the launch of several high-profile websites, namely Coursera,[55] edX,[56] and Udacity.[57]

Student interest in the educational content provided by MOOCs has been substantial, particularly outside the United States. For example, in 2011, Sebastian Thrun and Peter Norvig, both professors at Stanford University, attracted 160,000 students in 209 countries to the online version of their 200-student class on artificial intelligence.[58] Similarly, in the fall of 2012, eight public health classes offered by Johns Hopkins University on Coursera drew more than 170,000 students. However, initial high enrollments for some classes may be deceptive; participation and completion rates are often substantially lower. Coursera, for example, estimates that 40–60 percent of registered students attempt the first assignment, while only 10–15 percent will complete the course.[59]

Despite the initial surge of interest, many universities are reportedly wary of the MOOC phenomenon. Even universities that currently contribute educational content to MOOC platforms typically offer only a handful of classes and do not allow registered students to earn grades, credit, or academic degrees, although several MOOCs issue certificates of completion.[60] Such caution seems to stem from concerns that the large-scale delivery of educational instruction will erode academic and social reputations based upon selectivity and scarcity. Some universities, too, appear concerned that profits from their campus- based business model could be undercut by the low-cost delivery of education content over the Internet.[61]

Many universities and other observers are also reportedly concerned about the academic integrity of MOOC-based education, with issues like academic rigor, identity verification, and test security foremost among such worries. In response, some MOOCs are attempting to mimic the classroom experience by introducing quizzes, online forums, instructor email access, and final exams.[62] Several MOOCs are also experimenting with various schemes aimed at ensuring test security and identity authentication. Coursera, for example, plans to form partnerships with online proctoring companies that use webcams and software to monitor tests remotely, whereas edX and Udacity plan to require students to take exams at specific testing centers.[63]

Although most classes are currently free, many MOOCs, particularly those backed by venture capital funding, are exploring ways to generate revenues. One potential source of revenue may be the payment of licensing fees for educational content, likely survey courses and remedial classes produced by traditional universities. Antioch University, for example, has agreed to grant educational credit for students completing two Coursera courses on poetry and mythology produced at the University of Pennsylvania.[64] Similarly, in early 2013 Udacity announced a pilot project to offer remedial and introductory courses in algebra and statistics at San José State University (and several community colleges and high schools) in California.[65] Other ideas that might generate revenue include offering branded certificates of completion as well as job placement services through which recruiters can access details about high-performing students.[66] Some MOOCs may also be able to earn revenues by offering their web platforms for private sector educational training. edX, for example, is allowing companies to use its website to offer in-house training courses.[67] Affiliate revenues may also be a possibility. Coursera, for example, is an Amazon.com affiliate, receiving a small commission for students who click through to the Amazon site to buy recommended textbooks and other products.[68]

Budget Cuts and Rising Tuition Drive U.S. Universities to Actively Recruit Foreign Students

The 2007–08 financial crisis and subsequent economic downturn significantly affected the funding of higher education in the United States, particularly at public institutions.[69] Many U.S. states, which suffered declining tax revenues over the last five or so years, have significantly reduced funding appropriations for public universities.[70] At the University of California, for example, appropriations by the State of California were cut by 28 percent between 2007 and 2011, an amount totaling nearly $1 billion, with cuts of an additional $100 million occurring in 2012.[71] Similarly, at the University of Michigan (U-M), state appropriations have decreased by 25 percent over the past decade, and now cover only 17 percent of the U-M budget compared to 33 percent in 2002–03.[72]

In response to deep and ongoing budget cuts, many public universities have raised tuition prices, now reportedly relying on tuition payments to cover more than half of their annual expenditures. To increase revenues, some universities have actively taken steps to increase the share of out-of-state students in their enrollments. The University of Washington, for example, decreased the number of in-state freshman by almost 500 between 2007 and 2011, even as the school enrolled larger numbers of students, causing the percentage of out-of-state students to increase from 19 percent to 34 percent. On average, residents of Washington state paid tuition of $10,346 during the 2011–12 academic year, whereas nonresidents paid $27,830.[73]

Although less reliant on government funding, private universities are also under financial pressure as parents and students balk at high tuition in the face of poor job prospects, stagnant wages, and large student debt loads. This trend appears to be having an effect on tuition increases; according to the National Association of Independent Colleges and Universities (NAICU), an association representing 960 private institutions in the United States, average tuition grew by only 3.9 percent during the 2012–13 academic year, the smallest percentage increase in at least 40 years.[74] In addition, 24 of NAICU's member colleges froze tuition, while 8 members cut tuition.[75]

As a way to shore up budgets, many U.S. universities, both public and private, are expanding their share of foreign students (box 3.1). Of the 2011–12 freshman class at the University of Washington, for example, more than half of the nonresident students were from foreign countries, with almost two-thirds of that number coming from China.[76] During that same year, foreign students also represented at least 10 percent of the freshman class at the flagship public universities of Illinois, Indiana, and Iowa, as well as at the University of California campuses in Berkeley and Los Angeles. Private universities are also reportedly increasing their intake of foreign students. In 2011–12, for example, foreign students represented at least 15 percent of the freshman classes at Boston University, Columbia University, and the University of Pennsylvania.[77] Some universities also charge international students extra fees. Purdue University, for example, had an international student fee of $1,000 in 2011–12, which doubled to $2,000 during 2012–13.[78] Similarly, the University of Illinois at Urbana-Champaign levied a surcharge of $2,800 on international students during the 2012–13 academic year.[79]

The growing number of international students on U.S. campuses may be due, in part, to markedly more aggressive recruiting by U.S. universities, with recruiting efforts reportedly spreading from large and/or well-known public and private institutions to small regional private colleges, non-flagship state universities, and even community colleges.[80] While many universities have upgraded websites aimed at foreign applicants, a growing number are also sending recruitment staff to foreign recruiting events. For example, the China Education Expo 2011, which toured seven Chinese cities, hosted 587 universities from more than 37 countries and was attended by more than 65,000 attendees.[81] A growing number of universities are also employing specialty agents and brokers to recruit students, particularly from China. At their best, foreign student recruiters, who are typically paid a per-student contingency fee, match foreign students with appropriate universities and help applicants with required college admissions tasks such as filling out applications, obtaining references, writing essays, and meeting deadlines. However, as a growing number of observers have noted, paying recruiters to funnel foreign students to universities—a practice that was outlawed in the United States for domestic students—creates incentives that have reportedly led to recurring incidences of questionable behavior, including not only placing unprepared students at inappropriate universities but also widespread academic fraud, overcharging, misrepresentation, and even intellectual property violations.[82]

As a result, some universities have taken steps to circumvent recruiting agencies. For example, a group of 15 U.S. universities—including Colorado College, Wake Forest University, and the University of Maryland at College Park—formed a partnership called CNA-USA to build relationships with select middle schools in China.[83] A number of state-based consortiums have also emerged over the past few years. Such consortiums, which include Study New Jersey, Study Wisconsin, and Study Oregon, actively promote in-state institutions of higher education by sponsoring websites and educational seminars, representing members at foreign recruiting fairs and conferences, and hosting exchanges for admissions staff and foreign educational counselors.[84]

BOX 3.1. INTERNATIONAL STUDENT TRENDS

Over the past decade, the number of students studying outside their home country grew by more than 95 percent, from 2.1 million in 2000 to 4.1 million in 2010, for a compound annual growth rate of 7 percent. In 2010, the United States hosted the most foreign students in absolute terms, taking 17 percent of all foreign students worldwide; the United Kingdom (13 percent), Australia (7 percent), Germany (6 percent), and France (6 percent) rounded out the top five spots. Other countries hosting a significant share of foreign students in 2010 included Canada (5 percent), Japan (3 percent), the Russian Federation (4 percent), and Spain (2 percent). Overall, 83 percent of foreign students studied in G-20 countries and 77 percent studied in OECD countries.

At the macro level, growing foreign student mobility results from several factors, ranging from a rising interest in promoting academic, cultural, social, and political ties between countries to reduced international transportation costs to the global expansion of tertiary institutions in developing countries. In addition, the increasing globalization of societies and economies, including the labor market, has provided students an incentive to gain international experience as part of their education. At the micro level, students choose institutions based upon language of instruction; national immigration policies; tuition costs; and perceived educational quality. Other factors that shape foreign students' decisions to study abroad include the likelihood that foreign degrees will be recognized; restrictive admission policies for home-country universities; geographic, trade, cultural, and historic linkages between countries; the opportunity; future job opportunities; and the opportunity to experience other cultures.

Source: OECD, *Education at a Glance 2012*, September 2012, 362–67.

Growing Numbers of Chinese Students Study Abroad

Over the past decade, mainland China has become the world's largest source of foreign students. By 2011, for example, approximately 340,000 Chinese students were studying outside of China, a figure that has grown by more than 20 percent per year over the past several years.[85] In recent years, the United States has been the destination of choice for Chinese students. More than 194,000 students studied at U.S. colleges, universities, and community colleges during the 2011–12 academic year, a figure that represented more than 25 percent of total U.S. foreign student enrollments.[86] In 2011–12, 46 percent of Chinese students were studying at the graduate level, while 38 percent were undergraduates; nondegree students and students engaged in "other practical training" represented 7 percent and 10 percent of the total, respectively.[87] The number of Chinese students studying in the United States has grown at an annual rate of 10 percent over the past 10 years.[88] Although growth has occurred at both the undergraduate and graduate levels, undergraduate enrollments have experienced the most significant growth over the last few years.[89]

Chinese students enrolled at U.S. universities are reportedly high performers with strong test scores[90] who tend to study business/management (29 percent), engineering (19 percent), math/computer science (11 percent), and physical/life sciences (10 percent).[91] Many Chinese students pay full tuition, including out-of-state tuition at public schools, contributing an estimated $5 billion to the U.S. economy for tuition and living expenses during the 2011–12 academic year.[92] Many Chinese students reportedly covered most or all education and living expenses through family resources.[93]

The growth of U.S.-bound Chinese students is driven by a combination of social, economic, and demographic factors. Many Chinese students study abroad in response to deficiencies in the Chinese higher education system. Such deficiencies include a shortage of universities, particularly top-quality universities;[94] fierce competition for university slots;[95] and the grueling, high-pressure *gaokao* college entrance exam, which some students and parents believe requires too much preparation and focuses on irrelevant topics.[96] An increasing number of Chinese students also want to study in the United States due to the belief that U.S. colleges and universities are the best in the world.[97] Some Chinese students, for example, believe that Chinese higher education overemphasizes memorization and repetition, preferring instead the U.S. approach, which they believe focuses on problem-solving, critical thinking, creativity, and innovative ideas.[98] Some observers also believe that some Chinese students choose to study in the United States because it offers unique, life-changing experiences.[99]

Recent economic changes in China may also play a role. Nearly 20 years of rapid economic growth, for example, have created a large and growing middle class whose members highly value university-level education and have the financial means to send their children abroad. While many middle-class Chinese families are not wealthy by U.S. standards—more than 75 percent of Chinese students studying abroad came from families that earned less than $47,000 per year[100]—one result of China's long-running one-child policy is that the resources of several generations can be focused on a single child.[101] In addition, the gradual decline in the value of the U.S. dollar vis-à-vis the Chinese yuan since 2005 has made a U.S. education more affordable for middle-class Chinese families.[102]

Trade Trends

Cross-border Trade

In 2011, the value of U.S. cross-border exports of education services (box 3.2), which reflects foreign students' expenditures for tuition and living expenses while studying in the United States, rose by 8.4 percent to $22.7 billion, exactly in line with the annual growth of 8.4 percent recorded during 2005–10 (figure 3.1). Such strong growth reflected not only an increase in the number of foreign students studying in the United States, particularly from China and India, but also tuition increases.[103] In 2011, the five leading markets for U.S. exports of education services were China ($4.9 billion), India ($3.3 billion), Korea ($2.3 billion), Canada ($925 million), and Taiwan ($782 million) (figure 3.2).[104] As noted, foreign students are drawn to the United States due to its reputation for having an extensive and top-quality system of higher education.[105] U.S. universities owe this reputation to several interrelated factors, including highly regarded professors, world-class facilities, cutting-edge research in a wide variety of fields, and decades of substantial funding from both public and private sources.

BOX 3.2. AN EXPLANATION OF BEA DATA ON CROSS-BORDER TRADE IN EDUCATION SERVICES AND TRANSACTIONS BY EDUCATION AFFILIATES

U.S. cross-border exports of education services reflect estimated tuition (including fees) and living expenses of foreign residents (which exclude U.S. citizens, immigrants, or refugees) enrolled in U.S. colleges and universities. Cross-border imports of education services represent the same expenses for U.S. residents studying abroad.[a]

Data on U.S. imports of education services are estimated by the BEA based on two pathways by which U.S. citizens and permanent residents study in a foreign country. In the first, U.S. residents receive academic credit for study abroad from accredited U.S. colleges and universities, whether or not the U.S. residents also receive academic credit from the foreign institution. The BEA does not include the tuition and living expenses of students whose academic credits for study abroad do not transfer to U.S. institutions (with three country exceptions, as explained below) or who study abroad on an informal basis. The second pathway—from 2002 onward—supplements U.S. import data on education services by also including estimated tuition and living expenses for U.S. permanent residents who enroll in a degree program at a university in Australia, Canada, or the United Kingdom and reside temporarily in these countries in order to pursue their education. Because only formal study for credit toward a degree is included in estimates of tuition and living expenses that account for U.S. imports of education services, the full extent of studying abroad by U.S. students is understated in the trade data and, accordingly, the U.S. trade surplus in education services is overstated.

Data on education services affiliate transactions are limited, especially data concerning transactions by education affiliates located in the United States but owned by a foreign firm. Because transaction data from education affiliates cover a wide range of education providers other than the higher education segment, which is the focus of this section, education affiliate transaction data are not presented here.

Sources: BEA representative, email to USITC staff, December 7, 2010, and February 9–10, 2009; Koh Chin, *Open Doors 2004*, 2004, 92.

[a] Estimates for cross-border online instruction are included in "Other business, professional, and technical services" in the balance of payments, rather than the education services category.

During the 2011–12 academic year, the number of foreign students studying in the United States grew by 5.7 percent to 764,495, slightly faster than the annual growth of 5 percent from 2005 through 2010. Approximately 25 percent of total number of foreign students came from China, with India (13 percent), Korea (10 percent), Saudi Arabia (5 percent), and Canada (4 percent) also accounting for large shares of foreign students. Overall, international students and their dependents contributed an estimated $21.8 billion to the U.S. economy during 2011–12.[106]

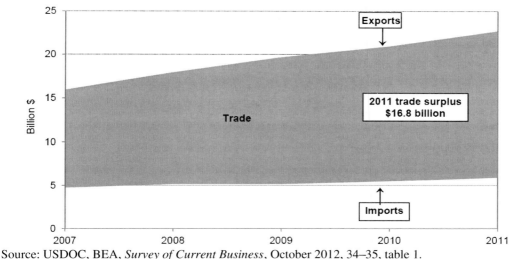

Source: USDOC, BEA, *Survey of Current Business*, October 2012, 34–35, table 1.

Figure 3.1. Education services: U.S. cross-border trade in private-sector services resulted in a U.S. trade surplus each year during 2007–11.

Students studying at the undergraduate and graduate levels each accounted for about 40 percent of total foreign students,[107] with business management (22 percent), engineering (19 percent), math and computer science (9 percent), social sciences (9 percent), and physical and life sciences (9 percent) being the most popular fields of study. During 2011–12, the most popular universities for foreign students were the University of Southern California, the University of Illinois at Urbana-Champaign, New York University, Purdue University, and Columbia University, with each university hosting approximately 1 percent of total foreign students.[108]

U.S. cross-border imports of education services, which reflect U.S. students' expenditures for tuition and living expenses while studying abroad, increased by 7.3 percent in 2011, roughly in line with the 7 percent annual growth recorded during 2005–10 but much lower than the 20 percent growth for foreign study in the United States that year.[109] As a result of these trends, the U.S. trade surplus in education services in 2011 widened by nearly 9 percent to $16.8 billion. The leading sources of U.S. imports of education services were the United Kingdom ($1.1 billion), Italy ($540 million), Spain ($498 million), France ($322 million), and Mexico ($294 million).[110]

During the 2011–12 academic year, roughly 274,000 U.S. students studied abroad, a figure that represented 1 percent growth over the previous year. Only 4 percent of U.S. students studied in foreign countries for at least one academic year, with the remainder studying for one semester (38 percent) or a shorter period (58 percent).[111] In general, U.S. students preferred destinations in Europe, with the United Kingdom (12 percent), Italy (11 percent), Spain (10 percent), and France (6 percent) hosting the largest numbers of students. China also hosted a large number of U.S. students, representing roughly 5 percent of the total. During 2011–12, the most popular fields of study for U.S. students abroad were programs in the social sciences (23 percent), business/management (21 percent), humanities (11 percent), fine or applied arts (8 percent), and physical and life sciences (8 percent).[112]

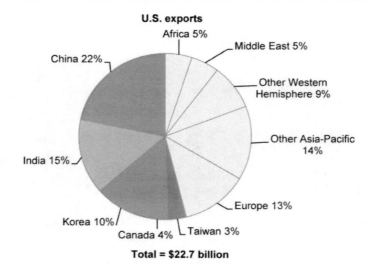

U.S. exports

Total = $22.7 billion

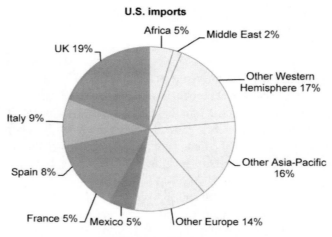

U.S. imports

Total = $5.9 billion

Source: USDOC, BEA, *Survey of Current Business*, October 2012, 46–47, table 5.2.
Note: Geographic regions are shaded in yellow. Figures may not total 100 percent due to rounding.

Figure 3.2. Education services: China was the leading source of U.S. exports of education services in 2011, while the United Kingdom was the leading source of imports.

Affiliate Transactions

Affiliate sales in education services occur when institutions of higher education serve foreign students by offering short-term educational programs abroad or by establishing campus facilities in other countries. The Harvard Business School, for example, offers a variety of short-term executive programs on topics like finance and marketing in Shanghai, China, to employees of Chinese companies.[113] Similarly, Michigan State University offers campus-based master's degree and executive education programs in Dubai, United Arab Emirates, in partnership with Dubai International Academic City.[114] In 2010, educational services supplied by U.S. universities in foreign countries totaled $3.5 billion, whereas services offered by foreign universities in the United States totaled $1.3 billion (figure 3.3).[115]

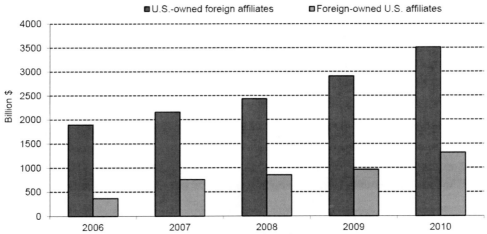

Source: USDOC, BEA, *Survey of Current Business*, various issues.

Figure 3.3. Education services: Services supplied by the affiliates of U.S. universities abroad exceeded services supplied by the affiliates of foreign universities in the United States in 2010.

Outlook

Over the next five years, the number of college students and revenues at U.S. colleges and universities are expected to grow in lockstep at a rate of about 1 percent per year. During this same period, flat or declining tax receipts and competition from other social programs will likely continue to put downward pressure on state-level appropriations for higher education. International student enrollments at U.S. universities, however, are expected to grow over the next five years, driven by rising disposable income levels in several developing countries, the solid reputation of the U.S. system of higher education, and many U.S. institutions' ongoing recruiting efforts abroad, particularly in China.[116] MOOC platforms like edX, Udacity, and Coursera will likely serve a growing number of students around the world as they expand course offerings and improve Web-based services, although many may struggle to monetize their services and attract enough revenues to survive and expand. Traditional universities may use MOOCs to deliver introductory or remedial courses, but will likely continue to resist the complete migration of educational instruction to online venues because of concerns about education quality and academic integrity, as well as reluctance to undercut lucrative business models and prized academic and social reputations.

SECTION 4. HEALTHCARE SERVICES

SUMMARY

Global demand for healthcare services (services provided by doctors, nurses, or other professionals in medical facilities such as hospitals, medical offices and clinics, or residential care facilities) has continued to grow.

As a result, global spending on healthcare—the best proxy figure available for healthcare services—has steadily risen since 2006. Although the United States and Europe are still the largest markets, they have grown more slowly than the global average. The fastest-growing markets are in developing countries, where private spending on healthcare is increasing dramatically. Healthcare systems around the world have developed new methods of service delivery and increased their use of information technology in response to both growing demand and the trend of "healthcare consumerism," in which patients take a more active role in their healthcare decisions. Governments have implemented policies to encourage investment in healthcare services; however, the shortage of healthcare workers remains a constraint in many countries.

The United States continues to maintain a trade surplus in healthcare services, which totaled $1.9 billion in 2011. In contrast, services supplied by foreign-owned U.S. affiliates significantly exceed services supplied by foreign affiliates of U.S. firms, largely due to the opportunities available in the U.S. market. However, U.S. healthcare organizations, particularly academic medical centers and hospitals, have increased their global presence in recent years by entering into a growing number of international affiliations and partnerships. Looking ahead, global healthcare demand will continue to grow, but growth in spending will be driven by developing economies, as growth in developed markets, particularly in the United States and Europe, continues to slow.

Introduction

Healthcare services[117] are demanded by almost all populations and provided in every market around the world. Service provision requires cooperation and coordination among a variety of different parties, including public and private providers, financiers, and regulators. Governments take an interest in the healthcare industry, in part, due to its critical role in economic growth[118] and development.[119] Further, in many countries, access to healthcare is considered a constitutional right, requiring these governments to play a larger role in the healthcare industry.[120] However, comprehensive healthcare coverage often requires a wide range of resources, beyond the scope of most governments. As a result, private firms, particularly healthcare providers and insurers, have found opportunities for profit in meeting demand for services outside of public systems. Hence most countries' healthcare systems comprise a mix of public and private providers, financed by a combination of public and private sources.

Market Conditions in Global Healthcare Services

Global healthcare expenditures continued their steady growth in recent years. This rise has been driven by sustained growth in public spending, which has counterbalanced less robust trends in private spending (figure 4.1).[121] Global spending grew at a compound annual rate of 7.5 percent from 2006 through 2010, as total spending rose from $4.9 trillion to $6.6 trillion, or over 10 percent of global GDP.[122] However, this relatively high average annual rate masks an abrupt deceleration in growth in 2009 and 2010 following the financial crises and ensuing recession.[123] Growth in global spending declined from almost 10 percent annually in 2008 to 2.5 percent in 2009, driven primarily by slower growth in private spending, and remained slow in 2010.[124] As a result, public spending accounted for a rising share of global healthcare expenditures, growing from 59 percent in 2006 to 63 percent in 2010.[125]

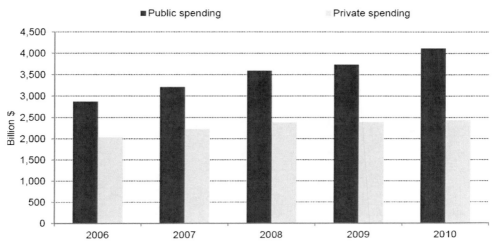

Source: USITC staff calculations based on data from World Bank, World Development Indictors database (accessed December 7, 2012).

Figure 4.1. Healthcare services: Global healthcare spending continued to rise during 2006–10 due to growth in public expenditures.

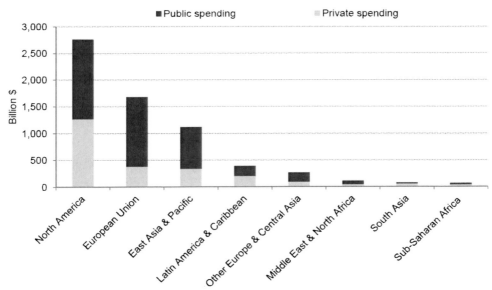

Source: USITC staff calculations using data from World Bank, World Development Indicators database (accessed November 1, 2012).

Figure 4.2. Healthcare services: Developed countries drive global healthcare spending, particularly public spending, 2010.

Table 4.1. Healthcare services: Top 10 global healthcare markets by total and private spending, 2010

Country	Total spending (billion $)	CAGR, 2006–10	Rank	Country	Private spending (billion $)	CAGR, 2006–10
United States	2,584.2	5.19%	1	United States	1,213.1	1.05%
Japan	520.7	9.92%	2	China	139.5	17.46%
Germany	379.2	5.28%	3	Brazil	102.3	17.39%
France	302.9	4.89%	4	Japan	91.0	5.54%
China	300.6	24.91%	5	Germany	86.9	4.54%
United Kingdom	217.0	1.17%	6	France	67.1	5.98%
Italy	194.7	3.76%	7	Canada	52.6	8.07%
Brazil	193.0	20.24%	8	India	48.4	13.76%
Canada	178.1	8.73%	9	Italy	43.6	2.59%
Spain	132.0	6.34%	10	Spain	35.9	4.91%

Source: Commission calculations based on data from WHO, Global Health Expenditures database, and World Bank, World Development Indicators database (accessed December 7, 2012).
Note: CAGR is the compound annual growth rate.

Developed markets—particularly North America (primarily the United States) and the European Union, which account for the bulk of healthcare expenditures (figure 4.2)—have largely driven the slowdown in global spending. The United States is by far the world's largest healthcare market (table 4.1), with per capita spending reaching $8,362 in 2010, compared to $3,368 in the European Union and $221 in China.[126] Although this level of spending represents growth of just under 6 percent since 2009, growth in expenditures in the U.S. healthcare market continues to lag growth in the global market. Market fluctuations and economic uncertainty led many consumers to curb spending, and the spike in unemployment resulted in a substantial loss in insurance coverage; both of these trends shrank private healthcare spending.[127] As a result, although the United States remains the world's largest private healthcare market, for the first time in decades private expenditures no longer accounted for the majority of U.S. healthcare spending; its share fell from 55 percent in 2006 to 47 percent in 2010.[128]

Many other developed countries also experienced healthcare spending growth that was slower than the global average of 7.5 percent during this period.[129] In contrast to the historical trend of sustained growth in healthcare expenditure, spending in many European countries actually declined from 2008 to 2010.[130] European markets have been hit particularly hard by the recession. In the face of budgetary pressures and financial constraints, governments have reduced labor forces, curtailed public spending by cutting wages and administrative costs, and in some cases increased cost sharing.[131] Additionally, countries with compulsory employment-based health insurance, such as France, have seen private expenditures on healthcare decline as unemployment has risen.[132]

In contrast, healthcare spending in developing markets continued to grow rapidly, driving the continued (albeit slower) growth in global healthcare spending. From 2006 through 2010, healthcare expenditures in developing countries in East Asia and the Pacific grew at an annual rate of 23 percent, and spending in developing Latin American and Caribbean countries grew by 15 percent.[133] Private spending has driven rapid growth in these markets, due to expanding insurance coverage and burgeoning middle-class populations with rising incomes and a growing desire for better care and advanced treatments. The expansion of China's healthcare industry has been driven by government policies aimed at improving access to care and expanding insurance coverage,[134] and by an aging population that is facing a growing incidence of chronic diseases. In China and Brazil, private spending on healthcare nearly doubled between 2006 and 2010, growing from $73.3 billion to $139.5 billion and from $53.9 billion to $102.3 billion, respectively. Although both China and Brazil have some form of national healthcare that provides free services to citizens, many patients are dissatisfied with the system and are willing to pay for high-quality private care.[135] As a result, China and Brazil were among the top 10 largest global healthcare markets in 2010, and (along with India) are among the largest private healthcare markets in the world.

The world's largest healthcare organizations continue to be located in the United States, and, in contrast to those in other countries, most are private.[136] In 2011, only 2 of the top 10 healthcare companies were located outside the United States, and both (the Japanese Red Cross Society and Alberta Health Services) were publicly funded (table 4.2). The leading healthcare company, based on operating revenue, was Express Scripts, a U.S.- based pharmacy benefit management service. (Pharmacy benefit managers are third-party managers of prescription drug programs.[137]) In 2012, Express Scripts solidified its role as market leader by acquiring Medco, the second-largest U.S. pharmacy benefit manager, increasing its share to 40 percent of the market.[138] The remaining leading healthcare companies, with the exception of Alberta Health Services, were all hospital systems, and other than the HCA hospital system (HCA Holdings, Inc.), none operate outside their home markets. Operations of the leading healthcare companies illustrate the degree to which the global healthcare system is fragmented along national borders.[139] Both patients and healthcare providers focus primarily on opportunities available in the domestic market.

In response to a variety of pressures, including smaller budgets, rising use of healthcare, and strained healthcare resources, many countries have undertaken healthcare reform. Motivated by cost concerns and a growing incidence of chronic disease, both the United States and the United Kingdom have recently passed major healthcare legislation. In the United States, the 2010 Patient Protection and Affordable Care Act (PPACA) endeavors to increase access to care by providing insurance coverage to previously uninsured individuals beginning in 2014 and by applying significant regulatory changes to the health insurance industry and the healthcare sector.[140] In the United Kingdom, where the National Health Service (NHS) provides universal healthcare to all residents,[141] the British Health and Social Care Act 2012 represents the largest reform of the NHS system in its history, as it targets rising healthcare costs by reorganizing and streamlining the system.[142]

Efforts to contain costs are not limited to developed markets. China has been progressively overhauling its healthcare system since 2009 in an effort to increase access by creating a competitive network that provides affordable care. The program began with the expansion of health insurance to over 95 percent of the population in 2011. More recently it has implemented new regulations to encourage private investment and begun efforts to reduce patients' costs by preventing providers from selling marked-up pharmaceuticals.[143] The implications of reforms for the global healthcare services market remain ambiguous.

Table 4.2. Healthcare services: Top 10 healthcare services companies, 2011

Rank	Company	Country	Operating revenue (thousand US$)
1	Express Scripts, Inc.	U.S.	46,128,300
2	St. Vincent Randolph Hospital, Inc.	U.S.	33,770,183
3	HCA Holdings, Inc.	U.S.	29,682,000
4	Methodist Healthcare Memphis Hospitals	U.S.	[a]27,000,000
5	Regents of the University of California (Nevada Cancer Institute)	U.S.	[b]14,938,600
6	Kaiser Foundation Hospitals	U.S.	[c]14,795,250
7	Japanese Red Cross Society	Japan	14,108,888
8	Community Health Systems, Inc.	U.S.	13,626,168
9	Catholic Health Initiatives	U.S.	[c]13,360,714
10	Alberta Health Services	Canada	11,951,494

Note: This table is drawn from firms for which Orbis reported ambulatory healthcare services, hospitals, or nursing and residential care facilities as a primary industry. It does not include all public healthcare systems.
[a] Most recent revenue data available are from 2010.
[b] Figure is an estimate. The Nevada Cancer Institute closed on January 31, 2013.
[c] Most recent revenue data available are from 2009.

Demand and Supply Factors

A wide range of factors affect the demand for and supply of healthcare services. Global demand for such services is primarily driven by population growth and other demographic trends, such as rising incomes. The global supply of healthcare services tends to be driven by government policy objectives, as well as by the development of new and innovative technologies. Although these supply and demand factors tend to have the greatest impact on national markets, they also often affect international trade in healthcare services.

The factors discussed below focus on four emerging trends and their effects on either demand or supply in the healthcare services industry. Healthcare IT is changing the way healthcare services are supplied, not only within domestic healthcare systems, but also across borders (mode 1).[144] Consumer-driven medical care has shifted the types of healthcare demanded and has also led to the rise of the medical travel industry (mode 2). Government policies that seek to increase healthcare services by boosting investment (mode 3) and encouraging the migration of foreign health professionals (mode 4) are responses to growing healthcare demand.

Rapid Adoption of Healthcare Information Technology (IT) Is Changing the Delivery of Healthcare

The widespread adoption of IT is changing the way healthcare is delivered and transforming the patient-provider relationship.[145] Healthcare IT refers to the use of information and communication technology by consumers, providers, governments, and insurers to store, share, or analyze healthcare data. The purpose of healthcare IT is to manage information more efficiently and increase communication between stakeholders in the healthcare industry—patients, providers, and payers—in order to improve outcomes while at the same time lowering costs.[146] For example, electronic health records, electronic referrals, and e-prescribing software can streamline communications and reduce administrative burdens.[147] Other healthcare IT applications such as telemedicine involve remote monitoring or computerized decision systems.[148] They directly support treatment and make positive outcomes more likely by providing information that helps providers make better decisions about the method of care.[149] It is difficult to characterize the size or effectiveness of telemedicine programs due to a scarcity of data. However, globally, the most commonly provided service via telemedicine is teleradiology—the remote viewing or diagnosis of images that were obtained in another location.[150] Other commonly provided remote services include dermatology, pathology, and cardiology/electrocardiology.[151]

High-income countries are, and are expected to remain, the main users of telemedicine. Currently, the global leaders in use of healthcare IT are Denmark, Sweden, and New Zealand. Such countries have widespread advanced IT infrastructure, and use healthcare IT to address challenges such as flat or declining budgets and shortages of healthcare professionals. Healthcare IT also helps reduce disparities and improve the overall quality of care. For example, electronic health records strengthen continuity of care across providers and make it easier to gather information on treatment and outcomes.[152] Other applications improve access to care by reaching traditionally underserved areas and populations, such as remote or rural regions.[153] For example, Japan uses remote health monitoring programs to provide its aging citizens with an alternative to hospital-based care. Patients can submit test results to providers over the Internet without having to visit an office. As of 2009, 70 percent of these Japanese telecare initiatives were carried out in rural areas.[154]

Some health IT applications facilitate international trade (particularly cross-border trade) in healthcare services. For example, telemedicine offers the opportunity for more collaboration between healthcare domestic and foreign professionals through remote training and sharing of information through international partnerships. While these programs are useful to professionals in developing countries, they also enable providers in developed countries to consult on diseases they may not see in person, such as neglected tropical diseases.[155] Greater portability of electronic or personal health records also supports continuity of care for patients who seek health treatments or procedures abroad by facilitating information sharing between foreign practitioners and their primary physicians. And remote diagnosis or treatment enables service providers to directly treat patients across borders or outsource certain functions, such as medical transcription or radiology readings.[156]

Governments of many high-income countries continue to support the adoption of IT in their healthcare systems, but face a number of challenges. The slow adoption of health IT in the United States is largely due to market fragmentation within and across states, networks, and care settings.[157] Other obstacles include budgetary constraints; resistance on the part of clinicians and end users due to a dislike of change, reluctance to learn new technologies, or concerns about increased liability; increased implementation costs for physicians; and problems with software functionality; and concerns over data privacy and security.[158] Researchers have identified policy elements common to a successful telemedicine program,[159] and many countries have implemented some or all of these elements. For example, the United States passed the Health Information Technology for Economic and Clinical Health Act (part of the American Recovery and Reinvestment Act in 2009), which provided incentives for the adoption of electronic health records. However, as of 2011, only 55 percent of U.S. providers had adopted an electronic health record system.[160]

Trend among Patients toward Healthcare Consumerism

Over the past decade, the composition of healthcare services demand has changed as the trend toward healthcare consumerism has intensified. Healthcare consumerism (or consumer-driven healthcare) refers to a shift in the healthcare delivery model, in which patients take a more active role in their healthcare decisions.[161] A number of factors have supported this transition, particularly health IT and the Internet, which offer patients access to vast amounts of information that increasingly influence their healthcare decisions.[162] Trends in health insurance policies have also supported this shift. In an attempt to contain rising healthcare costs, new insurance products such as healthcare saving accounts and high-deductible healthcare plans increase the exposure of consumers to the true cost of healthcare services, reducing some of the market distortion from the third-party payer system and encouraging consumers to become their own healthcare advocates. As a result, many patients are playing a larger role in determining the quality and cost of care they receive.

In the United States, one result of healthcare consumerism is the rise of retail clinics. Retail clinics are healthcare facilities found in retail stores, grocery stores, or pharmacies. They generally offer a set list of limited services, often provided by a nurse-practitioner, and are open for more hours than a traditional medical office.[163] These clinics are not owned by traditional healthcare companies; in October 2012, the United States' largest operators of clinics were CVS-owned MinuteClinic (588 clinics), Walgreens (356 clinics), and Wal-Mart (143 clinics).[164] The number of retail clinics in the United States has grown rapidly in recent years, from around 300 in 2007 to nearly 1,200 in 2010,[165] and more consumers are increasingly choosing to receive care from these clinics rather than from traditional healthcare facilities such as physicians' offices, urgent care facilities, or emergency rooms.

The number of visits to retail clinics grew from 1.5 million in 2007 to nearly 6 million in 2009.[166] The two factors leading consumers to prefer retail clinics are the convenience of longer hours and walk-in appointments, and lower costs.[167] A recent study using data from the three largest retail clinic operators found that over 44 percent of all clinic visits occurred outside of normal physician office hours.[168] Additionally, clinic visits tend to be significantly less expensive than other healthcare visits; estimated savings tend to range between $50 to $279 dollars per visit.[169] Although initially retail clinics targeted the uninsured population, insurance companies increasingly encourage beneficiaries to patronize retail clinics by either requiring only small co-payments or waiving co- payments entirely.[170] Between 2007 and 2009, over 70 percent of all retail clinic patients had some form of either private or public insurance.[171]

The emergence of patient choice and consumerism is also a key driver in the medical travel industry, which relies on patients making their own healthcare decisions.[172] Medical travel, or traveling to seek specific healthcare services, has long existed, as wealthy individuals in developing countries have traveled to receive advanced procedures and treatments from healthcare leaders in the United States and other developed countries. However, in the past decade, middle-class patients have become increasingly able to travel for medical care, both in developed and developing countries, as many countries have positioned their healthcare industries as medical destinations.[173] It is difficult to quantify the number of individuals who travel for care, as there are no comprehensive data available;

estimates range from 60,000 to 50 million travelers each year.[174] Despite the lack of consensus over the size of the market, the medical travel industry appears to be growing, as evidenced by the rising number of countries seeking to enter the market and the development of medical travel facilitators and related services providers. Generally, patients who seek care abroad tend to be uninsured individuals seeking affordable care, individuals seeking economical care for uncovered expenses, or informed patients seeking new or advanced treatments either where they are available or where expertise is greater.

Governments Encourage Healthcare Investment to Meet Rising Demand for Healthcare Facilities

Many governments seek to expand their facilities and meet rising demand for healthcare services by encouraging private sector investment. Although data are limited regarding the quantity and source of foreign direct investment in healthcare, anecdotal evidence suggests that cross-border investment is growing. For example, in October 2012, UnitedHealth Group, the largest U.S. health insurer, purchased a 90 percent share in Amil, Brazil's largest health insurer and healthcare provider. During that same month, the Indian hospital group Fortis raised over $400 million in international funds through an initial public offering on the Singapore stock exchange.[175] These deals also highlight a shift in geographic trends.

Although the United States remains the leading destination for healthcare investment activity, the recent trend towards consolidation, coupled with continued economic uncertainty and steady downward pressure on profit margins, has reduced the number of viable opportunities in the U.S. market.[176] Investors are now drawn to emerging markets, which have growing middle classes, expanding health insurance coverage, and a rising incidence of chronic disease. In turn, many governments, such as China, see private investment as a means to expand access to healthcare, and have encouraged privatization and investment. In January 2012, the Chinese government removed equity caps on foreign investment in healthcare institutions and allowed patients insured under the national system (over 400 million individuals) to receive treatment at private hospitals. In March 2012, Beijing's local government announced preferential taxes and preferential treatment regarding land use and energy consumption (the same afforded state-owned institutions) for private medical institutions.[177] These policies, as well as rapid economic growth, have attracted some private equity firms.[178] In June 2012 Carlyle-backed Concord Medical Holdings purchased a majority share (52 percent) of China's Chang'an Hospital, and in August 2012, Carlyle bought a 14 percent stake in China's largest private medical check-up firm.[179]

Developed countries like the United States also have policies favorable to foreign investors. The U.S. federal immigrant investment (EB-5) program was established in 1990 to "stimulate the U.S. economy through job creation and capital investment by foreign investors."[180] Under the program, U.S. Citizenship and Immigration Services can allocate up to 10,000 visas annually for entrepreneurs who make sizable investments that create a designated number of jobs.[181] Programs such as EB-5 that successfully attract foreign investment provide benefits to both parties and are increasingly seen as a potential source of funding for healthcare facilities. For example, in Hawaii, the Hawaiian Islands Regional Center (an immigrant investment center established under EB-5) is the primary lender in multiple healthcare projects, including a nursing home in Hilo and a hospital center in Maui.[182] Additionally, the Cleveland International Fund is hoping to fund an expansion of

Cleveland's University Hospitals by attracting investors from China, India, and Brazil under the EB-5 program.[183]

Widespread Shortages of Healthcare Professionals Increase Movement of Healthcare Workers around the World

Many governments face not only budgetary challenges in meeting rising demand for healthcare services, but also human resource constraints. The United Nations has estimated the global shortfall of healthcare workers at 4.3 million.[184] However, this figure was based on the minimum requirements to meet Millennium Development Goals[185] and thus underestimates total demand for healthcare professionals, as it does not account for shortages in developed countries or for professionals needed to provide services beyond immunizations and childbirth in low-income countries.[186] In many high-income countries, such as the United States, the domestic healthcare workforce has been unable to meet demand for years, and instead has been supplemented with international recruitment. The past decade has seen a rising number of healthcare professionals moving across borders, as more governments have enacted policies and agreements to attract foreign professionals.[187]

The United States is the world's leading destination for foreign healthcare workers,[188] and continues to pass legislation that facilitates the migration of foreign physicians. In 2010, U.S. demand for physicians exceeded supply by 13,700 physicians, with the greatest shortfall in primary care positions.[189] During that same year, 22 percent of U.S. physicians were graduates of medical schools outside of the United States or Canada, with the largest share graduating in India.[190] The United States' need for healthcare providers continues to grow, driven by rising consumption of healthcare and recent healthcare reform,[191] and it is projected that U.S. medical schools will not be able to produce enough graduates to meet the demand. As a result, foreign caregivers are allowed to practice in the United States under specific programs. For example, Congress recently extended a visa waiver program which allows U.S.-trained international medical graduates to stay in the United States if they practice in a medically underserved area for three years. To date, an estimated 9,000 physicians have worked under the program.[192]

Other countries that have not used foreign workers in the past are also changing their laws to encourage foreign workers. For instance, Japan is facing a rapidly aging population that will require many more caregivers in the near future[193] and so has begun to open its labor markets to foreign healthcare workers. Nurses and caregivers from the Philippines and Indonesia are allowed to work in Japan under trade agreements signed in 2008, and in 2013 Japan is expected to allow Vietnamese healthcare workers to enter as well.[194] Opportunities such as these are exacerbating healthcare shortages in some other countries, as the potential for higher salaries motivates health professionals to leave even when their home country is experiencing a shortage. For example, Indonesia is a major exporter of nurses to other Muslim countries and throughout Asia, but does not produce enough nurses to meet both domestic and foreign demand for caregivers.[195] Consequently, Indonesia faces a shortage of healthcare professionals, particularly in rural areas. However, the government continues to maintain and support a policy of sending healthcare workers to foreign markets,[196] citing benefits such as improved medical skills and expanded job opportunities, while also acknowledging that wage disparities underlie the shortages in remote areas.[197]

There are differing viewpoints on the impact of healthcare migration. Most frequently, workers move from low-income to high-income areas, whether from rural to urban areas or from developing to developed countries.[198] This often exacerbates shortages of workers in the neediest areas, leaving rural populations underserved. Additionally, if the government financed their education, workers who migrate permanently represent a lost public investment.[199] However, at the same time, migration may have positive impacts on a country's economy through the significant remittances that migrant workers send home. Additionally, if workers migrate for only a limited time, healthcare systems can benefit from their skills and experience on their return; it is argued that some of these workers might not have chosen a healthcare profession without the possibility of migration and higher wages.[200]

Trade Trends

Cross-border Trade

The United States continued to run a surplus in trade in healthcare services, as cross-border exports of healthcare services (box 4.1) exceeded imports every year from 2007 through 2011 (figure 4.3). In 2011, the United States exported just over $3.0 billion of healthcare services while imports totaled $1.1 billion.[201] Both imports and exports of healthcare services have grown steadily over the past five years, although both slowed slightly in 2011. Exports grew 5 percent that year, compared to 7 percent annual growth during 2006 through 2010, and imports grew 12 percent in 2011, slower than the annual growth of 15 percent from 2006 to 2010.[202] Overall, the U.S. trade surplus increased from $1.7 billion in 2007 to $1.9 billion in 2011.

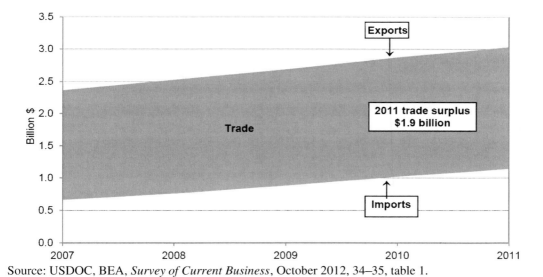

Source: USDOC, BEA, *Survey of Current Business*, October 2012, 34–35, table 1.

Figure 4.3. Medical services: U.S. cross-border trade in private-sector services resulted in a U.S. trade surplus each year during 2007–11.

BOX 4.1. UNDERSTANDING AVAILABLE DATA ON TRADE IN HEALTHCARE SERVICES

Healthcare services are traded via all four modes of services delivery,[a] but data on global trade in these services are limited. Statistics that are available often are not comparable across countries due to diverse methods of healthcare financing, large disparities in pricing, and the absence of an international standard for data collection.[b] Further, trade in healthcare services may be included with trade in other services. For example, healthcare services provided using information and communication technologies may be reported as trade in computer services.

This section's discussion of cross-border trade primarily uses data from the Bureau of Economic Analysis (BEA) of the U.S. Department of Commerce (USDOC), supplemented by United Nations (UN) data for analysis of specific export markets. The BEA data on cross-border trade in medical services estimate spending on healthcare services purchased abroad (consumption abroad or mode 2) through 2011.[c] The BEA does not provide U.S. bilateral healthcare trade data.

U.S. export figures, or receipts, estimate spending by foreign residents on medical services provided by U.S. hospitals, and include both emergency services required during travel and services for individuals who travel to the United States for the express purpose of receiving medical treatment. Data from a BEA study on patient headcounts and associated charges from medical facilities in major foreign-visitor destinations are used to estimate medical receipts for other U.S. hospitals that are likely to serve smaller volumes of such patients, and then such estimates are extrapolated forward using price indexes each year.[d]

Data on U.S. imports, or payments, estimate medical expenditures by U.S. residents traveling abroad. These statistics are based on estimates of the share of U.S. travelers requiring medical care from foreign providers. Import statistics include spending by U.S. residents on medical travel in Mexico or Canada (i.e., those who travel specifically seeking medical services); for all other destinations, statistics estimate spending on emergency care.[e]

Cross-border trade data reported in the UN Service Trade database likewise estimate spending by those traveling for medical reasons through 2010. However, unlike the BEA, the UN offers information on bilateral trade flows between the United States and selected countries.

Data on affiliate transactions in medical services also come from the BEA. Such statistics capture sales to foreign consumers by foreign healthcare affiliates of U.S. firms and purchases by U.S. consumers from U.S. healthcare affiliates of foreign firms.

---

[a] For example, foreign specialists provide remote consultations using information and communication technologies (mode 1); individuals seek treatment outside their home countries (mode 2); healthcare facilities establish branches in foreign markets (mode 3); and individual medical professionals migrate across borders (mode 4). For a more detailed explanation of the modes of services trade, see box 1.2 on page 1-7.

[b] Helble, "The Movement of Patients across Borders," November 26, 2010.

[c] BEA also collects data on trade in healthcare services via mode 1, which occurs when the service supplier and consumer remain in their respective countries. Discrete data on such trade are not

available, but are included in the subcategory "Other" within "Other business, professional, and technical services." USDOC, BEA representative, email to USITC staff, October 22, 2008.

[d] The comprehensive 1995 BEA study used to collect data was updated in 2005. Price indexes from the U.S. Consumer Price Index series are used to extrapolate estimates forward. The resulting export estimates do not include spending on ambulatory treatment or prescriptions received outside the hospital setting. USDOC, BEA, *U.S. International Transactions Accounts*, June 2011, 33; USDOC, BEA representative, email message to USITC staff, October 22, 2008.

[e] USDOC, BEA, *U.S. International Transactions Accounts*, June 2011, 33.

The majority of U.S. trade in healthcare services is likely with regional neighbors.[203] In 2010 (the most recent year for which data are available), Canada was the largest reported market for U.S. imports and exports of healthcare services,[204] importing $368 billion of healthcare services from the United States and reporting exports of $98 billion.[205] Regional trade is supported by limited but growing cross-border coverage by health insurance plans. For example, three programs offered by Canadian insurer Assured Diagnosis, Inc., cover services provided at the U.S.-based Mayo Clinic.[206] Similarly, in California, insurance plans are available that offer comprehensive healthcare coverage for services provided by private hospitals in the Mexico's Baja California region.[207] Additionally, many U.S. hospitals and medical centers position themselves as regional destinations for foreign patients. For example, the Baptist Health system in South Florida opened an office in the Cayman Islands in 2009 to facilitate patient outreach, and indicated plans for additional offices in other Caribbean and Latin American countries.[208] Baptist Health treats about 12,000 foreign patients a year, nearly 70 percent of whom come from nearby Caribbean and Latin American countries.[209]

Affiliate Transactions

Affiliate transactions illustrate the significance of the U.S. market for global healthcare firms, as well as the growing market power of U.S. firms as they expand abroad. Purchases of healthcare services from U.S.-based affiliates of foreign firms typically exceed sales of healthcare services by foreign-based affiliates of U.S. firms by a substantial amount, although available data are limited. Foreign companies have been more aggressive in expanding into the U.S. market than U.S. healthcare firms have been in expanding into foreign markets,[210] in part because the U.S. healthcare market has long been the most desirable destination for healthcare investment due to its size. The diversity, availability, and profitability of private sector healthcare firms attract both domestic and foreign merger and acquisition activity, as well as private equity investment.[211]

It can be challenging for foreign firms to enter the U.S. market, due to state-level regulation and licensing requirements, as well as difficulties qualifying for reimbursement from third-party payers. Nonetheless, foreign firms continue to expand into the U.S. market, either by acquiring U.S. healthcare firms or establishing new U.S. affiliates. For example, in 2007, Indian hospital operator Wockhardt acquired Radiant Research, a U.S. clinical trial services company.[212] Similarly, Northstar Healthcare, a Canadian owner and operator of ambulatory surgical centers, acquired majority shares in two U.S. ambulatory surgical centers in 2007.[213] Acquisitions such as these increase services supplied by U.S. affiliates of foreign firms because spending by U.S. consumers at these facilities is now considered a purchase from a U.S. affiliate of a foreign firm.

At the same time, foreign affiliates of U.S. firms have also been increasing their provision of healthcare services in foreign markets, which reached $2.6 billion in 2010 for an annual growth rate of 13.5 percent during the 2006–10 period. Some U.S. healthcare firms see opportunities overseas, while others are driven to consider investing abroad by the need for new revenue streams associated, in part, with the ambiguity surrounding the effects of recent U.S. healthcare reform, continuing downward pressure on reimbursement rates, and limited domestic opportunities.[214] To set up foreign operations, U.S. firms most often either invest in an existing facility or enter into a joint venture with local partners.[215] Between 2006 and 2011, the majority of foreign healthcare operations acquired by U.S. firms were European.[216]

BOX 4.2. THE GROWING GLOBAL FOOTPRINT OF LEADING U.S. ACADEMIC AND TEACHING MEDICAL CENTERS

Leading U.S. academic and teaching medical centers are increasing their presence in the global healthcare services market by entering into a growing number of international affiliations and partnerships.[a] For example, Johns Hopkins International, which earlier had focused primarily on international consulting, has become a partner in a number of long-term management contracts with hospitals around the world. The Cleveland Clinic, an academic medical center in Cleveland, Ohio, is in the process of building a hospital in the United Arab Emirates, and the University of Pittsburgh Medical Center manages and operates service-providing centers throughout Europe and Asia.[b]

Many academic medical centers have traditionally entered into international collaborations for training and education purposes. However, new international strategies are increasingly motivated by profit.[c] Most of these organizations previously focused exclusively on exporting healthcare services to foreign patients who traveled to the United States seeking treatment from these providers based on their advanced expertise and good reputations. However, after September 11, 2001, it became more challenging for patients, particularly those from the Middle East, to get visas for the United States.[d] Additionally, as the global medical travel industry developed, U.S. providers faced increased competition for international patients. By partnering with foreign institutions, U.S. providers were able not only to capture a growing share of medical travelers, but also to bolster their reputations in the global market,[e] which in turn draws foreign patients to their U.S. facilities for specialized care.[f]

[a] PricewaterhouseCoopers, *Global Healthcare Deals Quarterly*, 3Q 2012, 5.
[b] PricewaterhouseCoopers, *Global Healthcare Deals Quarterly*, 3Q 2012, 5; Lee, "Foreign Relations," June 11, 2012, 32.
[c] Dunn, "International Partnership Opportunities Gaining Interest," April 5, 2011.
[d] Van Dusen, "America's Top Hospitals Go Global," August 25, 2008; Are, "Global Expansion of US Health Care System and Organizations," February 13, 2009.
[e] Van Dusen, "America's Top Hospitals Go Global," August 25, 2008; Are, "Global Expansion of US Health Care System and Organizations," February 13, 2009.
[f] Dunn, "International Partnership Opportunities Gaining Interest," April 5, 2011.

Nevertheless, governments in many emerging economies are seeking to improve their domestic healthcare systems, and this trend has encouraged the expansion strategies of prominent U.S. academic and teaching medical centers.[217] Academic healthcare systems such as those of Johns Hopkins University and the University of Pittsburgh have traditionally led participation in the global market, either through new collaborations to expand education and research or through non-equity forms of investment, such as consulting agreements or alliances to develop healthcare networks.[218] Now these organizations are expanding their global footprint further (box 4.2), increasingly via equity-based cross-border collaborations.[219] For example, since the Chinese government announced plans to expand private hospital beds by 300 percent by 2015, the University of Pittsburgh Medical Center has entered into three joint ventures in China and recently opened a new Beijing office.[220]

Outlook

The trade outlook for the healthcare industry in the United States remains uncertain due to the ambiguity over how the U.S. industry and patients will respond to the increased demand generated by the PPACA. In particular, it is unclear to what degree foreign services will be substituted for domestic services.[221] Slow growth in spending is expected through 2014 as consumers continue to bear rising shares of healthcare costs, leading them to forego or defer attention for some health conditions. However, beyond 2014, spending is forecast to accelerate, since the PPACA is expected to increase demand for healthcare services in the United States by expanding health insurance coverage to 33 million previously uninsured individuals by 2022.[222] Globally, healthcare spending is forecast to grow moderately in the near future, as slow growth in developed economies tempers more rapid spending increases in fast-growing developing economies.[223] However, demand for healthcare services across the globe is expected to rise as populations increasingly become older, wealthier, and subject to more chronic diseases. For example, in the United States, it is estimated that the population over the age of 65 will nearly double by 2030.[224] As a result, both developed and developing economies could face a shortfall in healthcare financing in coming years, requiring other ongoing reforms of healthcare systems, such as limitations on care or increased contributions from patients.[225] These budgetary considerations are likely to continue to drive the adoption of healthcare IT, as governments and health insurers alike seek to cut costs further through remote monitoring and care.[226]

SECTION 5. LEGAL SERVICES

SUMMARY

The global legal services market grew modestly in 2011, with markets in the Asia-Pacific region outperforming the U.S. and European markets. Increasing growth rates for U.S. cross-border trade in 2011 reflected recovery from the economic downturn and rising demand for legal services. Although U.S. imports of legal services grew much faster, in percentage terms, than U.S. exports, the U.S. legal services trade surplus grew in 2011.

U.S. legal services exports were concentrated in Europe, Japan, and Canada, but the fastest-growing destinations were South and Central America and the Middle East. In response to slower demand in developed-country markets, law firms have opened new offices and merged with other law firms in fast-growing economies across Asia, Africa, Latin America, and the Middle East. Sales by foreign affiliates of U.S. law firms continued to exceed purchases from U.S. affiliates of foreign law firms, but after growing from 2006 to 2009, affiliate transactions in both directions declined in 2010. Europe continued to be the largest market for U.S. foreign affiliate sales of legal services, though its share declined from 2006 through 2010. The economic downturn accelerated certain trends in the U.S. legal services market, such as the rise of nontraditional suppliers and the internationalization of law firms, which have increased competition among legal services providers.

Introduction

Legal services[227] are a key input to international commerce: they facilitate trade and investment by increasing predictability and decreasing risk in business transactions.[228] In recent years, overall demand for legal services was depressed by the economic downturn; the global legal industry experienced a decline in 2009, and growth fluctuated in 2010 and 2011. Nonetheless, growth has varied across geographic regions, causing law firms to expand into markets with rapidly growing demand for legal services. This section discusses (1) the restructuring and growing competitiveness of the U.S. legal services industry since the downturn, including the rise of nontraditional providers of legal services; (2) the intense competition for employment in the U.S. legal services industry, especially among new graduates; (3) and the increasing internationalization of law firms.

Market Conditions in Global Legal Services

As noted above, the global legal services market fluctuated during 2008–11. Overall, the market grew at a 3 percent compound average annual rate between 2007 and 2010, but slowed to only 0.03 percent between 2010 and 2011 (when the market grew from $623.1 billion to $623.3 billion).[229] Annual growth rates during these years varied widely by region; Europe's legal services market grew by 4 percent in 2011 (compared to 3 percent during 2007–10), while the U.S. market declined by 7 percent in 2011 (compared to 2 percent annual growth during 2007–10).[230] Legal services markets in the Asia-Pacific region outperformed the U.S. and European markets during this period, growing by 5 percent in 2011 (equal to the region's average annual growth rate during 2007–10).[231] Expanding middle classes with rising incomes are driving growth in Asian markets.[232]

Although the United States continued to have the largest single-country legal services market in 2011, its share of the world market has declined in recent years as a result of growth abroad. In 2007, the United States and Europe accounted for 43 percent and 33 percent, respectively, of the global legal services market, while the Asia-Pacific region accounted for 12 percent. However, in 2011, the United States held only 39 percent, while

Europe, the Asia-Pacific, and the rest of the world increased their shares modestly (rising from 33 to 34 percent, 12 to 14 percent, and 12 to 13 percent, respectively).

Firms in the United States and the United Kingdom accounted for 76 and 14 of the world's 100 top-grossing firms, respectively, and all of the world's top 10 law firms in 2012 (table 5.1).[233] A recent flurry of mergers has resulted in new entrants on the top 100 list and increased the concentration of revenue, especially among the top 25 firms.[234] The largest global firms, where the average number of lawyers per firm was over 1,100 in 2011, are also largely U.S. and UK firms, but include six Australian firms and five Chinese firms.[235] A recent merger between an Australian and a Chinese firm created a company with approximately 1,700 lawyers, which will likely place the firm high in future rankings. Recent cross-border merger activity has coincided with new office openings in foreign markets, illustrating the continuing globalization of large law firms.

Demand and Supply Factors

The U.S. Legal Services Industry Is Restructuring after the Economic Downturn

The economic downturn significantly affected the U.S. legal services industry. It impacted trade flows (see "Trade Trends" below) and ushered in changes in firm structures, practices, and industry composition.[236] After averaging 4 percent growth during 2005–08, U.S. demand for legal services declined in 2009 and grew only modestly thereafter, rising by 0.5 percent in 2012.[237] From 1986 (the first year for which data are available) until the downturn, revenue per lawyer at the 100 highest-grossing firms steadily increased, then declined in 2008 and leveled off thereafter.[238] Productivity in U.S. law firms also fell in 2008, and despite staff cuts in 2009 and 2010, productivity has stagnated.[239] In 2011, the 100 highest-grossing law firms saw increases in gross revenue and revenue per lawyer, but performance diverged between the top and bottom 50 firms.[240] Similarly, among a broader set of firms, there was positive average growth in 2012 but large variance in performance.[241]

Table 5.1. Legal services: Top 10 global law firms, by gross revenue, 2012

Rank	Firm	Country	Gross revenue (million $)
1	Baker & McKenzie	U.S.	2,313
2	DLA Piper	U.S.	2,247
3	Skadden, Arps, Slate, Meagher & Flom	U.S.	2,165
4	Latham & Watkins	U.S.	2,152
5	Clifford Chance	U.K.	2,090
6	Linklaters	U.K.	1,936
7	Allen & Overy	U.K.	1,898
8	Freshfields Bruckhaus Deringer	U.K.	1,827
9	Kirkland & Ellis	U.S.	1,750
10	Hogan Lovells	U.S.	1,665

Source: *American Lawyer*, "The 2012 Global 100," October 2012.
Notes: Revenue figures refer to firms' most recently completed fiscal year.

Underlying market trends—including the rise of nontraditional service providers, the growing role of in-house counsel, and technology-driven commoditization of legal services—

have driven competition among the supply of legal services and increased the bargaining power of clients. Nontraditional providers of legal services include legal process outsourcers as well as other types of companies, discussed in more detail below.[242] In-house legal teams at business firms handle legal tasks and outsource them as needed.[243] "Commoditization" refers to the creation of a legal package or another legal consumable made available online for the end user to purchase from a number of potential suppliers.[244] Commoditized legal goods lie at the opposite end of the spectrum from "bespoke" legal services, which are tailored for specific cases or clients.[245]

Stagnating demand and productivity have been particularly important in creating a more challenging and competitive environment for big law firms.[246] In the past, firms typically downsized the number of their associates,[247] but now firms are placing higher performance expectations on partners: entering into equity partnerships increasingly depends on the candidate's ability to generate business,[248] and equity partners with lower productivity may be de-equitized or asked to leave.[249] Among the firms responding to *American Lawyer*'s 2012 annual survey, 45 percent said they had de-equitized partners in 2012 and 46 percent plan to de-equitize partners in 2013, significant increases compared to the previous year's survey.[250]

Other trends that have increased competitiveness in the supply of legal services include the emergence of nontraditional providers of legal services and a rise in the use of alternative fee arrangements. Nontraditional providers of legal services include firms that carry out tasks such as document review at lower prices than law firms.[251] For example, Axiom, originally a firm that placed attorneys at corporations on a temporary basis, recently hired a staff of attorneys to handle typically outsourced work.[252] Axiom is offering higher-tier legal services as well, though it faces some restrictions on the type of work it can do as it is not a law firm.[253] Additionally, in the past a client would likely turn to one firm to handle all aspects of litigation; now they may turn to a nontraditional vendor to handle the discovery piece of the litigation and thereby disaggregate their legal needs.[254] Finally, the market for alternative fee arrangements (such as charging flat fees for particular services and other billing arrangements not based on hourly rates) has also grown since the economic downturn as corporations seek to reduce their legal costs.[255] Such alternative fee arrangements offer incentives for efficiency and can increase cost savings and predictability.[256] A survey of 218 firms and 206 corporate law departments found that although traditional billing arrangements still dominate, alternative arrangements are increasingly common: between 2010 and 2011, 63 percent of firms and 50 percent of legal departments saw a rise in such arrangements, and about three-quarters of both firms and departments expect they will increase further by 2016.[257]

Competition in the U.S. Legal Employment Market

Recent U.S. law school graduates face a threefold quandary. While their law school debt is high and growing,[258] the number of high-paying legal jobs has declined, and the oversupply of graduates relative to available jobs is projected to continue, sharpening job competition in the industry. The proportion of jobs at law firms with more than 250 lawyers (which typically pay higher salaries than smaller firms) declined from 33 percent to 21 percent between 2009 and 2011, and correspondingly the median starting salary for the graduating class of 2011 fell about 17 percent during that time.[259] Nine months after graduating, only 55 percent of the 2011 graduating class had full-time jobs that required passing the bar exam.[260] Additionally, there was a wide disparity between high job placement rates for graduates of top-tiered schools and low placement rates (often under 50 percent) for graduates of lower-tiered schools.[261]

Legal services employment is anticipated to grow by 10 percent between 2010 and 2020—from 728,200 to 801,800[262]—but not enough to accommodate the 45,000 students graduating from law school each year.[263] While demand for legal services will not diminish,[264] demand growth for lawyers will be constrained by the increased use of paralegals, nontraditional providers, and other alternatives to lawyers.[265]

Partly for these reasons, law schools have seen declining applications:[266] the number of applicants dropped by 12 percent from 2010 to 2011,[267] and preliminary statistics show a 15 percent drop in first-year enrollment between 2010 and 2012.[268] The combination of rising law school costs and dim job prospects for new graduates has led to what some have called a crisis in U.S. legal education.[269] As a result, a number of legal education reforms have been proposed that may offer more practical legal training at reduced cost.

Continuing Globalization of Law Firms

The increasing globalization of law firms stems from two factors. Presence in foreign markets allows firms to better provide services to international clients.[270] And, by expanding into higher-growth markets in Africa, Asia, Latin America, and the Middle East, globalization helps firms offset relatively low growth in demand for legal services in the United States and Europe.[271]

Law firms expand internationally by opening new offices and executing cross-border mergers. In 2012, U.S. law firms opened 56 new offices in foreign markets: 28 in Asia (primarily China and the Republic of Korea [Korea]), 15 in Europe (primarily Germany and Russia), 6 in the Middle East and Africa, and 7 in Latin America and the Caribbean.[272] In some cases firms have entered these markets following liberalization[273] (see "Trade Trends" below).

Mergers offer a faster route to international expansion than opening a new office, but hinge on the ability to successfully meld two firms together.[274] In 2012, 96 cross-border mergers were announced, many more than in previous years.[275] For example, in March 2012, China's King & Wood merged with Australia's Mallesons Stephen Jaques to form the firm of King & Wood Mallesons, the first international merger for a Chinese law firm.[276] Among the top 100 global firms by revenue, many have pursued mergers with firms in Australia, as the country is seen as a point of entry into Asia (and especially China).[277] These mergers commonly result in looser organizational structures called vereins, in which merged entities remain financially independent. Mergers have also increased concentration in the international legal services market.[278]

Trade Trends

Cross-border Trade

U.S. imports of legal services grew at a much higher rate than U.S. exports in 2011, but because U.S. imports increased from a relatively small base, the U.S. legal services trade surplus grew to $5.7 billion (figure 5.1) (box 5.1).[279] Overall, U.S. cross-border exports of legal services increased by 4 percent to $7.5 billion in 2011, mirroring the annual growth rate of 4 percent from 2007 through 2010. U.S. imports of legal services increased by 16 percent to about $1.8 billion in 2011, compared to essentially no growth from 2007 through 2010.[280] Trends in cross-border trade reflect the impacts of the economic downturn and slow recovery in 2011: both imports and exports declined in 2009 and 2010, and exports in 2011 ($7.5 billion) were just above the 2008 level ($7.3 billion), while 2011 imports ($1.8 billion) were just under the 2008 level ($1.9 billion). U.S. exports of legal services are concentrated among a small number of foreign markets. In 2011, the top five export markets for legal services accounted for 50 percent of total U.S. exports of such services, down from 55 percent in 2007. The United Kingdom and Japan were the two leading export markets in 2011, accounting for 16 percent and 14 percent of such exports, respectively (figure 5.2), while Canada, Germany, and Switzerland also ranked in the top five.[281] Other notable single-country export markets in 2011 included China, Korea, and the Netherlands.

Although regional shares of U.S. legal services exports remained relatively steady in the recent period, there were notable differences in rates of growth.[282] From 2007 through 2011, U.S. legal services exports to Africa and Europe grew the slowest (6 percent and 11 percent, respectively); by contrast, exports to the Asia-Pacific region grew by 18 percent, exports to South and Central America grew by 36 percent, and exports to the Middle East grew by 97 percent. Within the regions showing rapid growth during this period, seven countries—Chile, India, Indonesia, New Zealand, Saudi Arabia, Singapore, and Thailand—experienced especially high rates of growth in U.S. legal services exports.[283]

As noted earlier, fast-growing markets in Asia, Africa, Latin America, and the Middle East have attracted international law firms seeking to diversify away from developed markets with slower demand growth.[284] For example, while only a handful of U.S. law firms have a physical presence in Africa, most U.S. firms with an international focus are seeking to increase their involvement in Africa-related matters, and some are providing cross-border services to the region.[285]

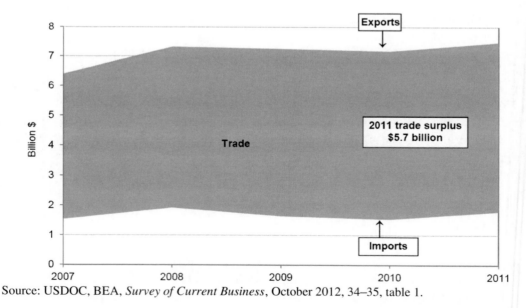

Source: USDOC, BEA, *Survey of Current Business*, October 2012, 34–35, table 1.

Figure 5.1. Legal services: U.S. cross-border trade resulted in a trade surplus each year during 2007–11.

BOX 5.1. BEA DATA ON CROSS-BORDER TRADE AND AFFILIATE TRANSACTIONS IN LEGAL SERVICES

This section's data on cross-border trade and affiliate transactions are prepared by the Bureau of Economic Analysis (BEA) of the U.S. Department of Commerce (USDOC). Data on legal services capture services provided when legal professionals travel abroad to provide services to clients, when clients travel abroad to engage the services of foreign attorneys, or when legal documents or advice are exchanged across national borders via the postal service, fax transmissions, the Internet, or other means.[a] Data are collected through surveys broken down by the type of service provided, and companies report their sales of legal services, defined as transactions involving "legal advice or other legal services."[b] The data do not differentiate among the specific categories of legal services that are traded. Cross-border sales of legal services therefore encompass all legal services rendered by U.S. companies through cross-border channels, irrespective of whether companies are law firms. For example, legal services rendered by a corporation's in-house counsel would be captured in cross-border trade data (though in-house attorneys would more commonly be dispensing advice internally).[c]

BEA data on legal service affiliate transactions capture sales by foreign legal services affiliates of U.S. law firms and purchases from U.S. affiliates of foreign law firms.[d] These data are also collected through surveys, but they are categorized based on the industry classification of the affiliate, rather than the type of service provided.[e] Thus, sales of legal services by foreign affiliates of U.S. firms include only sales by affiliates that are classified under NAICS code 5411 (legal services). Consequently, the data may theoretically exclude sales by affiliates of firms in other industries that also provide legal services or include sales by legal services affiliates with secondary activities in another industry. However, neither scenario is common in practice.[f]

[a] BEA representative, email messages to USITC staff, February 26, 2009.

[b] USDOC, BEA, form BE-125 (11-2011), Quarterly Survey of Transactions in Selected Services and Intangible Assets with Foreign Persons, 2011, 17; USDOC, BEA, form BE-120, Benchmark Survey of Transactions in Selected Services and Intellectual Property with Foreign Persons, n.d. (accessed April 29, 2013), 21; BEA representative, email messages to USITC staff, January 3, 2011, February 25, 2010, and February 26, 2009; BEA representative, telephone interview by USITC staff, May 13, 2010. Statistics for cross-border trade in legal services are collected quarterly through Survey BE-125, and every five years through Survey BE-120. Both surveys collect data on affiliated and unaffiliated cross-border trade. Data for affiliated cross-border trade in legal services became available for the first time beginning in 2006; such trade accounts for a very small share of total cross-border trade in legal services. Surveys BE-125 and BE-120 can be found at http://www.bea.gov/surveys/pdf/be125.pdf and http://www.bea.gov/surveys/pdf/ be120.pdf.

[c] BEA representative, email messages to USITC staff, January 3, 2011, and April 4, 2011. Similarly, any secondary (non-legal services) activity by a law firm would be classified as the type of service provided. However, the incidence of both activities (secondary activities by legal services providers, and legal services provided by firms in other industries) tends to be low.

[d] BEA reports "services supplied" by affiliates; for legal services, services supplied correspond to sales.

[e] BEA representative, telephone interview by USITC staff, May 13, 2010; USDOC, BEA, form BE-11B (rev. 8/2012), 2012 Annual Survey of U.S. Direct Investment Abroad, 2012, 3; BEA representative, email message to USITC staff, February 26, 2009. Statistics for transactions by majority-owned legal services affiliates are collected through BEA's surveys of U.S. direct investment abroad and foreign direct investment in the United States, which can be found at http://www.bea.gov/surveys/diasurv.htm and http://www.bea.gov/surveys/ fdiusurv.htm.
[f] BEA representative, email messages to USITC staff, January 3, 2011, and April 4, 2011.

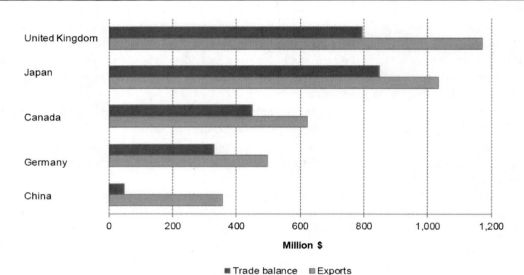

■ Trade balance	■ Exports

Source: USDOC, BEA, *Survey of Current Business*, October 2012, 52–53, table 7.2.

Figure 5.2. Legal services: The United Kingdom was the leading market for U.S. cross-border exports of legal services in 2011.

Liberalization in certain markets may ease entry to foreign markets and affect legal services trade. For example, Korea recently implemented free trade agreements with the European Union and the United States that contained provisions removing barriers to trade in legal services.[286] Additionally, an Indian high court ruled that foreign lawyers are permitted to provide advice on international law or international arbitration in India on a "fly in, fly out" basis (though foreign firms are not permitted to establish a presence or practice Indian law).[287] There has also been liberalization in the legal services markets in Israel and Malaysia.[288]

Five countries accounted for more than half (56 percent) of U.S. legal services imports in 2011: the United Kingdom (21 percent), Japan (10 percent), Canada (10 percent), Germany (9 percent), and China (5 percent) (figure 5.3). The share of the top five markets remained mostly unchanged from 2007, when those same countries accounted for 55 percent of U.S. legal services imports. Regional shares of U.S. legal services imports also remained fairly similar from 2007 through 2011, with the exception of the Asia-Pacific's share (which increased from 28 percent in 2007 to 31 percent in 2011). Growth rates during that time were highest in the Asia-Pacific, Middle East, and African regions. The source countries with the highest 2007–11 growth rates were China, India, Malaysia, New Zealand, the Philippines, Saudi Arabia, Thailand, and Venezuela.[289]

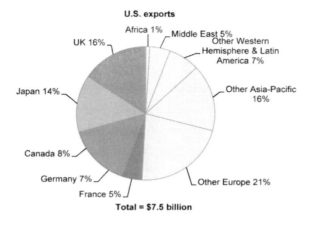

U.S. exports

Total = $7.5 billion

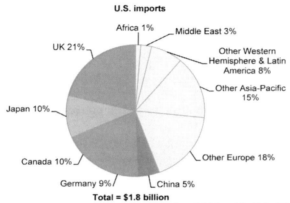

U.S. imports

Total = $1.8 billion

Source: USDOC, BEA, *Survey of Current Business*, October 2012, table 7.2, 52–53.
Note: Geographic regions are shaded in yellow. Figures may not total 100 percent due to rounding.

Figure 5.3. Legal services: Developed countries were the leading foreign suppliers of legal services in 2011.

Affiliate Transactions

Sales by foreign affiliates of U.S. law firms (foreign affiliate sales) greatly exceeded sales by U.S. affiliates of foreign law firms in recent years (figure 5.4). Nonetheless, foreign affiliate sales declined in 2010, falling by 2 percent to $5 billion. The 2010 decline in foreign affiliate sales growth stands in stark contrast to their average annual growth rate of 24 percent from 2006 through 2009. In 2010, Europe accounted for 73 percent of foreign affiliate sales, led by the United Kingdom (34 percent), France (11 percent), and Germany (10 percent). Japan, with 7 percent, was the largest non-European market for foreign affiliate sales. The most significant change in these shares since 2006 is the decline in the European share (down from 80 percent in 2006) and the rise of the share of other countries, from 12 percent in 2006 to 18 percent in 2010.[290]

Foreign affiliate sales growth has coincided with growth in U.S. direct investment abroad in the legal services sector. Investment abroad by U.S. law firms increased by 37 percent in 2011 and rose at an average annual rate of 16 percent from 2007 through 2010.[291] On average, U.S. direct investment abroad was highest in Latin America, Africa, and the Asia-Pacific region between 2009 and 2011.[292]

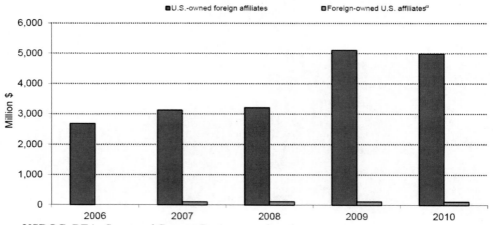

Source: USDOC, BEA, *Survey of Current Business*, various issues.
[a] Data for foreign-owned U.S. affiliates for 2006 was suppressed to avoid disclosure of data of individual companies.

Figure 5.4. Legal services: Services supplied by U.S.-owned foreign affiliates exceeded services supplied by foreign-owned U.S. affiliates.

Although country-specific data on affiliate sales are available for only a small number of countries, including Canada, some European countries, Australia, and Japan, anecdotal information suggests that certain markets have become increasingly important for international law firms. For example, Singapore has emerged as an attractive market from which foreign law firms may provide legal services to other parts of Asia,[293] and the country recently announced it will accept additional applications from foreign firms seeking to provide advice on Singapore law.[294] Mexico, with a growing economy, expanding middle class, burgeoning domestic investment opportunities, and increasing outbound investment into other Latin American countries, has also recently attracted foreign law firms, and an increasing number of U.S. firms are establishing a presence there.[295]

U.S.-owned foreign affiliate sales of legal services in 2006–09 grew at a faster pace than domestic purchases of legal services from U.S. affiliates of foreign law firms in 2007–09.[296] During 2010, the latest year for which affiliate data are available, purchases from U.S. affiliates actually declined by 4 percent to $111 million, in contrast to the average annual increase of 5 percent from 2007 through 2009. Purchases had grown only modestly in the previous year (0.9 percent in 2009). This pattern resembles trends in cross-border imports, for which growth declined in both 2009 and 2010.

Outlook

The legal services industry will likely continue to see increases in the use of alternative fee arrangements and nontraditional providers of legal services. A majority of respondents to a survey of U.S. law firms indicated that they had not changed how they conducted business in 2012 in order to increase efficiency,[297] but that such changes were likely in the future. A majority of respondents to a 2012 survey of leading law firms said that they expected price competition, commoditization of legal work, non-hourly billing, fewer equity partners, more contract lawyers, lower profits per partner, outsourcing of legal work, and smaller first-year classes at law schools to become more common.[298]

Most observers expect demand, revenue, and profits to increase only modestly in the U.S. legal services industry, while competition promises to be more intense. Firms that adjust their business structures will be most likely to succeed when the U.S. economy strengthens.[299] Foreign markets will continue to be attractive, and demand for legal services in higher-growth regions like Asia will become increasingly important.[300] Cross-border mergers will likely continue, as firms combine practice strengths (such as expertise in a particular industry) with global reach.[301] However, international expansion has not necessarily led to higher profits,[302] and emerging economies may not stimulate the global demand for legal services to the same extent as in the past.[303]

SECTION 6. SERVICES ROUNDTABLE

The Commission hosted its sixth annual services roundtable on November 13, 2012, with Commission Chairman Irving A. Williamson presiding and Commissioners Meredith Broadbent and Shara L. Aranoff moderating. These roundtables are held to encourage discussions among individuals from government, industry, and academia about important issues affecting services trade. This year's discussion focused on the relationship between services liberalization and regulation, as well as the prospects for upcoming services trade agreements.

Services Liberalization and Regulation

The panel discussed the impact of regulations on the provision and consumption of services. One participant pointed out that the quantity of services regulations is not necessarily related to their quality; for example, life insurance is not only a highly regulated industry, it is often a well-regulated one, inasmuch as governments focus on consumer protection and market stability while maintaining neutrality between domestic and foreign companies. On the subject of regulations that discriminate against foreign companies, another participant noted that state-owned enterprises (SOEs) are a significant impediment to liberalization, since governments try to exclude SOEs from regulations and international standards. For example, governments concerned about declining revenue from postal delivery services have tried to insulate such services from competition.

The panel considered whether countries' reluctance to liberalize services may be due to concerns that they have too little regulatory capacity to manage increased competition. One participant expressed a wish that countries could be convinced that liberalization implies neither deregulation nor the regulation of formerly unregulated sectors. Another panelist noted that regulations designed to ensure market access address only one type of market failure—specifically, concentration due to economies of scale in industries like telecommunications and logistics, which results in incumbents controlling infrastructure; other types of market failures are not covered under market access discussions. The participant pointed out that while the General Agreement on Trade in Services (GATS) ensures that regulations will not undermine commitments to expand market access (such as commitments to allow foreign telecommunication firms to access essential facilities), GATS does not address pure anticompetitive practices, such as the use of licensing and certification procedures for protectionist purposes.

The panel considered the question of countries' capacity to regulate. One participant said that developing countries seek rapid improvements in infrastructure services (especially finance, insurance, logistics, and telecommunications), and argued that these services need to be appropriately regulated before liberalization can occur. The participant cited Zambia, where liberalization did not necessarily lead to improved access to services, as an example of a country that prematurely liberalized without having enough prudential regulations in place. Another participant added that financial liberalization can shock domestic banking systems, as local firms often cannot compete with foreign firms that rely on revenue streams from their home-country operations. The panel discussed whether development requires not just the absence of access-impeding regulations but frameworks to ensure that regulators are not captured by oligopolistic interests that can appropriate the gains from liberalization. One participant suggested that there is no obviously optimal regulatory sequencing for industries like financial services and telecommunication, and it is difficult for countries to pinpoint the moment when they can safely liberalize.

Participants went on to discuss the diversity in size, development level, regulatory capacity, and reliance on SOEs of countries involved in trade negotiations. One participant noted that even among countries that are members of the Organization for Economic Co-operation and Development (OECD), regulations differ markedly (e.g., some countries do not significantly regulate professional services), and there are increasing regulatory divergences in industries like telecommunications as such services become more Internet-based. Another participant pointed out that low-income countries are very different from middle-income countries; for example, some low-income countries have not regulated cross-border banking at all, as they haven't had the resources to address it, while most middle-income countries have done so. The panelists contrasted informal retail sectors in sub-Saharan Africa, which are largely unregulated, to the retail sector in India, where regulatory measures block foreign entrants. One participant emphasized that low-income countries do not lack the will to regulate services optimally—in fact they are more interested in services and services competitiveness than they are often given credit for—but they lack expertise. The participant drew the inference that incremental liberalization can pave the way for incremental efficiency gains and incremental development in low-income countries.

The panel discussed ways of standardizing regulations across countries. Examples offered by the participants included UN advisory committees that help countries set financial regulations in accordance with anti-money-laundering guidelines; the International Telecommunication Union, which promotes conversations among regulators that can lead to best practices; and mutual recognition agreements. One participant noted that even though regulatory convergence is difficult, given that countries require both incentives and regulatory capacities to implement international standards, discussions among regulators nevertheless can lead to progress and a "meeting of minds." The panel noted that firms selling services abroad (or trying to) often just want a predictable regulatory environment and reasonable terms for market access, rather than having U.S. or EU regulations (even if they are more open) replicated line by line in every country where they operate. One participant added that harmonization is not practical in many situations due to differing cultural norms, and that if, in developed countries, there is a clash of sophisticated regulatory frameworks, interoperability rather than harmonization may be sufficient. Another participant suggested that if more countries adopt principle-based (or outcome-based) regulatory approaches, the regulatory environment may improve without it being necessary to get all countries to adopt a standard set of laws. One participant emphasized that the goal of setting international standards is to remove regulatory arbitrage (wherein firms seek to maximize profit by taking advantage of regulatory loopholes in certain countries). This participant cited financial services as an example of an industry where liberalization, instead of driving better regulation, led to regulatory cherry-picking by financial firms.

One participant emphasized the need to consider the impact of liberalization on professional workers and on labor standards, especially now as the United States faces high long-term unemployment.

The panel considered the spectrum of liberalization processes, ranging from a large, slow negotiation with many countries and points of contention, to individual countries simply deciding that "self-liberalization" is in their interest. A participant cited the example of a project in Romania that engaged local stakeholders to file antimonopoly lawsuits against the state's Internet service providers, which resulted in more Internet service providers and lower costs for consumers, illustrating the point that liberalization driven by domestic constituencies can be more successful than top-down liberalization. Another participant argued that attempts to open markets through "tough" negotiations may be unsustainable, as regulators prefer to be driven by a competition agenda rather than a trade agenda. The participant explained that in trade negotiations, countries often agree to commitments on services in order to get provisions they want on manufactured or agricultural exports— but they then find they lack the capacity to implement their services commitments well. One participant countered that regulators are often interested in pressuring their own societies for change, and use trade agreement negotiations as a source of leverage. Another added that there may be a perverse incentive for countries that might have been inclined to liberalize unilaterally to say instead, "I want to see what I can get for this through the negotiation process."

Prospects for Future Services Trade Agreements

In discussing forthcoming trade agreements, one participant expressed the belief that agreements among small groups of like-minded countries were more achievable than a broader International Services Agreement (ISA). The participant cited the fact that recent international efforts on trade and climate change have ended in a standoff between the United States and the BRIC countries (Brazil, Russia, India, and China), and there is little reason to expect the negotiations for an ISA to end differently. Another participant agreed that the trade negotiation process becomes less useful when it drags on for years and becomes bogged down in controversies and disagreements; instead, it may be more desirable to focus on something that can be accomplished quickly, such as getting a group of countries together to ratify existing levels of liberalization.

A third participant, citing high levels of protection in fast-growing Southeast Asian countries (particularly in transport and professional services), added that negotiators should deal with the levels of protection that exist, rather than developing an ideal agreement among like-minded countries and then looking for recruits. The participant contrasted the current environment with that of the late 1990s when China joined the WTO, suggesting it is much less likely today that negotiators can conceive a perfect agreement and then have large emerging markets simply accede to it. For this reason, the participant continued, it is not clear that the ISA will succeed where other proposed agreements have failed.

However, expressing skepticism that a smaller deal would be easier to achieve, a participant suggested that the presence of additional countries in the negotiation process may be an incentive to potential signatories. It was noted that an ambitious agreement that attracted a growing list of negotiating countries could lead to growing benefits and additional countries calculating that they are better off inside rather than outside the agreement. One participant mentioned the example of the General Agreement on Tariffs and Trade (GATT), which was originally ratified through bilateral agreements and then expanded into a multilateral agreement. Another participant expressed the view that even when final deals are elusive, working on broad agreements is worthwhile, remarking that the World Trade Organization (WTO) is an important institution and that negotiations build confidence and benefit the United States' geopolitical position.

The panel discussed the ISA in more depth, questioning exactly how many countries are seriously committed to the prospective agreement at this point. A participant speculated that if the Doha Round eventually collapses, the ISA may be the only ongoing major trade project involving trade in services, other than a proliferation of negotiations toward bilateral agreements. Partly for this reason, the participant emphasized that ISA negotiations need to be future-oriented, as they may set the tone for the next decade of services discussions (though the participant added that this consideration does not imply that negotiators should hold out for a perfect agreement).

The panel discussed ways to address differing levels of ambition among countries and differing levels of enthusiasm among industries, wondering whether these differences would lead to a "gerrymandered" agreement. One participant said that the reluctance of some countries to negotiate stems from political resistance, but also from three regulatory issues: the fear of the loss of regulatory freedom when countries do not know how commitments will be interpreted (such as what happened in the United States-Antigua online gambling dispute); general regulatory weakness (especially in developing countries that are not prepared to deal with competition); and the lack of mechanisms for regulatory cooperation. A participant suggested that industries might not anticipate many benefits from further trade negotiations because there simply are not many benefits left to be had; for example, the United States-EU economic relationship is already the most successful partnership in the world, and industries within the United States and the EU are able to work around the barriers that do exist.

The panel talked about the need for a new framework that integrates goods and services, as trade is, in practice, conducted by firms that provide both. One participant emphasized that the GATS is an artificial construction, categorizing the same activity (such as crossing borders to supply services) differently depending on whether it is done by General Motors or by Citi. Another participant said that market access in retail services is not meaningful without market access in goods, as well as market access for several non- retail services. Expanding on this point, the participant pointed out that retailers rely on a huge array of ancillary services, such as telecoms and financial services, to serve their customers; that retail services additionally require express delivery services to cross the "last mile" and get products to the customer; and that because customers want electronic platforms to learn about prices and products, data flows are involved as well.

List of external participants at the Commission's services roundtable held on November 13, 2012

Name	Title / Affiliation
Peter Allgeier	President Coalition of Services Industries
Erik Autor	Vice President and International Trade Counsel National Retail Federation
Christopher Benscher	Manager of Government Affairs Halliburton
Christine Bliss	Assistant U.S. Trade Representative for Services and Investment USTR
Maria Borga	Assistant Division Chief for Research and Analysis Bureau of Economic Analysis, Department of Commerce
Ralph Carter	Managing Director, Legal, Trade, and International Affairs FedEx Express
David Cohen	Executive Director, Department of Professional Employees AFL-CIO
Greg Frazier	Executive Vice President Motion Picture Association of America
Ed Gresser	Director Global Works Foundation
Adam Hemphill	Senior Manager of Federal Government Relations Walmart Stores Inc.
Charles R. Johnston	Director and Senior Vice President, International Government Affairs Citigroup
David LeDuc	Senior Director of Public Policy Software and Information Industry Association
David Long	Director Office of Services Industries, U.S. Department of Commerce
Aaditya Mattoo	Research Manager, Trade and Integration World Bank
Hildegunn Nordas	Senior Policy Analyst OECD
Lisa Rohrer	Director of Research Hildebrandt Baker Robbins
Jeffrey Schott	Senior Fellow Peterson Institute
Richard Self	Trade Policy Consultant World Trade Organization
Ben Shepherd	Principal Developing Trade Consultants Ltd.
Laurie Sherman	Senior Legal Advisor Transparency International USA
Brad Smith	Chief International Officer American Council of Life Insurers
James Wallar	Senior Vice President Nathan Associates

APPENDIX A. SELECTED SERVICES RESEARCH

This appendix highlights selected research by USITC staff on the services industry that were completed since the last *Recent Trends* was published. This year's report provides abstracts and links to four recent research papers and an executive briefing on trade (EBOT):

- "Policy Challenges of Cross-Border Cloud Computing" *(Journal of International Commerce and Economics)*
- "Liberalization of Retail Services in India: A CGE Model" (working paper)
- "Nontariff Measures in the Global Retailing Industry" (working paper)
- "An Overview and Examination of the Vietnamese Service Sector" (working paper)
- "China: A Leading Growth Market for U.S. Services Exports and Investment" (EBOT)

Cloud Computing Article

Policy Challenges of Cross-Border Cloud Computing
Renee Berry and Matthew Reisman, *Journal of International Commerce and Economics*, May 2012. http://www.usitc.gov/journals/policy_challenges_of_cross-border_cloud_computing.pdf.

Abstract
Providers of cloud computing services are increasingly serving customers outside their home country markets and using service delivery models that require the transmission of data across borders. In this article, we present an overview of the global market for cloud services and explore the role of cloud computing in U.S. exports. We then examine the main policy challenges associated with cross-border cloud computing—ensuring data privacy, security, and the free flow of information—and the ways that countries are ad- dressing them through domestic policymaking, international agreements, and other cooperative arrangements. Finally, we identify the particular challenges faced by developing countries as they seek to participate in the market for cloud computing services. Our discussion includes case studies of two of the most important emerging markets for such services—China and India.

India Services Modeling Paper

Liberalization of Retail Services in India: A CGE Model
Csilla Lakatos and Tani Fukui, Office of Economics Working Paper No. 2013-03A, March 2013. http://www.usitc.gov/publications/332/working_papers/EC201303A.pdf.

Abstract
In order to address the significant increase in importance of foreign direct investment (FDI) and of multinational corporation (MNC)-related policies, we have developed an extended Global Trade Analysis Project (GTAP) model and associated global database that

accounts for both FDI and MNCs, differentiated by the region of ownership. The model is calibrated on the GTAP v8 database, augmented by global foreign affiliate data described in Fukui and Lakatos (2012) and the FDI stocks data of Boumellassa, Gouel, and Laborde (2007). To illustrate the model's behavior, we examine the recent policy debate with respect to allowing FDI in multi-brand retailing in India. We find that the unilateral reduction of barriers to FDI in distribution services in India benefits the economy as a whole, consumers, and foreign producers, but hurts domestic distributors. Nevertheless, when we consider the associated productivity improvements documented in the literature to downstream and upstream industries, we find that domestic producers are expected to benefit from the liberalization of the distribution sector as well.

Retailing Working Paper

Nontariff Measures in the Global Retailing Industry
Matthew Reisman and Danielle Vu, USITC Office of Industries Working Paper ID-30, May 2012. http://www.usitc.gov/publications/332/working_papers/nontariff_measures_in_the_globa l_retailing_industryWP_NoID-30.pdf.

Abstract
This paper introduces a new measure of policies and regulations affecting the retailing industry. Our retail restrictiveness index addresses 13 categories of nontariff measures (NTMs), including market entry restrictions and operational regulations. We produce index scores for 75 countries. Southeast Asian countries, including Indonesia, Malaysia, and Thailand, are among the most restrictive retail markets as measured by our index, while the United States is one of the world's most open. We use econometric gravity models to examine how restrictiveness affects sales of multinational retailers' foreign affiliates, and find that high (restrictive) scores on our index are associated with decreased affiliate sales.

Vietnam Working Paper

An Overview and Examination of the Vietnamese Service Sector
Isaac Wohl, ed. USITC Office of Industries Working Paper ID-033, August 2012. http://www.usitc.gov/publications/332/working_papers/Vietnam_working_Paper_final2a. pdf.
Contributors: Lisa Alejandro, Eric Forden, Erick Oh, Joann Peterson, Samantha Pham, Matthew Reisman, George Serletis, Danielle Vu, and Isaac Wohl.

Abstract
Vietnam is growing rapidly as it transitions from a state-planned economy to a hybrid economy with an expanded private sector. Besides broadening its international trade relationships, in recent years Vietnam has committed to liberalizing its industries and strengthening its intellectual property laws through bilateral treaties, regional associations, and accession to the World Trade Organization. Service industries account for a growing share of Vietnam's economy, as new businesses seek services like banking and logistics while consumers with rising income demand education, retail, and telecommunication services.

Liberalization and foreign investment have increased the supply of services in Vietnam, but many industries are still hampered by shortages of skilled workers and good infrastructure, and by a weak business environment in which regulations impede commerce and state-owned enterprises have many advantages.

U.S-China Services Trade EBOT

China: A Leading Growth Market for U.S. Services Exports and Investment

George Serletis, USITC Executive Briefing on Trade, March 2013. http://usitc.gov/publications/332/executive_briefings/China_ServicesEBOT_ExternalFina l.pdf.

Abstract

U.S. cross-border exports of private services to China more than doubled in 2006–11, growing more rapidly than exports to all other leading U.S. services markets except Brazil. In 2011, U.S. exports of services to China were nearly $27 billion, which ranked China as the United States' fifth-largest services export market, up from ninth in 2006. Export growth was spread among a broad array of services industries. Sales of services by affiliates of U.S. firms operating in China also more than doubled during the period. China's recent focus on stimulating domestic demand through service sector growth, as well as the relatively small current share of services in its economy, suggests future growth of U.S. services trade in the market.

REFERENCES

Abelson, Reed. "The Face of Future Health Care." *New York Times*, March 20, 2013. Accenture. *Making the Case for Connected Health*, 2012.

Aldridge, Alex. "Law Students: 'And What Else Do I Get with My Masters?'" *Guardian*, October 4, 2012. http://www.guardian.co.uk/law/2012/oct/04/legal-education-llm-law-schools.

Allen, Greg. "South Florida Hospitals Compete for Foreign Patients." NPR.org, August 13, 2009. American Association of Medical Colleges. "Physician Shortages to Worsen without Increases in Residency Training," n.d. https://www.aamc.org/download/153160/data/pysician_shortages_to_worsen_without_ increases_in_residency_tr.pdf (accessed May 16, 2013).

ALM Legal Intelligence. "Speaking Different Languages: Alternative Fee Arrangements for Law Firms and Legal Departments," April 2012. http://www.lexisnexis.com/counsellink/documents/ALM- Survey-Alternative-Fee-Arrangements.pdf.

Altman Weil. "2012 Law Firms in Transition: An Altman Weil Flash Survey," 2012. http://www.altmanweil.com/dir_docs/resource/1667e5c8-b99e-4557-93ac-73174118ea29_ document.pdf.

American Lawyer. "The Global 100 Profit Picture: An Interactive Chart," n.d. http://www.americanlawyer.com/PubArticleTAL.jsp?id=1202514395288 (accessed March 13, 2013).

———— "Law Firm Leaders Survey 2012: Vote of Confidence," November 30, 2012. http://www.americanlawyer.com/PubArticleTAL.jsp?id=1202579030652&thepage=2.

————. "A Guide to Our Methodology," June 2012. Association for Legal Career Professionals. "Median Private Practice Starting Salaries for the Class of 2011 Plunge As Private Practice Jobs Continue to Erode." Press release, July 12, 2012. http://www.nalp.org/classof2011_salpressrel.

————. "The 2012 Global 100: Most Revenue," October 2012. http://www.americanlawyer. com/PubArticleTAL.jsp?id=1202571228982&The_2012_Global_100_Most_Revenue&s lreturn=20130201112831.

————. "The 2012 Law Firm Leaders Survey," n.d. http://www.americanlawyer. com/PubArticleTAL.jsp?id=1202579458620 (accessed February 21, 2013).

Anderson, Nick. "Elite Education for the Masses." *Washington Post*, November 5, 2012. http://www.washingtonpost.com/local/education/elite-education-for-the-masses/2012/11/ 03/c2ac8144-121b-11e2-ba83-a7a396e6b2a7_story_2.html.

Are, Chandrakanth. "Global Expansion of U.S. Health Care System and Organizations." Society of American Gastrointestinal Endoscopic Surgeons, February 13, 2009. Bain & Company. *Global Healthcare Private Equity Report 2012*, 2012.

Barnes, C. & Co. *Worldwide Colleges and Universities Industry (NAICS 61131)*. Barnes Reports, 2012.

Bartlett, Tom; Karin Fischer. "The China Conundrum." *Chronicle of Higher Education*, November 3, 2012. http://chronicle.com/article/The-China-Conundrum/129628/.

Becker, Scott; Kristian A Werling; Holly, Carnell. "Private Equity Investing in Healthcare: 13 Hot and 4 Cold Areas." McGuireWoods, August 16, 2011.

Bennett, William. "Why the Chinese Are Flocking to U.S. Colleges." *CNN*, May 31, 2012. http://www.cnn.com/2012/05/31/opinion/bennett-china-us-schools.

Bloom, David E; David, Canning. "Population Health and Economic Growth." Commission on Growth and Development. Working Paper No. 24, 2008.

Bloomberg News. "China Medical Services Market Seen Hitting $500 Billion," June 25, 2012. Bowden, Marilyn. "Medical Tourism Fills Hospital Beds." *Miami Today*, August 23, 2012.

Bronner, Ethan. "Law Schools' Applications Fall As Costs Rise and Jobs Are Cut." *New York Times*, January 30, 2013. http://www.nytimes.com/2013/01/31/education/law-schools-applications-fall- as-costs-rise-and-jobs-are-cut.html?smid=pl-share&_r=0.

Buntin, Melinda Beeuwkes; Matthew, F Burke; Michael, C. Hoaglin, and David Blumenthal. "The Benefits of Health Information Technology: A Review of the Recent Literature Shows Predominantly Positive Results." *Health Affairs*, 30, no. 3 (2011): 464–471.

Bureau of Labor Statistics (BLS). "Occupational Outlook Handbook: Job Outlook," n.d. http://www.bls.gov/ooh/Legal/Lawyers.htm#tab-6 (accessed February 5, 2013).

Bureau van Dijk. Orbis Companies Database. https://orbis.bvdep.com (accessed February 11, 2013).

————. Zephyr mergers and acquisitions database. https://zephyr2.bvdep.com (accessed February 14, 2013).

Butkeviciene, Jolita. "Temporary Movement of Natural Persons (Mode 4) under the GATS." United Nations Conference on Trade and Development (UNCTAD), n.d. (accessed December 4, 2012). http://unstats.un.org/unsd/tradeserv/db/docs/Doc42-CPM-091-Berlin-ISI.pdf.

Campos, Paul. "The Crisis of the American Law School." University of Colorado Law School Legal Studies Research Paper Series. Working Paper Number 12-13, July 9, 2012. http://papers.ssrn.com/sol3/papers.cfm?abstract_id=2102702.

Carlson, Scott. "What's the Payoff for the 'Country Club' College?" *Chronicle of Higher Education*, January 28, 2013. http://chronicle.com/blogs/buildings/whats-the-payoff-for-the-country-club- college/32477.

Carpenter, Dick M; II, Lisa Knepper; Angela, C Erickson; John, K Ross. "License to Work: A National Study of Burdens from Occupational Licensing." Institute for Justice, May 2012. https://www.ij.org/licensetowork.

Castro, Daniel. "Explaining International IT Application Leadership: Health IT," September 22, 2009. http://papers.ssrn.com/sol3/papers.cfm?abstract_id=1477486.

Cattaneo, Olivier; Peter, Walkenhorst. "Legal Services: Does More Trade Rhyme with Better Justice?" In *International Trade in Services: New Trends and Opportunities for Developing Countries*, edited by Olivier Cattaneo, Michael Engman, Sebastián Sáez, and Robert M. Stern, 67–97. Washington, DC: World Bank, 2010.

Chan, Cathy. "Carlyle Buys Stake in Chinese Private Medical Company." *Bloomberg Businessweek*, August 14, 2012.

Chee, Heng Leng. "Medical Tourism in Malaysia: International Movement of Healthcare Consumers and the Commodification of Healthcare." Asia Research Institute Working Paper No. 83, January 1, 2007.

Chikotie, Taurai; Jonathan, Oni; Vesper, Owei. "Factors Determining the Adoption of ICTs in Healthcare Service Delivery: A Developing Country Context." Paper presented at the 2nd International Conference on Information Management and Evaluation, Ryerson University, Toronto, Canada, April 27–28, 2011.

CNN Wire Staff. "Record Number of Chinese Attend College in the US." *CNN*, November 15, 2010. http://www.cnn.com/2010/WORLD/asiapcf/11/15/us.foreign.students/index.html.

Combs, Drewy. "Disruptive Innovation." *American Lawyer*, June 27, 2012. http://www.americanlawyer.com/PubArticleTAL.jsp?id=1202560242148&Disruptive_Innovation (subscription required).

Commonwealth Fund. *International Profiles in Health Care Systems, 2012*, November 2012.

Corkery, Michael. "Pressure to Rein in Tuition Squeezes Colleges." *Wall Street Journal*, December 30, 2012. http://online.wsj.com/article/SB10001424127887323777204578189881498443700.html.

Decker, Christopher; George, Yarrow. "Understanding the Economic Rationale for Legal Services Regulation." Regulatory Policy Institute, October 31, 2010. http://www.legalservicesboard.org.uk/news_publications/latest_news/pdf/economic_rationale_for_Legal_Services_Regulation_Final.pdf.

Deloitte. *2011 Survey of Health Care Consumers in Brazil: Key Findings, Strategic Implications*, 2011.

———. "Consumerism in Health Care: Trends and Implications for Health Industry Stakeholders." Webinar, June 12, 2012.

———. *Retail Clinics*, 2008.

Denning, Steve. "Why Is Your Doctor Typing? Electronic Medical Records Run Amok." *Forbes*, April 25, 2013.

Docquier, Frédéric; Hillel Rapoport. "Globalization, Brain Drain and Development." IZA Discussion Paper No. 5590, March 2011.

Dunn, Lindsey. "International Partnership Opportunities Gaining Interest, but Challenges Await Hospitals." *Becker's Hospital Review*, April 5, 2011.

Economist Intelligence Unit (EIU) and Eucomed. "Contract for a Healthy Future," October 2012. http://www.reforminghealthcare.eu/.

Economist Intelligence Unit (EIU). "Middle East and Africa: Healthcare and Pharmaceuticals Outlook." *Industry Briefing*, August 20, 2012.

―――. "Western Europe: Healthcare and Pharmaceuticals Outlook." *Industry Briefing*, August 8, 2012.

―――. "World: Healthcare Outlook." *Industry Briefing*, October 8, 2012.

Economist. "America's Lawyers: Guilty As Charged," February 2, 2013. http://www.economist.com/news/leaders/21571141-cheaper-legal-education-and-more-liberal- rules-would-benefit-americas-lawyersand-their.

―――. "Reforming America's Legal Education: The Two-year Itch," February 2, 2013. http://www.economist.com/news/business/21571213-could-law-schools-be-ready-change-their- ways-two-year-itch.

―――. "Homebodies Rule," October 15, 2011. http://www.economist.com/node/21532313.

Economist. "Bigger Means Cheaper," April 7, 2012.

―――. "Heroes Dare to Cross," July 21, 2012.

Edgecliffe-Johnson, Andrew; Chris, Cook. "Education: From Blackboard to Keyboard." *Financial Times*, January 17, 2013. http://www.ft.com/intl/cms/s/0/8de6072c-60a0-11e2-a31a-00144feab49a.html#axzz2MIjqcxvR.

Evans, Melanie. "Record Slowdown, Bigger Share." *Modern Healthcare*, January 10, 2011.

Faizal, Elly Burhaini. "RI to Export More Healthcare Workers despite Shortage at Home." *Jakarta Post*, January 7, 2012.

Farrar, Lara. "Smaller U.S. Colleges Try to Crack Chinese Market." *New York Times*, December 14, 2012. http://www.nytimes.com/2012/12/17/world/asia/17iht-educlede17.html?pagewanted=all&_r=0.

Fischer, Karen. "Number of Foreign Students in U.S. Hit a New High Last Year." *Chronicle of Higher Education*, November 16, 2012. http://chronicle.com/article/Number-of-Foreign-Students- in/49142/.

Freedman, Joshua. "Foreign Firms Set Sights on Israel As Legal Market Frees Up." *The Lawyer*, August 6, 2012. http://www.thelawyer.com/foreign-firms-set-sights-on-israel-as-legal-market-frees- up/1013776.article.

―――. "The Promising Land." *Lawyer*, August 6, 2012. http://www.thelawyer.com/the-promising- land/1013706.article.

Georgetown Law Center for the Study of the Legal Profession and Thomson Reuters Peer Monitor. "2013 Report on the State of the Legal Market," n.d. http://www.law.georgetown.edu/continuing-legal-education/executive-education/upload/2013-report.pdf (accessed February 21, 2013).

Global Ticker. "Chinese Students Regard U.S. Higher Education as Top Quality, but Also Confusing." *Chronicle of Higher Education*, March 16, 2012. http://chronicle.com/ blogs/ global/chinese-students-regard-u-s-higher-education-as-top-quality-but-also-confusing/ 32526.

Golden, Daniel. "China Rush to U.S. Colleges Reveals Predatory Fees." Bloomberg, May 22, 2011. http://www.bloomberg.com/news/2011-05-22/china-rush-to-u-s-colleges-reveals-predatory-fees.html.

Gonzales, Frédéric; Bradford Jensen, J; Yunhee, Kim; Hildegunn Kyvik Nordås. "Chapter 5: Globalisation of Services and Jobs." In *Policy Priorities for International Trade and Jobs,* edited by Douglas Lippoldt. OECD, 2012. http://www.oecd.org/site/tadicite/50258009.pdf.

Graham, Scott. "The Ten Year View." *National Law Journal*, March 26, 2012. http://www.law.com/jsp/nlj/PubArticleNLJ.jsp?germane=1202489565842&id=1202546791878 (subscription required).

Gross, Ames. "Forecast: Asia's Rising Middle-Class to Drive 10 Year Healthcare Growth." Pacific Bridge Medical, March 1, 2012.

Gryta, Thomas. "What Is a 'Pharmacy Benefit Manager?'" *Wall Street Journal*, July 21, 2011. Hamilton, Chris. "West Maui Hospital Could Be Finished by 2015." *Maui News*, October 15, 2012.

Hansel, Jeff. "Mayo Clinic Included in New Canadian Insurance Options." *PostBulletin.com*, April 17, 2012.

Hansen, Mark. "US Law Schools Expanding Clinical, Professionalism Offerings, Survey Shows." *ABA Journal*, July 5, 2012. http://www.abajournal.com/news/article/us_law_schools_expanding_clinical_professionalism_of ferings_survey_shows/?utm_source=maestro&utm_medium=email&utm_campaign=daily_email.

HealthIT.gov. "Basics of Health IT." http://www.healthit.gov/patients-families/basics-health-it (accessed October 10, 2012).

Helble, Matthias. "The Movement of Patients across Borders: Challenges and Opportunities for Public Health." *Bulletin of the World Health Organization*, November 26, 2010.

Henderson, William D. "Rise and Fall." *American Lawyer*, May 31, 2012. http://www.americanlawyer.com/PubArticleTAL.jsp?id=1202555054300&Rise_and_Fall (subscription required).

Henderson, William D; Rachel, M. Zahorsky. "The Law School Bubble: How Long Will It Last If Law Grads Can't Pay Bills?" *ABA Journal*, January 1, 2012. http://www.abajournal.com/magazine/article/the_law_school_bubble_how_long_will_it_last_if_law_grads_cant_pay_bills/.

Hensley, Scott. "For Simple Care, Retail Clinics Are a Popular Choice." *NPR.org*, November 5, 2012.

Hildebrandt Institute. "Law Firm Merges Rebound Strongly in 2011; Trend Predicted to Continue in 2012," January 4, 2012. http://hildebrandtblog.com/2012/01/04/law-firm-mergers-rebound- strongly-in-2011-trend-predicted-to-continue-in-2012/.

Hildebrant Consulting and Citi. "2013 Client Advisory." n.d. (accessed February 21, 2013). http://hildebrandtconsult.com/uploads/Citi_Hildebrandt_2013_Client_Advisory.pdf.

Hille, Kathrin. "Chinese Set Course for Foreign Universities." *Financial Times*, April 3, 2012. http://www.ft.com/intl/cms/s/0/bde3d892-7d6f-11e1-81a5-00144feab49a.html#axzz2MIjqcxvR.

Hook, Alison. "Sectoral Study on the Impact of Domestic Regulation on Trade in Legal Services." Paper prepared for the Sixth Services Experts Meeting, "Domestic Regulation and Trade in Professional Services," Paris, February 15–16, 2007. http://www.americanbar.org/content/dam/aba/migrated/cpr/gats/alison_hook.authcheckdam.pdf.

Hurford, Kathryn. "Going Global: The Case for Enhancing Global Trade in Professional Services." Barton, Australia: Institution of Engineers, 2003. http://www.engineersaustralia.org.au.

IBISWorld. "Law Firms in the US: 54111." *IBISWorld Industry Report*, September 2012.

IIE. "International Students: Fields of Study by Place of Origin." *Open Doors*, November 12, 2012. http://www.iie.org/Research-and-Publications/Open-Doors/Data/International-Students/Fields-of- Study-Place-of-Origin/2011-12.

Institute for International Education (IIE). "Open Doors 2012 Fast Facts." *Open Doors*, November 12, 2012. http://www.iie.org/Research-and-Publications/Open-Doors/Data/Fast-Facts.

Jamoom, Eric; Paul, Beatty; Anita, Bercovitz; David, Woodwell; Kathleen, Palso; Elizabeth, Rechtsteiner. "Physician Adoption of Electronic Health Record Systems: United States, 2011." U.S. Department of Health and Human Services, Centers for Disease Control and Prevention, National Center for Health Statistics. NCHS Data Brief No. 98, July 2012.

Johnson, Chris. "The Hustlers." *American Lawyer*, October 1, 2012. http://www.americanlawyer.com/PubArticleTAL.jsp?id=1202572358339&slreturn=20130201114919.

Johnson, Jenna. "U.S. Colleges Seek Foreign Students for Intellectual Stimulus, Bottom Line." *Washington Post*, September 2, 2011. http://www.washingtonpost.com/local/education/us-colleges-seek-foreign-students-for-intellectual-stimulus-better-bottom-line/2011/08/22/gIQAFeVlwJ_story.html.

Jowit, Juliette. "NHS Reform: Health and Social Care Bill Passes Its Final Hurdle." *Guardian*, March 20, 2012.

Kaiser Family Foundation. "Summary of New Health Reform Law." Publication No. 8061, April 15, 2011.

Kanchanachitra, Churnrurtai; Magnus, Lindelow; Timothy, Johnston; Piya, Hanvoravongchai; Fely, Marilyn Lorenzo; Nguyen, Lan Huong; Siswanto, Agus Wilopo; Jennifer, Frances dela Rosa. "Human Resources for Health in Southeast Asia: Shortages, Distributional Challenges, and International Trade in Health Services." *Lancet*, 377, no. 9767 (February 26, 2011): 769–81.

Keehan, Sean P; Gigi, A Cuckler; Andrea, M Sisko; Andrew, J Madison; Sheila, D Smith; Joseph, M Lizonitz; John, A Poisal; Christian, J Wolfe. "National Health Expenditure Projections: Modest Annual Growth Until Coverage Expands and Economic Growth Accelerates." *Health Affairs*, July 2012, 1600–12.

Kerr, Simeon. "Saudis Lead Healthcare Spending Spree." *Financial Times*, February 18, 2013.

Kinney, Eleanor D; Brian, Alexander Clark. "Provisions for Health and Health Care in the Constitutions of the Countries of the World." *Cornell International Law Journal*, 37, no. 285 (2004): 285–355.

Kliff, Sarah. "Health-Care Spending Slowdown (Choose Your Own Adventure Edition)." *WashingtonPost.com*, August 10, 2012.

Koh Chin, Hey-Kyung, ed. *Open Doors 2004*. New York, NY: Institute for International Education, 2004.

Korn, Melissa; Jennifer, Levitz. "Online Courses Look for a Business Model." *Wall Street Journal*, January 1, 2013. http://online.wsj.com/article/SB10001424127887324339204578173421673664106.html.

Krupa, Carolyne. "Congress Extends Visa Waiver Program for IMGs." *Amednews.com*, October 3, 2012. Lee, Jaimy. "Foreign Relations." *Modern Healthcare*, June 9, 2012.

Lane, Charles. "Book Review: 'Failing Law Schools' by Brian Z. Tamanaha." *Washington Post*, August 3, 2012. http://www.washingtonpost.com/opinions/book-review-failing-law-schools-by-brian-z-tamanaha/2012/08/03/e7054c9c-c6df-11e1-916d-a4bc61efcad8_story.html.

Lattman, Peter. "9 Graduates Lose Case against New York Law School." *New York Times DealBook*, March 22, 2012. http://dealbook.nytimes.com/2012/03/22/9-graduates-lose-case-against-new- york-law-school/.

———. "N.Y.U. Plans Overhaul of Students' Third Year." *New York Times Dealbook*, October 16, 2012. http://dealbook.nytimes.com/2012/10/16/n-y-u-law-plans-overhaul-of-students-third-year/.

Lawyer. "Local Firms Can Thrive in Malaysia," November 5, 2012. http://www.thelawyer.com/local- firms-can-thrive-in-malaysia/1015256.article.

Lee, Don. "Worries Grow As Health Jobs Go Offshore." *Los Angeles Times*, July 25, 2012. http://articles.latimes.com/2012/jul/25/business/la-fi-healthcare-offshore-20120725.

Leichter, Matt. "Clever Plans to Reform Legal Education Won't Make Legal Services Any Cheaper." *Am Law Daily*, January 30, 2012. http://amlawdaily.typepad.com/amlawdaily/2012/01/clever-plans-to-reform-legal-education-wont-make-legal-services-any-cheaper.html.

Lewin, Tamar. "Illegal in U.S., Paid Agents Overseas Help American Colleges Recruit Students." *New York Times*, February 4, 2012. http://www.nytimes.com/2012/02/05/education/smaller-colleges- rely-on-paid-student-recruiters-overseas.html.

———. "Students Rush to Web Classes, but Profits May Be Much Later." *New York Times*, January 6, 3013. http://www.nytimes.com/2013/01/07/education/massive-open-online-courses-prove- popular-if-not-lucrative-yet.html?pagewanted=all.

———. "Taking More Seats on Campus, Foreigners Also Pay the Freight." *New York Times*, February 4, 2012. http://www.nytimes.com/2012/02/05/education/international-students-pay-top-dollar-at-us- colleges.html?pagewanted=all.

Lewin, Tamar; John, Markoff. "California to Give Web Courses Big Trial." *Wall Street Journal*, January 15, 2013. http://www.nytimes.com/2013/01/15/technology/california-to-give-web- courses-a-big-trial.html.

Liu, Jie. "Overseas Money Shot in the Arm." *China Daily*, February 29, 2012.

Love, Julia. "Firms Beef Up Singapore Offices as a Launching Pad for Other Markets." *Law.com*, January 7, 2013. http://www.law.com/jsp/article.jsp?id=1202583488399&Firms_Beef_Up_Singapore_Offices_as_a_Launching_Pad_for_Other_Markets&slreturn=20130213112801.

Lunt, Neil; Richard, Smith; Mark, Exworthy; Stephen, T Green; Daniel, Horsfall; Russel, Mannion. *Medical Tourism: Treatments, Markets and Health System Implications; A Scoping Review*. Organisation for Economic Co-operation and Development. Directorate for Employment, Labour and Social Affairs. Paris: OECD, 2011.

MarketLine. "MarketLine Industry Profile: Global Legal Services." EBSCOhost Business Source Complete database, October 2012.

———. "MarketLine Industry Profile: Legal Services in Asia-Pacific." EBSCOhost Business Source Complete database, October 2012.

————. "MarketLine Industry Profile: Legal Services in Europe." EBSCOhost Business Source Complete database, October 2012.

————. "MarketLine Industry Profile: Legal Services in the United States." EBSCOhost Business Source Complete database, October 2012.

Mathews, Anna Wilde; Jon, Kamp. "UnitedHealth to Buy 90% of Brazil's Amil for $4.3 Billion." *Wall Street Journal*, October 8, 2012.

Matsuyama, Kanoko. "Aging Baby Boomers Face Losing Care As Filipinos Go Home." *Bloomberg.com*, September 14, 2012.

McFee, Michelle Jarboe. "Cleveland International Fund Eyes UH Projects after Raising $45 Million for the Flats East Bank." *Plain Dealer* via Cleveland.com, February 15, 2011.

McKinsey & Company. *Healthcare in China: Entering Uncharted Waters*, July 2012.

McMurtrie, Beth. "China Continues to Drive Foreign-Student Growth in the United States." *Chronicle of Higher Education*, November 16, 2012. http://chronicle.com/article/China-Continues-to- Drive/135700/.

Mehrotra, Ateev; Judith, R Lave. "Visits to Retail Clinics Grew Fourfold from 2007 to 2009, Although Their Share of Overall Outpatient Visits Remains Low." *Health Affairs*, 31, no. 9 (September 2012): 2123–29.

Mehrotra, Ateev; Margaret, C Wang; Judith, R Lave; John, L Adams; Elizabeth, A McGlynn. "Retail Clinics, Primary Care Physicians, and Emergency Departments: A Comparison of Patients' Visits." *Health Affairs*, 27, no. 5 (September 2008): 1272–82.

Mellman, Ira. "Chinese Top List of International Students in US." *Voice of America*, November 13, 2011. http://www.voanews.com/content/china-tops-list-of-international-students-in-us-133841133/168204.html.

Mihart, Bianca. "The Financial Crisis and the Crisis within European Health Insurance Systems." *Finante—provocarile viitorului* [Finance—Challenges of the Future] 1, no. 13 (December 2011): 218–24.

Mong, Adrienne. "Chinese Applications to U.S. Skyrocket." *MSNBC*, January 11, 2012. http://behindthewall.nbcnews.com/_news/2012/01/11/9679479-chinese-applications-to-us-schools-skyrocket?lite.

Mortensen, Jon. "International Trade in Health Services: Assessing the Trade and the Trade-Offs." Danish Institute for International Studies. DIIS Working Paper no. 2008/11, 2008.

NAFSA: Association of International Educators. "The Economic Benefits of International Students to the U.S. Economy: Academic Year 2011–12." November 2012. http://www.nafsa.org/Explore_International_Education/Impact/Data_And_Statistics/What_Is_the_Value_of_International_Students_to_Your_State_in_2012_/.

National Association of Independent Colleges and Universities (NAICU). "Private College Tuition Slows to Lowest Rate in at Least Four Decades." News release, October 4, 2012.

————. "New Affordability Measures at Private, Non-Profit Colleges and Universities: Academic Year 201-13," December 28, 2012.

Neil, Martha. "Law School Apps Drop 11.5 Percent, a 10-Year Low." *ABA Journal*, March 16, 2011. http://www.abajournal.com/news/article/law_school_apps_drop_11.5_percent_a_10-year_low/?utm_source=maestro&utm_medium=email&utm_campaign=weekly_email.

Netland,Torbjörn H; Erland, Alfnes. "Internationalisation of Professional Services: A 1999–2005 Literature Review." College of Service Operations Conference, July 2007. http://www.poms.org/conferences/cso2007/talks/47.pdf.

New South Wales Government. "Chronic Disease Management Office," n.d. http://www. health.nsw.gov.au/cdm/pages/default.aspx (accessed February 19, 2013).

New York Times. "Legal Education Reform," November 25, 2011. http://www.nytimes.com/ 2011/11/26/opinion/legal-education-reform.html?_r=0.

Nguyen-Hong, Duc. "Restrictions on Trade in Professional Services." Productivity Commission Staff Research Paper. Canberra, Australia: AusInfo, August 2000. http://www.pc.gov.au/data/assets/pdf_file/0016/8080/rotips.pdf.

O'Brien, Paula; Lawrence, O. Gostin. *Health Worker Shortages and Global Justice*. New York: Millbank Memorial Fund, October 2011.

Organisation for Economic Co-operation and Development (OECD) and World Health Organization. "International Migration of Health Workers." *OECD Policy Brief*, February 2010. http://www.oecd.org/migration/mig/44783473.pdf.

Organisation for Economic Co-operation and Development (OECD). "Health: Growth in Health Spending Grinds to a Halt," June 28, 2012. http://www.oecd.org/health/ healthgrowthinhealthspendinggrindstoahalt.htm.

Organisation for Economic Co-operation and Development (OECD). *Education at a Glance 2012: OECD Indicators*. Paris, France: OECD, 2012.

Orlik, Rose. "DLA's Mexico Entrance Flags Growing Interest in Burgeoning LatAm Markets." *Legal Week*, March 9, 2012. http://www.legalweek.com/legal-week/news/ 2157983/dlas-mexico-entrance-flags-growing-burgeoning-latam-markets (subscription required).

Outreville, J François. "Foreign Direct Investment in the Health Care Sector and Most-favoured Locations in Developing Countries." *European Journal of Health Economics*, 8, no. 4 (December 2007): 305–12.

Overseas Development Institute (ODI). "The Contribution of Services to Development and the Role of Trade Liberalisation and Regulation." ODI Briefing Notes, Department for International Development, UK. OECD Global Forum on International Investment, March 27–28, 2008. http://www.oecd.org/investment/globalforum/40302909.pdf.

Palazzolo, Joe. "India Supreme Court OKs 'Fly in, Fly Out.'" *Wall Street Journal Law Blog*, July 5, 2012. http://blogs.wsj.com/law/2012/07/05/india-supreme-court-oks-fly-in-fly-out/?KEYWORDS=lawyers.

———. "When a Company Sounds Suspiciously like a Law Firm." *Wall Street Journal*, January 19, 2012. http://blogs.wsj.com/law/2012/01/19/when-a-company-sounds-suspiciously -like-a-law- firm/?KEYWORDS=lawyers.

———. "Why Hire a Lawyer? Computers Are Cheaper." *Wall Street Journal*, June 18, 2012. http://online.wsj.com/article/SB10001424052702303379204577472633591769336.html? KEYWORDS=lawyers.

———. "Law Grads Face Brutal Job Market." *Wall Street Journal*, June 25, 2012. http://online.wsj.com/article/SB10001424052702304458604577486623469958142.html? KEYWORDS=lawyers.

———. "Report: Law Schools Still Stingy with Job-Placement Data." *Wall Street Journal Law Blog*, January 17, 2012. http://blogs.wsj.com/law/2012/01/17/report-law-schools-still-stingy-with-job- placement-data/.

Palin, Adam. "Law and Business: A Marriage of Convenience." *Financial Times*, November 25, 2011. http://www.ft.com/intl/cms/s/2/866327a0-1641-11e1-a691-00144feabdc0.html.

————. "International Law: Legal Studies in a Globalised Era." *Financial Times*, November 19, 2012. http://www.ft.com/cms/s/2/655c092a-29b7-11e2-a604-00144feabdc0.html #axzz2KF1R9sxl.

Parente, Stephen T; Jeffrey, S McCullough. "Health Information Technology and Patient Safety: Evidence from Panel Data." *Health Affairs*, 28, no. 2 (2009): 357–360. http://content.healthaffairs.org/content/28/2/357.full.pdf+html.

Pearson, Sophia; Phil, Milford. "New York, Chicago Law Schools among Group Sued by Graduates over Job Data." *Bloomberg News*, February 1, 2012. http://www.bloomberg. com/news/2012-02-01/new-york-chicago-law-schools-among-group-sued-by-graduates-over-job-data.html.

Phipps, Chelsea. "Cooley Law Grads' Lawsuit Dismissed." *Wall Street Journal Law Blog*, July 20, 2012. http://blogs.wsj.com/law/2012/07/20/cooley-law-grads%E2%80%99-lawsuit-dismissed/.

PricewaterhouseCoopers. *Emerging Trends in Chinese Healthcare*, 2010.

————. *Global Healthcare Deals Quarterly*, 1Q, 2012.

————. *Global Healthcare Deals Quarterly*, 3Q, 2012.

Ramstad, Evan. "Justice Ministry Approves First Foreign Lawyers." *Wall Street Journal Blog*, May 7, 2012. http://blogs.wsj.com/korearealtime/2012/05/07/justice-ministry-approves-first-foreign-lawyers/.

Randazzo, Sara. "Survey Says Outliers Helped Push Large Law Firm Revenue Up 5 Percent in 2012." *Am Law Daily*, January 29, 2013. http://www.americanlawyer.com/ PubArticleALD.jsp?id=1202586204617&Survey_Says_Outliers_Helped_Push_Large_L aw_Firm_Revenue_Up_5_Percent_in_2012.

Reisinger, Sue. "Training for Trouble." *Corporate Counsel*, November 2012. http:// www.corpcounsel-digital.com/corpcounsel/201211?sub_id=vUtDesViNWVL#pg77.

Ring, Suzi. "King & Wood Mallesons Emerges as Post-Merge Name As Partners Vote on Union." *Legal Week*, November 23, 2011. http://www.legalweek.com/legal-week/news/ 2130113/king-wood- partners-confirm-mallesons-tie-firm-live (subscription required).

Seah, Jessica. "Have QFLPs Worked for Singapore?" *Law.com*, May 21, 2012. http://www.law.com/jsp/article.jsp?id=1202555185632&slreturn=20130213113226.

Seddon, Nick. "As the Chinese Legal Market Expands, Western Law Firms Have a Narrow Window of Opportunity." *Legalweek.com,* November 24, 2011. http://www. legalweek.com/legal-week/analysis/2126980/chinese-legal-market-expands-western-law-firms-narrow-window- opportunity (subscription required).

Segal, David. "Law School Economics: Ka-Ching!" *New York Times*, July 16, 2011. http:// www.nytimes.com/2011/07/17/business/law-school-economics-job-market-weakens-tuition-rises.html?pagewanted=all.

————. "What They Don't Teach Law Students: Lawyering." *New York Times*, November 19, 2011. http://www.nytimes.com/2011/11/20/business/after-law-school-associates-learn-to-be-lawyers.html?_r=2&adxnnl=1&ref=business&adxnnlx=1323184992-ANKq CxfwRZ74i394O+1L8g.

Shimogawa, Duane. "Hilo to Get 100-bed Nursing Home." *Pacific Business News*, April 27, 2012. Suhrcke, Marc, Martin McKee, Regina Sauto Arce, Svetla Tsolova, and Jørgen Mortensen. "The Contribution of Health to the Economy in the European Union." European Commission, Health and Consumer Protection Directorate-General, August 23, 2005.

Smith, Jennifer. "Companies Reset Legal Costs." *Wall Street Journal*, April 8, 2012. http://online.wsj.com/article/SB10001424052702304587704577331711808572108.html (subscription required).

———. "India to Foreign Lawyers: C'mon In but Don't Stay Too Long." *Wall Street Journal Law Blog*, February 23, 2012. http://blogs.wsj.com/law/2012/02/23/india-to-foreign-lawyers-cmon-in-but- dont-stay-too-long/?mod=google_news_blog.

———. "Law Firms Follow Business to Mexico." *Wall Street Journal Blog*, February 21, 2012. http://online.wsj.com/article/SB10001424052970204131004577235261479 621288.html.

———. "Law Firms Keep Squeezing Associates." *Wall Street Journal*, January 30, 2012. http://online.wsj.com/article/SB10001424052970203363504577186913589594038.html? KEYWORDS=lawyers.

———. "Law-Firms' Partners Face Layoffs." *Wall Street Journal*, January 6, 2013. http://online.wsj.com/article/SB10001424127887323689604578221891691032424.html (subscription required).

———. "Stark Choice for Lawyers—Firms Must Merge or Die." *Wall Street Journal*, January 20, 2012. http://online.wsj.com/article/SB10001424052970203750404577171115 3838217514.html (subscription required).

———. "With Cross-Border Mergers, Law Firms Enter Arms Race." *Wall Street Journal*, December 9, 2012. http://online.wsj.com/article/SB10001424127887324433920457 8169393188242764.html?mg=id- wsj (subscription required).

Smith, Mitch. "Prestigious Law School Reduces Admissions, Marks New Trend." *USA Today*, May 1, 2012. http://usatoday30.usatoday.com/news/education/story/2012-05-01/hastings-law-school- admissions/54662710/1.

Sparkman, Robin. "The Haves and the Haves Less." *American Lawyer*, April 26, 2012. http://www.americanlawyer.com/PubArticleTAL.jsp?id=1202549688766   (subscription required).

Staley, Oliver. "Lure of Chinese Students Squeezes Out Asian-American Students." *Bloomberg Businessweek*, January 4, 2012, http://www.businessweek.com/news/2011-12-29/lure-of-chinese- tuition-squeezes-out-asian-american-students.html.

Stevens, Elizabeth Lesly. "Will Law School Students Have Jobs After They Graduate?" *Washington Post Magazine,* November 1, 2012. http://www.washingtonpost.com/ lifestyle/magazine/will-law-school-students-have-jobs-after-they-graduate/2012/10/31/ f9916726-0f30-11e2-bd1a- b868e65d57eb_story.html.

Stewart, James. "Dewey's Fall Underscores Law Firms' New Reality." *New York Times*, May 4, 2012. http://www.nytimes.com/2012/05/05/business/deweys-collapse-underscores-a-new-reality-for-law-firms-common-sense.html?adxnnl=1&adxnnlx=1361308100-jKAOSgI25xr8NJuqeCdS4Q&_r=0.

Study New Jersey. "A World of Options. A State of Mind." Presentation, NAFSA 2011 Conference, June 2, 2011.

Sullivan, William M; Anne, Colby; Judith, Welch Wegner; Lloyd, Bond; Lee, S. Shulman. "Education Lawyers: Preparation for the Profession of Law." Summary of complete report. Carnegie Foundation for the Advancement of Teaching, 2007. http://www. carnegiefoundation.org/sites/default/files/publications/elibrary_pdf_632.pdf.

Susskind, Richard. *The End of Lawyers? Rethinking the Nature of Legal Services*. New York: Oxford University Press, 2010.

Swiss Re. "Health Protection Gap in the Asia-Pacific Region Will Hit USD 197 Billion in 2020," November 28, 2012.

———. "To Your Health: Diagnosing the State of Healthcare and the Global Private Medical Insurance Industry." *sigma* no. 6/2007, 2007.

Tamanaha, Brian Z. "How to Make Law School Affordable." *New York Times*, May 31, 2012. http://www.nytimes.com/2012/06/01/opinion/how-to-make-law-school-affordable.html.

Tan, Andrea. "Singapore to License More Foreign Law Firms As Fees Fall." *Bloomberg News*, April 24, 2012. http://www.bloomberg.com/news/2012-04-23/singapore-to-license-more-foreign-law- firms-as-fees-fall.html.

The Advisory Board Company. "U.S. Hospitals Eye Chinese Market For Expansion." *Daily Briefing*, February 7, 2013.

Thomas, Ian. "McDermott to Open Seoul Law Practice Following Trade Agreement." *Bloomberg News*, February 14, 2012. http://www.bloomberg.com/news/2012-02-14/mcdermott-to-open-seoul-law- practice-following-trade-agreement.html.

Thrall, James, H. "Teleradiology Part I. History and Clinical Applications." *Radiology*, 243, no. 3 (June 2007): 613–17.

Thurm, Scott. "Who Can Still Afford State U?" *Wall Street Journal*, December 14, 2012. http://online.wsj.com/article/SB10001424127887323501404578163290734542674.html.

Thygeson, Marcus; Krista, A Van Vorst; Michael, V. Maciosek, and Leif Solberg. "Use and Costs of Care in Retail Clinics versus Traditional Care Sites." *Health Affairs*, 27, no. 5 (September 2008): 1283–92.

Torres, Ida. "Japanese Still Wary of Asian Health Care Workers." *Japan Daily Press*, October 16, 2012.

Triedman, Julie. "Appearances May Be Deceiving." *American Lawyer*, September 28, 2012. http://www.americanlawyer.com/PubArticleTAL.jsp?id=1202572359253.

———. "Hot Spot." *American Lawyer*, September 28, 2012. http://www.americanlawyer.com/PubArticleTAL.jsp?id=1202572359205&Hot_Spot&slreturn=20130114133610.

U.S. Citizenship and Immigration Services. "Green Card through Investment," March 30, 2011. http://www.uscis.gov/portal/site/uscis/menuitem.eb1d4c2a3e5b9ac89243c6a7543f6d1a/?vgnextoid=cf54a6c515083210VgnVCM100000082ca60aRCRD&vgnextchannel=cf54a6c515083210Vgn VCM100000082ca60aRCRD.

U.S. Department of Commerce (USDOC). Bureau of Economic Analysis (BEA). "Full-Time Equivalent Employees by Industry." Interactive tables: Gross Domestic Product by Industry Accounts, August 12, 2012. http://www.bea.gov/iTable/iTable.cfm?ReqID=5&step=1.

———. "Real Value Added by Industry." Interactive tables: Gross Domestic Product by Industry Accounts, November 13, 2012. http://www.bea.gov/iTable/iTable.cfm?ReqID=5&step=1.

———. "Wage and Salary Accruals per Full Time Equivalent Employee by Industry." Interactive tables: National and Product Accounts, August 2, 2012. http://www.bea.gov/iTable/iTable.cfm?ReqID=5&step=1.

———. *Survey of Current Business*, 89, no. 10 (October 2009).

———. *Survey of Current Business*, 91, no. 10 (October 2011).

———. *Survey of Current Business*, 92, no. 10 (October 2012).

U.S. Department of Commerce (USDOC). Bureau of Economic Analysis (BEA). "Full-Time Equivalent Employees by Industry." Interactive tables: Gross Domestic Product by

Industry Accounts, August 12, 2012. http://www.bea.gov/iTable/iTable.cfm?ReqID =5&step=1.

————— ."Real Value Added by Industry." Interactive tables: Gross Domestic Product by Industry Accounts, November 13, 2012. http://www.bea.gov/iTable/iTable.cfm?ReqID =5&step=1.

—————. "Wage and Salary Accruals per Full Time Equivalent Employee by Industry." Interactive tables: National and Product Accounts, August 2, 2012. http://www.bea.gov/ iTable/iTable.cfm?ReqID=5&step=1.

—————. *Survey of Current Business*, 89, no. 10 (October 2009).

—————. *Survey of Current Business*, 91, no. 10 (October 2011).

—————. *Survey of Current Business*, 92, no. 10 (October 2012).

U.S. Department of Commerce (USDOC). Bureau of Economic Analysis (BEA). *Survey of Current Business*, 92, no. 10 (October 2012).

U.S. Department of Commerce (USDOC). Bureau of Economic Analysis (BEA). *U.S. International Transactions Accounts: Concepts and Estimation Methods*, June 2011.

—————. Bureau of Economic Analysis (BEA). *Survey of Current Business*, 92, no. 10 (October 2012). U.S. Department of Commerce. U.S. Census Bureau. "State and County Quick Facts." http://quickfacts.census.gov/qfd/index.html (accessed December 13, 2012).

U.S. Department of Commerce (USDOC). U.S. Census Bureau. "Industry Statistics Sampler: NAICS 5411–Legal Services." http://www.census.gov/econ/industry/def/d5411.htm (accessed February 26, 2013).

—————. Bureau of Economic Analysis (BEA). "Gross Output by Industry." http://www.bea. gov/iTable/iTable.cfm?ReqID=5&step=1#reqid=5&step=4&isuri=1&402=15&403=1 (accessed May 8, 2013).

—————. Bureau of Economic - Roundtable" (unpublished notes). USITC, Washington, DC, November 13, 2012.

U.S. International Trade Commission (USITC). *Sixth Annual Services Roundtable*, Washington, D.C., November 13, 2012.

U.S. News & World Report. "Clinical Training," 2013. http://grad-schools.usnews. rankingsandreviews.com/best-graduate-schools/top-law-schools/clinical-training-rankings (accessed March 13, 2013).

U.S. Trade Representative. United States-Korea Free Trade Agreement, Annex II: Non-Conforming Measures for Services and Investment. http://www.ustr.gov/webfm_send/ 2790 (accessed March 13, 2013).

United Nations (UN). *Manual on Statistics of International Trade in Services 2010*. Geneva, Luxembourg, New York, Paris, Washington, DC: UN, 2012. http://unstats.un.org/unsd/ tradeserv/tfsits/manual.htm.

United Nations Conference on Trade and Development (UNCTAD). "Trade and Development Aspects of Professional Services and Regulatory Frameworks." TD/B/COM.1/EM.25.2, November 25, 2004. http://unctad.org/en/Docs/c1em25d2_ en.pdf.

United Nations. UN Service Trade Database. http://unstats.un.org/unsd/servicetrade/ (accessed February 15, 2013).

—————. Department of Economic and Social Affairs. Population Division. "Health Workers, International Migration and Development." *Population Facts*, no. 2010/2/Rev, August 2010.

Van Dusen, Allison. "America's Top Hospitals Go Global." *Forbes.com*, August 25, 2008.

Vargas, Bustamante; Arturo, Miriam Laugesen; Mabel, Caban; Pauline, Rosenau. "United States- Mexico Cross-border Health Insurance Initiatives: *Salud Migrante* and Medicare in Mexico." *Revista Panamericana de Salud Publica*, 31, 1 (2012): 74–80.

Waldmeir, Patti. "Chinese Students Buck Export Slowdown." *Financial Times*, September 27, 2012. http://www.ft.com/intl/cms/s/0/9e70f9cc-0537-11e2-8f0d-00144feabdc0.html# axzz2MIjqcxvR.

Want ChinaTimes. "260 Million Chinese Suffer Chronic Diseases: Report," July 10, 2012.

Weinick, Robin M; Craig, Evan Pollack; Michael, P Fisher, Emily, M Gillen; Ateev Mehrotra. "Policy Implications of the Use of Retail Clinics." RAND Technical Report, 2010.

Weiss, Debra Cassens. "Law Prof Sees 'Huge Opportunity' in Labor Projections Highlighting Law Grad Oversupply." *ABA Journal*, April 5, 2012. http://www.abajournal.com/ news/article/law_prof_sees_huge_opportunity_in_labor_projections_highlighting_law_gr ad/?utm_source=maestro&utm_medium=email&utm_campaign=daily_email.

———."1L Enrollment Dropped at Three-Fourths of Accredited Law Schools This Year." *ABA Journal*, November 28, 2012. http://www.abajournal.com/news/article/enrollment_ dropped_at_three- fourths_of_accredited_law_schools_this_year_pre/.

White, Chapin; James, D Reschovsky. "Great Recession Accelerated Long-Term Decline of Employer Health Coverage." Center for Studying Health System Change. NIHCR Research Brief No. 8, March 2012.

World Bank. World Development Indicators database. http://databank.worldbank.org/ ddp/home.do (accessed various dates).

World Health Organization (WHO). Global Health Expenditures database. http://www.who. int/nha/expenditure_database/en/ (accessed December 7, 2012).

———. National Health Accounts. "Glossary of Terms and Financing Flows," n.d. http://www.who.int/nha/glossary/glossary_english.pdf (accessed October 31, 2012).

———. *Telemedicine: Opportunities and Developments in Member States*. Global Observation for eHealth Series 2, 2010.

———. *The Right to Health in the Constitutions of Member States of the World Health Organization South-East Asia Region,* 2011.

———. "Health Topics: Chronic Diseases," n.d. http://www.who.int/topics/chronic_diseases/ en/ (accessed February 15, 2013).

———. "Migration of Health Workers." Fact sheet no. 301, July 2010.

World Trade Organization (WTO). *International Trade Statistics 2012,* n.d. Table A8: World Exports of Commercial Services by Region and Selected Economy, 2001–2011. http://www.wto.org/english/res_e/statis_e/its2012_e/its12_appendix_e.htm. (accessed January 20, 2013).

———. n.d. Table A9: World Imports of Commercial Services by Region and Selected Economy, 2001–2011. http://www.wto.org/english/res_e/statis_e/its2012_e/its12_ appendix_ e.htm. (accessed January 20, 2013).

World Trade Organization (WTO). *International Trade Statistics 2012*. Table A8: World Exports of Commercial Services by Region and Selected Economy, 2001–2011. http://www.wto.org/english/res_e/statis_e/its2012_e/its12_appendix_e.htm.

———. Table A9: World Imports of Commercial Services by Region and Selected Economy, 2001–2011. http://www.wto.org/english/res_e/statis_e/its2012_e/its12_appendix_e.htm.

Wotapka, Dawn. "Resort Living Comes to Campus." *Wall Street Journal*, December 6, 2012. http://online.wsj.com/article/SB10001424127887323830404578145591134362564.html.

Wozniak, Vanessa. "China's Yingke Continues Expansion with Launches in Poland and Turkey." *Lawyer*, January 27, 2012. http://www.thelawyer.com/chinas-yingke-continues-expansion-with-launches-in-poland-and-turkey/1011110.article.

Yang, David. *Colleges & Universities in the US*. IBISWorld, August 2012.

Yoon, Eddie. "2013 Outlook: Health Care." *Fidelity Leadership Series: Investment Insights*, December 2012.

Young, Aaron, Humayun J. Chaudhry, Janelle Rhyne, and Michael Dugan. "A Census of Actively Licensed Physicians in the United States, 2010." *Journal of Medical Regulation*, 96, no. 4 (2010): 10–20.

Young, Jeffrey. "MOOCs Take a Major Step toward Qualifying for College Credit." *Chronicle of Higher Education*, November 23, 2012. http://chronicle.com/article/MOOCs-Take-a-Major-Step/135750/.

Zywiak, Walt. "U.S. Healthcare Workforce Shortage: Caregivers." Computer Sciences Corporation, 2010.

End Notes

[1] This report uses the most recent data available. For example, BEA annual data on cross-border trade are available through 2011, while data on affiliate transactions are available only through 2010. Cross-border trade occurs when suppliers in one country sell services to consumers in another country, with people, information, or money crossing national boundaries in the process. Affiliate trade occurs when firms provide services to foreign consumers through affiliates established in the host (i.e., foreign) countries. A more detailed description of the different modes of services trade is provided in section 1.

[2] Beginning in 2013, *Recent Trends* will cover three industries per year, rotating on a quadrennial basis between professional services (education, healthcare, and legal or management consulting); electronic services (telecommunication, computer, and audiovisual services); financial services (banking, insurance, and securities or leasing); and distribution services (retail, logistics, and transportation services).

[3] Beginning in 2013, Recent Trends reports will cover three services industries per year, rotating on a quadrennial basis between professional services (education, healthcare, legal, or management consulting); electronic services (telecommunication, computer, and audiovisual services); financial services (banking, insurance, securities, or leasing); and distribution services (retail, logistics, and transportation).

[4] For more information, see USDOC, BEA, *Survey of Current Business*, October 2012.

[5] Data on affiliate transactions lag those on cross-border trade by one year. Thus, while analyses of cross-border trade data compare performance in 2011 (the most recent year for which data are available) to trends from 2006 through 2010, analyses of affiliate transactions compare performance in 2010 to trends from 2006 through 2009. Note also that in 2009, BEA changed its method of reporting affiliate trade data. New affiliate data report "services supplied," a measure that better reflects services output than the prior measure, "sales of services." The change is retroactive for data from 2005–08. For more information, see USDOC, BEA, *Survey of Current Business*, October 2009, 34–36.

[6] USDOC, BEA, "Real Value Added by Industry," November 13, 2012; USDOC, BEA, "Full-Time Equivalent Employees by Industry," August 2, 2012; USDOC, BEA, "Wage and Salary Accruals," August 2, 2012. Value added is a measure of an industry's contribution to GDP; it is the difference between the value of an industry's gross output and the cost of its intermediate inputs.

[7] This discussion draws on WTO trade data to help compare U.S. trends with those of other countries. The term "commercial services," used by the WTO, is roughly equivalent to "private services" used by the BEA: both refer to services offered by the private, rather than the public, sector. However, there are differences between the two values. These differences are the result of a lagged time period used for the WTO estimate and small differences in the activities captured by the two measures. USDOC, BEA representative, telephone interview by USITC staff, February 23, 2012.

[8] WTO, *International Trade Statistics 2012*, 2012, table A8.

[9] Ibid., table A9.

[10] Note that the $193.8 billion trade surplus estimated by the BEA differs from the $215.8 billion WTO estimate presented above in the "Global Services Trade" section. See footnote 5.

[11] For the purposes of this discussion, trade data for cross-border trade in professional services capture education services; management and consulting services; research, development and testing services; accounting, auditing, and bookkeeping services; advertising; architectural, engineering, and other technical services; industrial engineering services; installation, maintenance, and repair of equipment; legal services; medical services; and training services.

[12] USDOC, BEA, *Survey of Current Business*, October 2012, 34–35. Travel services are measured through the purchase of goods and services, such as food, lodging, recreation, local transportation, and entertainment, while traveling abroad. For information on the composition of cross-border trade, affiliate sales, and GDP data, see appendix B.

[13] In this study, all multiyear growth rates are expressed as compound annual growth rates. Cross- border services trade, as reported in the current account, includes both private and public sector transactions. The latter principally reflect operations of the U.S. military and embassies abroad. However, because public sector transactions are not considered to reflect U.S. service industries' competitiveness and may introduce anomalies resulting from events such as international peacekeeping missions, this report will focus solely on private sector transactions, except as noted.

[14] A form of risk management whereby insurance companies buy insurance contracts from other insurers to protect themselves from unexpected large claims.

[15] U.S.-owned foreign affiliates are affiliates owned by a U.S. parent company and located abroad; conversely, foreign-owned U.S. affiliates are affiliates located in the United States and owned by foreign parent companies.

[16] The main source for this section is the USDOC, BEA, *Survey of Current Business*, October 2007– October 2011.

[17] Data for professional services are underreported due to the suppression of data by BEA to avoid disclosing confidential company information.

[18] For the purposes of this report, affiliate transactions in professional services capture education services; management and consulting services; research, development, and testing services; accounting, auditing, and bookkeeping services; advertising services; architectural, engineering, and other technical services; industrial engineering services; installation, maintenance, and repair of equipment; legal services; medical services; and training services.

[19] USDOC, BEA, *Survey of Current Business*, October 2012, tables 8–10.2.

[20] Data for professional services are underreported due to the suppression of data by BEA to avoid disclosing confidential company information.

[21] UNCTAD, "Trade and Development Aspects of Professional Services," November 25, 2004, 3.

[22] Hurford, "Going Global," 2003, 3.

[23] Netland and Alfnes, "Internationalisation of Professional Services," July 2007, 5–6.

[24] USITC, "Sixth Annual Services Roundtable," November 13, 2012. Cross-border services trade that is facilitated by information technology has grown increasingly widespread, and will likely be an important topic for discussion in any future trade negotiations on services.

[25] Butkeviciene, "Temporary Movement of Natural Persons (Mode 4)," n.d. (accessed December 4, 2012). Under mode 4 of the GATS, temporary entry and stay of foreign personnel is typically granted for an initial period of one, three, or five years, and may be extended beyond these limits.

[26] ODI, "The Contribution of Services to Development," March 27–28, 2008, 16.

[27] Hurford, "Going Global," 2003, 3; USITC, "Sixth Annual Services Roundtable," November 13, 2012.

[28] Nguyen-Hong, "Restrictions on Trade in Professional Services," August 2000, 13.

[29] Hook, "Sectoral Study on the Impact of Domestic Regulation," February 2007, 4; Decker and Yarrow, "Understanding the Economic Rationale for Legal Services Regulation," October 31, 2010. "Information asymmetry" refers to the inability of consumers to assess the quality of a service they intend to buy because they know too little about the service provider. Popular websites such as Angie's List may be one way to correct for information asymmetries between consumers and service providers in the absence of (or in conjunction with) regulatory measures.

[30] Gonzales et al., "Chapter 5," 2012, 187. In the United States, licensing requirements also vary widely by state and may take nine months, on average, to complete. See Carpenter et al., "License to Work," May 2012.

[31] Hurford, "Going Global," 2003, 3.

[32] Gonzales et al., "Chapter 5," 2012, 177. See section 4, "Legal Services," for a full discussion of trade in this sector.

[33] Gonzales et al., "Chapter 5," 2012, 178.

[34] USDOC, BEA, *Survey of Current Business*, October 2011, table 1.

[35] All multiyear growth rates are expressed in compound annual growth rates.

[36] USDOC, BEA, *Survey of Current Business*, October 2012, table 7.2.

[37] Ibid. These services also ranked among the top three U.S. imports of professional services in 2011.

[38] The total is underreported due to the suppression of data by the BEA to avoid disclosing confidential company information.

[39] The total is underreported due to the suppression of data by the BEA to avoid disclosing confidential business information or individual company information.

[40] USDOC, BEA, "Full-Time Equivalent Employees by Industry," August 2, 2012; USDOC, BEA, Real Value Added by Industry," November 13, 2012.

[41] USDOC, BEA, "Full-Time Equivalent Employees by Industry," August 2, 2012; USDOC, BEA, Real Value Added by Industry," November 13, 2012.

[42] The global market is conservatively defined as revenues collected by colleges and universities in 47 countries, including countries in Africa (South Africa); Asia (including Australia, China, India, Indonesia, Japan, Malaysia, New Zealand, Pakistan, the Philippines, Singapore, the Republic of Korea, Taiwan, and Thailand); Europe (including Austria, Belgium, the Czech Republic, Denmark, Finland, France, Germany, Greece, Hungary, Ireland, Italy, the Netherlands, Norway, Poland, Portugal, Russia, Spain, Sweden, Switzerland, and the United Kingdom); Latin America (including Argentina, Brazil, Chile, Colombia, and Venezuela); the Middle East and North Africa (including Egypt, Iran, Israel, Saudi Arabia, and Turkey); and North America (including Canada, Mexico, and the United States).

[43] C. Barnes & Co., "Worldwide Colleges and Universities Industry," 2012, 8–101.

[44] Most modern universities were founded in the 1800s or the early to mid-1900s. Although the characteristics that define a university are subject to debate, the University of Bologna, which was founded in Bologna, Italy, in 1088, is generally considered to be the oldest university in the Western world. University of Bologna website, http://www.eng.unibo.it/PortaleEn/University/Our+History/default.htm (accessed April 29, 2013).

[45] Common academic degrees worldwide include bachelor's, master's, and doctoral degrees as well as specialized postgraduate degrees in the legal and healthcare fields.

[46] Yang, Colleges and Universities in the US, August 2012.

[47] Ibid.

[48] Yang, Colleges and Universities in the US, August 2012. During a recession, for example, the number of new students tends to increase even as existing students maintain enrollments. Such behavior is motivated by the students' desire to obtain new skills and/or "wait out" a recession. Conversely, during periods of strong economic growth, some potential applicants prefer to join the workforce.

[49] Ibid.

[50] The university's acceptance rate is defined as the number of students accepted divided by the number of students applying to attend the university.

[51] Metrics like average entrance-exam score, acceptance rate, student-to-teacher ratio, and student retention rate are often used as proxies for academic quality.

[52] Wotapka, "Resort Living Comes to Campus," December 6, 2012; Carlson, "What's the Payoff for the 'Country Club' College?" Chronicle of Higher Education, January 28, 2013.

[53] Yang, Colleges and Universities in the US, August 2012.

[54] Academic Earth website, http://www.academicearth.org/ (accessed various dates 2010 and 2011); Open Culture Web site, http://www.openculture.com/ (accessed various dates 2010 and 2011).

[55] Coursera, which received $16 million from venture capital firm Kleiner Perkins Caufield and Beyers, was founded in April 2012 in Mountain View, California. As of December 2012, Coursera offered 210 online classes from 33 universities. Coursera website, http://www.coursera.org (accessed December 19, 2012).

[56] edX, located in Cambridge, Massachusetts, is a nonprofit enterprise founded in May 2012 by Harvard and MIT, each of which have contributed $30 million to the project. Georgetown University; the University of California, Berkeley; the University of Texas system; and Wellesley College also recently joined the edX platform. As of December 2012, edX offers seven classes sourced from Harvard, MIT, and the University of California, Berkeley. edX website, http://www.edx.org (accessed December 19, 2012).

[57] Udacity, funded by venture capital firms Charles River Ventures (undisclosed amount) and Andreessen Horowitz ($15 million), was founded in February 2012 in Palo Alto, California. As of December 2012, Udacity offered 19 classes taught by leading experts, entrepreneurs, and university professors. Udacity website, http://www.udacity.org (accessed December 19, 2012).

[58] Edgecliffe-Johnson and Cook, "Education," January 17, 2013. Sebastian Thrun went on to found Udacity.

[59] Anderson, "Elite Education for the Masses," November 5, 2012.

[60] Coursera website, http://www.coursera.org (accessed December 19, 2012); edX website, http://www.edx.org (accessed December 19, 2012); Udacity website, http://www.udacity.org (accessed December 19, 2012).

[61] Anderson, "Elite Education for the Masses," November 5, 2012.

[62] Ibid

[63] Young, "MOOCs Take a Major Step," November 23, 2012, A23.

[64] Lewin, "Students Rush to Web Classes," January 6, 2013.

[65] Lewin and Markoff, "California to Give Web Courses a Big Trial," January 15, 2013.

[66] Korn and Levitz, "Online Courses Look for a Business Model," January 1, 2013; Lewin, "Students Rush To Web Classes," January 6, 2013.

[67] Korn and Levitz, "Online Courses Look for a Business Model," January 1, 2013.

[68] Lewin, "Students Rush to Web Classes," January 6, 2013.

[69] Lewin, "Taking More Seats on Campus," February 4, 2012.

[70] Thurm, "Who Can Still Afford State U?" December 14, 2012.

[71] Staley, "Lure of Chinese Tuition Squeezes Out Asian-American Students," January 4, 2012.

[72] Thurm, "Who Can Still Afford State U?" December 14, 2013.

[73] Staley, "Lure of Chinese Tuition Squeezes Out Asian-American Students," January 4, 2012.

[74] NAICU, "Private College Tuition Increases Slow," October 4, 2012.

[75] NAICU, "New Affordability Measures," December 28, 2012.

[76] Lewin, "Taking More Seats on Campus," February 4, 2012; Staley, "Lure of Chinese Tuition Squeezes Out Asian-American Students," January 4, 2012.

[77] Lewin, "Taking More Seats on Campus," February 4, 2012.

[78] Purdue University website, http://www.admissions.purdue.edu/costsandfinaid/tuitionfees.php (accessed December 27, 2012); Lewin, "Taking More Seats on Campus," February 4, 2012.

[79] University of Illinois at Urbana-Champaign website, http://admissions.illinois.edu/cost/tuition.html (accessed December 27, 2012).

[80] Farrar, "Smaller U.S. Colleges Try to Crack Chinese Market," December 14, 2012; Golden, "China Rush to U.S. Colleges Reveals Predatory Fees," May 22, 2012; Lewin, "Illegal in U.S., Paid Agents Overseas," February 4, 2012.

[81] China Education Expo 2012 website, http://www.chinaeducationexpo.com/english/exhibition/concept.html (accessed December 27, 2012).

[82] Golden, "China Rush to U.S. Colleges Reveals Predatory Fees," May 22, 2012; Lewin, "Illegal in U.S., Paid Agents Overseas," February 4, 2012. For example, some recruiting agencies engage in the unauthorized use of college logos in their marketing efforts.

[83] CAN-USA website, http://www.cna-usa.com (accessed December 27, 2012).

[84] Study New Jersey, "A World of Options," June 2, 2011.

[85] Waldmeir, "Chinese Students Buck Export Slowdown," September 27, 2012.

[86] IIE, "Open Doors 2012 Fast Facts," November 12, 2012.

[87] IIE, "International Students," November 12, 2012

[88] All multiyear growth rates are expressed as compound annual growth rates.

[89] IIE, "Open Doors Fast Facts," 2000–2012.

[90] Johnson, "U.S. Colleges Seek Foreign Students for Intellectual Stimulus," September 2, 2011.

[91] IIE, "International Students," November 12, 2012.

[92] McMurtrie, "China Continues to Drive Foreign-Student Growth," November 16, 2012, A18.

[93] Johnson, "U.S. Colleges Seek Foreign Students for Intellectual Stimulus," September 2, 2011.

[94] Fischer, "Number of Foreign Students in U.S. Hit a New High," November 16, 2009.

[95] Mong, "Chinese Applications to U.S. Schools Skyrocket," January 11, 2012; Hille, "Chinese Set Course for Foreign Universities," April 3, 2012; Bartlett and Fischer, "The China Conundrum," November 3, 2011.

[96] Waldmeir, "Chinese Students Buck Export Slowdown," September 27, 2012; Mong, "Chinese Applications to U.S. Schools Skyrocket," January 11, 2012.

[97] Bennett, "Why the Chinese are Flocking to U.S. Colleges," May 31, 2012.

[98] Mong, "Chinese Applications to U.S. Schools Skyrocket," January 11, 2012; CNN Wire Staff, "Record Number of Chinese Attend College in the US," November 15, 2010; Global Ticker, "Chinese Students," March 16, 2012.

[99] Mellman, "Chinese Top List of International Students in US," November 13, 2011; Mong, "Chinese Applications to U.S. Schools Skyrocket," January 11, 2012; Waldmeir, "Chinese Students Buck Export Slowdown," September 27, 2012.

[100] Waldmeir, "Chinese Students Buck Export Slowdown," September 27, 2012.

[101] McMurtrie, "China Continues to Drive Foreign-Student Growth," November 16, 2012, A18; Bartlett and Fischer, "The China Conundrum," November 3, 2012; Mellman, "Chinese Top List of International Students in US," November 13, 2011.

[102] Fischer, "Number of Foreign Students in U.S.," November 16, 2012. Many Chinese families believe that the prestige of a U.S. degree—as well as English-language skills and international experience—will lead to a good, high-paying job once their children return to China. Recruitment experts, however, question whether the time and money spent on a U.S. degree will pay off in the Chinese job market. For example, Zhaopin, a Chinese employment agency, recently reported that 70 percent of local Chinese companies did not give hiring preferences to candidates with foreign education credentials, while nearly 90 percent stated that they offered no salary premium, or only a small premium, for foreign-educated candidates. McMurtrie, "China Continues to Drive Foreign-Student Growth," November 16, 2012; Waldmeir, "Chinese Students Buck Export Slowdown," September 27, 2012.

[103] USDOC, BEA, Survey of Current Business, October, 2012, 23.

[104] USDOC, BEA, Survey of Current Business, October, 2012, 44.

[105] Rankings developed by QS Top Universities place U.S. universities in 13 of the top 20 spots worldwide, whereas Times Higher Education ranks them in 14 of the top 20. QS Top Universities website, http://www.topuniversities.com/university-rankings/world-university-rankings/2012 (accessed December 20, 2012); Times Higher Education website, http://www.timeshighereducation.co.uk/world-university-rankings/ (accessed December 20, 2012).

[106] NAFSA, "The Economic Benefits of International Students to the U.S. Economy," November 2012, 1.This figure includes both tuition and living expenses.

[107] The remaining 20 percent of students fell into categories labeled "non-degree" and "other practical training."

[108] IIE, "Open Doors 2012 Fast Facts," November 12, 2012.

[109] USDOC, BEA, *Survey of Current Business*, October, 2012, 24.

[110] Ibid., 45.

[111] I.e., a summer program or a program lasting eight weeks or less.

[112] IIE, "Open Doors 2012 Fast Facts," November 12, 2012.

[113] Harvard Business School website, http://www.exed.hbs.edu/programs/Pages/default.aspx (accessed December 20, 2012).

[114] Michigan State University website, http://dubai.msu.edu/ (accessed December 20, 2012).

[115] USDOC, BEA, *Survey of Current Business*, October 2012, 23–58.

[116] Yang, *Colleges & Universities in the US*, August 2012.

[117] This section focuses on the provision of healthcare services. However, due to the varied and complex relationships between healthcare providers, payers, and patients in global markets, healthcare markets are typically measured by total spending, which may include both healthcare services and goods. Global healthcare spending, as defined by the World Health Organization (WHO), includes spending on healthcare services and goods by governments, households, and private prepaid plans (insurers), as well as other private resources for health, such as nonprofit organizations. WHO, "Glossary of Terms and Financing Flows," n.d. (accessed April 29, 2013). Healthcare services encompass individualized and specialized services provided by doctors, nurses, and other healthcare professionals in medical facilities including hospitals; medical offices, clinics, and other ambulatory facilities; and nursing and residential care facilities. Swiss Re, "To Your Health," 2007, 8.

[118] Better population health has been found to increase national incomes by promoting higher levels of labor productivity, education, and saving and investment. The inverse relationship also holds; higher national incomes promote health through access to better nutrition, sanitation, and quality care. Bloom and Canning, "Population Health and Economic Growth," 2008, 1.

[119] Mortensen, "International Trade in Health Services," 2008, 5; Suhrcke et al., "The Contribution of Health," August 23, 2005, 22, 38, and 67; Swiss Re, "To Your Health," 2007, 10.

[120] See, for example, Kinney and Clark, "Provisions for Health and Health Care," 2004; WHO, *The Right to Health*, 2011.

[121] Global healthcare expenditures consist of public (government) spending and private spending. Private expenditure comprises spending by private prepaid plans, households' out-of-pocket spending, and spending by other private resources for health, such as nonprofit organizations that provide households with goods and services free or for negligible prices. WHO, "Glossary of Terms and Financing Flows," n.d. (accessed April 29, 2013).

[122] All multiyear growth rates are expressed as compound annual growth rates. The 2010 data are the most recent available. Data on healthcare expenditures are reported by the World Bank as ratios. USITC uses these ratios and GDP data to estimate healthcare expenditures. World Bank, World Development Indicators database (accessed October 31, 2012).

[123] As reported in the 2011 *Recent Trends* report, from 2003 through 2008, global healthcare spending grew at an annual rate of 9 percent. However, during the latter half of that period, the rate of growth diverged between public and private expenditures, as public spending rose 10.3 percent in 2008 while private spending rose only 6.7 percent.

[124] Growth in private spending measured less than 1 percent in 2009 and 2 percent in 2010, due to the continued effects of the financial downturn.

[125] World Bank, World Development Indicators database (accessed October 31, 2012).

[126] Per capita spending reported in current U.S. dollars. World Bank, World Development Indicators database (accessed December 7, 2012).

[127] U.S. private healthcare expenditure fell from $1.27 trillion in 2008 to $1.21 trillion in 2010. The percentage of children and working-age adults covered by employer-sponsored health insurance fell 10 percent between 2007 and 2010. USITC calculations using data from WHO's Global Health Expenditures database and the World Bank's World Development Indicators database (both accessed December 7, 2012); Evans, "Record Slowdown, Bigger Share," January 10, 2011, 6; White and Reschovsky, "Great Recession Accelerated Long-Term Decline of Employer Health Coverage," March 2012.

[128] Differing opinions exist regarding whether the slowdown in healthcare spending is a direct result of the recession. Some researchers argue that the slowdown began before the recession and that while the cause

remains unclear, it is not due to cyclical factors; others argue that an uptick in doctor visits following the recession indicates that the slowdown was due to consumers delaying healthcare visits. Kliff, "Healthcare Spending Slowdown," August 10, 2012. USITC calculations using data from WHO, Global Health Expenditures database, and World Bank, World Development Indicators database (accessed December 7, 2012).

[129] Developed countries that experienced particularly low average annual growth during 2006–10 include Greece (4.7 percent), Hungary (0.76 percent), and Ireland (3.1 percent). USITC calculations using data from WHO, Global Health Expenditures database, and World Bank, World Development Indicators database (accessed December 7, 2012).

[130] For example, Germany's total healthcare spending fell from $387.5 billion in 2008 to $379 billion in 2010. Similarly, in the United Kingdom, spending declined from $236.7 billion in 2007 to $217 billion in 2010. USITC calculations using data from WHO, Global Health Expenditures database, and World Bank, World Development Indicators database (accessed December 7, 2012).

[131] OECD, "Health," June 28, 2012; Mihart, "The Financial Crisis," December 2011, 219.

[132] Mihart, "The Financial Crisis," December 2011, 219.

[133] USITC calculations using data from WHO, Global Health Expenditures database, and World Bank, World Development Indicators database (November 7, 2010).

[134] PricewaterhouseCoopers, *Global Healthcare Deals Quarterly*, 1Q 2012, 11.

[135] Deloitte, *2011 Survey of Health Care Consumers in Brazil*, 2011, 5, 21; PricewaterhouseCoopers, *Emerging Trends in Chinese Healthcare*, 2010, 10.

[136] For example, the Japanese Red Cross Society, a government healthcare network that includes 104 medical institutions in Japan, had operating revenues of $14.1 billion in 2011, making it comparable in size to the U.S.-based Community Health Systems. Bureau van Dijk, Orbis Companies database (accessed February 11, 2013); Japanese Red Cross Society website, http://www.jrc.or.jp/english/index.html (accessed February 14, 2013).

[137] Such companies typically act as a middleman, negotiating with drug companies and pharmacies—a service increasingly in demand as firms and insurance companies seek to reduce costs. They are also expanding their services, looking for more ways to save their customers money, such as by increasing patient compliance with medication instructions. Gryta, "What Is a 'Pharmacy Benefit Manager?'" July 21, 2011.

[138] *Economist*, "Bigger Means Cheaper," April 7, 2012.

[139] In countries with sub-federal regulation, healthcare systems are also fragmented at a regional level. For example, in the United States, few healthcare companies provide services in all U.S. states.

[140] Kaiser Family Foundation, "Summary of New Health Reform Law," April 15, 2011.

[141] Care includes hospital and physician services and prescription drugs. Commonwealth Fund, *International Profiles of Health Care Systems*, November 2012, 32.

[142] Commonwealth Fund, *International Profiles in Health Care Systems*, November 2012, 36; Jowit, "NHS Reform," March 20, 2012.

[143] *Economist*, "Heroes Dare to Cross," July 21, 2012.

[144] See section 1 for a discussion of the four modes of services trade.

[145] WHO, *Telemedicine*, 2010, 9.

[146] Accenture, *Making the Case for Connected Health*, 2012, 3; Buntin et al, "The Benefits of Health Information Technology," 2011; Parente and McCullough, "Health Information Technology and Patient Safety," 2009.

[147] Chikotie, Oni, and Owei, "Factors Determining the Adoption of ICTs in Healthcare Service Delivery," 2011; HealthIT.gov, "Basics of Health IT" n.d. Although electronic health records have been associated with lower overall healthcare costs and improved outcomes, physicians have reportedly found it expensive and time consuming to implement such systems in their offices. Denning, "Why Is Your Doctor Typing?" April 25, 2013.

[148] The World Health Organization defines telemedicine as "the delivery of health care services, where distance is a critical factor, by all health care professionals using information and communication technologies for the exchange of valid information for diagnosis, treatment and prevention of disease and injuries, research and evaluation, and for the continuing education of health care providers, all in the interests of advancing the health of individuals and their communities." Accenture, *Making the Case for Connected Health*, 2012, 1.

[149] Accenture, *Making the Case for Connected Health*, 2012, 6.

[150] Thrall, "Teleradiology Part I," June 2007, 613.

[151] In a WHO survey, 60 percent of responding countries offered some form of teleradiology, and more than 30 percent had an established service. WHO, *Telemedicine*, 2010, 37, 43.

[152] Electronic medical records are "generally defined as computerized medical data that hospitals or physicians create to track patients' health." Electronic medical records are usually part of electronic health records, which refer to a "digital file capable of being shared across different healthcare settings, and may include such information as demographics, medical history, medications, immunization status, lab results, radiology images, vital signs and billing information." Accenture, *Making the Case for Connected Health*, 2012, 6. For example, in Denmark, each patient has an individual electronic "medical card" that provides each practitioner with a comprehensive list of prescriptions and treatments. The government is also implementing clinical

databases to "monitor quality in the primary care sector." Commonwealth Fund, *International Profiles of Healthcare Systems*, November 2012, 30.

[153] WHO, *Telemedicine*, 2010, 11, 13.

[154] Castro, "Explaining International IT Application Leadership," September 2009, 21.

[155] Neglected tropical diseases (NTDs) are a group of diseases endemic to developing countries in Africa, Asia, and the Americas that receive little attention in developed countries but cause significant sickness and death among the poor in low-income populations. The WHO classifies 17 diseases as NTDs, including dengue, leprosy, rabies, and yaws. USAID website, "About the NTD Program," http://www.neglecteddiseases.gov/about/index.htm (accessed December 5, 2012); WHO website, "Diseases Covered by NTD Department," http://www.who.int/neglected_diseases/diseases/en (accessed December 5, 2012); WHO, *Telemedicine*, 2010, 15.

[156] Some European countries engage in formal cross-border resource sharing (for example, the Baltic eHealth program creates a transnational infrastructure which allows shared resources, including teleradiology, between five countries—Denmark, Estonia, Lithuania, Norway, and Sweden). However, cross- border teleradiology is not particularly common in the United States, due to stringent licensing requirements and the lack of coverage by Medicare and Medicaid for services performed outside the United States. Castro, "Explaining International IT Application Leadership," September 2009, 22, 23; Baltic eHealth website, http://www.baltic-ehealth.org (accessed November 1, 2012).

[157] A 2012 Accenture study of the implementation and use of healthcare IT by eight developed countries (Australia, Canada, England, France, Germany, Singapore, Spain, and the United States) found that Spain and England were the leaders in incorporating IT into healthcare. Accenture, *Making the Case for Connected Health*, 2012, 6–7.

[158] Accenture, *Making the Case for Connected Health*, 2012, 9; Denning, "Why Is Your Doctor Typing," April 25, 2013.

[159] These factors are a governing body, or national agency, dedicated to development and promotion of telemedicine programs; a national telemedicine policy or strategy; involvement of scientific institutions in development of telemedicine solutions; and a dedicated evaluation process for the national use of telemedicine. WHO, *Telemedicine*, 2010, 50–60.

[160] Jamoom et al., "Physician Adoption of Electronic Health Record Systems," July 2012.

[161] Deloitte, "Consumerism in Health Care," June 12, 2012.

[162] Ibid.

[163] Deloitte, *Retail Clinics*, 2008, 5.

[164] Hensley, "For Simple Care," November 5, 2012.

[165] Mehrotra and Lave, "Visits to Retail Clinics Grew Fourfold," 2012.

[166] Ibid.

[167] Weinick et al., "Policy Implications of the Use of Retail Clinics," 2010, 10.

[168] Mehrotra and Lave, "Visits to Retail Clinics Grew Fourfold," 2012.

[169] Retail clinics are usually less expensive than other providers for most services, with the exception of vaccinations and prescriptions. For detailed comparisons, see Mehotra et al., "Retail Clinics, Primary Care Physicians, and Emergency Departments," September 2008; Thygeson et al., "Use and Costs of Care in Retail Clinics," September 2008; Weinick et al., "Policy Implications of the Use of Retail Clinics," 2010.

[170] Deloitte, *Retail Clinics*, 2008, 12.

[171] Mehotra and Lave, "Visits to Retail Clinics Grew Fourfold," 2012.

[172] Lunt et al., "Medical Tourism," OECD 2011, 15.

[173] Chee, "Medical Tourism in Malaysia," January 2007, 3.

[174] Upper estimates are based on a 2008 Deloitte study, while lower figures were estimated in a 2008 McKinsey & Co. study, which used a more conservative definition of medical travelers. Lunt et al., "Medical Tourism," 2011, 14.

[175] Mathews and Kamp, "UnitedHealth to Buy 90% of Brazil's Amil for $4.3 Billion," October 8, 2012; PricewaterhouseCoopers, *Global Healthcare Deals Quarterly*, 3Q 2012, 6.

[176] PricewaterhouseCoopers, *Global Healthcare Deals Quarterly*, 3Q 2012, 3.

[177] Liu, "Overseas Money Shot in the Arm," February 29, 2012; PricewaterhouseCoopers, *Global Healthcare Deals Quarterly*, 1Q 2012, 11.

[178] Becker, Werling, and Carnell, "Private Equity Investing in Healthcare," August 16, 2011.

[179] Chan, "Carlyle Buys Stake," August 14, 2012; Bloomberg News, "China Medical Services Market," June 25, 2012.

[180] U.S. Citizenship and Immigration Services, "EB-5 Immigrant Investor," July 3, 2012.

[181] The program requires a minimum $1 million investment (or $500,000 in a target employment area, defined as one with high unemployment or a rural area) that creates a minimum of 10 full-time jobs for U.S workers within two years. U.S. Citizenship and Immigration Services, U.S. Citizenship and Immigration Services, "Green Card through Investment," March 30, 2011. "EB-5 Immigrant Investor," July 3, 2012.

[182] Shimogawa, "Hilo to Get 100-bed Nursing Home," April 27, 2012; Hamilton, "West Maui Hospital Could Be Finished by 2015," October 15, 2012.

[183] McFee, "Cleveland International Fund Eyes UH Projects," February 15, 2011.

[184] United Nations, Department of Economic and Social Affairs, Population Division, "Workers," August 2010.

[185] The UN's Millennium Development Goals set a target of 2.28 doctors, nurses, and midwives per 1,000 people. The World Health Organization (WHO) notes that by comparison, the United States has a ratio of 2.42 doctors and 9.82 nurses and midwives per 1,000 people. WHO, *World Health Statistics 2012*, 128.

[186] O'Brien and Gostin, "Health Worker Shortages and Global Justice," October 2011.

[187] OECD and WHO, "International Migration of Health Workers," February 2010, 2.

[188] The United States has the largest number of foreign healthcare workers in absolute terms, although foreign professionals make up a greater share of the workforce in many European countries. O'Brien and Gostin, "Health Worker Shortages and Global Justice," October 2011.

[189] American Association of Medical Colleges, "Physician Shortages to Worsen without Increases in Residency Training," n.d. (accessed May 16, 2013).

[190] Licensing requirements involve passing board exams and an English language test, as well as completing a residency program in the United States. Reportedly, less than 40 percent of foreign-trained physicians who apply are accepted for U.S. residencies. For more information, see Giovannelli, "Foreign- Trained Doctors Kept Out of Practice in US," April 14, 2011; Krupa, "Foreign-trained Health Professionals Put on Path," July 25, 2011; Young et al., "A Census of Actively Licensed Physicians," 2011, 12.

[191] By 2030, the percentage of the population over age 65 is expected to grow to 20 percent (from 13 percent in 2011) and it is estimated that half the total population will have at least one chronic disease. Both factors will drastically increase the amount of healthcare services consumed. Additionally, the recently passed Affordable Care Act expanded health insurance coverage to an estimated 32 million patients, compounding the increase in demand for healthcare services. USDOC, U.S. Census Bureau, "State and County Quick Facts," March 14, 2013; Zywiak, "U.S. Healthcare Workforce Shortage," 2010, 2 (accessed December 13, 2012).

[192] Krupa, "Congress Extends Visa Waiver Program for IMGs," October 3, 2012.

[193] By 2025, it is estimated that one in three Japanese will be over 65 years of age. Matsuyama, "Aging Baby Boomers Face Losing Care," September 14, 2012.

[194] Although Japan has opened its labor market, healthcare professionals must pass a difficult examination in Japanese. Thus far only 7 percent of candidates from Indonesia and the Philippines have passed. Matsuyama, "Aging Baby Boomers Face Losing Care," September 14, 2012; Torres, "Japanese Still Wary of Asian Healthcare Workers," October 16, 2012.

[195] The Philippines, the regional leader in outward healthcare migration, produces 78 nurses per 100,000 population, while Indonesia produces only 15. Statistics are based on most recent year available—Indonesia (2008) and the Philippines (2007). Kanchanachitra et al., "Human Resources for Health in Southeast Asia," 2011, 771, 777.

[196] Indonesia has signed agreements to send health professionals to Japan and Timor-Leste, and has announced its desire to sign similar agreements with governments in Kuwait, Qatar, Saudi Arabia, Sudan, and other ASEAN countries. In 2012, the Indonesian government reported that requests for Indonesian healthcare professionals from foreign countries will total 13,000 professionals by 2014. Faizal, "RI to Export More Healthcare Workers despite Shortage," January 7, 2012.

[197] Faizal, "RI to Export More Healthcare Workers despite Shortage," January 7, 2012.

[198] WHO, "Migration of Health Workers," July 2010.

[199] Ibid.

[200] See, for example, Docquier and Rapoport, "Globalization, Brain Drain, and Development," March 2011; WHO, "Migration of Health Workers," July 2010.

[201] USDOC, BEA, *Survey of Current Business*, October 2012, 34–35, table 1.

[202] U.S. imports of healthcare services are expanding more rapidly than exports of such services. However, because imports are growing from a smaller base, the trade surplus continued to grow during 2007 through 2011.

[203] The BEA does not break down healthcare imports and exports by country. Data reported in the UN Service Trade Database appear to correspond to BEA estimates of cross-border trade, and thus are used to analyze major U.S. markets. However, very few countries report imports and exports of healthcare-related travel expenditure to the United States. Commission staff estimate that country-specific figures represent 20 percent or less of total healthcare imports and exports to the United States. USITC staff calculations are based on data from UN Service Trade Database (accessed February 15, 2013).

[204] Recent data are not available for U.S. trade with Mexico. However, historical data suggest that in the past, Mexico has surpassed Canada as the leading market for U.S. imports and exports of healthcare services.

[205] UN, UN Service Trade database (accessed February 15, 2013).

[206] Hansel, "Mayo Clinic Included in New Canadian Insurance Options," April 17, 2012.

[207] Bustamante et al., "United States-Mexico Cross-border Health Insurance Initiatives," 2012, 75.

[208] Allen, "South Florida Hospitals Compete for Foreign Patients," August 13, 2009.

[209] Ibid.," August 13, 2009; Bowden, "Medical Tourism Fills Hospital Beds," August 23, 2012.

[210] PricewaterhouseCoopers, *Global Healthcare Deals Quarterly*, 3Q 2012, 5.

[211] Among the 10 largest private equity deals announced in 2011, seven of the targets were U.S. companies. Bain & Company, *Global Healthcare Private Equity Report 2012*, 2012, 2, 4; PricewaterhouseCoopers, *Global Healthcare Deals Quarterly*, 3Q 2012, 5.

[212] Bureau van Dijk, Zephyr mergers and acquisitions database (accessed February 11, 2013).

[213] Bureau van Dijk, Zephyr mergers and acquisitions database (accessed February 11, 2013).

[214] Dunn, "International Partnership Opportunities Gaining Interest," April 5, 2011.

[215] Outreville, "Foreign Direct Investment in the Health Care Sector," 2006, 306.

[216] USITC staff calculations, based on data from Zephyr mergers and acquisitions database (accessed February 14, 2013).

[217] Dunn, "International Partnership Opportunities Gaining Interest," April 5, 2011.

[218] Outreville, "Foreign Direct Investment in the Health Care Sector," 2007, 306; Dunn, "International Partnership Opportunities Gaining Interest," April 5, 2011.

[219] PricewaterhouseCoopers, *Global Healthcare Deals Quarterly*, 3Q 2012, 5.

[220] Advisory Board Company, "U.S. Hospitals Eye Chinese Market for Expansion," February 7, 2013.

[221] It is unclear how the industry or patients will respond to this increased demand. Rising demand for primary care is expected to further strain the U.S. healthcare system and worsen the shortage of primary care physicians. One study predicts that the rise in the insured population will increase demand for primary care by between 15 and 24 million visits, which would require between 4,300 and 6,900 more primary care physicians. Hofer, Abraham, and Moscovice, "Expansion of Coverage under the Patient Protection and Affordable Care Act," March 2011, 69. Some sources speculate that implementation of the PPACA will encourage medical travel. Although expansion of health insurance or moderation of healthcare costs could reduce demand for foreign procedures from cost-conscious and uninsured patients (the primary categories of medical traveler), there is some speculation that the PPACA will have little effect on demand for elective procedures (such as dental care) that remain uninsured and could increase demand for foreign services if wait times increase due to the influx of newly insured patients. Further, resource bottlenecks in the United States could encourage more major U.S. health insurers to include foreign providers in their networks, despite the fact that few patients are using the foreign provider options offered thus far. Deloitte, "Medical Tourism: Update and Implications," 2009, 5; Lunt et al., "Medical Tourism: Treatments, Markets and Health System Implications," 2011, 17.

[222] U.S. Congressional Budget Office, "CBO and JCT's Estimates of the Effects of the Affordable Care Act," March 2012, 27.

[223] EIU, "World: Healthcare Outlook," October 8, 2012.

[224] It is estimated that the U.S. over-65 population will reach 72.1 million people in 2030, up from 39.6 million in 2009 (the last year for which data are available). U.S. Department of Health and Human Services, Administration on Aging, "Aging Statistics," n.d. (accessed February 19, 2013)

[225] Swiss Re, "Health Protection Gap in the Asia-Pacific Region," November 28, 2012; EIU, "Western Europe," August 8, 2012.

[226] EIU and Eucomed, "Contract for a Healthy Future," 15, October 2012; Abelson, "The Face of Future Health Care," March 20, 2013.

[227] UN, *Manual on Statistics of International Trade in Services* (MSITS), 2010, 67; USDOC, U.S. Census Bureau, "Industry Statistics Sampler" (accessed February 26, 2013). MSITS defines legal services as "legal advisory and representation services in any legal, judicial and statutory procedures; drafting services of legal documentation and instruments; certification consultancy; and escrow and settlement services."

[228] Cattaneo and Walkenhorst, "Legal Services," 2010, 69.

[229] All multiyear growth rates are expressed as compound annual growth rates. MarketLine, "Global Legal Services," October 2012. Growth increased to 3 percent during 2009–10.

[230] MarketLine, "Legal Services in the United States," October 2012, 8; MarketLine, "Legal Services in Europe," October 2012, 8.

[231] MarketLine, "Legal Services in Asia-Pacific," October 2012, 8. The legal services market in countries in the Asia-Pacific region has been growing from a smaller base in comparison to the United States and Europe: in the Asia-Pacific, the 2011 market value was $85.1 billion; in Europe, $209.4 billion; and in the United States, $246.2 billion. The term "Asia-Pacific" comprises Australia, China, India, Indonesia, Japan, New Zealand, Singapore, the Republic of Korea, Taiwan, and Thailand.

[232] Seddon, "As the Chinese Legal Market Expands," November 24, 2011.

[233] *American Lawyer,* "The 2012 Global 100," October 2012. Among the top 100 firms by gross revenue, there are also 6 Australian firms and 1 firm each from Canada, France, Spain, and the Netherlands.

[234] Johnson, "The Hustlers," October 1, 2012.

[235] Among the largest firms by number of lawyers, there are also three French, two Canadian, two Spanish, and one Dutch firm.

[236] Altman Weil, "2012 Law Firms in Transition Survey," 2012, 6. In a recent survey of 792 U.S. law firms with 50 or more lawyers, 90 percent of respondents from firms with over 250 lawyers indicated they believed "the recession served as a 'permanent accelerator of trends that already existed.'"

[237] Georgetown Law, "2013 Report on the State of the Legal Market," n.d., 2, 3 (accessed February 21, 2013). Demand for legal services is measured as total billable hours for 130 reporting law firms. Comparable revenue growth among U.S., UK, and continental European firms in 2012 suggest a similar pattern of demand growth in those markets, and distinct from higher demand for legal services in Asia and Latin America.

[238] Henderson, "Rise and Fall," June 2012.

[239] Georgetown Law, "2013 Report on the State of the Legal Market," n.d., 4 (accessed February 21, 2013). Productivity is measured as the ratio of the total number of billable hours to the total number of lawyers in each firm.

[240] Sparkman, "The Haves and the Haves Less," April 26, 2012.

[241] Randazzo, "Survey Says Outliers Helped," January 29, 2013.

[242] Georgetown Law, "2013 Report on the State of the Legal Market," n.d., 12–13 (accessed February 21, 2013).

[243] IBISWorld, "Law Firms in the US," 2012.

[244] Susskind, *The End of Lawyers?* 2010, 28–32.

[245] Ibid., 29.

[246] Most of the survey results in this paragraph refer to the participating firms among the 200 highest- grossing U.S. law firms.

[247] On the situation of associates since 2009, see Smith, "Law Firms Keep Squeezing Associates," January 30, 2012. According to *American Lawyer*'s survey, a majority of law firms expected the size of their associate class in 2012 to remain the same as the previous year and did not expect to lay off associates in 2012. *American Lawyer*, "The 2012 Law Firm Leaders Survey," n.d. (accessed February 21, 2013).

[248] Georgetown Law, "2013 Report on the State of the Legal Market," n.d., 10 (accessed February 21, 2013). Equity and non-equity are distinguished by the American Lawyer magazine as follows: "Equity partners are those who receive no more than half their compensation on a fixed-income basis while nonequity partners are those who receive more than half their compensation on a fixed-income basis." *American Lawyer*, "A Guide to Our Methodology," June 2012, 77.

[249] Smith, "Law Firms Partners Face Layoffs," January 7, 2013.

[250] *American Lawyer*, "The 2012 Law Firm Leaders Survey," n.d. (accessed February 21, 2013); *American Lawyer*, "Law Firm Leaders Survey 2012," November 30, 2012.

[251] Combs, "Disruptive Innovation," June 27, 2012. See also Palazzolo, "When a Company Sounds Suspiciously like a Law Firm," January 19, 2012. On the role of technology in the discovery process, see Palazzolo, "Why Hire a Lawyer?" June 18, 2012.

[252] Combs, "Disruptive Innovation," June 27, 2012.

[253] The attorneys at Axiom have worked for clients including Hewlett-Packard, Kraft, and Vodafone. Combs, "Disruptive Innovation," June 27, 2012.

[254] Industry representative, telephone interview by USTIC staff, May 14, 2012.

[255] Smith, "Companies Reset Legal Costs," April 8, 2012; *ALM Legal Intelligence*, "Speaking Different Languages," April 2012. According to the *ALM Legal Intelligence* article (page 10), a flat fee arrangement calls for the client to pay an agreed-upon amount of money for a given legal task, noting that "The firm, not the client, assumes the risk of cost overruns." Such an arrangement "encourages firms to perform distinct pieces of work efficiently." The discussion includes a list of alternative fee arrangements.

[256] *ALM Legal Intelligence*, "Speaking Different Languages," April 2012, 7.

[257] Ibid., 6.

[258] Ninety percent of law students rely on debt to finance law school, and student loan debt among private law school graduates has risen from an average of $70,000 in 2001 to $125,000 in 2011 (Bronner, "Law Schools' Applications Fall," January 30, 2013). It is reported that average law school debt surpasses $100,000; see Tamanaha, "How to Make Law School Affordable," May 31, 2012. The figures for 2010 show average debt for 85 percent of law graduates at $98,500, with average debt exceeding $120,000 for graduates at some schools; see Henderson and Zahorsky, "The Law School Bubble?" January 1, 2012 (this article also discusses the Department of Education's direct-lending program). The debt and uncertain job prospects faced by law school graduates has prompted some to question the return on investment from legal study (especially at lower-tier schools); see Stevens, "Will Law School Students Have Jobs After They Graduate?" February 21, 2013.

[259] Association for Legal Career Professionals, "Median Private Practice Starting Salaries," July 12, 2012. The total number of lawyers at the 250 largest U.S. law firms declined by 12,562 between 2008 and 2011 (from 133,723 to 124,161), with a modest gain in 2012 (to 126,721). Graham, "The Ten Year View," March 26, 2012.

[260] Bronner, "Law Schools' Applications Fall," January 30, 2013. The statistic on job placement comes from the American Bar Association (ABA), which now requires law schools to report specific job-placement data, including "whether graduates are in jobs funded by the schools, and whether graduates are in positions that require bar passage, or for which a J.D. is an advantage, and whether jobs are long-term or short-term." Palazzolo, "Report," January 17, 2012. These changes follow lawsuits against law schools alleging that law schools have distorted information about their graduates' employment and salaries. According to Pearson and Milford ("New York, Chicago Law Schools," February 1, 2012), as of February 2012, about 15 U.S. law

schools had been sued over such allegations, although two of these lawsuits were dismissed in 2012. See Lattman, "9 Graduates Lose Case against New York Law School," March 22, 2012; Phipps, "Cooley Law Grads' Lawsuit Dismissed," July 20, 2012.

[261] Palazzolo, "Law Grads Face Brutal Job Market," June 25, 2012.

[262] BLS, "Occupational Outlook Handbook" (accessed February 5, 2013). See Stevens, "Will Law School Students Have Jobs After They Graduate?" n.d. (accessed February 5, 2013), for a discussion of the BLS statistics.

[263] Weiss, "Law Prof Sees 'Huge Opportunity,'" April 5, 2012.

[264] Industry representative, telephone interview by USTIC staff, May 14, 2012.

[265] BLS, "Occupational Outlook Handbook" (accessed February 5, 2013).

[266] Bronner, "Law Schools' Applications Fall," January 30, 2013.

[267] Neil, "Law School Apps Drop 11.5 Percent," March 16, 2011.

[268] Weiss, "1L Enrollment Dropped," November 28, 2012.

[269] Campos, "The Crisis of the American Law School," July 9, 2012; industry representative, telephone interview by USITC staff, May 14, 2012.

[270] Georgetown Law, "2013 Report on the State of the Legal Market," n.d., 8 (accessed February 21, 2013).

[271] Ibid.; Johnson, "The Hustlers," October 1, 2012.

[272] Georgetown Law, "2013 Report on the State of the Legal Market," n.d., 8 (accessed February 21, 2013).

[273] Liberalization means the relaxation or elimination of legal barriers to trade and investment.

[274] Smith, "With Cross-Border Mergers," December 9, 2012.

[275] Georgetown Law, "2013 Report on the State of the Legal Market," n.d., 8 (accessed February 21, 2013). The number of the previous year's mergers were not available, but were reported as being "substantially more [in 2012] than in any prior year." In another publication, mergers are reported for previous years (48 in 2009, 44 in 2010, and 54 in 2011) and apparently refer to completed mergers "outside the U.S.;" this term appears to mean cross-border mergers, including U.S. law firms' mergers with law firms from other countries. Hildebrandt Institute, "Law Firm Merges Rebound Strongly in 2011," January 4, 2012. Also see Smith, "Stark Choice for Lawyers," January 20, 2012.

[276] Hildebrant Consulting and Citi, "2013 Client Advisory," n.d., 12 (accessed February 21, 2013); Ring, "King & Wood Mallesons," November 23, 2011.

[277] Johnson, "The Hustlers," October 1, 2012.

[278] Ibid.

[279] Both imports and exports decreased in 2009 and 2010, with imports decreasing at a higher rate than exports in those years. This decreased the base level of U.S. imports in 2010, and consequently, the higher rate of import growth in 2011 marginally depressed the growth of the U.S. legal services trade surplus. The surplus grew by 0.9 percent in 2011, as compared with annual growth of 5.1 percent during 2007–10. Trade data in this section are derived from USDOC, BEA, *Survey of Current Business*, October 2012; USDOC, BEA, "Table 7" (accessed November 26, 2012); USDOC, BEA, "Table 9" (accessed November 30, 2012); UDOC, BEA, "Table 10" (accessed November 26, 2012).

[280] As a fraction of gross output in legal services ($269.6 billion in 2011), exports ($7.5 billion in 2011) are relatively small. Data on gross output are reported by USDOC, BEA, "Gross Output by Industry" (accessed May 8, 2013).

[281] In 2007, the top five export markets were Canada, France, Germany, Japan, and the United Kingdom. In 2011, Switzerland had displaced France, becoming the fifth-largest export market.

[282] Europe's share declined from 51 percent in 2007 to 49 percent in 2011, South and Central America's share increased from 4 percent to 5 percent, and the Middle East's share increased from 3 percent to 5 percent. The Asia-Pacific's share remained the same during 2007–11 (30 percent), as did Africa's (1 percent) and Canada's (8 percent).

[283] Each of those countries accounted for less than 1 percent of total U.S. legal services exports in 2011. Other markets with growth rates of 30 percent or higher included Argentina (39 percent), Brazil (43 percent), Belgium-Luxembourg (32 percent), Mexico (34 percent), Norway (232 percent), Spain (38 percent), and Switzerland (63 percent).

[284] Triedman, "Hot Spot," September 28, 2012.

[285] Triedman, "Appearances May be Deceiving," September 28, 2012.

[286] See Ramstad, "Justice Ministry Approves First Foreign Lawyers," May 7, 2012; Thomas, "McDermott to Open Seoul Law Practice Following Trade Agreement," February 14, 2012. The free trade agreement between Korea and the United States includes liberalizing provisions related to legal services (see United States-Korea Free Trade Agreement, Annex II: Non-Conforming Measures for Services and Investment, 44–45). For example, U.S. law firms are allowed to establish foreign legal consultant offices, and U.S.-licensed attorneys are permitted to provide legal services regarding international law and laws of their home jurisdiction. Other provisions permit foreign legal consultant offices to enter into "cooperative agreements" with Korean law firms and permit U.S. law firms to form joint ventures with Korean law firms.

[287] Smith, "India to Foreign Lawyers," February 23, 2012; Palazzolo, "India Supreme Court OKs 'Fly In, Fly Out,'" July 5, 2012.

[288] Freedman, "The Promising Land," August 6, 2012; Freedman, "Foreign Firms Set Sights on Israel," August 6, 2012; *Lawyer*, "Local Firms Can Thrive in Malaysia," November 5, 2012.

[289] A wider group of markets with growth rates of 30 percent and higher include Australia (43 percent), Belgium-Luxembourg (43 percent), Brazil (31 percent), Hong Kong (33 percent), Italy (47 percent), and Korea (37 percent).

[290] Other countries include those outside Europe, Canada, Latin America and other Western Hemisphere, Australia, and Japan.

[291] USDOC, BEA, *Survey of Current Business*, September 2012, 64–66, table 15.

[292] Ibid., 43–45, tables 8.1–8.3. Country or regional data on direct investment abroad are not available for legal services.

[293] Love, "Firms Beef Up Singapore Offices," January 7, 2013.

[294] Tan, "Singapore to License More Foreign Law Firms," April 24, 2012; Seah, "Have QFLPs Worked for Singapore?" May 21, 2012; Love, "Firms Beef Up Singapore Offices," January 7, 2013.

[295] Smith, "Law Firms Follow Business to Mexico," February 21, 2012. For more specific information on the Mexican market (e.g., the insurance market and the relative ease of conducting business in the market for law firms) see Orlik, "DLA's Mexico Entrance," March 9, 2012.

[296] Data on purchases from foreign-owned U.S. affiliates were not available for 2006.

[297] Altman Weil, "2012 Law Firms in Transition Survey," 2012, 8.

[298] Ibid., i.

[299] Hildebrandt Consulting and Citi, "2013 Client Advisory," n.d. (accessed February 21, 2013), 11.

[300] Seddon, "As the Chinese Legal Market Expands," November 24, 2011.

[301] Hildebrant Consulting and Citi, "2013 Client Advisory," n.d. (accessed February 21, 2013), 11.

[302] *American Lawyer*, "The Global 100 Profit Picture," n.d. (accessed February 6, 2013); *Economist*, "Homebodies Rule," October 15, 2011.

[303] Georgetown Law, "2013 Report on the State of the Legal Market," n.d., 3 (accessed February 21, 2013).

In: U.S. Trade
Editor: Carina Vincent

ISBN: 978-1-63117-423-0
© 2014 Nova Science Publishers, Inc.

Chapter 2

RECENT TRENDS IN U.S. SERVICES TRADE: 2012 ANNUAL REPORT[*]

*George Serletis, Cynthia Payne, Lisa Alejandro,
Jennifer Powell, Joann Peterson, Matthew Reisman,
Martha Lawless, Eric Forden and Isaac Wohl*

ABSTRACT

Recent Trends in U.S. Services Trade: 2012 Annual Report focuses on exports and imports of infrastructure services, including banking, insurance, logistics, retail, securities, and telecommunications services. These services are essential inputs to firms in virtually every economic sector. The largest infrastructure service firms are located in developed countries and offer their services globally through cross-border trade and affiliate transactions. Economic growth in developing and emerging countries continues to create new opportunities for expansion and investment by infrastructure service firms, though many countries maintain regulations and policies that pose challenges for stakeholders in services trade.

Infrastructure service industries have shown signs of recovery following the recent financial crisis and ensuing economic downturn. Employment in infrastructure services continued to decline slightly in 2010, but wages, productivity, and value added grew strongly. While the United States had a small cross-border trade deficit in infrastructure services, it maintained a large trade surplus in affiliate sales, which accounted for the majority of infrastructure services trade.

ABBREVIATIONS AND ACRONYMS

3G	third generation (telecommunications services)
4G	fourth generation (telecommunications services)
3PL	third-party logistics

---

[*] This is an edited, reformatted and augmented version of U.S. International Trade Commission Publication, No. 4338, dated July 2012.

AIG	American International Group
ASEAN	Association of Southeast Asian Nations
ATM	automatic teller machine
BEA	Bureau of Economic Analysis
BLS	Bureau of Labor Statistics (U.S.)
BRIC	Brazil, Russia, India, and China
B2C	business-to-consumer (sales over the Internet)
CAFTA-DR	Dominican Republic-Central America-United States Free Trade Agreement
CAGR	compound annual growth rate
EIU	Economist Intelligence Unit
FDI	foreign direct investment
FIO	Federal Insurance Office
FTA	free trade agreement
FTEs	full-time equivalent employees
GATS	General Agreement on Trade in Services
GATT	General Agreement on Trade and Tariffs
GDP	gross domestic product
GM	General Motors
G7	Group of Seven (major economies, namely Canada, France, Germany, Japan, the Unite Kingdom, and the United States)
G20	Group of Twenty (major economies, namely Argentina, Australia, Brazil, Canada, China, the European Union, France, Germany, India, Indonesia, Italy, Japan, Mexico, Russia, Saudi Arabia, South Africa, South Korea, Turkey, the United Kingdom, and the United States)
IMF	International Monetary Fund
IT	information technology
M&A	merger and acquisition
MiFID	Markets in Financial Instruments Directive
NAIC	National Association of Insurance Commissioners
OECD	Organisation for Economic Co-operation and Development
OTC	over-the-counter (financial instruments)
QFII	Qualified Foreign Institutional Investor (China)
RFID	radio frequency identification
RTA	regional trade agreement
SIM	subscriber identity module
TIC	Treasury International Capital system
UNCTAD	United Nations Conference on Trade and Development
USDOC	U.S. Department of Commerce
USDOL	U.S. Department of Labor
USITC	U.S. International Trade Commission
USTR	Office of the U.S. Trade Representative
WTO	World Trade Organization

EXECUTIVE SUMMARY

The United States is the world's largest services market and was the world's largest cross-border exporter and importer of services in 2010.[1] In recent years, global trade in services showed signs of recovering from the economic downturn, with both U.S. exports and imports of services increasing rapidly.

The 2012 *Recent Trends in U.S. Services Trade* report, part of an annual series prepared by the U.S. International Trade Commission (Commission or USITC), provides an overview of U.S. trade in services. This year's report focuses primarily on recent developments in the banking, insurance, logistics, retail, securities, and telecommunication services industries.[2] These infrastructure services are critical inputs to every sector and directly affect the competitiveness and productivity of the overall economy. The United States remained a world leader in these industries, generating a cross-border trade surplus in all but the insurance and logistics industries in 2010.

During both the global economic downturn and the recent recovery in trade volumes, infrastructure services firms have continued to develop new technologies, test new business models, and otherwise adapt to changing commercial environments. New financial regulations have impacted the banking, insurance, and securities industries, while innovative technologies such as e-commerce platforms and smartphones have affected the retail and telecommunications industries. Most infrastructure services industries face relative maturity and saturation in developed markets, in contrast with rapid growth and fragmentation in developing markets.

Key Findings

Total U.S. Trade in Services

The United States Led the Global Services Market in 2009–10

Services industries make up the overwhelming majority of U.S. production and employment, accounting for 79 percent ($9 trillion) of total U.S. private-sector real gross domestic product and 82 percent (82 million) of U.S. private-sector full-time employees in 2010. The United States is highly competitive in the global services market and is the world's top exporter and importer of services. In 2010, the United States exported $518 billion of commercial services across borders (14 percent of the global total) and imported $358 billion of such services (10 percent of the global total). The U.S. services trade surplus of $160 billion was the world's highest. Other significant services traders included Germany (the second-largest services exporter and importer), the United Kingdom (the third-largest services exporter and fourth-largest importer), and China (the fourth-largest services exporter and third-largest importer). Royalties and license fees had the largest single-industry share of U.S. exports (20 percent of the total) and travel services had the largest single-industry share of U.S. imports (21 percent).

Affiliate transactions are the principal means of providing services to overseas customers, exceeding cross-border services trade. Services sold by foreign affiliates of U.S. parent firms totaled $1.1 trillion in 2009, while services purchased from U.S. affiliates of foreign parent firms totaled $669 billion. The largest purchasers of services from foreign affiliates were the United Kingdom, Canada, Ireland, and Japan, while the largest sellers of services through U.S. affiliates were the United Kingdom, Germany, and Japan.

U.S. Trade in Services Returned to Trend Following a Drop in 2009

In 2010, U.S. cross-border services exports increased by 9 percent, following a 2005–09 compound annual growth rate (CAGR) of 8 percent. This growth was spread across service industries, led by industrial engineering, passenger fares, and training services. U.S. services imports grew by 6 percent in 2010 (identical to the 2005–09 CAGR), led by advertising, database and other information services, and trade-related services. Cross- border exports and imports of services both fell in 2009 following the financial crisis, and the 2010 growth rates suggest a return to a longer-term trend. The 2009 figures for affiliate transactions show a decrease similar to that for cross-border trade in that year, as services supplied through foreign affiliates fell by 4 percent in 2009 while services purchased from U.S. affiliates fell by 5 percent.

Infrastructure Services

Infrastructure Services' Value Added Recovered in 2010 as Wages and Productivity Grew, but Employment Decreased

The value added by U.S. infrastructure services in 2010 was $3.8 trillion, equal to 43 percent of total value added by services. From 2005 to 2009, this value added declined at a compound rate of 0.4 percent annually as the financial crisis and ensuing recession weakened demand, but the sector's value added rebounded in 2010, growing by 5.7 percent as the economy improved. Stronger consumer and business spending drove growth in retail (which rose by 10 percent), finance and insurance (7 percent), and wholesale services (4 percent). Distribution services (retail and wholesale) accounted for 40 percent of infrastructure services and finance and insurance accounted for 29 percent in 2010.

Infrastructure services employed 30 million full-time-equivalent employees in 2010. Retail services accounted for 13 million workers, while finance and insurance employed 5.5 million workers. In contrast to professional services, where employment grew by 2.1 percent, infrastructure services employment shrank by 1.5 percent in 2010, following a compound annual decline of 1.3 percent during 2005–09. While employment declined, labor productivity grew; in 2010, infrastructure services was the second most productive U.S. sector (after manufacturing), with an average value added per worker of $127,396. Labor productivity varied substantially among infrastructure services industries, from under $70,000 in labor-intensive retail services to over $375,000 in capital-intensive utilities. Productivity in infrastructure services grew by over 7 percent in 2010, far exceeding its CAGR of 1 percent during 2005–09. Average wages for infrastructure services workers grew by 3.5 percent in 2010 to $55,611, exceeding the private sector average ($51,986) but trailing wages in the manufacturing ($60,003) and professional services ($60,864) sectors. Average wages varied from $32,036 in retail services to $91,787 in the publishing, utilities, and information and data processing industries.

Affiliate Transactions in Infrastructure Services Exceeded Cross-Border Trade in Such Services in 2009–10

Infrastructure services accounted for 25 percent of total U.S. cross-border services exports and 37 percent of U.S. cross-border services imports in 2010. Exports of such services totaled $132 billion while imports totaled $135 billion, resulting in a small cross-border trade deficit. Financial services led U.S. infrastructure services exports and accounted for a large trade surplus, while insurance services made up the largest share of U.S. infrastructure services imports and yielded a large trade deficit.

As in prior years, affiliate transactions accounted for the majority of U.S. trade in infrastructure services. Foreign affiliates supplied $641 billion of such services in 2009, while purchases of services from U.S. affiliates totaled $403 billion. This yielded a surplus of $238 billion, larger than the trade balance of professional services, agriculture, or manufacturing. Infrastructure services accounted for 60 percent of both sales through foreign affiliates and purchases from U.S. affiliates in 2009. Wholesale, finance, and information services accounted for three-quarters ($489 billion) of total infrastructure services provided through foreign affiliates and for two-thirds ($277 billion) of total infrastructure services purchased from U.S. affiliates.

Infrastructure Services Are Affected by Regulation and Liberalization

Regulation is a recurring theme in this report. In general, there is a natural tendency for infrastructure services to be supplied by monopolies or oligopolies, since they often require substantial capital investments, benefit from economies of scale, and have high barriers to entry. This has traditionally motivated governments either to operate them directly or subject them to extensive regulation. However, in some cases regulations can create inefficiencies, and in recent decades there has been a movement towards deregulation, in which government restrictions on economic activity are eased or eliminated to promote competition and attract new market entrants. Higher levels of competition have been associated with greater efficiency in some infrastructure services industries, but the outcomes of liberalization efforts have varied depending on the sequencing of reforms and the amount of stakeholder support. There is generally a correlation between competition, openness, and growth in infrastructure services industries, but there is no universal path by which deregulation, liberalization, and/or privatization lead to greater efficiency. Even after deregulation, governments typically maintain regulatory oversight to address negative side effects of providing the services (externalities) and to meet economic and social objectives.

The Outlook for U.S. Infrastructure Services Varies by Industry

The prospect for growth in each infrastructure service industry largely depends on overall economic growth, including changes in unemployment, consumer spending, and business investment. However, industry-specific factors such as regulatory reform, technological innovation, and market access will also have significant impacts. For instance, new regulations, such as Dodd-Frank and Basel III, could have substantial effects on banking, insurance, and securities services, though those effects are as yet unknown pending implementation. In addition, new technologies are expected to be adopted by many infrastructure services industries during the next few years; for example, mobile devices will likely become increasingly important for retailers. Finally, moves to expand market access, including joint ventures and mergers and acquisitions, are likely to proliferate as firms try to reduce costs and enter foreign markets. Access to foreign markets, in particular, will be increasingly important to industries such as banking, logistics, and retail that anticipate faster demand growth in developing countries than in developed countries.

Banking Services

The Banking Industry Continued to Recover from the Financial Crisis

After record losses incurred during the 2007–08 financial crisis, the global banking industry experienced its second straight year of growth in 2011, with revenues growing by 6 percent to $4.9 trillion. Much of the growth was driven by strong economic activity in Asia, where continued growth in personal income boosted demand for banking services. In comparison, the U.S. and European banking markets grew slowly. Many large U.S. banks registered significant profits in 2011, and only 92 banks were closed by the U.S. Federal Deposit Insurance Corporation that year, compared with 157 during 2010. However, banks are still deleveraging and replenishing the capital lost during the financial crisis, as well as preparing for the implementation of new financial regulations.

The United States Maintained a Cross-Border Trade Surplus in Banking Services

The United States maintained a large cross-border trade surplus in credit-related services and other financial services in 2010, with exports rising by 5 percent to $23 billion and imports rising by 24 percent to $6 billion. The increase in imports, largely due to growth in the U.S. refinancing market, reversed a decline starting in 2008. The steady growth in exports was partly driven by large U.S. banks marketing banking services in countries where the economic downturn did not have as strong an impact.

Insurance Services

The U.S. Insurance Market Remains the World's Largest but Grew Relatively Slowly in 2010

Global insurance premiums grew by 5.6 percent in 2010 to $4.3 trillion, exceeding the 2005–09 CAGR of 4.5 percent. The United States is the world's largest insurance market, accounting for almost 27 percent of global insurance premiums, but U.S. insurance premiums grew at a CAGR of only 0.4 percent from 2005 to 2010, more slowly than premiums in any other top 10 market (China's grew at a CAGR of 29 percent during this period). The economic downturn limited consumers' ability and willingness to purchase nonmandatory coverage such as life insurance, but raised demand for products such as credit insurance, which protects businesses against customer default. The Dodd-Frank Act established a new body, the Federal Insurance Office, to prevent systemic crises in the insurance industry. This change may affect life insurers by requiring higher capital reserves and limiting investments, though the impact of this and other new regulations is still uncertain.

Foreign Affiliate Sales Exceeded U.S. Cross-Border Exports of Insurance Services

The United States maintained a large cross-border trade deficit in insurance services, as 2010 exports totaled $15 billion while imports stood at $62 billion. Bermuda was the largest trading partner for both imports and exports of insurance services, likely due to corporate-related insurance trade. U.S. affiliate sales of insurance services greatly exceeded cross-border exports of such services, as affiliates of U.S. firms in overseas markets supplied $60 billion of insurance services in 2009, exceeding the $50 billion of such services supplied by foreign-owned U.S. affiliates by a significant and widening margin. While some Bureau of Economic Analysis data were suppressed to preserve confidentiality of figures for individual firms, it is likely that Japan was the top market for sales by U.S.-owned foreign insurance affiliates, despite the fact that Japan's insurance market is generally dominated by the state-owned Japan Post Holdings.

Logistics Services

Logistics Firms Expand Their Networks and Supply More Complex Services
The increasing globalization of production and supply chains continued to drive growth in global logistics revenues, which increased from $417 billion in 2006 to $551 billion in 2010. Global third-party logistics firms developed industry-specific supply chain expertise and expanded the reach of their transportation networks, and manufacturers outsourced a wider range of supply chain functions to such firms, including repairing laptops and managing the end-to-end transportation and distribution of pharmaceuticals. Although the United States remained the largest logistics market in 2010 with 23 percent of global revenues, this was a decline of 4 percentage points compared to 2006; during this period China and Brazil rapidly gained market share, becoming the second- and seventh-largest logistics markets respectively.

Merchandise Trade Drives International Trade in Logistics Services
Cross-border trade in logistics services (i.e., air and maritime freight transportation and port services) is highly correlated with merchandise trade, and recent increases in such trade resulted in an 18 percent increase in U.S. exports and imports of logistics services. The United States continued to run a trade deficit in freight transportation and port services, exporting $36 billion and importing $47 billion of such services in 2010. Affiliate transactions fell in 2009 as a result of the economic downturn.

Retail Services

Global Retail Sales Grew Rapidly as Emerging Markets Gained Market Share
Global retail sales grew sharply in 2010, rising 9 percent to $16 trillion. The United States remained the world's largest retail market with $3 trillion in sales (almost a fifth of the global total), but sales grew faster in developing and emerging countries; Brazil, Russia, India, and China together accounted for 24 percent of total retail sales in 2010, compared to 15 percent in 2005. Retailing over the Internet (e-commerce) is becoming increasingly common. Retailers are building smaller stores in the United States in order to reduce costs and enter city centers, and are using promotions and store brand merchandise to appeal to price-conscious consumers. U.S. retailers are expanding in Latin America, Asia, and Africa, even as some of them close stores in the United States.

Economic Conditions Impacted the Growth of U.S. Affiliate Sales
The value of services supplied by U.S.-owned foreign affiliates in the retailing industry grew by 5 percent to $68 billion in 2009, slower than the growth rate of nearly 11 percent in

2008. The slowdown was attributed to relatively weak retail sales growth in major developed-country destinations for U.S. foreign investment in retailing, such as Canada and the United Kingdom. Services supplied by foreign-controlled retailers in the United States shrank for the third consecutive year in 2009 to $34 billion; however, foreign investment positions in the U.S. retail industry continued to increase, suggesting that the decline was due to slow U.S. retail sales rather than reduced interest of foreign firms in the United States.

Securities Services

Global Investment Banking Revenues Remained below Their 2007 Peak

Global investment banking revenue recovered only slightly after the 2007–08 financial crisis, rising in 2010 but falling back in 2011 to $81 billion (close to the 2005 level). In 2011, about half of global investment banking revenue was generated in the United States and 30 percent was generated in Europe. Multinational investment banks continued to expand in emerging markets, serving both investors demanding wealth management services and global companies seeking financial assistance in cross-border transactions and mergers and acquisitions. U.S. investment banks remained global leaders: J.P. Morgan, Bank of America Merrill Lynch, Morgan Stanley, and Goldman Sachs were among the five largest investment banks by fees received, and about half of all global securities transactions took place in the United States.

The United States Maintained a Large Trade Surplus in Securities-Related Services

The United States has consistently had a large trade surplus in securities-related services, and in 2010 cross-border exports of securities transaction services and management and advisory services totaled $43.4 billion, while imports totaled $8.1 billion. Large volumes of securities and securities-related services are traded between countries with well- established financial centers, large issuer and investor bases, and active derivatives markets, such as the United States, the United Kingdom, France, Japan, and Switzerland. Affiliate trade heavily outweighed cross-border trade: the value of financial services (excluding insurance) sold through U.S.-owned foreign affiliates in 2009 was $166 billion, 5 percent lower than the 2008 peak, while purchases of such services from foreign-owned U.S. affiliates reached an all-time high of $97 billion.

Telecommunication Services

Growth in Global Telecommunications Revenues Slowed as Markets Became Saturated

Revenues of global landline, wireless, and Internet telecommunications markets grew by 6 percent in 2010 to $2 trillion. This represented a slowdown in growth compared to the 2005–09 CAGR of 7 percent, as telecommunications markets in both developed and developing countries became increasingly saturated. Despite this market maturity, firms continued to make substantial investments in expanding and upgrading network infrastructure, partly to accommodate growing data traffic. The United States remained the largest market for telecommunications services (accounting for 28 percent of global revenues), followed by China and Japan, and former incumbent operators (i.e., former state-owned or -designated service providers) in the United States, Europe, and Asia (including AT&T, NTT, and Verizon) remained the largest telecommunications firms.

The U.S. Trade Surplus in Telecommunication Services Was Driven by Value - Added Services

The United States had a $3 billion surplus in cross-border trade of telecommunications services in 2010, with exports growing by 10 percent to $11 billion and imports growing by 7 percent to $8 billion. Growth in such exports was mainly driven by value-added services such as satellite broadcasting, business communication, and data network management. The top five cross-border export markets were Brazil, the United Kingdom, Canada, Venezuela, and Argentina, while the top five sources of imports were the United Kingdom, Mexico, the Netherlands, Canada, and Germany. Most telecommunications trade takes place through affiliates of multinational companies, and the United States had a small trade surplus in 2009 affiliate transactions, as sales of foreign affiliates of U.S. parent companies totaled $32 billion and purchases from U.S. affiliates of foreign parent companies totaled $31 billion.

Recent USITC Roundtable Discussion

The Commission hosted its fifth annual services roundtable on November 3, 2011, with USITC Chairman Deanna Tanner Okun presiding and USITC Vice Chairman Irving Williamson moderating. Participants from government, industry, and academia discussed a range of issues affecting services trade, including the outcomes and prospects of multilateral trade negotiations, regional trade negotiations, and unilateral liberalization efforts, as well as the challenges and opportunities of achieving regulatory harmonization in services industries. Roundtable participants considered the tradeoffs between broad multilateral negotiations and smaller "coalition-of-the-willing" negotiations, emphasized the impact of clashing regulatory systems on services trade, and concluded with a discussion of services industries' contribution to employment and global economic activity.

SECTION 1. INTRODUCTION

This annual report examines U.S. services trade (both in the aggregate and in selected industries), identifies important U.S. trading partners, and analyzes global competitive conditions in selected service industries. This year's report focuses on the following infrastructure services: banking, insurance, logistics, retail, securities, and telecommunications.[3]

Data and Organization

The U.S. International Trade Commission (Commission or USITC) draws much of the services trade data used throughout this report from the Bureau of Economic Analysis (BEA) at the U.S. Department of Commerce (USDOC).[4] These data are supplemented with information from other sources, including individual firms, trade associations, industry and academic journals and reports, electronic media, international organizations, and other government agencies.

This section examines the U.S. services sector, global services trade, and U.S. services trade. It looks at both cross-border trade in services from 2005 through 2010 and affiliate sales of services from 2006 through 2009,[5] comparing the trade situation in recent years with previous trends. Section 2 examines services trade liberalization and trends affecting infrastructure service industries and examines the contribution of these industries to economic output, employment, labor productivity, and trade. Sections 3 through 8 analyze the banking, insurance, logistics, retail, securities, and telecommunication service industries. These sections provide an overview of global competitiveness and supply and demand factors, scrutinize recent trends in cross-border trade and/or affiliate transactions, and discuss measures that impede services trade. Finally, section 9 summarizes the information and views presented at the fifth annual USITC services trade roundtable, hosted by the Commission in November 2011.

The U.S. Services Sector

Service industries account for an overwhelming majority of U.S. production and employment. In 2010, private services-producing industries accounted for 79 percent (or $8.9 trillion) of total U.S. private industry real gross domestic product (GDP) and 82 percent (or 82.1 million) of U.S. private industry full-time employees, compared to 21 percent and 18 percent, respectively, for the goods-producing sector. Recent trends in the U.S. services sector have mirrored overall trends in the U.S. economy, as average annual increases in services sector GDP, employment, and wages were within 1 percent of the growth rates registered for the United States as a whole from 2005 through 2010.[6] An overview of production and labor trends in U.S. infrastructure service industries is provided in section 2.

Global Services Trade

The United States is highly competitive in the global services market. As the world's top exporter of services, the United States accounted for $518.3 billion, or 14 percent, of global cross-border commercial services exports in 2010 (figure 1.1).[7] Other top single- country exporters included Germany and the United Kingdom (each accounting for 6 percent). Although most of the world's top 10 services exporters in 2010 were developed countries, China was the fourth-largest services exporter, and India was the seventh largest. Overall, the top 10 exporting countries accounted for 51 percent of global cross-border services exports in 2010.[8]

The United States was also the world's largest services importer in 2010, with $358.1 billion, or 10 percent, of global commercial services imports. In that year, Germany was the next largest importer, accounting for 7 percent of such imports, and the top 10 importing countries together accounted for 48 percent of global commercial services imports. China was the third-largest importer of commercial services in 2010, and India was the seventh largest.

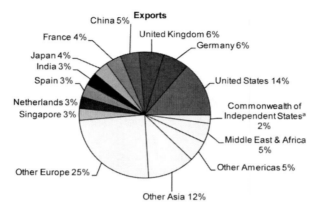

Total = $3.7 trillion

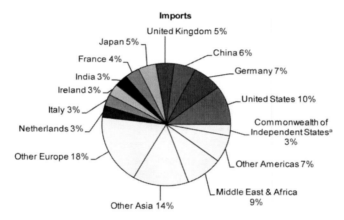

Total = $3.5 trillion

Source: WTO, *International Trade Statistics 2011*, 2011, tables A8 and A9.

Notes: Excludes public-sector transactions. Geographic regions are shaded yellow. Figures m ay not total 100 percent due to rounding.

a Includes Armenia, Azerbaijan, Belarus, Georgia, Kazakhstan, Kyrgyzstan, Moldova, Russia, Tajikistan, and Ukraine.

Figure 1.1. Global services: The United States led the world in cross-border exports and imports of services in 2010.

The World Trade Organization (WTO) reports that the U.S. services trade surplus in 2010 ($160.3 billion) was the world's highest, followed by that of the United Kingdom ($65.9 billion). Saudi Arabia and the United Arab Emirates had the world's largest services trade deficits, with imports exceeding exports by $40.7 billion and $29.9 billion, respectively.[9]

U.S. Trade in Services

The BEA annually publishes data on both cross-border trade and affiliate transactions in services, which together account for a substantial portion of the services provided through all four modes of supply specified in the General Agreement on Trade in Services (GATS) (box

1.1). The BEA publishes these data at the highest level of detail that its surveys allow. The agency also publishes quarterly cross-border trade data in highly aggregated form. "Cross-border trade" occurs when suppliers in one country sell services to consumers in another country, with people, information, or money crossing national boundaries in the process. Such transactions appear as imports and exports in a country's balance of payments. Firms also provide services to foreign consumers through affiliates established in host (i.e., foreign) countries, with the income generated through "affiliate transactions" appearing as direct investment income in the balance of payments report. The channel of delivery used by service providers depends primarily on the nature of the service. For example, retail services are usually supplied through affiliates located close to consumers. Conversely, air and maritime transport services are predominantly supplied to foreign consumers through cross-border trade, as passengers and freight are moved from one country to another. Affiliate transactions are the principal means of providing services to overseas customers, accounting for nearly 68 percent of overall U.S. services trade in 2009 (box 1.2).

BOX 1.1. SERVICES TRADE UNDER THE GENERAL AGREEMENT ON TRADE IN SERVICES

The GATS identifies four modes of supply through which services are traded:

Mode 1 is **cross-border supply.** In this mode, a service is supplied by an individual or firm in one country to an individual or firm in another (i.e., the service crosses national borders). WTO data for this mode of supply do not completely overlap with BEA's data for cross-border trade (see discussion below).

Mode 2 is **consumption abroad.** In this mode, an individual from one country travels to another country and consumes a service in that country.

Mode 3 is **commercial presence.** In this mode, a firm based in one country establishes an affiliate in another country and supplies services from that locally established affiliate.

Mode 4 is **the temporary presence of natural persons**. In this mode, an individual service supplier from one country travels to another country on a short-term basis to supply a service there—for example, as a consultant, contract employee, or intracompany transferee at an affiliate in the host country.[a]

Cross-border trade and affiliate transactions data reported by the BEA do not correspond exactly to the channels of service delivery reflected in the GATS of the WTO.[b] The BEA notes that mode 1 and mode 2 transactions, as well as some mode 4 transactions, generally are grouped together in its data on cross-border trade, while mode 3 transactions are included, with some exceptions, in affiliate transactions data.

[a] USDOC, BEA, *Survey of Current Business*, October 2009, 40–43, tables 1 and 2.
[b] For more information on the four modes of supply under the GATS, see WTO, "Chapter 1: Basic Purpose and Concepts," n.d. (accessed April 7, 2009).

BOX 1.2. THE RISE OF AFFILIATE TRANSACTIONS

Since 1986, when the U.S. Department of Commerce began collecting statistics on U.S. services trade, the relative importance of cross-border trade and affiliate transactions has shifted significantly.[a] In each of the 10 years from 1986 through 1995, U.S. cross-border exports of services exceeded sales by majority-owned foreign affiliates of U.S. firms. Since 1996, however, sales by U.S. firms' foreign affiliates have exceeded cross-border services exports. In 2009, services supplied by U.S. firms' affiliates abroad ($1.1 trillion) were more than double the value of U.S. cross- border exports of services ($487.9 billion). Similarly, services supplied to U.S. citizens by foreign-owned affiliates have exceeded cross-border services imports since 1989. In 2009, services supplied to U.S. citizens by the U.S. affiliates of foreign companies ($668.8 billion) were nearly twice the value of U.S. services imports ($346.0 billion).[b]

The growing predominance of affiliate transactions largely reflects the global spread of service firms, facilitated by liberalization—the removal or lessening of barriers to trade—in investment and services. Liberalization first occurred in developed countries and has occurred more recently in a growing number of low- and middle-income countries.

[a] USDOC, BEA, *Survey of Current Business*, October 2006.
[b] USDOC, BEA, *Survey of Current Business*, October 2011, 13.

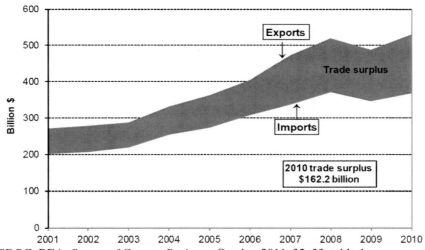

Source: USDOC, BEA, *Survey of Current Business*, October 2011, 32–33, table 1.

Figure 1.2. U.S. services: U.S. cross-border trade in private sector services resulted in a U.S. trade surplus each year during 2001–10.

Cross-border Trade, 2010

U.S. exports of private sector services totaled $530.3 billion in 2010, while U.S. imports totaled $368.0 billion, resulting in a $162.2 billion trade surplus (figure 1.2).[10] Infrastructure Services[11] accounted for 25 percent of exports and 37 percent of imports (figure 1.3).[12] Royalties and license fees (i.e., payments for U.S. intellectual property) were the largest single-category share of U.S. exports in 2010,[13] accounting for 20 percent of the total. Travel services were the largest single-category share of U.S. imports in 2010, accounting for 21 percent of the total.[14]

In 2010, U.S. cross-border services exports increased after falling in 2009 as a result of the global recession. U.S. cross-border services exports increased by 9 percent in 2010, compared to a compound annual growth rate (CAGR) of 8 percent during 2005–09.[15] This increase was spread across service industries, led by industrial engineering (22 percent); passenger fares (18 percent); training services (17 percent); and research, development, and testing (16 percent).

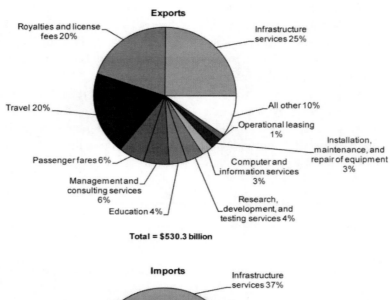

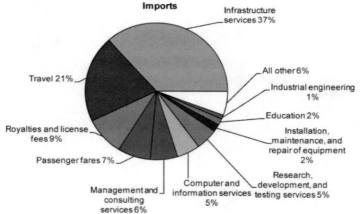

Source: USDOC, BEA, *Survey of Current Business*, October 2011, 31–32, table 1.

Note: As discussed in footnote 5, trade data exclude public-sector transactions. Figures may not total 100 percent due to rounding.

Figure 1.3. U.S. services: Infrastructure services accounted f or a large share of U.S. cross-border exports and imports of services in 2010.

The value of U.S. services imports grew by 6 percent in 2010, identical to the CAGR for U.S. services imports from 2005 through 2009. Import growth was particularly high for advertising (39 percent), database and other information services (29 percent), trade- related services[16] (21 percent), and transportation services[17] (20 percent).

As in most previous years, the majority of U.S. service industries registered cross-border trade surpluses in 2010. Royalties and license fees achieved the largest surplus in 2010 ($72.1 billion), followed by financial services ($52.6 billion), travel services ($28.0 billion), education services ($15.6 billion), and audiovisual services ($11.9 billion). Service industries that netted cross-border trade deficits in 2010 include insurance services ($47.2 billion); transportation services ($11.3 billion); computer and data processing services ($9.6 billion); and accounting, auditing, and bookkeeping services ($1.4 billion).

Several U.S. service industries recorded deficits, for a variety of reasons. The deficit in insurance services principally reflects U.S. primary insurers' payments to European and Bermudian reinsurers in return for their assuming a portion of large risks. The deficit in transportation services (i.e., freight transport and port fees) largely reflects the U.S. deficit in manufactured goods trade and the way in which U.S. imports of freight transportation services are measured. For example, Chinese shipments of manufactured goods to the United States typically exceed U.S. shipments of goods to China, and payments to Chinese or other foreign shippers for transporting U.S. merchandise imports are recorded by the BEA as U.S. imports of transportation services. Lastly, the deficit in computer and data processing services largely reflects U.S. firms outsourcing many of these services to Indian providers.[18]

A small number of developed countries account for a substantial share of U.S. cross-border services trade. Canada, the United Kingdom, and Japan collectively received 27 percent of total U.S. cross-border services exports in 2010 (10 percent, 9 percent, and 8 percent, respectively). The United Kingdom (11 percent), Canada (7 percent), Japan and Germany (6 percent each), and Switzerland (5 percent) supplied the largest single- country shares of U.S. services imports in 2010. The European Union (EU) accounted for 32 percent of U.S. services exports and 34 percent of U.S. imports in 2010.[19]

Cross-Border Trade, 2011

Preliminary data for 2011 suggest that the United States' services exports, services imports, and surplus in services trade continued to grow that year. Annual services exports in 2011 exceeded those in 2010 by 11 percent or $58.5 billion (table 1.1). Annual services imports in 2011 exceeded those in 2010 by about 7 percent, or $27.2 billion.

Annual services trade posted a surplus of $193.5 billion in 2011, or $31 billion more than in 2010.

Affiliate Transactions

In 2009, due to the global recession, services supplied by U.S.-owned foreign affiliates[20] decreased by 3.6 percent to $1.1 trillion, in stark contrast to the 12 percent CAGR registered from 2006 through 2008.[21] Infrastructure services accounted for 60 percent[22] of services supplied by U.S.-owned foreign affiliates in 2009 (figure 1.4). Sales of non- infrastructure services were led by administrative and support services, which accounted for approximately 4 percent of total services supplied by U.S.-owned foreign affiliates. The largest foreign purchasers of services from U.S.-owned affiliates were the United Kingdom (18 percent), Canada (9 percent), and Ireland and Japan (6 percent each). The EU accounted for 47 percent of total services supplied by U.S.-owned affiliates in 2009.[23]

Services supplied by foreign-owned affiliates in the United States decreased by 5 percent in 2009 to $668.8 billion as the U.S. economy contracted during the first half of the year. This decline contrasted with a 4 percent CAGR from 2006 through 2008. Infrastructure services supplied by foreign-owned U.S. affiliates accounted for 60 percent of total services supplied by such affiliates in 2009.[24] Administrative, support, and waste management services, accounting for 5 percent of purchases, were the largest type of non-infrastructure services supplied by foreign-owned affiliates in the United States. By country, the United Kingdom accounted for the biggest share of services supplied by foreign-owned affiliates in 2009 (18 percent), followed by Germany and Japan (13 percent each). Canada and France rounded out the top five with 10 percent each. Overall, 56 percent of services supplied by foreign-owned affiliates were from affiliates of EU- based parent firms.

Table 1.1. U.S. private services exports and imports to the world, by category, 2010–11

Service industry	2010	2011	% change 2010–11
	Million $		
Exports			
Business, professional, and technical services	126,296	137,862	9.2
Royalties and license fees	105,583	120,619	14.2
Travel	103,505	116,279	12.3
Financial services	66,387	72,988	9.9
Passenger fares	30,931	36,717	18.7
Education	21,291	22,823	7.2
Port services	20,168	21,309	5.7
Freight	19,768	21,145	7.0
Insurance services	14,605	15,350	5.1
Telecommunications	11,095	12,744	14.9
Other	10,645	10,983	3.2
Total	**530,274**	**588,819**	**11.0**
Imports			
Business, professional, and technical services	90,585	106,766	17.9
Travel	75,507	79,120	4.8
Insurance services	61,767	57,561	-6.8
Freight	37,915	40,340	6.4
Royalties and license fees	33,450	36,581	9.4
Passenger fares	27,279	31,104	14.0
Financial services	13,803	15,070	9.2
Port services	13,288	14,144	6.4
Telecommunications	8,006	7,822	-2.3
Education	5,677	5,970	5.2
Other	759	796	4.9
Total	**368,036**	**395,274**	**7.4**

Source: USDOC, BEA, U.S. International Transactions Accounts Data, March 14, 2012, table 3a.
Note: Data for 2011 are preliminary.

Services supplied by foreign affiliates of U.S. firms[a]

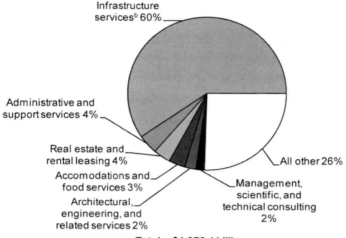

Total = $1,076.4 billion

Purchases from U.S. affiliates of foreign firms[c]

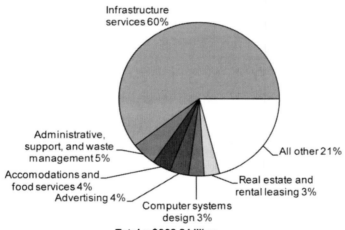

Total = $668.8 billion

Source: USDOC, BEA, *Survey of Current Business*, October 2011, 54, 56, tables 9.2 and 10.2.

Note: Trade data exclude public sector transactions. Figures may not total 100 percent due to rounding.

[a] Services supplied by majority-owned foreign affiliates of U.S. parent firms.

[b] Data are underreported due to suppression of data by the BEA to avoid disclosure of data of individual companies.

[c] Services supplied by majority-owned U.S. affiliates of foreign parent firms.

Figure 1.4. U.S. services: Infrastructure services led services transactions by affiliates in 2009.

SECTION 2. INFRASTRUCTURE SERVICES OVERVIEW

Infrastructure services are essential to the efficient functioning of modern economies. They are fundamental inputs to the production of other services and goods, and they facilitate trade and commerce. Firms in all sectors depend on access to reasonably priced, high-quality infrastructure services, such as communications, transportation, and financial services, to maintain or improve their competitive position.[25] Further, infrastructure services trade is associated with GDP growth and welfare gains, and there is a strong and growing body of evidence that liberalizing infrastructure services (i.e., opening them up to competition and reducing trade barriers) can boost efficiency and economic growth both at the sector level and in the broader economy.[26]

Services Regulation and Liberalization

Regulation is a recurring theme in the following sections. Certain infrastructure services have natural monopoly or oligopoly structures, in that they operate most efficiently (at the lowest average cost) when provided by a single or small number of suppliers.[27] These services generally require large capital investments, benefit from economies of scale, and have high barriers to entry that discourage outside firms from trying to compete. For instance, transportation services rely on costly networks of roads, railways, ports, and airports, while telecommunication services require extensive networks of fixed lines, cell towers, and satellites. The importance of infrastructure services, combined with the desire of monopolists to maximize profits by undersupplying and overpricing them, has traditionally motivated governments to directly operate or extensively regulate infrastructure services.[28]

In some cases, regulations go beyond preventing monopolies and end up protecting incumbents and creating inefficiencies. Additionally, technological innovation has changed the way many services are provided, giving providers new bases for competing with each other. As a result, there has been a movement towards deregulation in recent decades, in which government restrictions on economic activity are eased or eliminated in an effort to promote competition and attract new entrants into the market. Higher levels of competition have been linked to greater efficiency in infrastructure services industries; for example, in the air and maritime transport sector, competition is associated with lower costs and increased capacity.[29] In the United States, deregulation of the telecommunication sector speeded the commoditization of many telecommunication services and led to significantly lower prices (see section 8 for a discussion of the telecommunication sector).

However, the historical outcomes of liberalization efforts have varied, depending on factors such as the order in which reforms occur and the amount of stakeholder support. When South Africa tried to liberalize its telecommunication sector by partially privatizing the state-owned incumbent (existing provider), the enterprise became more productive, but prices for consumers did not fall.[30] When Costa Rica sought to liberalize its telecommunication sector in 2000, both unions and consumers (who anticipated higher prices and poorer service) opposed the reforms, and the government eventually halted the process.[31] While there is generally a correlation between competition, openness, and growth in infrastructure services industries,[32] there is no universal path by which deregulation, liberalization, and/or privatization automatically lead to greater efficiency.

Even in infrastructure services industries that have been deregulated, governments often continue their regulatory oversight to address negative externalities (undesirable side effects of supplying the service) and to meet economic and social objectives.[33] Regulators try to ensure that providers, including monopolists and oligopolists, supply services in sufficient amounts and at fair prices. In particular, they try to ensure that poor and rural consumers have access to essential services such as telecommunications, banking, and insurance.[34] They must also deal with the problem of asymmetrical information in cases when consumers cannot easily judge the quality of a service—for example, by assessing the safety of transportation networks.[35] Effective regulatory structures complement increased competition, given that liberalization may not improve access to services in the absence of prudential regulation.[36]

Some countries also set up regulations to monitor and control imports of infrastructure services. Examples include limits or quotas on foreign participation, licensing and certification requirements, and other regulations that prohibit or raise the cost of foreign-supplied services. Regulations that restrict foreign direct investment (FDI) can be a substantial barrier to services trade, as FDI is a key channel through which infrastructure services are provided by foreign suppliers in many countries.[37] These regulations can be used to protect incumbent providers such as state-owned enterprises from foreign competition.[38] In some cases, such regulations are nontransparent and differ substantially across countries.[39] The following sections include short discussions of nontariff measures that significantly affect international trade in infrastructure services.

Gross Domestic Product (GDP), Employment, Labor Productivity, and Salaries

The value added by U.S. infrastructure services in 2010 was $3.8 trillion, which represented 43 percent of the total value added by services.[40] From 2005 to 2009, the sector's value added declined at a CAGR of –0.4 percent, since the financial crisis and ensuing recession weakened demand for these services in the latter part of the period. In 2010, as the economy improved, infrastructure services' contribution to GDP rebounded: it grew 6 percent, surpassing all other sectors except manufacturing (which expanded by 11 percent). Stronger consumer and business spending in 2010 led to significant growth in several infrastructure services, including retail (which grew by 10 percent), finance and insurance (7 percent), and wholesale services (4 percent). Among all infrastructure services, only the information and data processing industry declined in 2010, after posting positive growth during 2005–09. Distribution services (retail and wholesale) accounted for about 40 percent of infrastructure services' contribution to GDP in 2010 ($1.6 trillion), followed by finance and insurance (29 percent, or $1.1 trillion) (figure 2.1). The shares of these industries remained relatively stable from 2005 to 2010. Infrastructure services accounted for the largest share of U.S. private sector employment in 2010. These services employed 30 million full-time-equivalent employees (FTEs), nearly 30 percent of the total U.S. private sector workforce. Retail services accounted for 12.6 million workers or 42 percent of infrastructure services employment in 2010, followed by finance and insurance (5.5 million) and wholesale services (5.3 million) (figure 2.2). Following the general trend in the economy during 2005–09, infrastructure services employment fell by 1.6 million FTEs (at a compounded annual rate of -1.3 percent) (table 2.1). This represented fewer job losses than in manufacturing (where employment fell by over 2.4 million FTEs), but contrasted dramatically with professional services, which gained over 2 million jobs during the period. The decline in infrastructure services employment was broad, with nearly all sectors shedding employees; the retail sector alone lost over 760,000 jobs during 2005–09 (table 2.2).

Table 2.1. United States: GDP, FTEs, wage and salary accruals, and labor productivity, by goods and service sectors, 2005–10

	2005	2009	2010	Compound annual growth rate, 2005–09 (%)	Percent change, 2009–10
GDP[a] (billion $)					
Private sector	11,037	10,965	11,355	–0.2	3.6
Goods	2,501	2,295	2,422	–2.1	5.6
Manufacturing	1,569	1,444	1,606	–2.1	11.2
Nonmanufacturing	932	851	816	–2.3	–4.1
Services	8,536	8,671	8,936	0.4	3.0
Professional services	2,042	2,196	2,262	1.8	3.0
Infrastructure services	3,689	3,629	3,838	–0.4	5.7
Other services	2,805	2,850	2,843	0.4	–0.3
FTEs (thousands)					
Private sector	105,572	101,349	100,539	–1.0	–0.8
Goods	22,894	19,176	18,458	–4.3	–3.7
Manufacturing	13,954	11,528	11,235	–4.7	–2.5
Nonmanufacturing	8,940	7,648	7,223	–3.8	–5.6
Services	82,680	82,173	82,080	–0.2	–0.1
Professional services	24,334	26,442	26,754	2.1	1.2
Infrastructure services	32,183	30,578	30,125	–1.3	–1.5
Other services	26,163	25,153	25,201	–1.0	0.2
Wage and salary accruals ($ per FTE)					
Private sector	44,717	50,411	51,986	3.0	3.1
Goods	48,196	55,454	57,385	3.6	3.5
Manufacturing	50,909	57,335	60,003	3.0	4.7
Nonmanufacturing	43,963	52,619	53,308	4.6	1.3
Services	43,753	49,234	50,773	3.0	3.1
Professional services	52,451	59,416	60,864	3.2	2.4
Infrastructure services	48,915	53,744	55,611	2.4	3.5
Other services	29,313	33,048	34,277	3.0	3.7
Labor productivity[b] ($ per FTE)					
Private sector	104,546	108,186	112,937	0.9	4.4
Goods	109,251	119,660	131,217	2.3	9.7
Manufacturing	112,462	125,243	142,937	2.7	14.1
Nonmanufacturing	104,239	111,245	112,986	1.6	1.6
Services	103,239	105,524	108,865	0.5	3.2
Professional services	83,924	83,050	84,541	–0.3	1.8
Infrastructure services	114,629	118,690	127,396	0.9	7.3
Other services	107,193	113,322	112,797	1.4	–0.5

Sources: USDOC, BEA, "Full-Time Equivalent Employees by Industry," interactive tables, December 13, 2011; USDOC, BEA, "Table 6.6D: Wage and Salary Accruals per Full-Time Equivalent Employee by Industry," interactive tables, August 8, 2011; USDOC, BEA, "Table 6.3D. Wage and Salary Accruals by Industry," interactive tables, August 8, 2011; USDOC, BEA, "Real Value Added by Industry," interactive tables, December 13, 2011.

[a] Real value added by industry using 2005 chained dollars.

[b] Labor productivity, calculated by USITC staff, is GDP by industry divided by the number of FTEs.

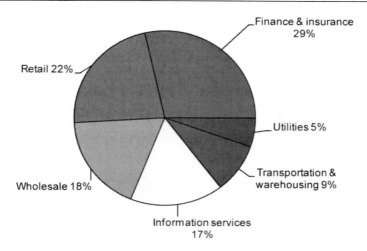

Total infrastructure services GDP = $3.8 trillion

Source: USDOC, BEA, "Real Value Added by Industry," interactive tables, December 13, 2011 (accessed December 14, 2011).

Note: Figures may not total 100 percent due to rounding.

Figure 2.1. U.S. Infrastructure services: Finance and insurance services had the largest contribution to GDP in 2010.

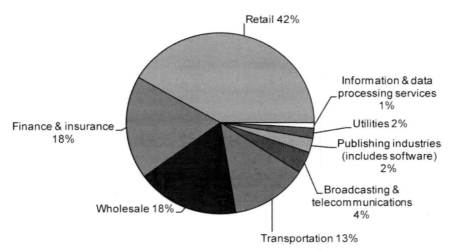

Total infrastructure services employment = 30 million workers

Source: USDOC, BEA, "Full-Time Equivalent Employees by Industry," interactive tables, August 8, 2011 (accessed December 5, 2011).

Note: Figures may not total 100 percent due to rounding.

Figure 2.2. U.S. Infrastructure services: Retail accounted f or the largest share of Infrastructure services employment in 2010.

Table 2.2. United States: GDP, FTEs, wage and salary accruals, and labor productivity, by service industries, 2005–10

	2005	2009	2010	Compound annual growth rate, 2005–09 (%)	Percent change, 2009–10
GDP[a] (billion $)					
Broadcasting & telecommunications	311	359	371	3.6	3.3
Finance & insurance	1,019	1,044	1,112	0.6	6.6
Information & data processing services	71	82	81	3.7	-1.3
Publishing industries (includes software)	150	138	143	-2.0	3.5
Retail	838	790	869	-1.5	10.1
Transportation	370	345	357	-1.7	3.5
Utilities	206	198	205	-0.9	3.3
Wholesale	726	674	700	-1.8	3.9
FTEs (thousands)					
Broadcasting & telecommunications	1,289	1,247	1,168	-0.8	-6.3
Finance & insurance	5,829	5,571	5,527	-1.1	-0.8
Information & data processing services	394	292	290	-7.2	-0.7
Publishing industries (includes software)	855	787	753	-2.1	-4.3
Retail	13,467	12,704	12,561	-1.4	-1.1
Transportation	4,194	4,009	3,976	-1.1	-0.8
Utilities	542	555	546	0.6	-1.6
Wholesale	5,613	5,413	5,304	-0.9	-2.0
Wage and salary accruals ($ per FTEs)					
Broadcasting & telecommunications	65,935	72,349	74,542	2.3	3.0
Finance & insurance	77,981	84,566	88,118	2.0	4.2
Information & data processing services	76,004	85,005	89,954	2.8	5.8
Publishing industries (includes software)	70,368	85,951	91,787	5.1	6.8
Retail	29,230	31,177	32,036	1.6	2.8
Transportation & warehousing	43,865	48,363	49,859	2.5	3.1
Utilities	77,409	87,764	89,676	3.2	2.2
Wholesale	57,922	64,833	67,187	2.9	3.6
Labor productivity[b] ($ per FTE)					
Broadcasting & telecommunications	241,040	287,570	317,295	4.5	10.3
Finance & insurance	143,436	165,546	170,567	3.6	3.0
Information & data processing services	179,188	280,137	278,276	11.8	-0.7
Publishing industries (includes software)	175,322	175,604	190,040	0.0	8.2
Retail	62,196	62,162	69,190	0.0	11.3
Transportation	88,102	86,131	89,864	-0.6	4.3
Utilities	379,889	357,477	375,458	-1.5	5.0
Wholesale	129,254	124,460	131,957	-0.9	6.0

Sources: USDOC, BEA, "Full-Time Equivalent Employees by Industry," interactive tables, December 13, 2011; USDOC, BEA, "Table 6.6D: Wage and Salary Accruals per Full-Time Equivalent Employee by Industry," interactive tables, August 8, 2011; USDOC, BEA, "Table 6.3D. Wage and Salary Accruals by Industry," interactive tables, August 8, 2011; USDOC, BEA, "Real Value Added by Industry," interactive tables, December 13, 2011.

[a] Real value added by industry using 2005 chained dollars.

[b] Labor productivity, calculated by USITC staff, is GDP by industry divided by the number of FTEs.

While employment has declined, labor productivity in infrastructure services (measured as output per FTE) has grown in recent years. In 2010, infrastructure services was the second most productive U.S. sector after manufacturing, with an average output per worker of $127,396 compared to $142,937 in manufacturing. By contrast, average output per worker in professional services was $84,541. However, productivity varied substantially among infrastructure services industries: average output per worker ranged from under $70,000 in labor-intensive retail services to over $375,000 in capital-intensive utilities. From 2005 to 2009, productivity in the infrastructure services sector grew at a compound annual rate of only 1 percent, reflecting the slight decline in sector output. However, productivity grew by over 7 percent in 2010, second only to manufacturing (14 percent), as GDP increased and the economy showed signs of recovery.

Infrastructure services workers earned an average wage of $55,611 in 2010, which exceeded the private sector average ($51,986) but trailed wages in goods manufacturing ($60,003) and professional services ($60,864). Average wages varied substantially within the sector. In 2010, average annual wages were $32,036 in retail services, where many jobs are part-time positions that do not require advanced education or training, compared to roughly $90,000 in the publishing, utilities, and information and data processing industries, which mostly employ highly skilled workers. During 2005–09, the CAGR of wages in infrastructure services was 2.4 percent, the slowest rate in the economy, though close to the overall average rate of 3 percent. In 2010, average wages rose by 3.5 percent, the second-largest increase after manufacturing (4.7 percent), which corresponded to the gains in productivity and output during the year.[41]

Table 2.3. U.S. infrastructure services:[a] Top five cross-border export and import markets and leading industries, 2010

Rank	Country	Export to country	Exports (million $)
1	United Kingdom	Financial services	9,348
2	Canada	Financial services	4,702
3	Japan	Financial services	3,059
4	Bermuda	Insurance services	2,735
5	Canada	Insurance services	2,617
Rank	Country	Import from country	Imports (million $)
1	Bermuda	Insurance services	29,940
2	Switzerland	Insurance services	6,590
3	United Kingdom	Insurance services	5,488
4	United Kingdom	Financial services	4,325
5	Germany	Insurance services	3,050

Source: USDOC, BEA, *U.S. International Trade*, "Table 5 Other Private Services," 2006–2010.

[a] Data for cross-border trade in infrastructure services are limited. Data for financial services, insurance services, and telecommunication services only were used to produce this table.

U.S. Trade in Infrastructure Services

Infrastructure services represented a significant share of U.S. services trade in 2010, accounting for 25 percent of total U.S. cross-border services exports (GATS mode 1) (see box 1.1) and 36.6 percent of U.S. cross-border services imports.[42] The United States posted a small cross-border trade deficit in infrastructure services of $2.8 billion in 2010, with imports of $134.8 billion and exports of $132.0 billion (figure 2.3).

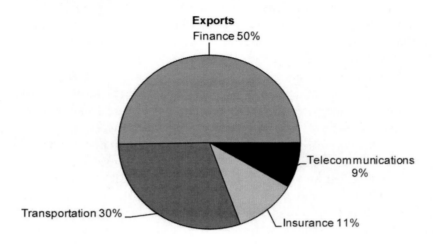

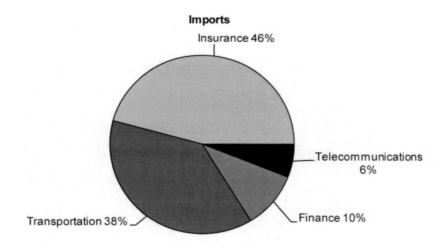

Source: USDOC, BEA, *Survey of Current Business*, October 2011, 31–32, table 1.
Note: Trade data exclude public-sector transactions. Figures may not total 100 percent due to rounding.

Figure 2.3. U.S. Infrastructure services: Finance led U.S. cross-border exports and insurance services led U.S. cross-border imports of Infrastructure services in 2010.

Among the principal infrastructure services subsectors, the trade situation varied substantially. Financial services (including banking and securities services) represented over half of U.S. sector exports ($66.4 billion) and generated a large trade surplus of $52.6 billion in 2010. Leading export markets for U.S. financial services were the United Kingdom, Canada, and Japan (table 2.3) (see section 3 for a discussion of banking services and section 7 for a discussion of securities services). Other leading exports were other transportation services ($39.9 billion), insurance services ($14.6 billion), and telecommunications ($11.1 billion). The United States ran a large trade deficit in insurance services of $47.2 billion, which represented 46 percent of total infrastructure services imports in 2010. A significant share of U.S. imports of insurance services was reinsurance services supplied by Bermuda ($28.2 billion), the leading provider of insurance services in 2010, along with Switzerland and the United Kingdom (see section 4 for a discussion of insurance services).

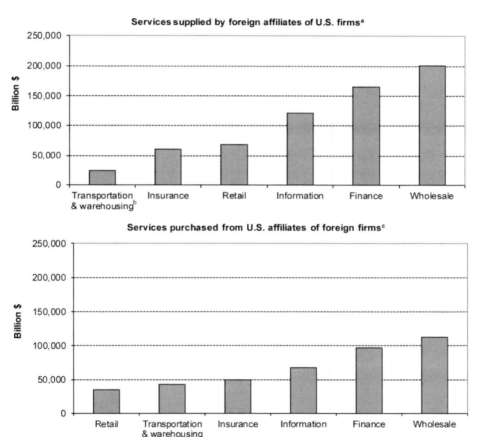

Source: USDOC, BEA, *Survey of Current Business*, October 2011, 54, 56, tables 9.2 and 10.2.
Note: Trade data exclude public sector transactions.
[a] Includes only services supplied by majority-owned foreign affiliates of U.S. parent firm s.
[b] The global total for transportation and warehousing sales was suppressed. This total represents the data for those countries that were made available.
[c] Includes only services supplied by majority-owned U.S. affiliates of foreign parent firms.

Figure 2.4. U.S. Infrastructure services: In 2009, trade in wholesale services led transactions by foreign affiliates of U.S. firms and U.S. affiliates of foreign firms.

Affiliate transactions (mode 3) accounted for a substantial majority of U.S. trade in infrastructure services. U.S.-owned foreign affiliates supplied $641.0 billion of such services in 2009, while the value of services provided by foreign-owned U.S. affiliates was $403.4 billion. This generated a trade surplus of $237.6 billion, the largest balance of any sector (including professional services, agriculture, and manufacturing) in the U.S. economy that year.[43] Infrastructure services also accounted for the largest share of affiliate transactions in services. In 2009 about 60 percent of both sales of services by foreign affiliates of U.S. firms and U.S. affiliates of foreign firms were infrastructure services. Wholesale, finance, and information services accounted for three-quarters ($488.5 billion) of total infrastructure services provided by U.S.-owned foreign affiliates in 2009. These sectors also represented the top three infrastructure services provided by foreign-owned U.S. affiliates, with a value of $276.6 billion, or over two-thirds, of such transactions in 2010 (figure 2.4).

SECTION 3. BANKING SERVICES

SUMMARY

In 2011, the global banking industry experienced its second straight year of growth since the end of the global financial crisis. Strong economic activity in Asia drove increased demand for banking services. The U.S. and European banking markets, in contrast, grew slowly due to weak balance sheets, sluggish economic growth, and reduced fee income. Large multinational banks continued to seek growth opportunities in emerging markets, particularly those in Asia.

The United States maintained a cross-border trade surplus in banking services, and services supplied by U.S.-owned affiliates abroad exceeded services purchased from foreign-owned affiliates in the United States. Overall, however, affiliate trade declined in 2009 as developed markets shrank and U.S. multinational banks scaled back foreign operations in an effort to strengthen their positions in the domestic market.

Introduction

For the purpose of this discussion, banking services are fee-based commercial banking services. These include financial management and transaction services; advisory services; custody services; credit card services; and other credit-related services, such as the provision of standby letters of credit for trade financing. Because they are not tracked in U.S. official data, deposit-taking and lending services are excluded from the trade discussion, but they are included in the industry analysis section of this section. Fee- based commercial banking services can be traded across borders or sold through affiliates.

Deposit taking and lending generate the majority of banking revenues. Banks actually lose money on deposit taking on its own, due to the costs of setting up and maintaining accounts and the interest paid on balances, but it generates the capital that banks use to invest and make higher-interest loans. Further, banks routinely sell additional products and services such as mortgages, credit cards, and other forms of financing to clients, all of which generate profits. Consumer and commercial deposits account for about 60 percent of industry products and services, while loans to those two groups account for a combined 34 percent.[44]

Globally, consumer and retail customers constitute the largest segment of the banking customer base (45 percent), followed by small businesses, corporations, and institutions (35 percent) and government clients (15 percent).[45] While corporate clients generally conduct higher-value transactions, the sheer volume of retail banking clients accounts for the size of that market segment.

Competitive Conditions in the Global Banking Services Market

The global banking industry generated an estimated $4.9 trillion in revenues in 2011, a 6 percent increase over the previous year.[46] It was the second consecutive year in which banks worldwide showed collective growth following the 2007–08 global financial crisis, which resulted in record losses for banks, particularly those in Europe and the United States. Extreme fluctuations in the market during 2006–10 had the cumulative effect of shrinking revenues at a compound annual rate of −1.8 percent during that time.[47]

Global industry assets were valued at $119.5 trillion in 2011, an increase of 5 percent over 2010 levels.[48] European firms continued to dominate the list of top 10 global banks by assets, with two U.S. banks maintaining a presence (table 3.1). One notable absence on the list is Citigroup, which has long been one of the top 10 banks but fell to number 12 in 2011 after taking substantial write-downs and reorganizing its business lines. Industrial and Commercial Bank of China held the 10th spot, while the other three large state-owned commercial Chinese banks (Bank of China, China Construction Bank, and Agricultural Bank of China) all entered the top 25, reflecting the growing size of these firms.

In 2011, Europe generated the majority of global bank revenues at 47.4 percent, followed by North America and Asia (22.6 and 16.5 percent, respectively) (figure 3.1). However, an estimated 40 percent of global banking enterprises are located in Asia, while 29 percent are in North America and just 15 percent in Europe.[49] This reflects the concentrated and saturated nature of the U.S. and European markets, compared to the more fragmented, emerging nature of the developing Asian financial systems.

Table 3.1. Banking services: Top 10 global banks by total assets, 2011 (million $)

Rank	Bank	Country	Total assets
1	BNP Paribas	France	2,671,334
2	Deutsche Bank	Germany	2,547,634
3	Mitsubishi UFJ Financial Group	Japan	2,480,778
4	HSBC Holdings	UK	2,454,689
5	Barclays	UK	2,331,213
6	Crédit Agricole	France	2,313,965
7	Royal Bank of Scotland (RBS)	UK	2,274,767
8	Bank of America	US	2,264,909
9	JP Morgan Chase & Co.	US	2,117,605
10	Industrial and Commercial Bank	China	2,032,196

Source: *The Banker*, "Top 25 Banks in 2011, Top 1000 World Ranking," January 25, 2012.

Banks worldwide began stabilizing in 2010–11. Many of the largest U.S. banks registered significant profits in 2011,[50] and fewer banks closed—the Federal Deposit Insurance Corporation shuttered 92 institutions that year, compared with 157 during 2010.[51] However, the banking industry, particularly in the United States and Europe, still faces challenges. Bank failures in the U.S. market are projected to cost about $45 billion during 2010–14.[52] This is in addition to the record losses suffered by banks during the peak of the financial crisis in 2008–09. Foreclosure rates have remained persistently high since 2008, representing a continuous stream of losses for banks. It is estimated that write-offs by U.S. banks totaled $744 billion during the 2008–11 period.[53] U.S. banks also face new regulations under the 2010 Dodd-Frank Wall Street Reform and Consumer Protection Act[54] that limit transaction fees, raise compliance costs, and expand minimum capital requirements. As a result, banks have in some cases sought to raise customer fees for certain accounts and transactions, and to reduce operating costs through staff cuts and branch closures. Banks are also increasingly outsourcing customer service and data processing (both domestically and abroad), along with higher value-added functions such as accounting and finance, in an effort to free capital. By one estimate, top U.S. banks will outsource about $5 billion worth of information technology and support projects to India in 2011–12.[55]

There were 55,082 commercial banks worldwide in 2011, down 9.6 percent from 2007.[56] The global banking industry, while still generally fragmented, has been consolidating for many years. Before the global financial crisis, merger and acquisition (M&A) activity was high: larger banks merged with smaller counterparts to gain market share in saturated developed-country markets, and they acquired firms in developing-country markets where economic growth is strong, disposable incomes are rising, and populations are underbanked, particularly in rural communities. After the financial crisis, mergers accelerated further as firms sought new growth and as bank failures and divestitures yielded opportunities for healthier banks to make acquisitions at bargain prices. At the same time, banks are beginning to see increased competition from nontraditional financial service providers such as retailers (box 3.1).

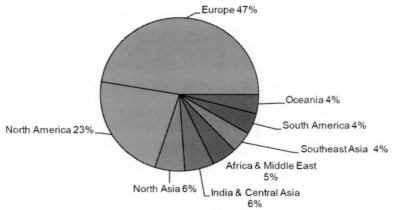

Source: IBIS World, "Global Commercial Banks," May 16, 2011, 11. Figures may not total 100 percent due to rounding.

Figure 3.1. Banking services: Europe and North America held the majority of bank assets in 2011.

BOX 3.1. RETAILERS INCREASINGLY PROVIDE FINANCIAL SERVICES

In the wake of the financial crisis, customers in many countries have reportedly become disenchanted with traditional banks.[a] At the same time, banks have reduced lending in order to rebuild capital and stem ongoing losses, resulting in credit shortages. As a result of both trends, customers are increasingly seeking banking services from nontraditional providers, particularly large retailers. Retailers have traditionally offered branded credit cards and financing for purchases through partnerships with banks, but some retailers are increasing the scope of financial services that they offer, including services that require banking licenses from regulatory authorities. For example, since 2007 Walmart has operated its own bank in Mexico, Banco Walmart, offering basic, low-cost banking services to households that do not typically participate in the formal financial system.[b] As of March 2011, Banco Walmart had more than 260 branches and collected deposits totaling $9.4 million. These branches do not necessarily compete directly with larger banking institutions, given their focus on underserved communities, but in other markets the retailer does compete with established banks. For example, Walmart obtained a banking license in Canada in 2010 and is reportedly seeking a share of the country's mortgage and consumer loan market.[c] The retailer has not yet secured a banking license in the United States, but it does offer financial services across the country in a partnership with SunTrust bank, and it recently started offering small business loans of up to $25,000 through its Sam's Club stores.[d] Retailers in the United Kingdom have also begun offering financial services. The country's biggest retailer, Tesco, has had a banking license since 1997, when it launched Tesco Personal Finance in a joint partnership with the Royal Bank of Scotland. In 2008, Tesco bought out the bank's share and outlined larger plans to become "the people's bank."[e] The rebranded Tesco Bank has an estimated 6.5 million customer accounts and offers credit cards and savings and loan services, as well as insurance products.[f] Smaller retailers have also announced plans to offer financial services in the United Kingdom, but it remains to be seen whether the costs and complexity of establishing banking networks will prove to be a deterrent.

[a] Felsted, "Retailers," April 28, 2010.
[b] Wal-Mart, "Banco Walmart Opens Its 1 Millionth Account," March 15, 2011.
[c] Canada MSN Money, "Will WalMart's Banking Push into Canada Succeed?" June 6, 2010.
[d] American Public Media, "Wal-Mart's Bank Ambitions in Mexico," August 6, 2010.
[e] Felsted, "Retailers," April 28, 2010.
[f] Tesco Bank Web site. http://mediacentre.tescofinance.com/help/about_us/key_facts/ (accessed March 15, 2012).
[f] Felsted, "Retailers," April 28, 2010.

Demand and Supply Factors

Economic Growth Drives Demand for Banking Services in Developing Asian Countries

As prosperity increases, both corporate and personal wealth tend to rise, creating greater demand for loans (particularly real estate and credit card loans), as well as more sophisticated investment vehicles. Divergence in income growth has caused a geographic divergence in the growth of demand for banking services, as advanced economies are anticipated to grow by 2.5 percent annually in 2011 and 2012, while emerging and developing economies are expected to grow at an estimated 6.5 percent.[57]

In the United States, Europe, and Japan, high unemployment has accompanied slow or flat economic growth in recent years, resulting in lower personal income and reduced demand for most financial services. In much of developing Asia, however, personal incomes have continued to rise steadily, as countries such as China, India, the Philippines, and Indonesia experienced positive economic growth in 2008 and 2009. This income growth is due in large part to China's sustained economic performance, as well as the fact that banks in this region had relatively low exposure to the toxic assets that precipitated the financial downturn. Strong economic growth in these countries contributed to greater demand for banking services and attracted multinational banks. This phenomenon is reflected in the changing shares of global bank loans. In 2006, North America and Western Europe accounted for an estimated 31 and 40 percent of global bank loans, respectively, while Asia and Australasia[58] accounted for 26 percent; however, in 2011, North America and Europe held 29 and 32 percent, and Asia and Australasia had 34 percent.[59] Loan activity is expected to increase in all markets in the coming years, though less so in Western Europe than in North America. However, growth in Asia is projected to continue to outpace growth in developed markets outside Asia, and the region may account for 41 percent of global bank loans by 2015.[60]

Availability of Capital Influences Supply of Banking Services

When banks are profitable and can access large amounts of capital, they are able to lend more money and take bigger risks. Conversely, when access to capital is limited, banks are forced to be more selective in their activities. In the financial crisis, banks incurred significant losses and write-downs due to exposure to bad mortgage-backed assets, which limited their holdings of and ability to borrow capital. Many banks have stabilized their balance sheets and recovered from these losses in the past three years, but their capital supplies have not been fully replenished due to sluggish economic growth. Furthermore, new regulations have raised capital reserve requirements: domestic regulations such as those recently enacted in the United States and Europe, and the anticipated Basel III international standards, significantly increase the amount of reserve capital that banks must hold, with larger institutions required to hold more capital. These obligations ultimately protect consumers but constrain banks' activities to some degree. To illustrate, while demand for banking services has grown rapidly in many Asian markets, several large multinational banks have lessened their exposure in these markets in recent years in order to conserve capital. Bank of America, for example, reduced its stake in China Construction Bank in 2009 from 19.15 percent to 11 percent, raising $10.1 billion in the process.[61]

Regulatory Environments Affect the Way Banks Do Business

In most countries, banking is a highly regulated industry, and government regulations often determine a financial firm's commitment to a given market. In some markets, regulations are nontransparent and may discriminate against foreign firms. In certain cases, such as China, if the market is dynamic, multinational banks may be willing to navigate a complex regulatory environment in exchange for access to a large and increasingly wealthy population. In 2010, the 360 foreign banking institutions in China— including headquarters, branches, and subsidiaries—accounted for just under 2 percent of total assets in the banking system.[62] However, in other cases, the regulatory costs of doing business can outweigh the potential long-term benefits for banks, particularly if there are large, deeply entrenched incumbents and small, less affluent populations.

Since 2008, many countries have imposed new rules to strengthen their banking sectors and avert future financial crises. In the United States, as mentioned earlier, the Dodd- Frank Wall Street Reform and Consumer Protection Act established new requirements that will affect banks' capital and revenues primarily by limiting investment activity, raising reporting and compliance costs, and placing restrictions on fees charged to customers (see box 7.1 in section 7). An example is Title VI of the Dodd-Frank Act, known as the Volcker Rule. Intended to keep banks from taking excessive risks, this rule limits the amount of capital that banks can invest in hedge funds and private equity funds (not counting investments made on behalf of customer accounts). The Office of the Comptroller of the Currency estimated that this rule may impose $1 billion in compliance and capital costs on the industry.[63] Further, financial firms determined to be "too big to fail" are required to develop roadmaps for their own liquidation in the event of bankruptcy, a measure intended to avoid Federal bailouts of nonviable firms. Preparing such plans, as well as making required contributions to a liquidation fund, could add more costs.

Other provisions of the Dodd-Frank Act reduce some of the fees that banks can charge. The Durbin amendment, for example, requires the Federal Reserve System to lower interchange fees that banks collect from debit and credit card transactions.[64] Other measures designed to protect consumers include changes to the way overdraft fees are levied and limits to the late fees and interest rate hikes that credit card companies can charge to customers that miss payments. The combination of new costs and fee reductions resulting from the legislation could affect some banks' ability or willingness to supply certain financial services.

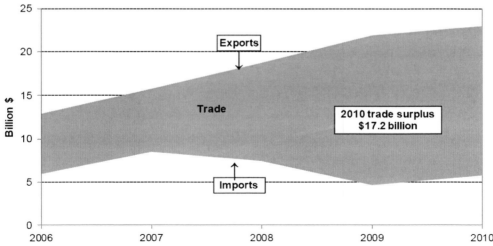

Source: USDOC, BEA, *Survey of Current Business*, October 2011, 20–21, tables G and H; USDOC, BEA, *Survey of Current Business*, October 2010, 25–25, tables G and H; USDOC, BEA, *Survey of Current Business*, October 2009, 31, table E.

Figure 3.2. Banking services: U.S. cross-border trade in private-sector services resulted in a U.S. trade surplus each year during 2006–10.

Trade Trends

Cross-border Trade

U.S. cross-border exports[65] of banking services (box 3.2) rose by 5.0 percent to $23.0 billion in 2010 (figure 3.2). While the 2008 financial crisis disrupted the global banking sector, U.S. cross-border exports of banking services still grew at a CAGR of 19.2 percent during 2006–09.[66] This is partly because large U.S. banks continued to market financial management services to clients in countries where the economic downturn did not have as strong an impact. At the same time, cross-border imports of banking services rose to $5.8 billion in 2010,[67] reversing a decline that accompanied the onset of the financial crisis in 2008. This amounted to an increase of 23.8 percent from 2009 levels, a departure from the compound annual decline of 7.8 percent during 2006–09. Imports of other financial services and credit services increased in 2010, largely due to growth in the U.S. refinancing market.[68] As a result, the financial services trade balance remained flat in 2009–10, but the CAGR during 2006–09 was 35.2 percent.

BOX 3.2. UNDERSTANDING BEA DATA ON CROSS-BORDER TRADE AND AFFILIATE TRANSACTIONS IN BANKING SERVICES

BEA data on cross-border trade in banking services are included in its "financial services" category. The financial services data are broken down into four subcategories: (1) securities transactions services, including brokerage services and underwriting and private placement services; (2) management and advisory services, including financial management services and financial advisory and custody services; (3) credit card and other credit-related services (such as the provision of standby letters of credit for trade financing); and (4) other financial services, including securities lending and electronic funds transfer.[a] These data exclude both deposit-taking and lending services. Although there is some overlap between securities services and banking services in these data, subcategories 1 and 2 likely comprise predominantly securities services, as these include the traditional investment banking functions of broking, dealing, and underwriting, while subcategories 3 and 4 likely comprise predominantly banking services. Data on total U.S. imports and exports of these services, whether between unrelated parties or between affiliates in a single corporate group, are available beginning in 2006 (older statistics reflect unaffiliated trade only).[b] However, in its reporting of U.S. exports and imports by country, the BEA combines the four subcategories into a single category of "financial services," itself a component of the larger category "Other Private Services" in the International Services Accounts. The BEA captures this data largely through mandatory quarterly and benchmark surveys of business services, supplemented by survey data from U.S. government agencies, private sector sources, and BEA estimates.[c]

In addition, the BEA publishes data on financial services (excluding insurance) supplied abroad through foreign affiliates of U.S. majority-owned groups and financial services supplied in the United States by affiliates of foreign- owned corporations. For financial services, as for many other services, direct investment in local affiliates represents a significant avenue for sales in foreign markets. The BEA data include revised measures for sales of affiliates starting in 2004.

The data include sales by, and purchases from, firms that primarily provide non-depository credit intermediation and related services; securities, commodity contracts, and other intermediation and related activities; and funds, trusts, and other financial vehicles. Country breakdowns are provided for the financial services category, but the data do not distinguish securities-related services from banking services.[d]

[a] USDOC, BEA, *Survey of Current Business*, October 2009, 31.
[b] USDOC, BEA, *Survey of Current Business*, February 2010, 44.
[c] USDOC, BEA, *Survey of Current Business*, February 2010, 44.
[d] USDOC, BEA, *Survey of Current Business*, October 2009, 37–38.

The largest markets for U.S. exports of non-insurance financial services[69] in 2010 were the United Kingdom (which purchased $9.3 billion of such services), Canada ($4.7 billion), Japan ($3.1 billion), France ($2.3 billion), and Australia ($2.1 billion).[70] These figures represent year-on-year increases for all countries except the United Kingdom, reflecting economic recovery in those markets.[71] The leading suppliers of such services to the United States in 2010 included the United Kingdom (which sold services valued at $4.3 billion), Canada ($958 million), France ($818 million), Japan ($735 million), and Germany ($640 million). Imports from Canada, France, and Japan increased over 2009 levels, while those from the United Kingdom and Germany declined possibly due to increasing financial market challenges in Europe.

Nontariff Measures Affecting Trade

Multinational banks routinely face nontariff barriers when entering foreign markets, especially in certain developing countries that may see their local banks as unprepared to compete with large global banks. Some of the more common measures place limits on branching, form of establishment, licensing, issuing debit and credit cards, and joint ventures. Branch networks are critical for banks, as they enable the collection of more deposits, and banks sometimes complain that branching rules in foreign markets are designed to limit their deposit bases and protect domestic banks from competition. For example, foreign banks operating in India are required to submit annual branch expansion proposals, but nontransparent quotas on expansion prevent such plans from being enacted. Only six new foreign branch licenses were granted from April 2009 to March 2010.[72] Multinational banks may also encounter obstacles to obtaining licenses. In some cases governments have either limited or stopped issuing new licenses to foreign banks altogether, effectively closing the market to new entrants. Further, restrictions on the legal form of establishment are common; in such cases a bank may be required to incorporate locally, may only be permitted to establish a representative office, or may only be allowed to establish in one form (e.g., only branch offices, no subsidiaries). Such rules can make it difficult for foreign banks to tailor their operations to market conditions and compete with local firms.

Regulations increasingly target electronic transactions. For example, some countries limit the ability of foreign banks (but not domestic banks) to issue credit and debit cards. Such regulations may completely prevent foreign banks from issuing cards, ban them from issuing cards in the target country currency, or delay the approval of cards. Additionally, some countries restrict the operation or establishment of automatic teller machines (ATMs). In some markets, foreign banks are not allowed to operate ATMs, are only allowed to operate a certain number of ATMs, or have to count ATMs as branches (in cases where there is a branch quota).[73]

Outlook

Global demand for banking services is forecast to increase, but geographic disparities in growth will likely persist as developing economies continue to expand faster than developed markets. Banks anticipate challenges in the coming years as they continue to manage nonperforming assets resulting from the financial crisis, while searching for fresh revenue sources as fee incomes are reduced by new regulations. In an effort to streamline costs, banks will likely stop offering some services and focus on the bread-and-butter activities of deposit taking and lending, while continuing to reduce staff where feasible. Banks also may increasingly outsource certain functions, domestically or abroad, in an effort to free up capital.[74]

SECTION 4. INSURANCE SERVICES

SUMMARY

The United States is the world's largest insurance market, accounting for almost 27 percent of global insurance premiums. However, U.S. insurance premiums grew at a CAGR of only 0.4 percent from 2005 to 2010, more slowly than premiums in any other top 10 market. A number of factors affect supply and demand for insurance services, such as changes in personal income, investment returns, demographic trends, natural disasters, and government regulation. In recent years, the financial downturn has led to lower demand for life insurance and other non-mandatory insurance products, as well as weak investment returns, decreased willingness to hire or expand operations, and the continuance of low premium rates in the property and casualty segment. Although increasing economic stability and rising interest rates could lead to growth in industry revenues, economic conditions will likely continue to depress investment income and insurance demand in the near term. Additionally, insurers may confront significant compliance costs related to new regulations.

U.S. affiliate sales of insurance services far exceed cross-border exports of such services, and while the United States continues to run a deficit in cross-border trade in insurance services, insurance services provided by the affiliates of U.S. firms in overseas markets exceeded such services supplied by foreign- owned U.S. affiliates by a widening margin. However, a variety of provisions hamper U.S. insurers' ability to participate in foreign markets, such as discriminatory regulation, local partnership requirements, and foreign equity caps.

Although recently signed free trade agreements have provisions that may facilitate the operations of U.S. insurance firms in certain countries, there has been little significant liberalization of measures affecting the foreign provision of insurance services in recent years.

Introduction

The insurance industry is a critical component of the global economy, in terms of both its size and its contribution to economic growth and development.[75] The industry underwrites financial risk for life and nonlife (property/casualty) products, and provides many specialty products. The latter include reinsurance (the transferring of risk between insurance companies), marine and transportation insurance (for goods in transit, hulls, aviation, and offshore oil rigs), and brokerage services (the packaging of policies from several underwriters to cover a given risk).

Such activities encourage economic activity by mitigating the potential risks of project failure, lessen social threats by offering discounts for low-risk behavior,[76] and increase the overall volume of investable funds by pooling the premiums of many smaller investors.[77] Insurance firms' revenues are largely a product of collected premiums and investment income, less claims paid to policyholders.

Competitive Conditions in the Global Insurance Services Market

From 2009 to 2010, global insurance premiums grew by 5.6 percent to $4.3 trillion, slightly faster than the CAGR of 4.5 percent recorded during 2005 to 2009.[78] Accelerated growth was principally driven by the life insurance segment of the industry, which accounted for the largest and fastest-growing share of global premiums during 2009 to 2010. Specifically, life insurance premiums grew by 6.4 percent to reach $2.5 trillion, while nonlife premiums grew by 4.4 percent to $1.8 trillion.

While 9 of the world's top 10 insurance markets are high-income countries, several middle-income countries account for significant and rapidly growing shares of the global insurance market. The United States is, by far, the world's largest insurance market, having accounted for $1.2 trillion, or almost 27 percent, of global insurance premiums in 2010 (table 4.1). However, U.S. insurance premiums grew at a CAGR of only 0.4 percent from 2005 to 2010, more slowly than premiums in any other top-10 market. By contrast, China—the only middle-income country among the world's top 10 insurance markets— recorded premium growth of 29.0 percent per year, much higher than the 0.4–9.7 percent growth rates posted in other top 10 insurance markets. Annual premiums have also grown rapidly in several other large middle-income countries during the period, including India (25.6 percent), Brazil (21.8 percent), Russia (18.9 percent) (box 4.1), and South Africa (9.9 percent).[79]

Table 4.1. Insurance services: Top 10 insurance markets, by total premiums, 2005–10

Rank	Country	2005	2006	2007	2008	2009	2010	CAGR,[a] 2005 –10
				Million $				
1	United States	1,142,912	1,170,101	1,229,668	1,240,643	1,149,758	1,166,142	0.4
2	Japan	476,481	362,766	424,832	473,197	518,070	557,439	3.2
3	United Kingdom	300,241	311,691	463,686	450,152	312,165	310,022	0.6
4	France	222,220	177,902	268,900	273,007	283,070	280,082	4.7
5	Germany	197,251	94,911	222,825	243,085	239,941	239,817	4.0
6	China	60,131	45,092	92,487	140,818	163,046	214,626	29.0
7	Italy	139,194	89,576	142,328	140,689	169,360	174,347	4.6
8	Canada	78,723	39,212	100,398	105,174	98,496	115,521	8.0
9	South Korea	82,933	72,298	116,990	97,023	96,676	114,422	6.6
10	Netherlands	61,073	62,669	102,831	112,611	108,144	97,057	9.7

Source: III, *Fact Book*, various issues, 2007-2012.
[a] Compound annual growth rate.

BOX 4.1. THE RUSSIAN INSURANCE MARKET

Rising demand in an unsaturated market, together with recent insurance sector liberalization, would seem to make Russia particularly attractive to foreign insurance firms looking to expand their operations. However, measures limiting market access, as well as other factors that affect overall market development, continue to limit and discourage foreign participation in Russia's insurance market.

Russia is the 19th-largest insurance market in the world, with total premiums of $41.6 billion in 2010. From 2005 to 2010, total insurance premiums in Russia increased at an average annual rate of almost 19 percent—much faster than the 5 percent growth rates posted for global insurance premiums and only slightly slower than the 21 to 29 percent growth rates posted for other BRIC countries.[a] In addition, growth in Russian insurance premiums reportedly has recovered quickly following the global economic downturn. However, despite rapid growth, Russia accounted for less than 1 percent of global insurance premiums in 2010, and per capita spending on private insurance stands at only $62 per year.[b] The Russian insurance market remains underdeveloped due, in part, to its relatively recent emergence,[c] consumer distrust of insurers stemming from scandals and poor service quality, and a long-standing perception of insurance as a tax-like fee on private property.[d] Demand for life insurance is particularly low, accounting for only about 2 percent of total Russian insurance premiums in 2010. This is likely because banks currently offer more secure savings vehicles than insurers, and because life insurance—unlike certain types of nonlife insurance—is not required by law. Sustained high inflation has also had a negative effect on the returns of life insurance investments.[e]

Although liberalization and market reforms have facilitated foreign participation, only a small number of foreign firms operate in the Russian insurance market.[f] These include U.S. firm AIG (a leading participant in Russia's small life insurance market), French firm AXA (which provides property and casualty insurance through its 37 percent stake in Reso-Garantia), and German firm Allianz (which provides life and property and casualty insurance through its holdings in six Russian insurance firms), among others.

As part of its scheduled accession to the WTO, Russia liberalized or eliminated several measures that had barred foreign insurers from providing certain types of insurance, such as compulsory medical insurance and life insurance. Further, a substantial increase in the Russian insurance sector's statutory capital requirements—which took effect on January 1, 2012—may force many domestic insurers out of business, to the benefit of foreign insurance providers.[g] However, foreign insurers continue to face several obstacles in Russia. Foreign investment in a Russian insurance firm requires the approval of the regulator (the Federal Financial Markets Service); overall foreign equity in the industry is limited to 25 percent; and firms may enter the market only through an EU-based establishment.[h] Factors such as fraud, sharp rate decreases,[i] continued low demand, and the lack of a strong rule of law may also explain foreign insurers' minimal participation in the Russian market.[j]

[a] USITC staff calculations, based on data published by the Insurance Information Institute (III).
[b] Koshik, "Russian Insurance Market," December 2, 2011.
[c] Koshik, "Russian Insurance Market," December 2, 2011.
[d] Datamonitor, "Non-Life Insurance in Russia," September 2011, 14; Nikishenkov, "Insuring Russia," February 6, 2012.
[e] Koshik, "Russian Insurance Market," December 2, 2011.
[f] Top domestic insurance providers in Russia include Sogaz Insurance Group, Ingosstrakh Insurance Company, and Rosgosstrakh, among others. Datamonitor, "Insurance in Russia," September 2011, 20, 23, 24.
[g] EIU, *Country Commerce: Russia*, November 2011, 21; and SwissLife, *Russia,* 4.
[h] EIU, *Country Commerce: Russia*, November 2011, 20–21.
[i] Specifically, certain corporate insurance rates have decreased substantially in recent years, with some Russian insurance firms reportedly sustaining losses in order to gain market advantage. *Russia Briefing,* "Foreign Capital Raises Its Share," February 18, 2011.
[j] Koshik, "Russian Insurance Market," December 2, 2011; *Russia Briefing,* "Foreign Capital Raises Its Share," February 18, 2011; industry representative, telephone interview by USITC staff, March 1, 2012.

The world's leading providers of insurance changed little in recent years, as the same companies ranked among the world's top 10 insurance firms in both 2009 and 2010, and seven firms have numbered among the top 10 in most years since 2005 (table 4.2).[80] Japan Post Holdings—which provides life insurance coverage through its wholly owned subsidiary Japan Post Insurance—was the world's top insurance firm in 2010, with revenues of $204 billion. The firm has been the world's top insurance provider since 2008, following its privatization in 2005 and its establishment as a distinct subsidiary of Japan Post Holdings in 2006. The Japanese government remains the sole owner of Japan Post Insurance, as plans for an initial public offering were stopped in 2010. However, while this firm dominates the Japanese insurance market, it is unlikely that it significantly influences competition outside its home market, as its business operations are limited to Japan.

Two U.S. firms, Berkshire Hathaway and American International Group (AIG), ranked among the top 10 insurance firms in terms of global revenues in 2010. Berkshire Hathaway (which owns GEICO and General Re, among other insurance holdings) consistently ranked among the world's top 10 insurers between 2005 and 2010, and was the world's top property and casualty insurance firm in 2010. AIG, which was the world's sixth largest insurer in

2010, ranked among the top 10 in every year during the period except 2008. (Between FY2007 and FY2008, the company's revenues fell from $110.1 billion to $34.9 billion, and the U.S. government extended an $85 billion line of credit to AIG in exchange for a 79.9 percent company share in an effort to prevent the firm's failure.[81]) Two other U.S. firms— State Farm Insurance Cos. and Liberty Mutual Insurance Group—ranked among the world's top 10 property and casualty insurers in 2010. No U.S. firms ranked among the world's top 10 life insurance firms; U.S.-based MetLife was among the top 10 from 2005 to 2008, but fell out of this group when its revenues fell 25 percent in 2009.[82]

Merger and acquisition (M&A) activity increased in 2010, as firms attempted to gain market share in emerging markets, strengthen their presence in established markets, and supply new and higher-quality services to customers. Many of the high-value deals announced during 2010 involved buyers and target firms based in developed countries.[83] However, expansion into Middle Eastern, Latin American, and Asian countries reportedly also increased, due to these markets' relatively quick recovery from the global economic downturn and slow growth in mature markets.[84] Examples of such deals include Sompo Japan Insurance Inc.'s acquisition of a majority stake in the Turkish firm Fiba Sigorta AS in 2010 (valued at $337 million), and Japanese firm Mitsui Sumitomo Insurance Co.'s acquisition of a minority stake in the Takaful[85] business of Malaysia- based Hong Leong Assurance BHD in 2011.[86] Agents, brokers, and other distribution firms accounted for 350 of the 721 M&A deals announced in 2010, while in terms of value, life insurance firms accounted for more than half of M&A activity in that year.[87]

Demand and Supply Factors

Economic and Demographic Trends Affect the Composition of Insurance Demand
Several factors shape insurance demand. Because life insurance products tend to be similar, demand for the product offerings of particular firms is often based on price, service quality, and brand awareness.[88] Demand for life insurance also can be affected by the investment performance of these products as compared to other savings vehicles.[89] One recent study suggests that demand for nonlife insurance coverage may be affected by cultural differences between countries, such as the extent of perceived economic and political inequality, individualism, tolerance for uncertainty, and predominant religious beliefs.[90]

Property and casualty insurance—particularly auto, property, and business insurance—is often required by law or deemed necessary by policyholders. Demand for many types of property and casualty insurance is therefore typically steady, with policy renewals accounting for the vast majority of increases in insurance exposure in these business segments. However, price considerations can lead consumers to increase or decrease coverage levels or deductibles, and factors that affect consumer perceptions of risk, such as severe weather events, may raise demand for certain types of insurance.[91]

In recent years, decreases in personal income following the financial crisis have significantly reduced demand for certain types of insurance. High unemployment and a struggling housing market have lessened consumers' ability or willingness to buy insurance coverage, particularly life insurance, annuities, and other nonmandatory insurance products.[92] For example, sales of individual life insurance products fell 15 percent in 2009. While such sales rebounded the following year, growing by 4 percent, average policy face values[93] fell 4 percent from 2009 levels as customer willingness to spend large sums on individual policies remained low.[94] Job losses have also limited the volume of life insurance and other coverage that is distributed through the workplace.[95] By contrast, continued economic uncertainty has increased demand for products such as credit insurance, which protects businesses against customer default.[96]

Table 4.2. Insurance services: Top 10 global insurance companies, by revenue, 2010[a]

Rank	Company	Country	Revenues[b] (million $)	Industry
1	Japan Post Holdings	Japan	203,958	Life/health
2	AXA	France	162,236	Life/health
3	Berkshire Hathaway	U.S.	134,185	Property/casualty
4	Allianz	Germany	127,379	Property/casualty
5	Assicurazioni Generali	Italy	120,234	Life/health
6	American International Group	U.S.	104,417	Property/casualty
7	Aviva	UK	90,211	Life/health
8	Nippon Life Insurance	Japan	78,571	Life/health
9	Munich Re Group	Germany	76,220	Property/casualty
10	Prudential	UK	73,598	Life/health

Source: Insurance Information Institute, World Rankings, 2012.
[a] Based on an analysis of companies in the Global Fortune 500. Includes stock and mutual companies.
[b] Revenues include premium and annuity income, investment income, and capital gains or losses, but excludes deposits; includes consolidated subsidiaries, but excludes excise taxes.

Demographic trends, particularly population aging and relatively low marriage rates, have cut into the demand for certain types of insurance coverage, particularly in the life insurance segment of the industry. Longer lifespans and declining marriage rates and birthrates have all led insurers to decrease their traditional emphasis on products that pay survivor benefits and focus more on retirement products.[97] For example, among individuals in their 20s and 30s (Generation Y), a weak economy has reportedly contributed to historically low marriage rates, and these factors have made traditional life insurance products both less affordable and less necessary.[98] Hence the marketing of life insurance products to younger consumers often stresses relatively low-cost term coverage.[99] At the same time, demand for annuities and other products that contribute to retirement savings has risen among older consumers.[100] These trends have led insurers to increase their focus on retirement-planning products and develop new investment vehicles for the baby boom generation, such as products that offer lifetime income guarantees.[101] The aging of the population may also increase demand for property and casualty insurance, as disposable income and holdings of insurable assets typically grow throughout an individual's lifetime,[102] and for long-term care policies.[103]

Insurance Supply Is Affected by Overall Economic Conditions, Regulatory Change, the Frequency of Catastrophes, and Changing Business Models

The weak economic climate has affected insurers' investment returns and employment levels which, in turn, have lessened firms' willingness to establish or expand operations.[104] In the property and casualty insurance industry, lower insurance demand, together with a surplus of underwriting capacity, has intensified competition and has compelled insurance firms to keep premium rates low, thus undermining industry revenues.[105] By contrast, the life insurance market, excepting the group life segment, has become less price competitive in recent years, enabling firms to raise prices and restore capital holdings that were depleted as a result of defaults, credit downgrades, and other factors that marred insurer balance sheets during the financial crisis.[106] Nonetheless, higher costs, increased risk, and the current lack of high-yield investment vehicles (which limits insurers' ability to offer products yielding high interest) have also led life insurers around the world to modify product lines or reduce new business in certain product segments, such as variable annuities,[107] and return their focus to non-variable wealth accumulation products.[108] In both the life and property and casualty segments of the industry, reduced interest rates, a high rate of delinquencies on debt instruments (such as loans), and other equity market factors have depressed investment income, which accounts for a significant share of industry revenues.[109]

Changes in regulations and standards have a significant effect on insurers; as such changes may necessitate new business strategies, impact capital accumulation or product offerings, or involve other adjustment costs.[110] As noted in sections 3 and 7, one of the most notable developments in recent years is the 2010 Dodd-Frank Wall Street Reform and Consumer Protection Act (Dodd-Frank),[111] which was designed to reduce systemic risk in the financial sector. Although this law has begun to take effect, the extent of its impact on insurers remains unclear.[112] Other changes that are expected to affect insurance firms' operations in the near future include revised accounting standards, a National Association of Insurance Commissioners (NAIC) initiative on reserves, and Europe's Solvency II guidelines.[113]

Property and casualty insurers' ability to supply affordable coverage is heavily influenced by natural and manmade disasters, as actual and potential losses from such events have a substantial impact on insurers' capital stock, insurers' willingness to provide coverage in certain locations, and the price of such coverage. Global insurance losses from natural and manmade disasters were $43 billion in 2010, higher than losses in the previous year ($27 billion), but in line with average annual losses during the preceding 10 years.[114] However, growing asset values and urban and coastal population densities have contributed to an upward trend in insured losses.[115] Earthquakes, for example, have accounted for a large and growing share of insured losses[116] as urban population growth has increased the assets and the number of people that can be affected by a single event.[117] One industry representative argues that globalization has contributed to the growth in catastrophe-related insurance losses, as insurers' international business increasingly extends to markets where they are less familiar with catastrophe risks.[118] In response to the increase in losses from natural and manmade disasters, credit-rating agencies have compelled insurers to increase their surplus holdings, which provide a cushion against losses, but may impair their ability to write policies.[119]

In addition, changes in business models, customer buying patterns, and technology have affected the way insurance is supplied. A growing share of insurance is sold by banks and brokerages, which leverage the efficiency and reach of their distribution networks.[120] The workplace has become an increasingly important venue for the sale of a wide range of insurance products, such as dental, auto, and homeowners' insurance, among others. This arrangement benefits insurer firms (due to economies of scale and access to a relatively young and healthy client base), employers (which may be perceived as providing enhanced employee benefits), and consumers (who may prefer the convenience or perceived security associated with purchasing insurance at work).[121] One firm sells insurance through auto dealerships, bundling coverage in a vehicle's overall purchase price.[122] In addition, insurers are using Internet sites and other technologies to increase the speed and efficiency of business transactions.[123]

Insurance firms are also developing new products for emerging niche markets, as well as redesigning existing lines to distinguish their product offerings. For example, insurers are beginning to offer policies that address new concerns, such as green building,[124] decreasing home values, cyber-liability, and nanotechnology, among others. Some auto insurance providers offer cheaper insurance rates to drivers that allow companies to monitor their driving habits electronically.[125] For example, customers that opt for the Progressive Snapshot program (offered in 20 states) or the Allstate Drive Wise program (offered in Illinois) can qualify for discounts as high as 30 percent based on their speed, braking, and mileage patterns.[126] Similarly, State Farm is expanding its Drive Safe & Save program (offered in eight states) to provide discounts based on a growing number of driver behaviors.[127]

Trade Trends

Cross-border Trade

The United States continues to have a significant trade deficit in insurance services, although it shrank slightly between 2009 and 2010 due to a small decrease in U.S. imports of such services (box 4.2). In 2010, U.S. exports of insurance services totaled $14.6 billion while imports stood at $61.8 billion, resulting in a trade deficit of $47.2 billion (figure 4.1). U.S. exports of insurance services rose by 1.2 percent from 2009 to 2010, much slower than the CAGR of 17.5 percent posted during 2005–09. By comparison, U.S. insurance services imports fell by 2.9 percent from 2009 to 2010, following a CAGR of 22.0 percent between 2005 and 2009. This decrease in imports is largely due to a decline in U.S. premium payments to foreign reinsurers. One source reports that several factors, such as high levels of surplus capital and relatively low insurance losses, led to a decline in renewal rates for reinsurance policies in 2010.[128]

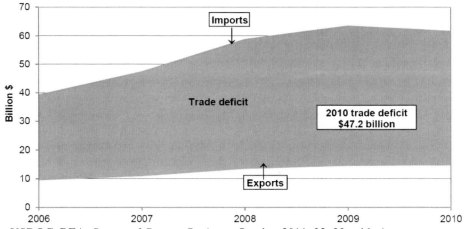

Source: USDOC, BEA, *Survey of Current Business*, October 2011, 32–33, table 1.

Figure 4.1. Insurance services: U.S. cross-border trade in private-sector services resulted in a U.S. trade deficit each year during 2006–10.

BOX 4.2. UNDERSTANDING BEA DATA ON CROSS-BORDER TRADE AND AFFILIATE TRANSACTIONS IN INSURANCE SERVICES

The BEA publishes discrete cross-border trade data for "primary and other insurance" (principally life and property/casualty insurance) and reinsurance.[a] BEA data on cross-border trade in insurance services are the sum of premium income (adjusted for "normal" losses), investment income, and auxiliary services. BEA estimates of "normal" losses—which are subtracted from total premiums—are derived by averaging the difference between total premiums and losses over a certain period of years.[b] These data also incorporate an estimate of the investment income that insurance firms derive from their technical reserves (insurance premium supplements).[c] Auxiliary services include earnings from the provision of actuarial, agency and brokerage, claims adjustment, and salvage administration services, as well as agents' commissions.[d]

In 2008, the BEA changed the way it calculates affiliate transactions in insurance services. Beginning with data for the year 2004, the BEA revised its estimates of affiliate transactions in the insurance industry to reflect "services supplied through affiliates" rather than "sales of services," creating a new measure that is more similar to output than sales value. Much like cross-border trade data for this industry, affiliate transactions data derived using this approach reflect sales (adjusted by "normal" losses) and incorporate premium supplements.[e]

[a] USDOC, BEA, *Survey of Current Business*, October 2007, 130–32.
[b] USDOC, BEA, *Survey of Current Business*, October 2007, 99.
[c] USDOC, BEA, "Catalog of Major Revisions," June 3, 2009.
[d] USDOC, BEA, *Survey of Current Business*, October 2007, 99.
[e] USDOC, BEA, *Survey of Current Business*, October 2008, 18–19, 34–35.

In 2010, Bermuda was the United States' top export market for insurance services, accounting for $2.7 billion, or 18.7 percent, of such exports and surpassing Canada, which was the United States' top export market from 2006 to 2009 (figure 4.2).[129] This may be due, in part, to U.S. exports of corporate-related insurance to Bermuda; unlike exports to other markets, these exports remained strong during the global economic downturn.[130] Canada fell to second place with 17.9 percent of U.S. insurance services exports in 2010, while the United Kingdom and Japan ranked third and fourth respectively, accounting for 10.7 and 9.6 percent of such exports (figure 4.3). All three of these countries also ranked among the top four markets for such exports throughout 2005–09. Mexico, which accounted for almost 4 percent of exports in 2010, became the fifth-largest market for U.S. insurance services exports in that year due to a 32 percent average annual decline in exports to Switzerland between 2008 and 2010. This decrease affected exports of both insurance and reinsurance, and may be attributable to the economic downturn and the acquisition of U.S. firm 21st Century by Swiss-owned Zurich Financial Services in 2009 (which impacted the volume of cross-border insurance services transactions between the two countries), among other factors.

In 2010, the top five source countries for U.S. imports of insurance services were Bermuda (which accounted for 49 percent of U.S. insurance services imports in that year), Switzerland (11 percent), the United Kingdom (9 percent), Germany (5 percent), and Ireland

(4 percent). The United States posted substantial insurance services deficits with each of these countries, principally due to U.S. reinsurance services imports from these markets. Reinsurance services accounted for more than 67 percent of insurance services imports from the United Kingdom, and over 93 percent of such imports from each of the other top-five source countries. These five countries are global leaders in the reinsurance segment. One reason is that 6 of the world's top 10 reinsurance firms are based in these markets, including Munich Re and Hanover Re (Germany), Swiss Re Group (Switzerland), Lloyd's of London (UK), and Partner Re Ltd. and Everest Re Group Ltd. (Bermuda). Further, Ireland's favorable tax environment, EU membership, proximity to London's financial markets, and large supply of experienced professional services providers have made that country a particularly welcoming market to reinsurers, and a large share of the world's top reinsurance providers have established operations in that country.[131]

Affiliate Transactions

In the previous decade, services supplied by U.S.-owned foreign affiliates grew rapidly before registering a small decline due to the global economic downturn. From 2004 to 2008, insurance services supplied by U.S.-owned affiliates increased at a CAGR of 15 percent before decreasing by 2 percent during 2008–09, when they fell to $60.4 billion (figure 4.4). Services supplied by foreign-owned U.S. affiliates posted relatively slower growth from 2004 to 2008, increasing at a CAGR of 8 percent per year. However, unlike U.S.-owned affiliate sales abroad, sales by foreign-owned affiliates in the United States continued to grow during 2008–09, increasing by 3 percent to $49.9 billion. As a result of these trends, U.S.-owned foreign affiliates' sales surpassed services supplied by foreign-owned U.S. affiliates in 2005, and by a widening margin until 2009, before this margin decreased by over $3 billion during 2009–10.

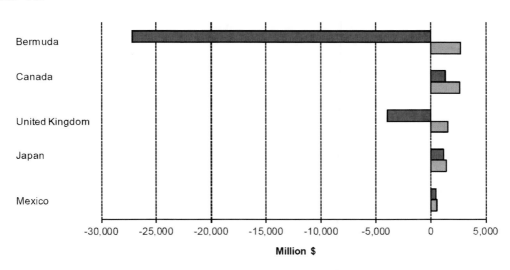

Source: USDOC, BEA, *Survey of Current Business*, table 5.2, October 2011, 44–45.

Figure 4.2. Insurance services: U.S. cross-border insurance trade yielded significant deficits with Bermuda and the United Kingdom in 2010.

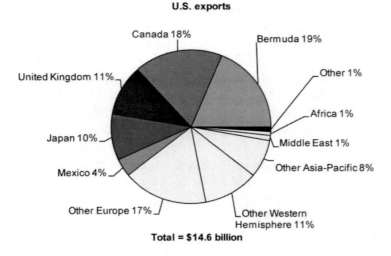

U.S. exports

Canada 18%

Bermuda 19%

Other 1%

United Kingdom 11%

Africa 1%

Japan 10%

Middle East 1%

Mexico 4%

Other Asia-Pacific 8%

Other Europe 17%

Other Western Hemisphere 11%

Total = $14.6 billion

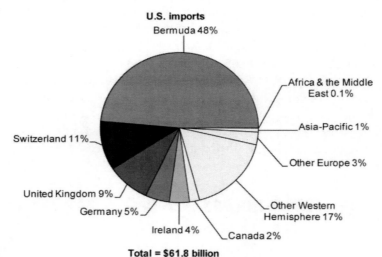

U.S. imports

Bermuda 48%

Africa & the Middle East 0.1%

Asia-Pacific 1%

Switzerland 11%

Other Europe 3%

United Kingdom 9%

Germany 5%

Other Western Hemisphere 17%

Ireland 4%

Canada 2%

Total = $61.8 billion

Source: USDOC, BEA, *Survey of Current Business*, October 2011, 44–45, table 5.2.
Note: Geographic regions are shaded in yellow. Figures m ay not total 100 percent due to rounding.

Figure 4.3. Insurance services: Bermuda and Canada were the top markets f or U.S. exports, while Bermuda supplied the most insurance services imports in 2010.

Japan was likely the top market for sales by U.S.-owned foreign insurance affiliates during the years under review. Although data on sales in Japan were suppressed in order to avoid disclosure of information on individual firms, Japan accounted for the largest share (21 percent) of services provided by U.S.-owned foreign affiliates in 2008. The United Kingdom, Canada, and Germany also accounted for substantial shares of U.S.- owned foreign affiliate sales, with 17 percent, 9 percent, and 3 percent, respectively, in 2009. Despite Japan's high share of U.S. foreign affiliate sales, it is unlikely that U.S. firms play a significant role in Japan's insurance market. Foreign participants account for a small share (approximately 6 percent) of the non-life segment of the Japanese insurance market,[132] and Japan's life insurance market is dominated by Japan Post Holdings.

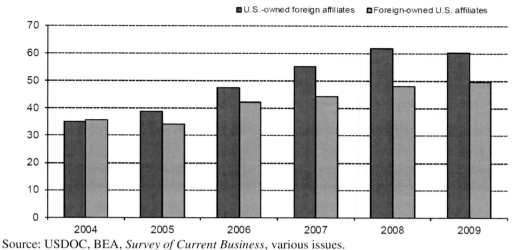

Source: USDOC, BEA, *Survey of Current Business*, various issues.

Figure 4.4. Insurance services: Services supplied by U.S.-owned foreign affiliates exceeded services supplied by foreign-owned U.S. affiliates beginning in 2005.

By contrast, foreign firms are key market players in the UK insurance industry, with firms such as AXA (France), Zurich Insurance (Switzerland), and Allianz (Germany) accounting for substantial shares of the market. Although data are not available on U.S.-owned firms' overall share of the UK market, U.S.-firm AIG ranks among the United Kingdom's top 10 providers of property and casualty insurance, accounting for almost 2 percent of revenues in that market segment.[133]

Available data indicate that Canada, Germany, and Switzerland accounted for substantial shares—18 percent, 15 percent, and 13 percent, respectively—of services supplied by foreign-owned U.S. affiliates in 2009.[134] It is likely that Canada's share of the U.S. insurance market has further increased due to the $1.4 billion acquisition of U.S.-firm Zenith National Insurance Corp. by Canadian-owned Fairfax Financial Holdings Ltd. in May 2010.[135]

Nontariff Measures Affecting Trade

A variety of provisions limit U.S. insurers' ability to participate in foreign markets, particularly cumbersome regulations, local partnership requirements, and foreign equity caps. Although strong regulations are necessary for the efficient operation of the insurance industry, the recent financial crisis has been followed by a significant increase in both domestic and overseas regulation.[136] Insurers are concerned that the large volume of new regulations may create high compliance costs and hinder trade. Additionally, the impact of regulation on competitiveness has become a top industry concern as liberalization has eliminated many market access and national treatment barriers.[137]

Although markets are largely open, certain countries still maintain measures that apply specifically to foreign insurance suppliers, including limits on the size and form of a firm's market presence. India and China limit foreign equity in insurance firms to 26 and 50 percent, respectively. Several sources indicate that China maintains a number of measures that disadvantage foreign firms; for example, China applies different branching rules to foreign firms, and limits the types of investments in which foreign insurers can engage.[138] Several foreign firms have reportedly exited the Chinese market due to frustration with that country's bureaucratic obstacles.[139] Other barriers that insurers face in overseas markets include privacy measures that may affect the cross-border flow of customer data, market participation by state-owned insurance firms (such as the postal insurers in Japan and Korea), nationality requirements, provisions requiring insurers to place all or part of their reinsurance business with local firms, and prohibitions on participating in certain market segments.[140]

During the past five years, there have been some efforts to liberalize measures affecting the foreign provision of insurance services. In February 2012, China announced that it will remove its restriction on foreign participation in the third-party liability auto market.[141] Additionally, recently enacted free trade agreements with Colombia, Korea, Panama, and members of the Dominican Republic-Central America-United States Free Trade Agreement (CAFTA-DR) contain provisions that may make it easier for U.S. insurance firms to operate in these countries. For example, as a result of its commitments under CAFTA-DR, Costa Rica opened its insurance market in 2010 following 84 years of monopoly provision of such services.[142] At the same time, liberalization through the WTO has not progressed; in fact, a few countries have established measures that further restrict the foreign provision of insurance services. Notably, both Argentina and Brazil established measures in 2011 that prohibit firms established in those countries from reinsuring with overseas companies, and Argentina passed a resolution requiring insurance firms that operate in that country's market to repatriate overseas investments.[143]

Outlook

The near-term outlook for the U.S. insurance industry is unclear, as persisting economic uncertainty, imminent regulatory changes, catastrophe trends, and increased consolidation may have a substantial—but unknown—effect on insurers. Low interest rates, equity market volatility, high unemployment, and other economic factors will likely continue to weigh down investment income, life insurance demand, and property and casualty insurance premiums through 2012.[144] If the economy continues to stabilize and interest rates rise, insurance revenues will likely grow during the next five years in both the life and the property and casualty segments of the industry. Higher employment would boost demand for commercial coverage, such as workers' compensation insurance, while a recovery in the housing market would increase demand for title insurance and benefit the investment income of U.S. life insurers, which typically maintain substantial holdings of mortgage-backed securities.[145]

Several significant and interrelated regulatory changes will likely present challenges to insurers in the next five years, as compliance with new regulations may entail significant costs, redirect management focus, and impair insurers' ability to operate in certain market segments.[146] Dodd-Frank introduces federal regulation of insurance firms that are systemically important and that own thrifts or banks, and establishes the Federal Insurance Office (FIO) which will monitor and coordinate policy for the insurance industry and examine insurance-related issues.[147] Although Dodd-Frank was signed into law in 2010, the impact of FIO oversight remains unclear.[148] The FIO currently has a small staff, and its initial report on insurance law modernization was delayed past its January 21, 2012, deadline.[149]

While Dodd-Frank could subject life insurers to new obligations—such as higher capital requirements, investment limitations, and greater prudential standards—the law is expected to have little effect on property and casualty insurers.[150]

The EU's Solvency II requirements, which are scheduled to take effect in 2013, are intended to guarantee that all insurers in the European market hold adequate capital reserves. These requirements will impose compliance costs on U.S. insurers with European operations,[151] and may affect insurers' pricing strategies and product offerings. Solvency II could also intensify competition in the global insurance market or alter the expectations of rating agencies as these standards become increasingly widespread in EU and non-EU markets.[152] These standards have already influenced the development of the NAIC revised guidelines on reserve requirements, which NAIC plans to complete in 2012.[153] Additionally, the International Accounting Standards Board and the Financial Accounting Standards Board are establishing new accounting standards that would alter the way insurance policies are valued and require greater transparency in insurers' financial statements. These changes may increase the complexity of insurers' financial statements—particularly among property and casualty insurers, for whom one-time events can have a major impact on financial results— and may impact the formation and cost of new products.[154]

Catastrophes will continue to have a substantial but unpredictable impact on property and casualty insurers. Globally, insured losses from natural and manmade disasters increased from $152 billion in 2010 to $380 billion in 2011,[155] and average yearly losses increased from $75 billion during 1981–2010 to $113 billion during 2001–10.[156] The cost of such events is expected to grow as an increasing number of people live in disaster-prone areas.[157] Additionally, rising temperatures associated with climate change may raise flooding and wildfire risks in certain areas, increasing the risk of property loss.[158] At the same time, recent mitigation efforts may lessen the costs of future catastrophes. For example, some U.S. states have taken steps towards improving building standards, and demand for homes that have been strengthened against disasters has grown in the wake of Hurricane Katrina.[159]

The industry also anticipates increases in both mergers and acquisitions and globalization. M&A activity is expected to increase moderately, particularly in overseas markets, as firms attempt to become more competitive by achieving greater economies of scale.[160] Such activity is often faster and less expensive than "organic" growth, and may be motivated by recent drops in the value of insurance company shares, which can effectively reduce the price of acquisitions.[161] However, it is also possible that low share values will discourage M&A activity by decreasing the value of the assets available to purchasing firms.[162] Increasing globalization will likely be spurred by U.S. market saturation, new opportunities in emerging markets, and risk diversification efforts.[163]

SECTION 5. LOGISTICS SERVICES

SUMMARY

Global logistics revenues grew by nearly one-third during 2006–10 to reach $551 billion, as manufacturers continued to outsource a wider range of supply chain functions to third-party logistics (3PL) firms.

Although the United States remained the largest logistics market in 2010, accounting for 23 percent of global revenues, this share declined by 4 percentage points during 2006–10. By contrast, logistics revenues in the fast-growing economies of Brazil and China rose sharply during the period, indicating an upward trend in logistics demand in these markets. In recent years, all of the leading global 3PL firms have developed industry-specific supply chain expertise and expanded the reach of their transportation networks to improve their competitiveness.

Trade in logistics services consists primarily of cross-border transactions (i.e., in air and maritime freight transportation and port services), which are correlated with merchandise trade. In 2010, U.S. exports and imports of logistics services rose by nearly 18 percent, prompted by the large increase in U.S. merchandise trade. Affiliate transactions also grew during the 2006–10 period, and continue to account for a growing proportion of logistics services trade. Despite the potential for increased trade in logistics services, especially in emerging markets, significant infrastructure and regulatory barriers remain in place.

Introduction

Logistics services are a collection of activities that oversee the end-to-end transport of raw, intermediate, and final goods between suppliers, producers, and consumers.[164] These services typically include freight forwarding; multimodal transport (i.e., transport by air, ship, truck, or rail); warehousing and storage; tracking and tracing; and customs brokerage. They also include other value-added services, such as order fulfillment, product repair, and supply chain management.[165] Firms may outsource some or all of these activities to third-party logistics service providers (3PLs) in order to focus on their core competencies and reduce costs, removing the need to develop in-house logistics capacity.[166] Firms thus gain a competitive advantage by using the resources and expertise of a 3PL.[167] Each firm makes an individual decision as to which and how many logistics functions to outsource, ranging from the low-value-added functions (e.g., warehousing and storage) to the strategic (e.g., supply chain management).[168] In some cases, a firm may contract with multiple 3PLs to provide an array of services, although it can be more expensive to manage a network of service providers.[169]

Most firms outsource some portion of their logistics needs to 3PL firms. For instance, although large multinational firms such as Procter & Gamble, Wal-Mart, and Toyota have sophisticated in-house logistics operations, they still use 3PL providers for some services due to capacity and cost considerations.[170] By contrast, other firms, such as U.S. heavy equipment manufacturer Caterpillar, have in-house logistics arms large enough to function as 3PL service suppliers to external clients. For the most part, however, the logistics industry comprises dedicated logistics services firms, ranging from small companies offering a few "bread and butter" services (e.g., freight forwarding, warehousing, and trucking services) to large, integrated service providers such as DHL and UPS. In many cases, these large providers started as freight transportation firms and, over time, added logistics and supply chain management capabilities.

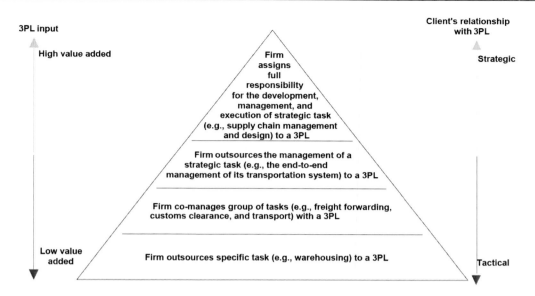

Source: Adapted from "The Emerging Role of the Third-Party Logistics Provider (3PL) as an Orchestrator," *Journal of Business Logistics*, 2011.

Figure 5.1. Logistics services: Scope of 3PL engagement with client varies.

The competitive landscape for 3PL firms has changed significantly within the past decade due to the rapid globalization of production and supply chains.[171] As a result, the role of 3PLs has shifted: instead of interacting with a fixed group of suppliers, producers, and consumers, 3PLs increasingly coordinate a constantly changing mix of supply chain participants. Hence, successful 3PLs are those with the capacity to design and manage their customers' supply chains and the ability to connect those supply chains to complex, global IT and transportation networks.[172] These networks facilitate the transport of goods between any two geographic points in an efficient and seamless manner.[173] At the same time, traditional logistics functions such as trucking and warehousing services have become commoditized; consequently, customers are less willing to pay a premium for these services (figure 5.1).[174]

Competitive Conditions in the Global Logistics Services Market

In 2010, global revenues for the logistics services industry totaled $550.9 billion, compared to $417.1 billion in 2006.[175] The United States is by far the largest market for logistics service providers, although growth in the U.S. 3PL market has been tempered by the recent economic downturn.[176] In 2010, the revenues of U.S. logistics firms reached $127 billion, accounting for 23 percent of global logistics revenues, down from 27 percent in 2006 (table 5.1). By contrast, China, which ranked 2nd in logistics revenues ($74.5 billion), accounted for nearly 14 percent of the global total, up from 9 percent in 2006. Brazil also increased its status as a supplier of logistics services, moving in rank from 10th place in 2006 to 7th place in 2010. Among leading logistics markets, Brazil achieved the third-largest absolute dollar increase in revenues (after China and the United States) during the 2006–10 period: its revenues rose from $7.8 billion to $19.9 billion.[177]

Logistics costs, calculated as a percentage of GDP, are another way to gauge the competitiveness of a country's logistics sector (table 5.2). Generally, as countries become more developed, their logistics sectors become more efficient and their logistics expenditure ratios decrease. Conversely, a high expenditure ratio indicates inefficiencies in a country's logistics market that may result from inadequate transportation infrastructure, a poor customs environment, or lack of expertise in logistics management.[178] In 2010, U.S. logistics costs accounted for 8.3 percent of the country's GDP. By this measure, the United States is nearly the most efficient logistics market in the world (edged out slightly by the Netherlands, whose ratio was 8.1 percent).

Table 5.1. Logistics services: Top 10 countries by global revenues, 2010

Rank	Country	3PL revenues ($ billion)	Percent of total global 3PL revenues
1	United States	127.3	23.0
2	China	74.5	13.5
3	Japan	41.8	7.6
4	Germany	27.8	5.0
5	France	24.0	4.4
6	Italy	20.5	3.7
7	Brazil	19.9	3.6
8	United Kingdom	19.1	3.5
9	Canada	13.1	2.4
10	Australia	12.8	2.3
	Total	380.8	69.0

Source: Armstrong & Associates, Inc., "Global 3PL Market Size Estimates," n.d. http://www. 3plogistics.com/3PLmarketGlobal.htm (accessed November 14, 2011).

Table 5.2. Logistics costs as a percentage of GDP for top 10 global logistics markets in 2010, and percentage change for 2006–10

Rank	Country	Logistics expenditure ratio (percent)		2006–10 change (percentage points)
		2006	2010	
1	United States	9.9	8.3	(1.6)
2	China	21.0	18.1	(2.9)
3	Japan	8.7	8.7	—
4	Germany	8.0	8.3	0.3
5	France	9.5	9.2	(0.3)
6	Italy	10.6	9.4	(1.2)
7	Brazil	14.9	11.6	(3.3)
8	United Kingdom	10.0	8.5	(1.5)
9	Canada	10.4	9.9	(0.5)
10	Australia	N/A	10.5	—
	World average	11.5	11.1	(0.4)

Source: Armstrong & Associates, Inc., "Global 3PL Market Size Estimates," n.d. http://www. 3plogistics.com/3PLmarketGlobal.htm (accessed November 14, 2011).

Conversely, the logistics expenditure ratios of Brazil (11.6 percent), China (18.1 percent), and India (13.0 percent) in 2010 were higher than the global average of 11.1 percent. Nonetheless, logistics costs in these and other emerging economies decreased notably in the last five years. Policy reforms and infrastructure improvements may be partially responsible for this decline. In countries where logistics costs fell most dramatically during 2006–10, especially Brazil and China, logistics revenues increased significantly, suggesting a strong relationship between efficiency and market size.

The leading logistics providers in 2010 were a diverse set of firms in terms of geographical base, core business, name recognition, and ownership structure. In that year, German- and U.S.-based firms topped the list of the 10 largest global 3PL providers (table 5.3).

Two of the top three German firms are government-affiliated: DHL Supply Chain & Global Forwarding is a subsidiary of express services firm, DHL, which is owned by Germany's national postal agency, Deutsche Post; and DB Schenker Logistics is a subsidiary of the government rail transportation entity, Deutsche Bahn. The largest U.S. 3PL in 2010 was C.H. Robinson Worldwide, a non-asset-based logistics firm (i.e., it does not own transportation equipment). Although its name is less recognizable than DHL or UPS, C.H. Robinson has a more than 100-year history in the logistics industry and currently operates in over 200 countries worldwide. CEVA Logistics, a Netherlands- based 3PL, is also a non-asset-based logistics firm, and was formed in 2007 as a joint venture between U.S. air freight forwarder, EGL, and the Dutch firm TNT Logistics. German-based Kuehne + Nagel and the Swiss firm Panalpina are well-established international freight forwarders with strong ties to the maritime transport industry. GLOVIS is the logistics arm of Korea's leading automobile manufacturer, Hyundai. In addition to serving the automobile industry, the company provides logistics services for heavy goods such as steel, rail cars, and construction equipment. GLOVIS operates in 10 countries outside of Korea, including the United States, Canada, China, and India.[179]

In recent years, leading global logistics firms have developed supply chain management capabilities that moved from the periphery to the core of companies' service offerings. For example, Panalpina increasingly provides customers with strategic plans to optimize the flow of goods within their supply chains, and implements such plans using Panalpina's network of transportation and IT services providers.[180] Kuehne + Nagel leverages its experience in transportation management by offering customized logistics services that extend along the value chain from resource procurement to aftermarket services.[181] UPS has established a consulting practice to provide clients with both customized and off-the-shelf products for supply chain design, and as a result, supply chain management services have become an integral and growing part of the company's business.[182]

Demand and Supply Factors

Globalization of Supply Chains Increases Demand for High-Value Logistics Services

The globalization of manufacturing has been one of the largest demand drivers for logistics services in recent years. Illustratively, the global volume of merchandise exports grew by more than 50 percent between 2000 and 2010, in part reflecting increased international trade in manufactured parts and components.[183] Globalization not only means that suppliers, producers, and consumers reside in separate geographic locations, but that these locations are subject to change depending on resource availability, manufacturers' costs, and consumer trends. Such fluid supply chains are challenging to manage and require a high level of logistics expertise and network capabilities that often only the largest multinational firms possess.[184] For example, Caterpillar's global footprint includes more than 100 manufacturing plants, 70 parts distribution centers, and 4,000 independent dealers in nearly every country worldwide. By managing its own geographically dispersed value chain, the company has developed sophisticated supply chain expertise, which it has developed into a separate logistics business.[185]

However, most manufacturing firms increase efficiencies in their global supply chains by outsourcing logistics functions to 3PLs that provide holistic services, thereby increasing the demand for these services. For instance, in 2000, General Motors (GM) formed a joint venture with U.S. logistics provider CNF to create software that enables GM to monitor costs at key nodes in its value chain, including procurement, distribution, and sales and marketing. Where costs are high, the program helps GM reconfigure its global supply chain network for greater efficiency.[186] Similarly, in 2003, the Japanese electronics firm Hitachi hired UPS to design and implement a global distribution system for its hard drives that involved moving the company's disparate inventory and account data to a single IT platform.[187]

In Emerging Markets, Demand for Logistics Services Is Increasing

As emerging markets mature, they increasingly demand logistics services. Significant emerging markets include the BRIC economies (Brazil, Russia, India, and China) as well as Mexico, South Korea, Thailand, Turkey, and the United Arab Emirates (UAE).[188] GDP growth in many of the emerging economies has exceeded GDP growth in major developed countries in recent years, and it is forecast to continue to do so through 2015.[189] The primary driver of such growth—an increase in the domestic production of goods and services—presents significant potential for the expansion of these countries' logistics sectors as more imports, exports, and domestically produced goods are being moved to, from, and within these markets.[190] For example, Thailand has become an important location for many of the world's largest manufacturers: computer firms Apple and Dell produce hard disk drives in Thailand,[191] while Japanese automobile manufacturers Honda, Mitsubishi, and Toyota produce automotive parts there. Rising demand for logistics services in these markets has led to an expanded supply of such services. Netherlands- based CEVA Logistics reportedly has 48 warehousing and distribution facilities located near Bangkok, and global maritime firms Maersk (Denmark) and NYK (Japan) provide container shipping services between Thailand and its trading partners.[192]

In many emerging economies, however, the domestic logistics sector remains highly fragmented, even when significant infrastructure improvements have been made. In these markets, small logistics firms supply individual services such as trucking and warehousing, but there is little coordination among service providers. For example, in Vietnam, there are reportedly more than 800 separate firms that supply shipping, trucking, and customs clearance services, many of which are characterized as "mom-and- pop" operations with as few as five employees.[193] The underdeveloped nature of the logistics industry in Vietnam, and in some other emerging countries, means that providers in these markets are unable to achieve the network and scale economies necessary to drive down domestic logistics costs.[194]

Table 5.3. Top 10 global 3PL firms by revenue, 2010

Rank	Company	Country	Revenues ($ million)	Parent company (if subsidiary of larger firm)	Core business of firm or firm's parent
1	DHL Supply Chain & Global Forwarding	Germany	30,486	Deustche Post	Postal services
2	Kuehne + Nagel	Germany	19,476	——	Freight forwarding
3	DB Schenker Logistics	Germany	18,999	Deutsche Bahn	Rail transportation
4	Nippon Express	Japan	18,450	——	Express delivery
5	C.H. Robinson Worldwide	United States	9,274	——	Contract logistics
6	CEVA Logistics	Netherlands	9,091	——	Contract logistics
7	UPS Supply Chain Solutions	United States	8,670	UPS	Express delivery
8	DSV	Denmark	7,587	——	Road transportation; freight forwarding; and contract logistics
9	Panalpina World Transport	Switzerland	6,887	——	Freight forwarding
10	Hyundai GLOVIS	Korea	6,303	Hyundai Motor Corporation	Automobile manufacturing

Source: Armstrong & Associates, "A&A's Top 50 Global Third-Party Logistics Provider (3PL) List,"
n.d. (accessed November 14, 2011).

Note: A state-owned Chinese transportation services firm, Sinotrans, ranked 11th after Hyundai
GLOVIS, with revenues of $6.286 billion in 2010.

3PLs Continue to Develop Industry-Specific Expertise to Supply a Diverse Client Base

3PLs establish practice areas that reflect the principal industries of their clients in order to provide more valuable supply chain services. For example, Panalpina has developed expertise in the automotive, healthcare, high-tech, retail, and oil and gas industries.[195] Similarly, UPS's supply chain management services focus on the industrial manufacturing, computer, pharmaceutical, and biotechnology industries, among others (box 5.1).[196] In some cases, the industry expertise developed by 3PLs permit them to partner with client firms. For instance, Toshiba hired UPS to perform repairs on the company's laptop computers in an effort to improve the timeliness of Toshiba's aftermarket service: UPS accepts broken computers at its retail outlets, forwards the computers to a facility near its Louisville hub for repair, and then ships the computers directly back to customers.[197] Using their sector-specific knowledge,

3PLs also adapt logistics processes to clients in a range of industries. For example, CEVA Logistics developed a standardized process for transporting component parts and finished goods from suppliers to producers, aimed at minimizing transit time between locations, and adapted this supply chain management tool to customers in the automotive, energy, and high-tech industries.

BOX 5.1. 3PL FIRMS BECOME IMPORTANT PLAYERS IN THE HEALTHCARE INDUSTRY

In recent years, the logistics requirements of the healthcare industry have grown in complexity, stimulated in part by the global activities of large biotechnology and pharmaceutical companies. According to one study, an individual healthcare service provider spends an average of $100 million a year, or approximately one-third of its annual operating budget, on supply-chain-related expenses. Many of the leading global logistics firms—including UPS, DHL, and FedEx—provide services to a range of healthcare clients and have developed a portfolio of logistic and supply chain services tailored specifically to healthcare providers. In addition to biotechnology and pharmaceuticals, 3PL firms have established practice areas related to medical devices and hospital services.[a]

Logistics firms principally provide warehousing, distribution, and inventory management services to their healthcare clients, with a particular emphasis on temperature-controlled or cold chain supply. However, the role of logistics firms in the healthcare industry has gradually deepened, as healthcare companies shed in-house distribution and warehousing assets in favor of outsourcing logistics management functions to 3PL firms. For example, UPS manages the distribution, transportation, and warehousing of pharmaceutical products manufactured by U.S. firm Merck both in the United States and in foreign markets such as Brazil and China. The UPS warehousing facilities used by Merck adhere to the U.S. Food and Drug Administration's temperature and environmental guidelines for the storage of vaccines and other specialized pharmaceuticals.[b] Currently, UPS has 30 healthcare distribution facilities worldwide.[c] Similarly, DHL, through its contract logistics subsidiary Exel, manages product distribution for U.S. pharmaceutical company Bristol-Myers Squibb, including finished goods, pharmaceuticals used in clinical trials, and products for export. Four of Exel's 14 logistics hubs are dedicated to serving clients in the healthcare and life sciences industries.[d]

Other examples of services provided by 3PL firms to healthcare clients include the implementation of RFID-enabled[e] inventory management systems to track equipment use within a hospital, and packaging and quality inspection services for medical device manufacturers.[f] 3PL firms are also increasingly performing quality assurance and regulatory compliance tasks, especially for their biotechnology and pharmaceutical clients.[g]

[a] UPS, "Supply Chain Solutions for Healthcare Providers," 2005, 2; Nachtmann and Pohl, "The State of Healthcare Logistics," July 2009, 5.

[b] UPS, "UPS and Merck Expand Their Distribution and Logistics Agreement," June 28, 2011. Other U.S. and foreign government regulations that pertain to the transport, storage, and distribution of pharmaceuticals and that a logistics services provider like UPS would follow include those under the U.S. Food and Drug Administration, the U.S. Drug Enforcement Agency, Health Canada, and the European Medicines Agency (EMA). UPS, "Pharmaceuticals and Biotech," n.d. (accessed January 24, 2012).

[c] UPS, "UPS to Acquire Italian Pharma Logistics Company Pieffe," December 1, 2011.

[d] FiercePharma Manufacturing, "BMS Offloads U.S. Distribution to Exel," March 29, 2011; Pharmaceutical Commerce, "Exel Wins Bristol-Myers Squibb's 3PL Services Contract," April 8, 2011.

[e] "RFID" refers to a radio frequency identification system. RFID uses a wireless radio to read and transmit data (over a distance of several yards) that is stored on an electronic tag attached to a warehouse item.

[f] UPS, "Supply Chain Solutions for Healthcare Providers," 2005, 6: Federal Express, "Supply Chain Customer Success Story," n.d. (accessed January 17, 2011).

[g] UPS, "UPS to Acquire Italian Pharma Logistics Company Pieffe," December 1, 2011.

Network Capabilities of 3PLs Grow in Importance as New "Hotspots" for Logistics Activity Emerge

The ability of 3PL firms to effectively supply services to their global clients is also determined by the size and scope of 3PLs' transportation networks. The transportation networks of large, asset-based 3PL firms generally consist of a major air hub connected to a collection of smaller, regional air hubs, often supported by ground transportation fleets. Over the years, these networks have grown in size and geographic scope to include multiple locations abroad. For example, in addition to its global hub in Louisville, Kentucky, UPS has 10 air hub facilities worldwide, including a newly established intra- Asia hub based in Shenzhen, China.[198] Likewise, FedEx has 9 domestic and international air hubs—including those in Paris (France) and Dubai (UAE)—that each connect to the company's main hub in Memphis, Tennessee.[199]

As noted, the globalization of manufacturing activity has stimulated the demand for cross-border logistics services; in turn, 3PLs' global network expansion has facilitated the geographic fragmentation of the manufacturing base. In recent years, certain countries have emerged as new "hotspots" of both manufacturing and logistics activity—China and India are two prominent examples, but Saudi Arabia, Turkey, and Vietnam are also among such hotspots. For instance, Turkey and Vietnam are growing centers of textile and other manufacturing operations as well as transportation gateways for the larger economies of the European Union and China, respectively.[200] Similarly, Saudi Arabia is now home to nearly 2,700 manufacturing companies and is also a gateway for goods transported between Asia, Africa, and Europe.[201] 3PL firms DHL and Kuehne + Nagel are already present in Saudi Arabia, Turkey, and Vietnam, and other large logistics firms are likely to follow.[202]

Trade Trends

Cross-Border Trade

In 2010, U.S. exports of freight transportation and port services (box 5.2) reached $36.0 billion and U.S. imports equaled $47.4 billion, yielding a U.S. trade deficit of $11.4 billion (figure 5.2). Prompted by the beginning of the recovery from the economic downturn, U.S. exports in 2010 increased by 13.6 percent over the previous year—far faster than the 2.9 percent CAGR recorded during 2005–09. The increase in U.S. exports of freight transportation and port services in 2010 is consistent with an increase in U.S. merchandise exports, which rose by 21 percent to nearly $1.3 trillion in the same year.[203] However, U.S. imports of freight and port transportation services rose even faster than exports of such services, increasing by 21.3 percent in 2010, compared to a compound annual decrease of 6.1 percent during 2005–09. As with exports, the large increase in U.S. imports of freight transportation and port services in 2010 reflects a sizable increase in U.S. merchandise imports—23 percent—compared to 2009.[204]

The leading recipient countries for U.S. exports of freight transportation and port services in 2010 were the United Kingdom, accounting for 10 percent of total U.S. exports, followed by Japan (9.6 percent), Germany (7.3 percent), China (6.1 percent), and Korea (5.2 percent) (figure 5.3). In 2010, China ranked first and Japan, Germany, the United Kingdom, and Korea ranked fourth through seventh, respectively, among the top 10 countries for U.S. merchandise exports.[205] At the same time, the United States posted a deficit with each of these countries in freight transportation and port services; the largest U.S. deficits were with Japan ($2.2 billion) and Korea ($1.1 billion) (figure 5.4). In particular, U.S. imports of ocean freight services from Japan rose 37 percent in 2010; those from Korea rose by 32 percent. These increases were likely driven in part by growth in U.S. imports of automobiles and heavy machinery from these countries.

BOX 5.2. AN EXPLANATION OF BEA DATA ON CROSS-BORDER TRADE AND AFFILIATE TRANSACTIONS IN LOGISTICS SERVICES

Official data on cross-border trade in logistics services are unavailable. Therefore, data on trade in air and maritime freight transportation services and port services are used as proxies, since they account for a substantial portion of trade in logistics services. Cross-border trade in air and maritime freight transportation and port services stems from merchandise trade, and thus tends to expand and contract in tandem with merchandise trade.

Cross-border trade in air and maritime freight transportation services can be broken down into two components:

- Exports of air and maritime freight transportation services refer to the transport of U.S. merchandise on U.S. air or ocean carriers to foreign destinations or between foreign ports.
- Imports of air and maritime freight transportation services refer to the transport of merchandise to the United States by foreign air and ocean carriers.

Similarly, U.S. exports of port services reflect the value of goods (except fuel) and services procured by foreign carriers at U.S. ports, while imports of port services reflect the value of goods and services procured by U.S. carriers at foreign ports.[a]

Due to the absence of official data on logistic services affiliates, data on transportation and warehousing affiliates serve as proxies. However, the BEA estimates include sales of all services by transportation and warehousing affiliates, not just those pertaining directly to transportation and warehousing. For 2005, the BEA reported that certain foreign affiliates were reclassified from the manufacturing sector to the transportation and warehousing sector because of changes in the composition of their principal activities. The reclassification therefore increased BEA's figures for sales of services overall in 2005, in particular for sales of services by transportation and warehousing affiliates.

Source: BEA, *Survey of Current Business*, 2007, 96; BEA *Survey of Current Business*, 2011, 17–18, 27.

[a] In 2011, the BEA reported that transactions between the U.S. postal service and foreign postal entities for the cross-border delivery of letters, printed matter, and parcels were reclassified from U.S. government miscellaneous services to freight transportation services. This reclassification was done as part of a larger effort by BEA to more closely align government services with the type of activity performed. The reclassification resulted in an increase in exports and imports of private freight transportation services in 2011.

Japan was the leading source of U.S. imports of freight transportation and port services in 2010, accounting for 11.9 percent of total U.S. imports, followed by Germany (7.6 percent), the United Kingdom (6.5 percent), Korea (6.3 percent), and China (6.1 percent). U.S. imports of freight transportation and port services from China increased by a combined total of nearly 40 percent. The increase in U.S. logistics imports from China was due to a significant rise in the provision of air freight services (57.4 percent) and ocean freight services (43.7 percent) by logistics firms located in China, a result of expanding U.S.–China merchandise trade. By contrast, U.S. imports of freight transportation and port services from Germany and the United Kingdom increased at the relatively slower rate of 15.5 percent each, driven principally by growth in imports of ocean freight services.

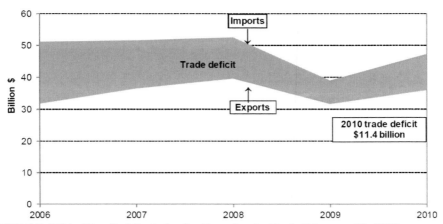

Source: USDOC, BEA, "Detailed Statistics for Cross-border Trade," January 25, 2012.

[a] Logistics services include ocean and air freight and ocean and airport services.

Figure 5.2. Logistics services: a U.S. cross-border trade in logistics services resulted in a U.S. trade deficit each year during 2006–10.

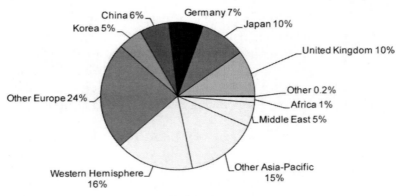

U.S. exports

Total = $36.0 billion

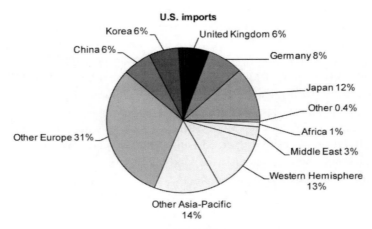

U.S. imports

Total = $47.4 billion

Source: USDOC, BEA, "Detailed Statistics for Cross-border Trade," January 25, 2012.
Note: Geographic regions are shaded in yellow. Figures may not total 100 percent due to rounding.
[a] Logistics services include ocean and air freight and ocean and airport services.

Figure 5.3. Logistics services: a The United Kingdom was the top market for U.S. exports, while Japan was the leading source of U.S. imports in 2010.

Affiliate Transactions

Total sales for foreign affiliates of U.S. transportation and warehousing companies were not reported in 2009 to avoid disclosure of individual company data.[206] However, available data indicate that such sales were at least $44.3 billion.[207] At the same time, total purchases from U.S. affiliates of foreign transportation and warehousing companies in 2009 equaled $42.6 billion. Available data indicate that the top five markets for foreign affiliate sales in 2009 were the United Kingdom ($5.4 billion), Germany ($4.0 billion), the Netherlands ($2.5 billion), France ($2.1 billion), and Switzerland ($1.5 billion). Foreign affiliate sales in the United Kingdom and Germany fell by a combined total of 17 percent in 2009, likely the result of reduced trade flows during the economic downturn which dampened demand for logistics services.[208]

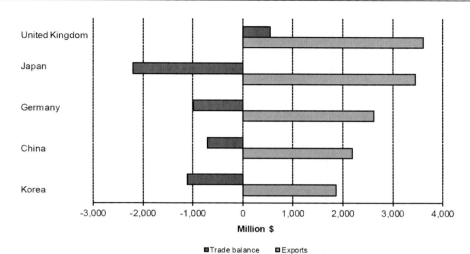

Source: USDOC, BEA, *U.S. International Services*, "Detailed statistics for cross-border trade: 3. Travel, passenger fares, and other transportation," found at http://www.bea.gov/international/international_services.htm, January 25, 2012.

[a] Logistics services include air and m aritim e freight transportation and port services.

Figure 5.4. Logistics services: a Among the top five U.S. trading partners in logistics services, the United Kingdom was the only country with which the United States posted a trade surplus in 2010.

In 2009, purchases from U.S. affiliates of foreign transportation and warehousing companies decreased by 13 percent over the previous year, compared to a CAGR of 9.5 percent during 2004–08.[209] According to available data, purchases from U.S. transportation and warehousing affiliates were primarily from those with parents in Germany ($10.3 billion), the United Kingdom ($6.3 billion), and Japan ($3.1 billion). The high volume of purchases from U.S. affiliates of German firms likely reflects the activity of German-based logistics firms DHL, Kuehne + Nagel, and DB Schenker in the U.S. market. Overall, purchases from U.S. affiliates of Europe-based companies fell by 17.3 percent in 2009, and purchases from U.S. affiliates with parents in the Asia-Pacific region decreased by 15.7 percent. These decreases were offset slightly by purchases from U.S. affiliates with parents in Canada, which rose by 2.2 percent in 2009.

Nontariff Measures Affecting Trade

Global 3PL firms typically operate in a large number of countries where they are subject to government policies on foreign direct investment, cargo security, licensing, and air traffic rights. Such policies influence where logistics firms set up local ventures, how they operate, and what services they provide. Policies that limit air transportation rights or foreign direct investment in particular undercut the ability of 3PL firms to serve new markets or to expand service in countries where they are already present. For example, U.S. logistics firms may be unable to provide air freight or air express services to a country with which the United States does not have a bilateral air transport agreement.[210] In addition, the frequency and scope of such service may be limited in countries with which the United States does not maintain "open skies" agreements that permit unrestricted air service.[211]

Some countries also place restrictions on commercial establishment (GATS mode 3) by foreign logistics firms. For example, before its accession to the WTO, China enforced joint venture requirements on foreign firms supplying road freight transport services, storage and warehousing services, freight forwarding services, and courier services.[212] However, the Chinese government eliminated joint venture requirements on these entities in 2006 and now permits wholly foreign-owned enterprises in logistics services.[213] Similarly, Vietnam removed joint venture requirements on express delivery firms as of January 2012, permitting 100 percent foreign ownership of such entities.[214] In Mexico, joint venture requirements on foreign firms providing freight transportation services were phased out in 2004. However, port services firms must still receive government approval to establish companies in which foreign investment exceeds 49 percent.[215]

The operation of 3PL firms in developing and emerging markets may also be limited by lack of access to adequate transportation infrastructure (i.e., roads, railways, and air and sea ports) and poor customs environments. For instance, India's road network is in disrepair, and it has relatively few major airports and seaports.[216] Moreover, India's burdensome customs procedures add inefficiency to the country's supply chain operations.[217] As a result, India's logistics costs are higher than the global average, in part reflecting the physical and bureaucratic challenges faced by 3PL firms such as DHL and FedEx that operate in the Indian market.[218]

In the past, multilateral services negotiations under the WTO addressed some of the above issues, although such negotiations are currently at a standstill. Previous WTO efforts under the GATS focused on developing a checklist for logistics services, and setting milestones for WTO members to eliminate restrictions on each of the services identified in the checklist.[219] More recent WTO negotiations have focused on revising the text of customs-related provisions under Articles V, VIII, and X of the General Agreement on Trade and Tariffs.[220] In addition, logistics services may be one of several sectors targeted for plurilateral negotiations among WTO members in the absence of further progress under the GATS. However, while the United States, the European Union and other economies may favor plurilateral negotiations, emerging economies such as Brazil, China, and India have indicated that they prefer a broader multilateral forum, thus adding uncertainty to the future of liberalization efforts.[221]

Outlook

The growth in merchandise trade has accelerated the globalization of supply chains. Goods now cross borders several times during the production process, and this has led to an increase in the demand for logistics services.[222] Large 3PL firms have responded to globalization by extending the geographic reach of their information and transportation networks, as well as by developing industry expertise so that they can offer more valuable supply chain services to their customers. Specialization and network expansion will likely remain trends for the foreseeable future as competition within the logistics industry intensifies.[223] At the same time, developing and emerging economies will likely continue to increase their demand for logistics services, as manufacturing and consumer activity in these countries grow.[224] Significant logistics barriers in these markets remain, however, especially those related to infrastructure, commercial establishment, and customs administration. Some have suggested that, given the stalemate on logistics services liberalization under the GATS, the best prospect for removing some of these barriers may be through bilateral or plurilateral negotiations, as mentioned above. However, other barriers (such as inadequate transportation infrastructure) may be best addressed through unilateral efforts.[225]

SECTION 6. RETAIL SERVICES

SUMMARY

Retailing is one of the principal commercial activities in most economies and accounts for more than a tenth of all employment in the United States. Global retail sales grew by 9.0 percent in 2010 after falling amid the economic downturn in 2009. The United States remained the world's largest retail market in 2010, but sales grew faster in developing and emerging countries such as China and Brazil. Around the world, retailing over the Internet (e-commerce) is growing rapidly, and traditional "brick-and-mortar" retailers are strengthening their online presence. Retailers are building smaller stores in the United States in order to reduce costs and enter new markets, such as city centers; in Europe, they are using low-cost store brands to appeal to pinched consumers. Meanwhile, faster-growing developing countries are central to multinational retailers' growth strategies. U.S. retailers are expanding in Latin America, Asia, and Africa, even as some of these same companies close stores in the United States.

Services supplied by U.S.-owned foreign affiliates in the retailing industry grew in 2009, but more slowly than in previous years: weak retail sales affected the leading destinations for U.S. foreign investment in retailing, including Canada and the United Kingdom. Services supplied by foreign-owned retailers in the United States shrank in 2009 for the third straight year amid the broader slowdown in U.S. retail sales, although foreign firms continued to invest. Numerous countries maintain barriers to foreign investment in retailing, including India's ban on foreign ownership in multibrand retailing and an opaque economic needs test in Vietnam. Bilateral and regional trade agreements have sometimes proven useful for easing such barriers. Going forward, retail sales will likely continue to grow more quickly in developing countries than in developed ones, while sales via mobile devices will grow around the world.

Introduction

Retailing is the final stage in the merchandise distribution process. Retailers buy goods from manufacturers or wholesalers, then resell them in small quantities to individual consumers. They operate via fixed points of sale (i.e., physical stores) or through other channels, such as catalogs, television, direct selling (e.g., door-to-door sales), and the Internet (e-commerce).[226] When shoppers make a retail purchase, they are paying for both the merchandise and the distributive services associated with it. These services include transporting the merchandise to the point of sale, maintaining inventories, and providing information about the merchandise.[227]

Retailing accounts for a substantial share of output and employment in many countries. In the United States in 2011, the retail industry employed 14.7 million people (11.1 percent of nonfarm employment)[228] and accounted for 6.1 percent of value added as a share of GDP ($884.9 billion). [229] Demand for retail services depends on broader factors in the economy, such as the rate at which consumers' incomes are growing and their willingness to consume (which in turn depends on their expectations about future income and the performance of the economy). Retailers' ability to supply their services depends on the quality of infrastructure, such as transport networks for moving merchandise to stores or warehouses; access to real estate suitable for store sites; the availability of workers to staff the stores; and policies and regulations, such as rules on store size, operating hours, and prices. Additional factors affect supply and demand for retailing via e-commerce, including consumers' access to broadband Internet and the tax treatment of online transactions versus in-store ones (see "Demand and Supply Factors" later in this section).

Competitive Conditions in the Global Retail Services Market

Global retail sales totaled $16.2 trillion in 2010, an increase of 9.0 percent from 2009. This exceeded the average annual rate of growth over the 2004–09 period (7.2 percent) and represented a sharp turnaround from 2008–09, when sales declined by 3.4 percent.[230] The United States was the world's largest retail market in 2010, with sales totaling $3.0 trillion— almost a fifth of the global total (figure 6.1).[231] But this represented a decline in share compared to 2005, when the United States accounted for nearly a quarter of global sales. Over this period, emerging markets grew in importance at the expense of the traditional leaders in the developed world. In 2005, the BRIC countries (Brazil, Russia, India, and China)[232] accounted for 15 percent of global retail sales; by 2010 their share had grown to 24 percent. Over the same period, the share of the G7 group of industrialized countries[234] fell from 52 percent to 42 percent.[235] These trends coincided with a period of rapid economic growth in developing countries: in 2005–10, their average annual GDP growth rate was 5.5 percentage points higher than in developed ones.[236] The world's top 10 retail firms in 2009 (the most recent year for which data were available) were all headquartered in Europe or the United States (table 6.1). All except two of them—the United States' Kroger and Target— also operated in countries outside their home markets.

Demand and Supply Factors

Growth of E-Commerce Drives Integration of Online and in-Store Sales Channels

The growth of retail sales over the Internet (e-commerce) over the past decade has been one of the most notable trends in the global retail industry (box 6.1). Online outlets offer consumers more choices and information, which may lead to greater competition, lower prices, and increased demand. It also may enable retailers to increase sales via an expanded base of potential customers.

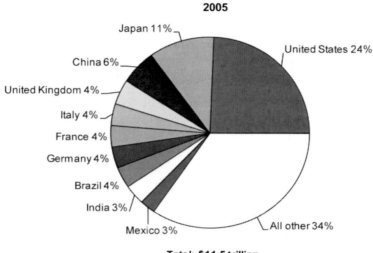

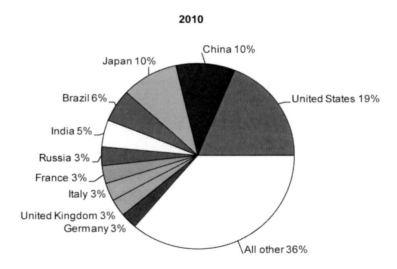

Source: Planet Retail database (accessed August 22, 2011).
Note: Figures may not total 100 percent due to rounding.

Figure 6.1. Retail services: Although the United States still held the largest share of global retailing revenues from 2005 to 2010, the share going to the BRIC countries (Brazil, Russia, India, and China) rose during that period.

In the United States, year-on-year growth of e-commerce has exceeded growth of overall retail sales in every quarter since the fourth quarter of 2000 (the first period for which data are available). E-commerce accounted for an all-time high of 4.8 percent of U.S. retail sales in the fourth quarter of 2011.[237] The expansion of U.S. e-commerce has been facilitated by the growth of broadband Internet infrastructure, which makes it faster and easier for consumers to connect to retailers' Web sites. In addition, online retailers enjoy a de facto exemption from sales taxes[238] and avoid store construction and maintenance expenses. As a result, they can offer competitive prices despite the extra costs of shipping to consumers.

Table 6.1. Top 10 retailers, by global retail sales, 2009

Company	Country[a]	Global retail sales (US$ billion)[b]	Number of countries[c]
Walmart	United States	405.0	15
Carrefour	France	119.9	35
Metro	Germany	90.9	33
Tesco	United Kingdom	90.4	14
Schwarz Group	Germany	77.2	25
Kroger	United States	76.7	1
Costco	United States	69.9	9
Aldi	Germany	[d]67.7	18
Home Depot	United States	66.2	5
Target	United States	63.4	1

Sources: Deloitte, "Leaving Home," January 2011; Planet Retail database (accessed September 28–29, 2010).

[a] Country represents location of headquarters.

[b] Some figures are adjusted from those reported by companies to exclude nonretail sales.

[c] Hong Kong is counted within China; Puerto Rico is counted within the United States. Taiwan is counted as a separate country.

[d] Estimate.

BOX 6.1. CROSS-BORDER E-COMMERCE EMERGES AS AN AVENUE FOR ENTERING NEW MARKETS

Researchers and statistical agencies frequently downplay suggestions that cross-border retailing is important. For example, a 2005 study into the tradability of various services defined retailing as primarily nontradable,[a] and as recently as November 2010, one study claimed that "there is little evidence to indicate that B2C (business to consumer) e-commerce involving conventional physical products has been viewed strategically by the retail TNCs [transnational corporations] as a low cost or 'virtual' form of international market entry."[b] The BEA does not publish separate statistics on cross-border retail trade (see box 6.2).[c]

Yet a growing body of evidence suggests that retailers are increasingly using international e-commerce to enter new markets. Since 2009, several multinational retailers have unveiled strategies to expand sales via the Internet in markets where they do not have physical stores. For example, Gap announced in August 2010 that it would make international shipping available to 65 countries by the end of the year, including several countries where it did not have stores.

The company's president described the strategy as "an efficient way to reach new international customers and test the waters for our brands."[d]

The U.S. department store Nordstrom only has physical stores in the United States, but offered shipping to 41 other countries as of December 2011,[e] and the department store John Lewis, which only has stores in the United Kingdom, offered shipping to 33 other countries as of December 2011.[f]

The expansion of cross-border e-commerce is due to a number of factors. First, it offers retailers a relatively low-risk way to pursue new growth opportunities. They can explore new markets without making large upfront investments in store construction and personnel. Secondly, the expansion of broadband service worldwide has created a larger pool of potential customers. Finally, retailers have access to specialized service providers that can help them design and implement their international e-commerce strategies. One example is the U.S. consulting firm FiftyOne. Its clients include many of the best-known names in U.S. retail, including Nordstrom, Sears, Aéropostale, and Macy's. FiftyOne's services include customization of Web sites for shoppers in different countries; calculation of prices in various currencies, factoring in duties, taxes, and exchange rates; and shipping of merchandise to international customers from a hub in the United States.[g]

[a] Jensen and Kletzer, "Tradable Services," September 2005, 9.
[b] Wrigley and Lowe, "The Globalization of Trade in Retail Services," November 17, 2010, 29.
[c] Borga, "Improved Measures of U.S. International Services," March 2, 2008, 24–25.
[d] Gap Inc., "Gap Inc. Expands E-commerce Reach," August 12, 2010.
[e] Nordstrom Company Web site, http://shop.nordstrom.com/c/international- shopping?origin=footer &previousUrl=http%3A%2F%2Fshop.nordstrom.com%2F (accessed December 5, 2011). Hong Kong and Taiwan are counted as individual countries.
[f] John Lewis Company Web site, http://www.johnlewis.com/Help/Help.aspx?HelpId=55&intcmp =HP_header_international_021211 (accessed December 5, 2011).
[g] FiftyOne Company Web site, http://www.fiftyone.com (accessed December 5, 2011).

E-commerce is also growing rapidly outside the United States: in Korea, e-commerce grew sevenfold between 2001 and 2010, and in Australia, such transactions grew eightfold from 2001 to 2008. The growth of e-commerce has been especially impressive in China, where e-commerce sales totaled ¥476 billion ($70.2 billion) in 2010, nearly quadruple the total in 2008 (¥128 billion). China has the second-largest population of Internet shoppers in the world (145 million, compared to 170 million in the United States). One study projects that the number of Internet shoppers in China will increase by more than 30 million per year through 2015, by which time China will be the world's leading market for e-commerce sales.[239]

The influence of the Internet on retail sales is even greater than these figures suggest. When consumers make purchases in physical stores, they increasingly research merchandise online before or during their shopping trips, often using mobile devices such as smartphones and tablet computers ("m-commerce" or mobile commerce). One senior U.S. retail executive estimated that consumers use the Web to do research for more than half of their significant purchases,[240] including comparing prices across retailers.[241] E-commerce's growth has forced traditional brick-and-mortar retailers to shift their business models. Many have sought to become "multichannel" retailers with integrated physical and Web operations. For example, a growing number of retailers (such as the U.S. department store chain JCPenney) allow customers to order online and pick up their orders in-store,[241] while the department stores

Sears and Kohl's have in-store kiosks where customers can order directly from the companies' Web sites. Others are integrating online and physical channels at the level of individual sales staff: outdoor apparel retailer Moosejaw recently equipped employees with iPod Touch devices that they use to research customers' past purchases, generate product recommendations, and complete sales with attached credit card readers.[242]

Retailers in Developed Countries Adjust to Sluggish Economic Conditions

In 2009, retail sales in the G7 countries (Canada, France, Germany, Japan, the United Kingdom, and the United States) declined for the first time since 2001, as weak economic conditions lowered consumer confidence and disposable incomes. While sales growth in these countries turned positive (3.3 percent) in 2010, it remained below its average annual growth rate of 5.7 percent between 2003 and 2008,[243] amidst high unemployment and fears of a return to recession.[244] The 2011 holiday shopping season in the United States yielded some tentative signs of recovery, with sales during the period increasing by an estimated 3.8 percent over the previous year. Yet some observers suggested that the economy's entrenched weaknesses might render such growth unsustainable.[245]

Retailers in developed countries have taken a number of steps to adjust to these difficult conditions, such as adopting smaller store formats and expanding their private label (store brand) offerings. In the United States, retailers in categories ranging from electronics (e.g., Best Buy) to office supplies (Staples)[246] to department stores (Bloomingdale's) are building smaller stores, which reduce costs for real estate, inventory, and labor (as fewer staff are required).[247] The smaller formats have an additional advantage: they are easier to set up in large cities. "Big-box" retailers such as Walmart and Target have typically built their stores in suburban areas where land is less expensive than in central cities. As a result, markets for big-box retailing in cities are less saturated than in suburban areas, making the cities attractive targets for growth. For example, Target plans to open scaled-down stores in Chicago, Los Angeles, San Francisco, and Seattle in 2012,[248] and Walmart has announced plans for six stores in Washington, DC (its first in the city).[249] There has been opposition to some of these projects, with some community leaders arguing that the big-box retailers pose a threat to smaller retailers and do not pay high enough wages. In contrast, supporters argue that the stores will bring jobs, investment, and lower-priced merchandise to struggling neighborhoods. The weak economy appears to be strengthening public sentiment in favor of the projects.[250]

In Europe, private labels were growing more popular even before the recession,[251] and retailers have continued to turn to them for growth. One study found that private label brands gained market share in 18 European countries in 2010.[252] Private label products typically sell for less than comparable brand-name goods, making them especially appealing to consumers during difficult economic times. Retailers like them, too, because they yield greater margins per sale than brand-name goods.[253] In the United Kingdom, traditional grocery market leaders such as Tesco and Sainsbury have broadened their offerings of private label merchandise in order to compete with the increasingly popular "hard discounters,"[254] such as the German-owned Aldi and Lidl chains. For example, in 2011, Sainsbury introduced a line of private-label refrigerated Mexican food, featuring items such as chicken quesadillas and fajita kits.[255]

Private labels have also grown more popular in the United States, for grocery as well as other market segments. For example, U.S. department stores such as Macy's, Bloomingdale's, and Saks Fifth Avenue have recently expanded their private label apparel offerings. They have developed these products in-house as well as through exclusive partnerships. An example of the latter is Macy's Material Girl line, developed in cooperation with the entertainer Madonna.[256]

Large Retailers Focus Expansion Efforts on Developing and Emerging Countries

In recent years large multinational retailers have focused increasingly on establishing and expanding operations in certain developing and emerging countries. These retailers have been attracted to the fast growth of personal income and consumer spending in these countries, as well as the opportunity to establish an early presence in less saturated markets.[257] This trend predates the recent economic downturn.

Retail sales in the BRIC countries grew at an average annual rate of 12.9 percent between 2000 and 2007, compared to 4.6 percent in the G7—a differential that caused many large retailers to devote more attention to emerging countries. The gap grew wider between 2007 and 2010; retail sales growth averaged 14.9 percent per year in the BRICs, compared to 1.5 percent in the G7.[258]

Developing and emerging countries figure prominently in U.S. retailers' growth strategies. For example, in 2011, clothing retailer Gap opened its first store in Latin America (Chile), announced that it would enter Colombia and Panama in 2012, and described plans to triple its stores in China between January 2012 and 2013. (By contrast, by the end of 2013, it plans to close 189 stores in the United States, where it was struggling even before the recession.)[259] During the same year, Walmart completed a high-profile takeover of Massmart, a South African retailer that operates in 13 African countries.[260]

However, retailers from the United States and other developed countries have also suffered setbacks in emerging countries. For example, Best Buy closed its stores in China in 2011 after struggling to compete against better-known chains,[261] and Swedish home furnishings retailer IKEA halted expansion outside Moscow in Russia in 2009 due to what it described as endemic corruption affecting the permitting process. (In some cases, countries use opaque procedures to protect domestic retailers from foreign competition— see "Nontariff Measures Affecting the Retailing Industry" later in this section.) However, IKEA's experience in Russia also exemplifies the enduring attractiveness of the emerging economies to retailers: IKEA resumed expansion in Russia outside Moscow in 2011 after clearing the bureaucratic bottlenecks.[262]

While multinational retailers have grown increasingly active in developing and emerging countries, they continue to pursue growth opportunities in developed ones. For example, Target, which presently operates stores only in the United States, bought real estate in Canada in 2011 that will allow it to open 100 to 150 stores there in 2013 and 2014.[263] Target believes its high brand recognition among Canadians will enable it to succeed there; the company's research showed that 10 percent of Canadians shopped at Target stores in the United States in 2010.[264]

Japan's Fast Retailing opened two of its Uniqlo apparel stores in New York City in 2011 as part of an aggressive plan to grow around the world. The company seeks to fill a niche for basics such as T-shirts and sweaters that are well-made and stylish but affordable.[265]

Trade Trends

Affiliate Transactions

U.S.-owned foreign affiliates supplied retail services (box 6.2) worth an estimated $67.9 billion in 2009, an increase of 4.6 percent over the previous year, but a sharp slowdown from growth of nearly 11 percent in 2008 (figure 6.2).[266] This slowing of growth reflects the broader slowdown of retail sales in developed countries in 2009. Countries in this group are some of the United States' most important foreign markets, including Canada, which accounted for 27.9 percent of U.S. retailers' services supplied via affiliates in 2009. Other leading markets include the United Kingdom, Japan, and Germany (figure 6.3).[267]

BOX 6.2. UNDERSTANDING BEA DATA ON RETAIL SERVICES

For its statistics on affiliate sales in the retail industry, the BEA examines the full range of industry segments, including general merchandise stores; stores specializing in specific merchandise categories (e.g., furniture, electronics, clothing, and sporting goods); and non-store retailers (e.g., telemarketers, online retailers, and vending machine operators). The BEA does not report separate data for cross-border supply of retailing services via e- commerce ("Mode 1" trade under the GATS). Instead, the value of such services is subsumed within the data for merchandise imports and exports.[a] Retail purchases by consumers outside their home country ("Mode 2" trade under the GATS) are counted within BEA's travel accounts, but are not disaggregated from other types of travel expenditures.

In 2008, the BEA introduced a major change in the way it calculates affiliate transactions in retail services, and revised its estimates of such transactions beginning in 2002 for foreign-owned affiliates and 2004 for U.S.-owned affiliates. Previously, the BEA reported only retailers' "sales of services," which included secondary services sold at an explicit price (e.g., an electronics retailer's sales of repair services) but not service attributes whose prices are usually bundled into the price of merchandise (e.g., customer service, the assortment of goods offered, and information about the goods).[b] For the revised measure, the BEA collects data on retail affiliates' sales, cost of goods sold, and beginning- and end-of-year inventories. It then calculates trade margins that capture the value of retail services associated with merchandise sales.[c] These adjustments led to a significant increase in BEA's estimates of affiliate activity in the retailing industry. To understand why, one can return to the example of electronics retailers: instead of simply reflecting their sales of specific services, the data now incorporate a portion of every merchandise transaction as retailing "services supplied."

[a] Borga, "Improved Measures of U.S. International Services," March 2, 2008, 24–25.
[b] Borga, "Supplemental Estimates of Insurance, Trade Services, and Financial Services," October 2007, 109–110.
[c] BEA representative, e-mail message to USITC staff, February 22, 2010. Data from the U.S. Census Bureau is used to calculate margins in instances where the requisite data are not available from BEA's surveys.

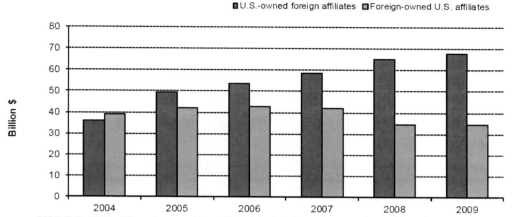

Sources: USDOC, BEA, "Supplemental Detail: Table 9;" "Supplemental Detail: Table 10;" "Table 9;" "Table 10."

Figure 6.2. Retail services: Services supplied by U.S.-owned foreign affiliates grew faster than retailing services supplied by foreign-owned U.S. affiliates in recent years.

Canada has long been a leading foreign destination for U.S. retailers because of its proximity and its cultural and economic ties to the United States, but its share of affiliate sales has dropped since 2007, when it had 30.8 percent of U.S.-owned retailers' affiliate sales. This reflects the increasing importance of emerging markets such as Brazil, China, and Mexico to U.S. retailers (see "Competitive Conditions" in this section). In Brazil and China, U.S. retailers face strong competition from domestic retailers and multinationals from other countries. For example, in Brazil, Walmart competes in the grocery market with France's Carrefour and Casino, the Netherlands' Makro, Chile's Cencosud, and the domestic retail cooperative Coop. In China, U.S. retailers across market segments (e.g., grocery, apparel, electronics, and home improvement) compete with firms from a variety of European and Asian countries as well as domestic firms. In contrast, U.S. multinational retailers face less competition from other multinationals in Mexico, where they enjoy the advantages of proximity and the two countries' extensive commercial links. Walmart, Best Buy, and The Home Depot are among the prominent U.S. retail chains active in the Mexican market.[268]

U.S. firms have dedicated an increasing amount of capital to retail operations abroad over the past decade. U.S. direct investment abroad in retailing more than doubled between 2000 and 2010, growing from $23.6 billion to $52.8 billion. The growth of non-store retailing operations abroad was particularly striking: direct investment in such businesses grew twentyfold over the period, and equaled 45 percent of all U.S. direct investment in retailing in 2010, compared to 5 percent in 2000.[269] The rapid growth of nonstore retailers likely reflects the international expansion of online retailers such as Amazon.com, which had "fulfillment centers" and other physical facilities in 14 countries outside the United States as of January 2012 (see "Competitive Conditions").[270]

Foreign firms' retail affiliates in the United States supplied services worth $34.4 billion in 2009, a decline of 0.2 percent over 2008. This was the third consecutive year in which foreign retailers' U.S. affiliate sales fell, although the drop was far less steep than the 18.2 percent decline in 2008. These declines in services supplied did not coincide with a decrease in foreign direct investment in the U.S. retail industry: after dropping slightly in 2007, foreign firms' direct investment positions rose in each subsequent year through 2009.[271] This suggests that the decline in services supplied was due to sluggish sales rather than a lessening of foreign firms' interest in the United States.

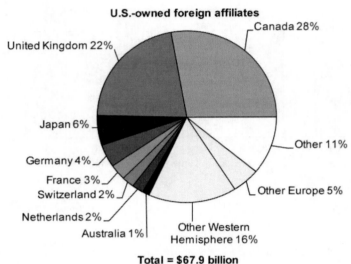

Total = $67.9 billion

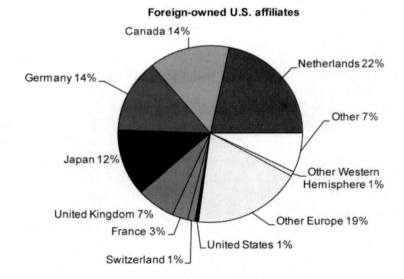

Total = $34.4 billion

Source: USDOC, BEA, *Survey of Current Business*, October 2011, 54 and 56, tables 9.2 and 10.2.
Note: Geographic regions are shaded in yellow. Figures may not total 100 percent due to rounding. These graphs show ownership by ultimate beneficial owner of affiliates. Unlike the foreign parent, the ultimate beneficial owner of a U.S. affiliate may be located in the United States.

Figure 6.3. Retail services: Canada and the United Kingdom accounted for nearly half of the retailing services supplied by U.S.-owned foreign affiliates in 2009, while more than one-fifth of all retailing services supplied by foreign-owned U.S. affiliates in 2009 involved affiliates from the Netherlands.

U.S. affiliates of Europe-based retailers accounted for 65 percent of the sales of U.S. affiliates of foreign firms in 2009. European firms own numerous grocery chains in the United States: for example, the Netherlands' Ahold owns Stop & Shop and Giant, Germany's Aldi owns the U.S. supermarket chain of the same name, and the United Kingdom's Tesco owns Fresh & Easy. However, Europe's share of affiliate sales is down slightly from 2006, when it was 70 percent. Over the same period, Japan's share increased from 7 percent to 12 percent. The Japanese company Seven & i Holdings controls one of the United States' largest convenience store chains, 7-Eleven.[272]

Nontariff Measures Affecting Trade

Most measures that explicitly restrict foreign participation in the retail industry are targeted at the establishment of "commercial presence" in the form of brick-and-mortar stores, or "Mode 3" trade under the GATS. While few countries fully prohibit foreign participation in some or all retail segments, there is a notable exception: India, which does not allow foreign direct investment in establishments selling more than one brand of merchandise. This restriction has prevented multinational operators of general merchandise stores, such as Walmart and Carrefour, from establishing retail outlets in the country.[273]

Several other countries restrict foreign ownership in retailing without banning it outright. For example, Malaysia caps foreign ownership at 70 percent, while Saudi Arabia limits it to 75 percent. In Thailand, foreign ownership is not permitted in retail investments under 100 million baht ($3.1 million) unless special permission is granted.[274] Vietnam allows 100 percent ownership of retail businesses, but all requests to build stores after the first outlet are subject to an "economic needs test" with unclear criteria.[275]

Most Organisation for Economic Co-operation and Development (OECD) countries do not explicitly ban foreign participation in retail, but many of these countries have regulations that may affect foreigners' willingness to invest, such as restrictions on the hours or days that stores may be open, permitting processes that are more burdensome for larger stores, and limitations on the times when discounts may be offered. For example, in France, openings on Sundays are limited, proposed stores over 1,000 square meters in surface area require special authorization, and sales may take place only at certain times of year.[276]

Retailing is underrepresented in countries' multilateral trade commitments. As of January 2008, 54 WTO members had made commitments in retail services.[277] The majority of these commitments contain no limits on market access and national treatment,[278] but some of the countries with the most notable barriers to foreign activity (e.g., India) have not made retailing commitments. In light of the prolonged impasse in the WTO's Doha Round of trade negotiations, the organization's most fruitful avenue for liberalization has arguably been the accession process: every new member since the Kyrgyz Republic (which acceded in December 1998) has made commitments in retailing, with the exception of Samoa.[279] While some of these countries allowed some foreign direct investment in retailing before accession, their GATS commitments gave investors more certainty that such policies would remain in place.

In some instances, countries have made commitments on retailing in their bilateral and regional trade agreements that are more liberal than their WTO commitments. One recent example is the United States-Panama Trade Promotion Agreement, signed by President

Obama in October 2011. Panama has a general ban on foreign participation in retailing, but this agreement creates an exception for U.S. retailers.[280]

Outlook

Industry observers suggest that growth conditions in the global retailing industry are likely to remain more challenging in developed than developing countries in the near future, with conditions particularly difficult in Western Europe.[281] In the largest retail markets in that region (France, Germany, Italy, and the United Kingdom), the International Monetary Fund projects slow economic growth or declines and little change in unemployment in 2012,[282] which will likely continue to depress consumer confidence and spending.

Analysts project that U.S. retail sales will grow more slowly in 2012 than in 2011, but faster than in Western Europe, due in part to economic growth that is expected to exceed that in the large Western European countries.[283] Higher-income Americans are expected to support healthy sales among luxury retailers, while discounters will benefit from shoppers with strained budgets hunting for bargains.[284]

Retailers will continue to focus on growing sales in developing and emerging countries in 2012, particularly in China. The luxury market there is expected to continue growing robustly.[285] Multinational retailers' interest in India may depend on whether the government loosens its restrictions on foreign direct investment. In Brazil, slower economic growth in 2011 may lead to slower retail sales going forward, although some observers believe that policy measures such as a minimum wage increase and relaxed credit regulations will support consumer spending in 2012.[286]

Mobile devices are expected to continue growing in importance as channels for retail sales in the coming years, as the use of smartphones and tablet computers increases in developed and developing countries alike.[287] Continued economic weakness in developed countries may also boost mobile commerce, as customers seek to find the best deals using their mobile devices.[288]

SECTION 7. SECURITIES SERVICES

SUMMARY

Roughly half of all transactions in global securities markets take place in the United States, and U.S. securities firms dominate in the provision of securities trading and investment banking services around the world. During the first nine months of 2011, U.S. firms occupied the top four positions in the global rankings of fees earned from investment banking activities.[289] Investment banking revenues are generally correlated with growth in the global economy as well as company share prices.[290] While the global bond markets are suffering the effects of uncertainty over European sovereign debt, and equity markets continue to struggle to make long-term gains due to low investor confidence, somewhat higher levels of corporate lending and merger and acquisition (M&A) activity are underpinning demand for securities services.[291]

Regulatory authorities around the world continue to make progress towards establishing tighter regulatory regimes, but uncertainty about future regulation may also dampen financial services innovation.[292]

Large volumes of securities and securities-related services are traded between countries with well- established financial centers, such as the United States, the United Kingdom, Japan, and Switzerland, where there are large issuer and investor bases as well as active derivatives markets. In 2008–10, the United States consistently achieved a trade surplus in securities-related services.

Introduction

Securities are financial instruments—e.g., stocks and shares in companies and government as well as corporate bonds—that may be bought and sold in various capital markets. They are the means by which capital is transferred from savers to users of capital. A variety of services exist to manage and trade in these essential financial tools, including investment banking (mainly debt and equity underwriting and financial advisory services, especially for M&A activity), securities dealing and brokering, proprietary trading, and asset management services. Investment banks broker and make markets in securities of all types, including derivative securities. As corporate finance advisors, investment banks help companies raise capital by underwriting equity or debt issues, locating potential private equity investors, and arranging M&A transactions. Before the impact of new regulation in recent years, investment banks also earned significant profits by investing their own equity capital (so-called "proprietary trading"). Asset management firms are fund managers for institutional investors such as pension funds and insurance companies, as well as for individuals seeking to invest their savings in mutual funds and other savings vehicles that enable them to access global stock and bond markets.

Securities-related services are often provided by intermediaries between securities issuers (companies, governments, and state-owned enterprises) and securities investors (individuals and institutional investors, such as mutual funds, pension funds, and insurance companies). The major providers of these services are large global investment banks such as Goldman Sachs, Morgan Stanley, and J.P. Morgan, although the industry also comprises many smaller firms and is only moderately concentrated.[293] Given the high volatility of earnings in this industry, many firms are part of larger "universal banks" that also provide commercial banking and/or retail banking services. Examples include Bank of America Merrill Lynch and Citigroup in the United States, and UBS, Deutsche Bank, and Barclays abroad. The main consumers of core investment banking services are industrial and natural resource companies, insurance companies, pension funds and other institutional investors, and government and municipal agencies, while small businesses and private individuals use the portfolio management services provided by investment banks' asset management arms.

In 2011, about half of global investment banking revenue was generated in the United States, about 30 percent in Europe, about 10 percent in Asian developed markets, and the remaining 10 percent in emerging economies.[294] This geographic breakdown of investment banking revenue reflects the relative size of financial markets around the world. For example, the total assets of mutual funds (important investment and savings avenues for individuals) under management in the United States represented 48 percent of the global total at the end of 2010, while 32 percent of the total was under management in Europe and 20 percent was under management in the rest of the world.[295] Looking at trading volumes in global equity markets, the breakdown is similar: in 2010, trading in U.S. stocks accounted for 48 percent of global equity market trading volume, Japanese trading accounted for 7 percent, UK trading accounted for 5 percent, and other developed markets accounted for 20 percent, with 21 percent of global equity market trading taking place in emerging markets.[296]

Competitive Conditions in the Global Securities Services Market

The 2008 financial crisis was a watershed for the securities industry, resulting in significant industry consolidation and government intervention. The subprime-mortgage crisis in the United States and the banking crisis in Europe caused investors to lose confidence and global securities markets to fall sharply.[297] Investors withdrew funds from capital markets around the world, making it difficult for banks and companies to refinance or replace capital lost from write-downs of asset values. The ensuing global economic downturn brought most corporate finance transactions to a near halt as equity valuations suffered from falls in share prices. Derivatives trading also contracted sharply with the collapse of the mortgage-backed securities market.[298] As investment banks' balance-sheet risks grew to unsustainable levels, the industry consolidated; for example, J.P. Morgan Chase took over Bear Stearns, Merrill Lynch was acquired by Bank of America, and, after its collapse, Lehman Brothers' U.S. and foreign operations were acquired by Barclays and Nomura.[299]

The U.S. government stabilized the financial system by using the Troubled Asset Relief Program to purchase deeply discounted assets from banks, thereby shoring up their balance sheets.[300] Although the U.S. monetary authorities allowed Lehman Brothers to fail and orchestrated the acquisition of other investment firms by healthier banks, significant support was extended by the U.S. government to several of the largest U.S. banks, such as Bank of America and Citibank.[301] At the same time, in Europe, several governments also assumed ownership stakes in some of their largest financial institutions, and in Japan, the government launched a large asset-relief program to bolster its banking system.[302]

Both revenues and profits of securities firms around the world plummeted in 2008, and the industry has recovered only slightly in the years since. Before the crisis, investment banks typically achieved a return on equity[303] of around 20 percent, but in the current market environment these rates have been roughly halved as banks have increased their equity capital and reduced their leverage.[304] Investment banking fee revenue rose in 2010, but fell back in 2011 to $81 billion worldwide, close to the 2005 level (figure 7.1).[305]

Reflecting the United States' large share of the global investment banking market, U.S. firms dominate in global rankings of investment banks by fees received (table 7.1). In the Americas,[306] the five largest U.S. investment banks (J.P. Morgan, Bank of America Merrill Lynch, Morgan Stanley, Goldman Sachs, and Citibank) earned 35 percent of total fees in 2011, and smaller top-20 U.S. firms accounted for another 5 percent of total fee earnings.[307] U.S. investment banks also have significant revenue and market share in most capital markets outside the United States, after expanding internationally in recent years.

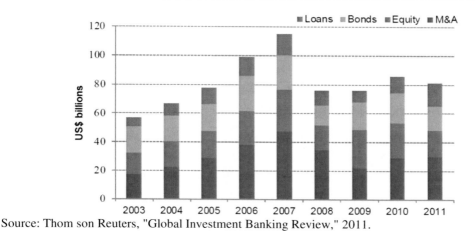

Source: Thom son Reuters, "Global Investment Banking Review," 2011.

Figure 7.1. Securities services: Global investment banking fees remain below their 2007 peak.

Table 7.1. Global investment banking: Top banks, 2011

Rank	Firm	Country	Fees (million $)	Market share (percent)
1	J.P. Morgan	United States	5,467	6.8
2	Bank of America Merrill Lynch	United States	4,925	6.1
3	Morgan Stanley	United States	4,104	5.1
4	Goldman Sachs & Co.	United States	3,981	4.9
5	Credit Suisse	Switzerland	3,429	4.2
6	Citi	United States	3,310	4.1
7	Deutsche Bank AG	Germany	3,224	4.0
8	Barclays Capital	United Kingdom	2,843	3.5
9	UBS	Switzerland	2,387	2.9
10	Wells Fargo & Co.	United States	1,576	1.9
11	RBC Capital Markets	Canada	1,438	1.8
12	BNP Paribas SA	France	1,424	1.8
13	HSBC Holdings PLC	United Kingdom	1,274	1.6
14	RBS	United Kingdom	1,228	1.5
15	Mizuho Financial Group	Japan	964	1.2

Source: Thomson Reuters, "Global Investment Banking Review," 2011, 5.

The five major firms generate up to half of their revenue outside the United States,[308] with a 20 percent market share in Europe, a 17 percent market share in Japan, and a 13 percent market share in the Asia-Pacific region excluding Japan. However, in geographic regions with strong, well-established financial sectors, local banks usually play the largest role. In Europe, Deutsche Bank is ranked first, and together the top 20 ranked European firms earned 39 percent of total fees in 2011. In Japan, Japanese banks dominate even more noticeably, with those in the top 20 earning almost two-thirds of total fees in 2011.[309]

Demand and Supply Factors

Emerging Markets' Demand for Securities Services Is Growing, While Demand for Securities Services in Developed Markets Is Likely to Remain Constrained

Foreign and domestic investors and corporations operating in emerging markets are underpinning worldwide demand for securities services, and global investment banks are looking to these markets for future revenue growth.[310] The significant business opportunities for global investment banks in emerging economies are illustrated by the fact that financial markets in these countries have grown faster than the countries' GDPs in recent years. Between 2005 and 2010, while nominal GDP roughly doubled in emerging markets, mutual funds and equity market capitalization both tripled, and contracts traded on derivatives exchanges increased fivefold. Domestic bond issuance and borrowing from international banks also doubled over the period.[311]

Many multinational companies see opportunities for new business in emerging markets, where there is relatively strong economic growth and significant ongoing investment in new infrastructure. They are moving to increase their presence in these markets by setting up local affiliates or acquiring local enterprises. In a recent survey, 81 percent of industrial company respondents said that expanding their geographical presence would be their primary rationale for M&A transactions in 2012, and close to two-thirds list Latin America, China, and India as the most attractive regions for corporate growth.[312] These activities require corporate finance advisory services, such as advising on negotiations with potential local partners, assisting in the establishment of local affiliates or joint ventures, and raising capital. Leading investment banks also see opportunities in emerging markets to help introduce foreign investment funding to local projects. For example, Morgan Stanley Infrastructure Partners (one of the U.S. investment bank's private equity arms) is reportedly in talks to invest in road projects in India, where the government has undertaken an ambitious highway development program.[313]

Global investment banks have expanded in major emerging economies such as China, India, and Brazil in order to increase their participation in those countries' domestic securities markets as well as to assist global companies making cross-border transactions. In China, where foreign investment banks operate through minority stakes in joint ventures, UBS, Goldman Sachs, and Deutsche Bank are the leading foreign firms, although their combined share of the domestic capital markets business remains limited.[314] Foreign investment banks provide a range of services to the Chinese market, such as share brokerage, corporate finance advice, foreign exchange, commodities and derivatives trading, debt underwriting, and asset management.[315] For example, foreign firms' investment management arms are doing more business in China as affluent Chinese increasingly shift their savings from property and cash into wealth management products.[316] In India, where foreign banks' rupee-denominated assets are relatively limited, foreign banks have concentrated on providing securities services, where they have a comparative advantage; foreign banks have roughly a 60 to 75 percent market share in M&A and in sales and trading in equity capital markets products.[317] In both China and India, however, the domestic bond market is restricted and relatively undeveloped, implying that securities firms are limited in their ability to provide debt capital markets products (such as interest rate swaps).[318]

At the same time, demand for securities services in developed markets is likely to remain constrained by the slow global economic recovery and high levels of individual debt. Core activities such as underwriting, M&A advice, and the arrangement of initial public offerings are now only beginning to recover from the lows seen in 2008–09 as investor confidence remains weak and capital for underwriting new deals remains restricted.[319] Companies that might normally need securities services in the course of investing and expanding their business are still wary of increasing their risk exposure and are therefore hoarding cash. Individuals' concerns about unemployment and high indebtedness are restricting demand for mortgages, which in turn reduces activity in the markets for mortgage-backed securities. However, not all securities services were affected by the downturn in the same way. For example, even in the midst of the financial crisis, securities brokerage activity (in which investment banks' fees are related to the number and size of securities trades) did not decline like other investment banking activities because the extreme volatility in bond and share prices led to a high volume of transactions.[320]

Investment Banks Are Scaling Back Product Offerings in Capital Markets and Increasing Provision of Investment Management Services

The European sovereign debt crisis, increased regulation, and the need to recapitalize their balance sheets has led many investment banks to scale back their product offerings in capital markets (such as debt securitizations) and to provide more investment management services instead. Because wealth managers trade on behalf of their clients and do not own the securities portfolios under management, regulators do not require securities firms to back up this activity by allocating large amounts of reserve capital to it. In contrast, investment banks have to reserve significant amounts of capital to support share underwriting, corporate lending, or sales and trading of equities, bonds, and derivatives, as these activities involve holding large trading positions in the normal course of business. When banks refocus their business away from trading and towards wealth management, they reduce risk and bolster their capital base.[321]

As global stock prices recovered after 2009, asset management activities provided a growing source of revenue for firms. Fees charged for asset management services are typically a percentage of the value of assets under management, so firms' revenues from this activity increase when asset prices (especially share prices) rise overall.[322] In 2010, an increase in performance fees earned by financial management firms likely explains the higher receipts for management and advisory services seen in the U.S. data on cross- border trade in financial services.[323]

Since 2010, the rate of asset write-downs by banks has slowed and bank balance sheets have strengthened (often with government help). However, in countries which are recovering from a sharp collapse in property prices, banks have limited ability to make new loans because of the increase in capital they need to reserve, owing to the overhang of property assets in a "negative equity" or "underwater" position (in which the outstanding balance on the loan exceeds the value of the property).[324] At the same time, due to the Eurozone crisis, many European banks holding sovereign debt obligations have seen these assets fall sharply in value despite the European Union's rescue packages for Greece, Ireland, and Portugal. As a result, European banks have been lowering risk exposure and preserving capital by reducing their sovereign and interbank lending, which has led to tighter credit markets both locally and around the world.[325]

Stronger Regulatory Oversight Is Being Implemented Around the World, Increasing the Cost of Capital for Securities Firms

Global regulators are carrying out a wide range of banking sector reforms as they try to reduce systemic risks to the world financial system, limit the chances of a major financial institution failing, and protect governments from having to bail out such institutions if they do fail. For example, regulators are tightening capital requirements, which prescribe the amount of capital that financial institutions must hold for a given level of risk exposure. The cornerstone of this effort is a new market-risk framework issued by the Basel Committee on Banking Supervision, known as "Basel III," which doubles or triples regulatory capital requirements for many securities market activities. Other important measures include higher charges for counterparty credit risk and more stringent liquidity and funding requirements.[326]

The Group of Twenty (G20) nations agreed to the Basel Committee's proposals in November 2010. These countries have made concurrent efforts at the national and regional levels. The United States' Dodd-Frank Act of 2010[327] tightened minimum capital requirements for all major banks and securities firms (box 7.1), and the EU's Capital Requirement Directive, along with national proposals from the Swiss government, the UK's Independent Commission on Banking, and others, made similar reforms. It is still unclear exactly how these national regulations will interact with the phase-in of the Basel III regime, but the United States and other G20 countries are coordinating their reform efforts.[328] Nevertheless, the reform process is complex and will take years to complete, during which time there will be uncertainty about the details and implementation of the new rules.[329]

BOX 7.1. THE DODD-FRANK ACT OF 2010 FUNDAMENTALLY REDEFINED FINANCIAL REGULATION IN THE UNITED STATES

The Dodd-Frank Wall Street Reform and Consumer Protection Act (Dodd-Frank Act) was signed into law on July 21, 2010, and implementation of its regulations, policies, and guidance is ongoing. It includes several measures of "macro-prudential regulation"—rules aimed at reducing overall risk to the financial system and therefore the risk of another severe disruption to the economy. Financial institutions identified as large enough to have systemic influence are subject to tighter supervision by the Federal Reserve Board and stricter risk-based capital and liquidity requirements, as well as new limits on leverage.[a] Among other things, these measures attempt to establish an orderly process for a nonbank financial institution, such as an investment bank, to be wound up in the case of bankruptcy, thus removing the moral hazard problem of being "too big to fail."

The Dodd-Frank Act also increases regulation and supervision of individual firms in order to prevent excessive risk taking. The new rules for securitizations require that the originating bank retain a percentage of the underlying assets (with the exact percentage being related to the quality of the underlying asset) to ensure that originators have "skin in the game."[b] The so-called Volcker Rule prohibits (with some exceptions) depository institutions from engaging in proprietary trading—that is, taking speculative market positions for the bank's own account and not for the benefit of clients—or from investing in a hedge fund or private equity fund.[c] This is a return to the policy of putting constraints on what activities banks may undertake, embodied in the Glass-Steagall Act of 1933 until the law was reinterpreted in 1996–97 and then repealed in 1999.

In another set of measures designed to limit trading risks, the Dodd-Frank Act increases regulation of derivatives trading. In order to increase transparency in the market, trading in many derivatives will now be subject to mandatory clearing through regulated exchanges.[d] Also, "over-the counter" (OTC) derivatives will be regulated for the first time and will have new reporting and registration requirements.

[a] Webel, "The Dodd-Frank Wall Street Reform and Consumer Protection Act," July 29, 2010, 1.

[b] The bank which first extends the loans being securitized remains exposed to some extent to the risk of nonpayment by the borrowers. Webel, "The Dodd-Frank Wall Street Reform and Consumer Protection Act," July 29, 2010, 8.

[c] Federal Reserve Bank of Philadelphia, "The Proposed Implementation of the Volcker Rule," 2011, 2; Ryan, "Financial Services Regulatory Highlights," 2010, 5. This idea was originally proposed by former U.S. Federal Reserve Chairman Paul Volcker.

[d] Ryan, "Financial Services Regulatory Highlights," 2010, 4; PricewaterhouseCoopers, "A Closer Look," July 2011, 2.

These higher capital requirements and liquidity ratios may limit the future profitability of firms' trading activities, especially trading in longer-maturity instruments such as bonds and asset-backed debt securitizations.[330] One study points to higher capital costs from new regulations as the chief factor reducing profit in securities business activities. Certain investment banking activities, such as structured credit and interest-rate derivatives trading, are likely to be particularly affected, as these activities require that more capital be set aside for them than for stockbroking or fund management. As a result, securities firms may decide to scale back on providing these types of products.[331] Most firms are already adopting a more conservative approach to lending and trading, holding more capital relative to their risk exposures, even though many of the new minimum capital guidelines have not yet been finalized. This may help to explain the fall in profits experienced by securities firms in 2011.[332] Over time, the prospect of lower profitability may discourage new suppliers from entering the industry.

Besides launching stricter capital requirements, both U.S. and European regulators are introducing regulations aimed at making trading in derivatives markets more transparent and orderly. Derivatives are financial instruments whose value reflects that of an underlying security (such as a U.S. Treasury bond, company share, or mortgage-backed security), or another financial price (such as an interest rate or spot foreign exchange rate). Credit derivatives are contracts that transfer credit risk, for example by promising a payment in case of a loan default or other credit event.[333] In the years leading up to the financial crisis, derivatives markets grew rapidly but were opaque and largely unregulated. One lesson learned by national regulators during the crisis was that the risks associated with complex, structured financial products were far greater than market participants had supposed.[334] As a result, regulatory authorities in several countries are now putting new rules into effect to discourage securities firms from developing or holding large amounts of complex, difficult-to-value derivatives.

Like the United States, the EU is increasing derivatives regulation in order to reduce systemic risks, via the mandatory clearing requirements imposed by the European Markets Infrastructure Regulation. In late 2011, the European Commission amended and extended the Markets in Financial Instruments Directive (MiFID). Under the proposed new regulations

("MiFID II"), trading of many types of derivative contracts will now have to go through central clearing via an exchange, instead of through two-party OTC trades in which many parties are indirectly exposed to the risk of default of other market participants.[335] The new derivatives trading regulations are likely to force a major change in the business model adopted by securities firms because a central clearing structure implies higher liquidity and funding costs, as well as lower profit margins from reduced trading opportunities.[336] These developments will affect all the major global investment banks, as they all have large trading operations in London and elsewhere in Europe.[337]

Additionally, some governments have restricted the types of activities in which deposit-taking financial institutions may engage, to keep retail and commercial banking services from being damaged by volatility in a bank's capital markets businesses. Efforts in the United States to separate securities trading and traditional banking activities (using the "Volcker Rule" discussed in box 7.1) are being mirrored abroad, although the methods of implementation differ.[338] For example, the UK Independent Commission on Banking has proposed a system to "ring-fence" the activities of retail and commercial banks—i.e., separate them from investment banking activities—in order to protect deposit-taking banks from being bankrupted by the failure of their investment banking subsidiaries.

These measures imply that investment banks in the United Kingdom, including wholly owned subsidiaries of large universal banks, will not enjoy the tacit guarantee of government support they relied on previously.[339] Switzerland has addressed the issue in a different way, by imposing capital requirements on Swiss banks substantially above internationally agreed minimums, rather than changing the structure or permissible activities of Swiss banks.[340] As a result, with government encouragement, both UBS and Credit Suisse, which are based in Switzerland, plan to reduce their exposure to risk by scaling back their investment banking operations and focusing more on wealth management.[341]

Trade Trends

Cross-border Trade

Although the global financial crisis and the ensuing economic downturn caused cross-border trade in financial services to contract sharply, over the past several years the United States has consistently had a large trade surplus in securities-related services and in securities themselves (box 7.2). In 2010, the United States exported $15.5 billion of securities transaction services (including brokerage, underwriting, and private placement services) and $27.9 billion of management and advisory services (including asset management, financial advisory, and custody services), totaling $43.4 billion of securities services exports (figure 7.2).[342] The United States imported $4.0 billion of transaction services and $4.1 billion of management and advisory services in 2010, totaling $8.1 billion of securities services imports. Cross-border trade in securities services in 2010 yielded a $35.4 billion surplus.

Both exports and imports of securities services jumped in 2007 before declining in 2008 and 2009. Securities services imports continued to fall in 2010, declining 10 percent, while securities services exports rose 7 percent. These latest year-on-year changes may be compared to a 2006–09 CAGR of 5 percent for exports and 1 percent for imports.[343]

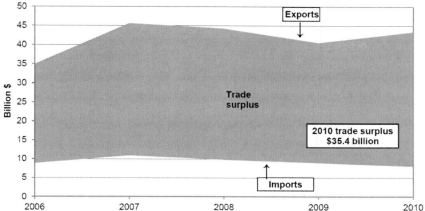

Source: USDOC, BEA, *Survey of Current Business*, October 2011, 20–21, tables G and H, USDOC, BEA, *Survey of Current Business*, October 2010, 25–25, tables G and H, and USDOC, BEA, *Survey of Current Business*, October 2009, 31–32, tables E and F.

Figure 7.2. Securities services: U.S. cross-border trade in securities services resulted in a U.S. trade surplus each year during 2006–10.

BOX 7.2. UNDERSTANDING DATA ON CROSS-BORDER TRADE AND AFFILIATE TRANSACTIONS IN SECURITIES SERVICES

BEA data on cross-border trade in securities services are included in its "financial services" category. The financial services data are broken down into four subcategories: (1) securities transactions services, including brokerage services and underwriting and private placement services; (2) management and advisory services, including financial management services and financial advisory and custody services; (3) credit card and other credit-related services (such as the provision of standby letters of credit for trade financing); and (4) other financial services, including securities lending and electronic funds transfer.[a] These data exclude both deposit-taking and lending services. Although there is some overlap between securities services and banking services in these data, subcategories 1 and 2 likely comprise predominantly securities services, as these include the traditional investment banking functions of broking, dealing, and underwriting, while subcategories 3 and 4 likely comprise predominantly banking services. Data on total U.S. imports and exports of these services, whether between unrelated parties or between affiliates in a single corporate group, are available beginning in 2006 (older statistics reflect unaffiliated trade only).[b] However, in its reporting of U.S. exports and imports by country, the BEA combines the four subcategories into a single category of "financial services," itself a component of the larger category "Other Private Services" in the International Services Accounts. The BEA captures this data largely through mandatory quarterly and benchmark surveys of business services, supplemented by survey data from U.S. government agencies, private sector sources, and BEA estimates.[c]

In addition, the BEA publishes data on financial services (excluding insurance) supplied abroad through foreign affiliates of U.S. majority-owned groups and financial services supplied in the United States by affiliates of foreign-owned corporations.

For financial services, as for many other services, direct investment in local affiliates represents a significant avenue for sales in foreign markets. The BEA data include revised measures for sales of bank affiliates starting in 2004. The data include sales by, and purchases from, entities that primarily provide nondepository credit intermediation and related services; securities, commodity contracts, and other intermediation, and related activities; and funds, trusts, and other financial vehicles. Country breakdowns are provided for the financial services category, but the data do not distinguish securities-related services from banking services.[d]

The U.S. Treasury reports data on international trade in securities, which give insight into the likely volume of services provided in order to execute these transactions. The U.S. Treasury's Treasury International Capital (TIC) data reporting system measures gross U.S. purchases of foreign long-term securities (government and corporate bonds and company stocks) and gross foreign purchases of U.S. long-term securities, in terms of the market value of portfolio holdings. Specifically, the TIC system records monthly and quarterly cross-border data as reported by banks and broker dealers, annual surveys of cross-border holdings of short- and long-term securities, and quarterly positional data reported by other financial institutions.[e]

[a] USDOC, BEA, *Survey of Current Business*, October 2009, 31.
[b] USDOC, BEA, *Survey of Current Business*, February 2010, 44.
[c] Ibid.
[d] USDOC, BEA, *Survey of Current Business*, October 2009, 37–38.
[e] Bertaut, "Understanding U.S. Cross-Border Securities Data," 2006, A60; U.S. Treasury, "U.S. Transactions with Foreigners in Long-Term Securities by Type and Country," n.d. (accessed January 19, 2012).

The trends in international trade in securities services move in parallel with the pattern of cross-border purchases of long-term securities,[344] although trade in securities demonstrates a markedly higher volatility. Because investment banks (or the capital markets arms of larger, universal banks) play an intermediary role, providing market liquidity and facilitating the transfer of securities between buyers and sellers, their revenue from the provision of dealing and brokerage services is related to the volume of securities transactions. The value of securities services provided cross-border is therefore likely to be related to the volume of cross-border securities transactions, although the value of the services will be only a small percentage of the transaction value. As data on securities traded cross-border are captured much more quickly than services trade data—the U.S. Treasury's TIC data is released each month for the prior month—this provides the most timely indication of trends in the trade of securities services. As mentioned above, the United States has maintained a surplus in securities trade, and therefore securities services trade, over a long period, although this surplus has narrowed recently to its lowest level in the 2005–11 period (figure 7.3). Foreign net purchases of U.S. long-term securities totaled $908 billion in 2010, moving in the direction of the highs seen in 2005–07, but then fell back in 2011 to $445 billion. Net purchases of foreign securities by U.S. investors decreased to $115 billion in 2010 from $187 billion in 2009, and fell further in 2011 to $58 billion. However, the total value of securities traded cross-border recovered to $70 trillion in 2011, up significantly from the 2009 level of $51 trillion, but still below the 2008 peak of $76 trillion.[345]

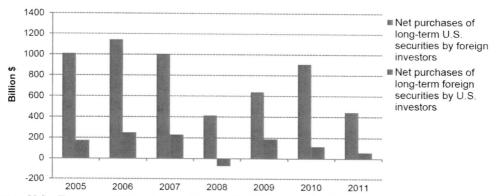

Source: U.S. Treasury, "U.S. Transactions with Foreigners in Long-term Domestic and Foreign Securities," n.d. (accessed January 19, 2012).

Figure 7.3. Securities services: The U.S. showed a cross-border trade surplus in purchases of long-term securities during 2005–11.

Large volumes of securities and securities-related services are traded between countries with well-established financial centers, large issuer and investor bases, and active derivatives markets, such as the United States, the United Kingdom, France, Japan, and Switzerland. Small-economy countries with major financial sectors, such as the Cayman Islands, Bermuda, Luxembourg, and Ireland, also figure prominently because, as in the United Kingdom, financial institutions in these locations often play a custodial role for third-country purchases of U.S. securities.[346] The United Kingdom also has a long history of direct investment in the United States and plays a leading role in the global insurance industry.[347] These factors help to explain why in 2009–10 the United Kingdom had the largest share of international activity in U.S. equities, with about 14 percent of foreign gross activity in U.S. company shares, and was the leading recipient of U.S. activity in foreign equities, with over 30 percent of U.S. gross activity in foreign stocks.[348] A significant share of international trading in company shares also takes place between the United States and the Latin America and Caribbean region,[349] which is likely related to the "custodial bias" referred to above, as well as the very large reinsurance trade flows between the United States and Bermuda, and the large number of entities whose equity has been issued in offshore locations such as Bermuda and the Cayman Islands (see section 4).[350]

Affiliate Transactions

Banks provide securities and other financial services to foreign markets far more through local affiliates than through cross-border trade. Financial services, excluding insurance, supplied to foreign persons by U.S. multinational corporations (MNCs) though their majority-owned affiliates in foreign markets totaled $165.9 billion in 2009, the latest year for which data are available. This was down 5 percent from the cyclical peak in 2008, but still above prior-year totals. Growth in U.S.-owned foreign affiliate sales of financial services during 2004–08 was 23 percent on an annualized basis, illustrating the market power of U.S. investment and commercial banks. Financial services, excluding insurance, supplied to U.S. persons by U.S.-based affiliates of foreign MNCs totaled $97.0 billion in 2009, up 2 percent from the year before and the highest level achieved to date. Growth in sales of financial services of foreign-owned U.S. affiliates was 11 percent on an annualized basis during 2004–

08, before the effects of the global financial crisis were fully felt. Given the importance of London as a global financial center, especially for securities and derivatives trading, it is not surprising that close to 40 percent of U.S.- owned foreign affiliates' sales of financial services have consistently been located in the United Kingdom, with another 20 percent located in other European markets. In the U.S. market, sales of financial services (excluding insurance) by UK majority-owned affiliates represented over 30 percent of total foreign affiliate sales, with another 40 percent coming from affiliates of MNCs based in other European countries.

Nontariff Measures Affecting Trade

Around the world, providers of securities firms face barriers to cross-border and affiliate trade. The complex regulatory landscape described above represents a significant nontariff impediment to trade. Securities firms also face limits on foreign ownership and joint venture participation, visa restrictions on employees and clients, and other hindrances to doing business.

In an effort to counterbalance these measures, countries negotiate financial services liberalization on a multilateral basis at the WTO, or as part of bilateral free trade agreements. However, many also undertake liberalization efforts on a unilateral basis, motivated by the prospect of greater economic growth stemming from increased integration with global capital markets. In Europe, beginning in 2007, the MiFID allowed investment firms established in any member state to operate in all other member states, with the goal of reducing barriers to the flow of capital within the EU. The directive has reportedly increased the entry of multinational trading companies in the EU.[351]

Since 2003, the Chinese government has allowed a limited and gradual opening of the local securities markets to foreign participants through its Qualified Foreign Institutional Investor (QFII) program.[352] The QFII program enables foreign securities firms to trade in public share markets, including the domestic renminbi-denominated A-share market, public debt markets, and certain derivatives markets (for example, QFIIs are allowed to trade stock index futures as of May 4, 2011). Such trading, however, is subject to government approval, specified lock-up periods, and strict investment quotas.[353] In addition, China has started to open its markets to foreign asset management firms. In May 2011, at the annual China-U.S. Strategic and Economic Dialog summit, China promised that it would amend relevant regulations to allow qualified locally incorporated foreign banks to enjoy the same rights as domestic banks to distribute mutual funds and to obtain custody licenses for mutual funds.[354]

However, the degree of foreign participation in China's securities markets remains small.[355] Foreign investments in financial companies (except for financial leasing companies) such as banks and securities firms are categorized by the government as "restricted" and therefore subject to stricter government scrutiny and administrative requirements. "Restricted" investments may require central government approval as well as local approvals, and may be denied at the discretion of the approving authorities.[356] Finally, China limits foreign participation in joint-venture securities companies, though in May 2012 the foreign ownership cap was raised from 33 percent to 49 percent.[357]

Outlook

Increased regulatory oversight in the investment banking sector is likely to have wide-ranging effects. Investment banks' profitability will likely decline as a result of stricter regulatory capital requirements and new rules for exchange clearing of derivatives. Also, any forced separation of retail banks and investment banks will increase the cost of capital for investment banks, as they will likely suffer significant downgrades in their perceived creditworthiness with their removal from a steady deposit base.

Most countries are moving towards implementing the Basel III risk-based capital framework for banks in a reasonably well coordinated fashion. However, regulatory reform of the financial sector is not progressing evenly around the world, with some countries or regions moving more quickly than others in some areas, such as derivatives market regulation, or choosing to implement regulations in excess of the minimum guidelines agreed by the G20. Industry studies have found that both regulatory burdens and legal risk drive activity towards competing locations,[358] and banks are likely to review the physical location of their activities as well as their product mix.[359] Even where firms remain stationary, profitability might suffer if they have trouble passing on higher costs to their clients, who can easily turn to providers based in a different country with less costly regulation.[360] Regulatory arbitrage—i.e., firms' strategic response to costs imposed by regulation—is therefore an issue for all countries with major financial centers. Differences in regulatory emphasis and uneven implementation of financial reform might induce migration of certain financial activities from North America to Europe or to Asia, a development that would significantly change the pattern of global trade in securities services. Reforms are being pursued concurrently in all major financial centers, however, which suggests that a full-scale realignment in the global securities industry is not likely to take place as the result of regulatory changes alone.[361]

SECTION 8. TELECOMMUNICATION SERVICES

SUMMARY

Over the past five years, the global telecommunications market has expanded at a moderate pace, with the United States accounting for the largest share of global revenues. Wireless services held the largest share of the world market in 2010, and have been the main driver of that market's growth in recent years. The largest service providers worldwide tend to be the former incumbent telecommunication operators in Asia, Europe, and North America. In most countries, the primary basis for competition is price, although handset subsidies, product differentiation, and customer service are also important factors. Major industry trends include ongoing network construction, growing merger and acquisition activity, and cost-reduction efforts, particularly the growing use of network sharing agreements.

The United States kept its trade surplus in telecommunication services in 2010, as U.S. exports continued to exhibit strong, albeit slowing, growth.

Affiliate transactions remained the predominant mode of international trade in telecommunication services, and the value of services supplied by U.S.- owned foreign affiliates in 2009 was more than three times the value of cross-border exports of U.S. telecommunication services that year. Over the next few years, the global telecommunication services market is expected to grow steadily, driven by the global economic recovery and robust demand for high-bandwidth services. Carriers are expected to continue efforts to cut costs and streamline operations, and to boost revenue and subscriber growth through both domestic and international mergers and acquisitions.

Introduction

Telecommunication services encompass basic and value-added services. Basic telecommunication services involve the end-to-end transmission of voice or data information from senders to receivers. The most widely used basic services are landline and mobile telephone calls and Internet access services; others include facsimile (fax) services and enterprise data services.[362] Value-added telecommunication services add value to basic telecommunication services by enhancing their form or content, or by offering ways to store or retrieve information. Examples include voice mail, e-mail, online data processing, and online data storage and retrieval.[363] Subscribers can also use telephone handsets to access other value-added services, thereby increasing service providers' revenues. Common examples include short message services (text messages), multimedia message services (e.g. sending digital photographs between mobile telephone handsets), and mobile telephone Internet access services.

With the advent of "smart phones," particularly Apple's iPhone, new varieties of value-added services have emerged, aided by the development of software tools ("applications" or "apps") that are designed for use with mobile handsets. In addition to the hundreds of thousands of smart phone applications currently in existence, new apps are released almost continuously. Common applications allow users to play games, read news stories, recommend restaurants, monitor weather forecasts and stock prices, and conduct basic banking operations.

Competitive Conditions in the Global Telecommunication Services Market

The global telecommunication services market, measured by revenues derived from landline, wireless, and Internet services,[364] was valued at about $1.9 trillion in 2010. Overall, the global market grew by 5.9 percent in 2010, slightly slower than the 6.6 percent CAGR of 2005–09.[365] All three market segments (landline, wireless, and Internet) showed slowing growth or declines in 2010. Revenues in the global landline segment, for example, fell by approximately 0.4 percent in 2010, following declines of 0.2 percent and 4.1 percent in 2008 and 2009, respectively. The global landline market experienced essentially no growth during 2005–10, largely due to two factors: declining average revenue per line and shrinking subscriber numbers, both of which stem from ongoing substitution of mobile devices for fixed ones in many countries. Although the wireless segment grew by 9.3 percent in 2010, largely due to a recovery in spending tied to improvements in the global economy, this fell short of the 12 percent CAGR during 2005–09. Slower growth reflected high wireless penetration levels, which already approach or even exceed 100 percent (due to users purchasing multiple phones and Subscriber Identity Module, or SIM, cards) in many developed and developing countries. Similarly, global Internet revenues grew by 6 percent in 2010, substantially slower than the CAGR of 11 percent during 2005–09. Slowing growth in this market over the past three years, particularly in the broadband segment, stemmed from global economic weakness and increasing market maturity.[366]

The size of a country's telecommunication services market is highly correlated with its GDP, and the list of the world's top 20 markets is dominated by large economies in Asia, Europe, and North America. In 2010, the United States was the largest country market in the global telecommunication services industry, accounting for 28 percent of total global revenues. Other large telecommunication services markets included China (8 percent), Japan (5 percent), Germany (5 percent), and the United Kingdom (5 percent) (table 8.1). These five countries were also the largest telecommunication services markets in 2005. China, however, rose from fifth place to second place from 2005 to 2010, achieving a CAGR of 20 percent in its wireless services market for those years. The 10 largest country markets represented about 50 percent of the global telecommunication services market in 2010, while the 20 largest markets represented 78 percent.

Table 8.1. Telecommunication services: Top 20 global telecommunications markets, by revenue and share of global revenues, 2010

Rank	Country	Revenues (million $)	Share of global revenues (%)
1	United States	558,016	28.1
2	China	149,418	7.5
3	Japan	97,536	4.9
4	Germany	96,258	4.9
5	United Kingdom	94,296	4.0
6	Brazil	66,594	3.4
7	Italy	64,462	3.2
8	France	58,337	2.9
9	South Korea	41,144	2.1
10	Canada	40,714	2.1
11	Spain	40,038	2.0
12	India	37,302	1.9
13	Russia	36,630	1.8
14	Mexico	32,751	1.7
15	Philippines	26,184	1.3
16	Ukraine	25,568	1.3
17	Australia	23,166	1.2
18	Saudi Arabia	20,853	1.1
19	Taiwan	19,614	1.0
20	Vietnam	18,787	0.9
	Total (Top 20)	1,547,668	78.0

Source: TIA, *TIA's 2011 Market Review and Forecast*, 2011.

The largest global telecommunication service firms, measured by revenue, tend to be the former telecommunication services incumbents (holders of government monopolies) in the United States, Europe, and Asia; prominent examples include AT&T, NTT, Verizon, Deutsche Telekom, Telefónica, and France Télécom (table 8.2). Overall, the global telecommunication services industry displays a relatively low level of concentration, with the largest four companies accounting for 22 percent of total global revenues in 2010. Such low concentration stems in large part from the fragmented structure of the global telecommunication services industry, in which most telecommunication services companies earn a large share of their revenues by providing services domestically. Those carriers that operate outside their home countries tend to focus on only one or two countries, or in some cases regions. Exceptions include France Télécom and Vodafone, each of which has interests of one form or another in more than 30 countries. Other companies that operate in several regions include Etisalat (United Arab Emirates), MTN (South Africa), Saudi Telecom (Saudi Arabia), Telefónica (Spain), and Vimpelcom (Russia) (table 8.3).

Table 8.2. Telecommunication services: Top 15 global telecommunication services firms, by revenue and employees

Rank	Company	Country	Revenue (million $)	Net income (million $)	Net profit Margin (%)[a]	Employees
1	AT&T	United States	124,174	20,162	16.2	206,590
2	NTT	Japan	118,502	8,072	6.8	219,343
3	Verizon	United States	106,474	10,209	9.6	194,400
4	Deutsche Telekom	Germany	83,585	2,357	2.8	246,777
5	Telefónica	Spain	81,330	13,487	16.6	285,106
6	China Mobile	China	73,551	18,194	24.7	164,336
7	Vodafone	United Kingdom	70,148	12,031	17.2	83,862
8	France Télécom	France	60,931	5,098	8.4	161,392
9	América Móvil	Mexico	49,205	8,006	16.3	148,058
10	KDDI	Japan	39,496	2,934	7.4	18,418
11	Telecom Italia	Italy	36,919	4,792	13.0	84,200
12	Softbank	Japan	34,247	2,823	8.2	21,799
13	China Telecom	China	33,622	2,428	7.2	312,322
14	Sprint	United States	32,535	(3,461)	(10.6)	40,000
15	BT	United Kingdom	30,693	2,299	7.5	92,600

Source: *Total Telecom*, Global 100, October 2011, 14–16.

Note: The end of the financial year is March 31, 2011, for BT, KDDI, NTT, Softbank, and Vodafone. For all other companies, the end of the financial year is December 31, 2010. Revenues were translated from foreign currencies to U.S. dollars at the exchange rate prevailing on the last day of each company's financial year.

[a] Net profit margin, calculated as net income/revenues, reports the profit available to shareholders, in percentage terms, after all expenses of the firm have been deducted; net income includes noncash expenses like depreciation and amortization.

Table 8.3. Telecommunication services: Telecommunication services firms' regional presence, selected, 2011

Americas	Africa	Asia	Western Europe	Eastern Europe	Middle East
América Móvil	Airtel	Airtel	BT	Deutsche	Batelco
Cable & Wireless	Etisalat	Digicel	Deutsche Telekom	Telekom	Etisalat
Digicel	France Télécom	Etisalat	France Télécom	France Télécom	France Télécom
France Télécom	MTN	France Télécom	Global Crossing	MTS	MTN
Global Crossing	Millicom	Hutchison	Hutchison	Tele2	Saudi Telecom
Millicom	Orascom	NTT	Tele2	Telefónica	Vodafone
Nextel	Saudi Telecom	Orascom	Telecom Italia	Telenor	Wataniya
Orascom	Vodafone	Singtel	Telefónica	TeliaSonora	Zain
Telecom Italia	Wataniya	Saudi Telecom	Telenor	Vimpelcom	
Telefónica	Vimpelcom	Telenor	TeliaSonora	Vodafone	
Vimpelcom		Vimpelcom	Vodafone		
		Vodafone	Vimpelcom		

Source: Hot Telecom, *Global Telecom Market Status and Forecast Report*, 2010–2015, July 2011, 19.

As noted above, telecommunication services fall into three broad segments: landline services, wireless services, and Internet access services. Landline service, mainly the traditional voice telephone call, has been the primary telecommunications service for more than a century; in 2010, it still accounted for 55 percent of global revenues.[367] In contrast, wireless voice services, which emerged as a broad-based, commercially viable choice in the mid-1990s, have experienced rapid worldwide adoption, growing to represent 36 percent of global revenues by the end of 2010.[368] In less than 20 years, wireless voice services have grown from a niche service offered only in select developed countries to one that is widely available, even in many of the world's poorest countries.

Internet access services, which allow users to connect to the Internet from their home, office, or public locations, experienced mainstream adoption starting in the mid-1990s, but represented only 9 percent of global revenues by the end of 2010.[369] Although such services have grown very rapidly in developed countries, low levels of personal computer ownership and low landline penetration have hampered adoption in developing countries.

In many countries, the price of telecommunication services is the primary basis of competition, largely due to the undifferentiated nature of such services. Intense industry competition and several years of global economic weakness have accelerated the commoditization of many services, particularly wireless voice services and entry-level broadband services. In the wireless segment, for example, carriers offer similar services and geographic coverage in most country markets. As a result, consumers focus heavily on service pricing and frequently switch carriers on the basis of price, a phenomenon referred to as "churn."[370]

To acquire and "lock in" customers, telecommunication carriers in many countries offer subsidized mobile handsets (cell phones), subject to the customer signing a one-year or, increasingly common, two-year contract. The handset subsidy is recovered over the duration of the contract. Many carriers also develop complex pricing packages that make it harder to compare services, thereby dissuading customers from switching to a competing carrier.[371]

Service is another important factor in the telecommunications industry. In the wireless segment, service coverage, defined as the percentage of the population covered by a carrier's network, can be a critical competitive factor. Wireless carriers are also expected to provide enough network capacity, a particularly important issue with the ever-wider deployment of high-bandwidth, third generation (3G) services; insufficient bandwidth can lead to dropped mobile telephone calls, slow download speeds, and other network quality issues. In the Internet segment, service levels are typically defined in terms of download speeds and monthly limits on downloaded data. High-income users, for example, often demand services that require fast download speeds and high monthly download limits. Service quality is also important, as consumers and businesses expect static-free telephone calls and minimal interruptions to their Internet access.[372]

Product differentiation on the basis of innovation is also an important competitive factor. In the telecommunications industry, product innovation typically requires companies to quickly incorporate the latest technologies and value-added features into products and services. Over the past few years, for example, wireless companies have completed 3G, 3.5G, and 4G (fourth generation) network upgrades, adopted Smart SIM technology, and rolled out ever-better mobile telephone handsets capable of Internet and television services. In the Internet segment, service providers have innovated by expanding service offerings, particularly Voice over Internet Protocol services and long distance calling minutes, as well as bundling Internet services with other telecommunication services. Many service providers also adopt innovative branding and marketing strategies to stand out from the competition.[373]

Demand and Supply Factors

Telecom Carriers Focus on Network Construction

Although rising levels of subscriber penetration have resulted in flat or declining rates of growth in fixed, wireless, and Internet market segments worldwide, most telecommunication companies have invested heavily over the past several years to expand and update their networks and thereby increase their capacity to supply telecommunication services (box 8.1). In developed countries, the growing use of smart phones and, increasingly, Internet tablets— particularly Apple's popular iPad—has caused a surge in data traffic which, in turn, has driven network development. As a result, over the past decade carriers have almost continuously upgraded their wireless networks from the second generation (2G and 2.5G) technologies prevalent during most of the 2000s to 3G technologies and above. In many developing countries, extensive network construction stemmed less from the need to accommodate surging data traffic than from the need to address strong latent demand for basic voice services resulting from decades of underdeveloped landline networks. Although many developing countries have constructed 3G networks over the past several years, such networks were often built to meet the huge demand for bandwidth stemming from rapid growth of first-time subscribers, as opposed to users of high-end, 3G services. Many mobile carriers have also taken steps to develop 4G networks, typically using Long Term Evolution technologies (a standard for high-speed wireless communications). By early 2012, more than 30 carriers had completed 4G networks and launched commercial services, although more than 100 deployments were still under development. In many cases, operators see 4G networks as a means of alleviating network congestion on overloaded 3G networks, rather than as a means of increasing revenue.[374]

Network construction has been fueled by both technology trends and public policy initiatives. For example, many carriers have rolled out networks capable of delivering all voice, data, and Internet services over one simplified network using Internet Protocol technologies (so-called "All-IP Networks"), as opposed to the plethora of networks and technologies that the industry has used for decades. This will allow the carriers to expand capacity and simplify network architectures. Additionally, national broadband plans developed by regulators and policymakers are stimulating network construction around the world. These plans, which aim to increase broadband access and adoption in rural and underdeveloped areas, are often cornerstones of countries' economic and development policies. Such efforts have led governments not only to mobilize private capital but also to subsidize network construction on an unprecedented scale. A large number of countries are developing national broadband plans, including Australia, Austria, Brazil, Botswana, Canada, France, Germany, Italy, Malaysia, Morocco, Singapore, South Africa, Uganda, the United Kingdom, and the United States.[375]

BOX 8.1. INTERNATIONAL SUBMARINE CABLES

Over the past six years, the submarine cable industry has grown dramatically in terms of both active systems and lit capacity[a] as existing cable systems have been upgraded and 49 new commercial networks have been launched. Such large-scale investment and construction has been driven by a surge in demand for Internet and broadband services, with total demand for international bandwidth growing by approximately 600 percent during 2006–10. Demand has grown most rapidly in emerging markets, with the capacity of systems connecting Africa, Latin America, and the Middle East collectively growing by more than 80 percent per year during this period. By contrast, international bandwidth usage in Europe grew by 63 percent per year during the period, while usage in the United States and Canada together grew by about 54 percent per year.[b]

During 2006–10, approximately $6.5 billion was invested in upgrades and new construction.[c] The cost of building a new submarine cable system varies widely, from less than $100 million for small regional systems to nearly a billion dollars for intercontinental systems, depending on system length, network configuration, the number of landing stations, and other factors. For example, the Lion 2 cable system, connecting two islands—Madagascar and Réunion—in the Indian Ocean, is estimated to cost around $74 million, whereas the estimated costs of the West African Cable System and the Africa Coast to Europe cables, both running from South Africa to Europe, are $600 million and $700 million respectively.[d]

Despite strong demand for international bandwidth, the flood of capacity entering the market has put downward pressure on prices. On average, bandwidth prices have fallen by about 25 percent per year over the past couple of years, with transpacific and transatlantic 10G wavelengths[e] among the cheapest routes on a price-per-mile basis, and Miami-São Paulo and Hong Kong-Tokyo among the most expensive.[f]

Although prices vary by circuit size, geographic location, route competition, activation schedule, and other factors, prices for high-capacity circuits have declined more rapidly than those for smaller circuits. Price drops are expected to continue. According to one estimate, the average cost of an annual lease for a 10G wavelength between Hong Kong and Tokyo will fall by 61 percent over the next three years, from $509,000 in 2011 to $197,000 in 2014. As demand for bandwidth grows, bandwidth buyers purchase greater amounts of bandwidth, with volume discounts pushing unit prices down even further.[g] Over the next few years, industry observers expect the bulk of submarine cable construction to shift away from heavily built regions like Asia, Africa, and the Middle East towards South America, which has experienced little construction activity over the last several years. Construction of new cables to diversify routes and reduce latency will likely continue in many regions worldwide.[h]

[a] The term "lit capacity" refers to fiber optic cable strands which have been activated (by installing transmission equipment at both ends of the strand) and are capable of carrying telecommunications traffic. Fiber optic strands are frequently left dormant ("dark") until sufficient demand justifies activation.
[b] *Capacity Magazine*, "Analysis," May 9, 2011.
[c] *Capacity Magazine*, "Analysis," May 9, 2011.
[d] Joanne Taaffe, "Submarine Cable Networks," *Total Telecom*, February 2011, 6; Orange, "France Telecom- Orange Sign Agreement," September 23, 2010.
[e] An optical wavelength capable of transmitting telecommunications traffic at a rate of 10 gigabits per second is referred to as a 10G wavelength.
[f] *Capacity Magazine*, "Analysis," May 9, 2011.
[g] TeleGeography, "New Cables and Falling Prices," February 29, 2012.
[h] *Capacity Magazine*, "Analysis," May 2011.

Merger and Acquisition Activity Resumes

Following the 2007–08 financial crisis, merger and acquisition (M&A) activity in the telecommunications industry slowed dramatically. Over the past couple of years, however, telecom M&A activity has picked up again as confidence in the economy and stock market has improved, a trend which has changed the roster of suppliers in the industry (table 8.4). In addition to consolidation deals within countries, many M&A agreements have taken place across borders, as large, multinational telecommunications firms sought to maintain revenue growth by acquiring existing companies (or boosting existing ownership positions) in high-growth emerging markets.[376] In 2010, for example, India's Bharti Airtel Limited purchased the African operations of Kuwait's Zain Group, acquiring mobile operations in 17 African countries for approximately $11 billion. In the United States, the $10.6 billion purchase of Qwest by rival CenturyLink was completed in 2011. UK-based Vodafone Group also closed a deal in 2011, paying $5.5 billion to buy out its joint venture partner (Essar) in mobile operator Vodafone Essar Limited.[377]

Table 8.4. Telecommunication services: Selected mergers and acquisitions, 2009–11

Announced	Completed	Activity	Value (billion $)
Q1 2011	Q1 2012: withdrawn	AT&T (U.S.) enters into agreement to purchase T-Mobile (U.S.); deal blocked by the U.S. Department of Justice and the U.S. Federal Communications Commission	39.0 (Withdrawn)
Q2 2011	Q4 2011	Level 3 (U.S.) acquires Global Crossing (U.S.)	3.0
Q2 2011	Q2 2011	Vimpelcom (Russia) increases ownership position in GTel (Vietnam) from 40% to 49%	0.2
Q2 2011	Q2 2011	Vodafone (UK) buys out joint venture partner (Essar; India) in Vodafone Essar (India)	5.5
Q1 2011	Q4 2011	PLDT (Philippines) acquires 51.6% of Digitel (Philippines)	1.7
Q1 2011	Q3 2011	América Móvil (Mexico) buys wireless operations in El Salvador and Honduras from Digicel (Ireland)	
Q1 2011	Q2 2011	France Télécom (France) secures 20% indirect stake in Korek Telecom (Iraq)	0.2
Q4 2010	Q2 2011	Cable & Wireless (UK) purchases 51% stake in Bahamas Telecom Company (Bahamas) from the government of the Bahamas	0.2
Q4 2010	Q4 2010	Telekom Austria (Austria) acquires remaining 30% stake in Velcom (Belarus)	0.5
Q2 2010	Q2 2011	CenturyLink (U.S.) and Qwest (U.S.) merge	10.6
Q1 2010	Q2 2010	Bharti Airtel (India) acquires the African operations of Zain Group (Kuwait) after two failed bids by MTN Group (South Africa)	10.7
Q1 2010	Q1 2010	STT (Singapore) acquires 33% stake in U Mobile (Malaysia)	0.3
Q4 2009	Q4 2010	Vimpelcom (Russia) and Kyivstar (Ukraine) merge	22.0
Q3 2009	Q3 2009	Sprint Nextel (U.S.) increases ownership position in Virgin Mobile USA to 100%	0.5
Q2 2009	Q3 2009	Etisalat (Egypt) acquires 100% of Tigo (Sri Lanka) from Millicom International Cellular (Luxembourg)	0.2
Q2 2009	Q2 2009	Vodafone (UK) purchases 70% stake in Ghana Telecom (Ghana)	0.9
Q2 2009	Q2 2009	Batelco (Bahrain) acquires initial 36.9% stake in S-Tel (India)	0.2
Q2 2009	Q2 2009	AT&T (U.S.) buys fixed-line assets from Verizon (U.S.) in rural areas in 18 U.S. states	2.4
Q2 2009	Q2 2009	France Télécom (France) lifts stake in Orange España (Spain) from 81.6% to 99.85%	1.8
Q1 2009	Q3 2009	Maroc Télécom (Morocco) purchases 51% of former monopoly operator SOTELMA (Mali)	0.4

Source: TeleGeography, Worldwide Telecoms M&A Timeline, GlobalComms Database, 2012.

Tight Margins Motivate Carriers to Adopt Network Sharing Arrangements

Over the past five years, wireless carriers in a growing number of countries have adopted network sharing agreements. Such arrangements, which involve two or more carriers sharing mobile network components, have become increasingly common in both developed and developing countries as they allow telecommunication services suppliers to reduce operating costs, minimize capital spending, expand network coverage, speed time to market, and respond to environmental and universal service regulations.[378] According to one estimate, network sharing can reduce network construction costs by 16–20 percent, with accumulated savings running into the billions of dollars.[379] Recent examples of network sharing deals include a 2010 joint venture between two Polish telecom companies, TPSA and PTC, in which the firms share mobile network infrastructure and radio frequencies. TPSA and PTC expect to save hundreds of millions of dollars over the next five years.[380] In 2011, Irish carriers O2 Ireland and eircom announced plans to share their mobile networks by consolidating existing sites and jointly building new ones. O2 and eircom plan to share site equipment, power supplies, technology, and transmission equipment; both companies also plan to contribute staff to roll out and maintain their tower networks.[381]

Trade Trends

Cross-Border Trade

In 2010, U.S. exports of telecommunication services (box 8.2) totaled $11.1 billion, while imports totaled $8.0 billion, yielding a trade surplus of about $3.1 billion (figure 8.1).[382] Exports increased by 10 percent in 2010, slower than the CAGR of 20 percent recorded during 2005–09.[383] Telecommunication exports rose mainly due to an increase in intrafirm receipts by U.S. parent companies from their foreign affiliates. Strong growth in such receipts over the past several years were largely due to a surge in value-added services, including satellite broadcasting, business communication, and data network management services. Such affiliated services now account for more than half of all telecommunication receipts.[384]

Box 8.2. Understanding BEA Data on Cross-Border Trade and Affiliate Transactions in Telecommunication Services

The BEA's data on cross-border trade in telecommunication services cover receipts and payments between U.S. and foreign telecommunication companies for the following services: message telephone services, telex, telegram, and other jointly provided basic services; private leased channel services; value-added services; support services; and reciprocal exchanges.[a] These figures are collected quarterly via Form BE-125 and reported on a gross basis.[b] Trade data by service type, however, are not available, as companies are instructed to report such data for the above-listed categories in the aggregate. In addition, the BEA periodically conducts benchmark surveys using Form BE-120, with the last such survey occurring in 2006. In 2006, following the introduction of revised forms BE-120 and BE-125, the BEA began collecting and reporting data for both affiliated and unaffiliated telecommunication transactions.

Before 2006, the BEA collected only unaffiliated cross-border telecommunications trade data.[c] Within the telecommunications industry, affiliated transactions represent trade within multinational telecommunication services companies—specifically, trade between U.S. parent companies and their foreign affiliates, and vice versa. By contrast, unaffiliated transactions represent trade with foreign partners that neither own, nor are owned by, a U.S. telecommunication services company.[d]

To survey services supplied through affiliates, the BEA collects data for the U.S. affiliates of foreign companies using forms BE-12 (Benchmark Survey) and BE-15 (Annual Survey) and for foreign affiliates using forms BE-10 (Benchmark Survey) and BE-11 (Annual Survey). Unlike cross-border data, which is collected by service type, affiliate data are collected and published according to the primary industry of the affiliate.[e] The BEA's *Survey of Current Business* reports on services supplied through telecommunication affiliates in three broad industry categories: wireline telecommunication carriers, wireless telecommunications carriers (except satellite), and other telecommunication services.[f]

[a] USDOC, BEA, Form BE-125 (1-2010), "Quarterly Survey of Transactions in Selected Services and Intangible Assets with Foreigners," 17. As mentioned earlier, value-added (enhanced) services are defined as telecommunication services that add value or function above and beyond the telecommunications transport services that deliver the value-added service to end users. Such services can include (1) e-mail, voice mail, code and protocol processing, and management and operations of data networks; (2) fax services and video conferencing; (3) Internet connections (online access service, including Internet backbone, router services, and broadband access services); (4) satellite broadcasting, business communication, and paging services provided by satellite connections; and (5) telephony, interactive voice response, virtual private networking, remote access service, and voice over Internet protocol services. Support services involve the maintenance and repair of telecommunications equipment and ground station services. Reciprocal exchanges include transactions involving barter.
[b] BEA representative, e-mail message to USITC staff, March 23, 2010. For example, if Company A in the United States owes Company B in France $100 million, and Company B owes Company A $20 million, Company A would report a receipt (export) of $20 million and a payment (import) of $100 million.
[c] BEA representative, various e-mail messages to USITC staff, March 12–23, 2010. For more information on affiliated/unaffiliated transactions pertaining to telecommunication services, see table 1, "Trade in Services, 1998–2008," footnote 7 in DOC, BEA, *Survey of Current Business*, October 2009, 41.
[d] USDOC, BEA, *Survey of Current Business*, October 2009, 29.
[e] BEA representative, e-mail message to USITC staff, March 12, 2010.
[f] USDOC, BEA, *Survey of Current Business*, October 2009, 22–64.

In 2010, U.S. imports of telecommunication services increased by 7 percent, slower than the 14 percent CAGR from 2005–09.[385] This slower growth represents efforts by U.S. carriers to reduce fees and payments to their foreign counterparts, including ongoing activities aimed at reducing mobile termination rates.[386] In 2010, the top five cross-border export markets for U.S. telecommunication services were Brazil (which accounted for 20 percent of the total), the United Kingdom (16 percent), Canada (6 percent), Venezuela (6 percent), and Argentina (5 percent) (figure 8.2). In that same year, the top sources of U.S. telecommunication services imports were the United Kingdom (which accounted for 22 percent of the total), Mexico (7 percent), the Netherlands (7 percent), Canada (6 percent), and Germany (3 percent). The United States maintained bilateral surpluses vis-à-vis its top five telecom markets in 2010 (figure 8.3).

Affiliate Transactions

International trade in telecommunication services occurs predominantly through the affiliates of multinational companies, although data on such transactions are frequently suppressed to avoid disclosing services supplied by individual companies.[387] In 2009, sales by U.S. foreign affiliates totaled $31.7 billion, 47 percent higher than such sales in 2006 (such data are unavailable for 2007 and 2008). Overall, U.S. foreign affiliate sales grew at a CAGR of 5 percent from 2004 through 2009.[388] In 2009, services supplied to U.S. customers by the U.S.-based affiliates of foreign telecommunication service companies totaled $30.9 billion, roughly the same level as in 2008. From 2006 through 2009, sales by U.S. affiliates of foreign companies grew at a CAGR of 13 percent.[389]

Nontariff Measures Affecting Trade

Firms seeking to offer services outside their home country typically face a number of barriers to market entry. In many countries, government regulation acts as a barrier. For example, governments often control the issuance of service licenses as a way to limit the number of competing firms. In the wireless segment, new entrants also need to obtain a license that authorizes the use of electromagnetic spectrum. In addition to the (often substantial) cost of obtaining such a license, spectrum availability is finite in all markets; once all available spectrum is allocated, mergers or acquisitions are typically the only way to enter the market. Government-imposed ownership restrictions, such as foreign equity caps on domestic telecommunication carriers, are another important type of barrier. In some countries, governments completely prohibit foreign companies from taking an ownership position in incumbent operators.[390]

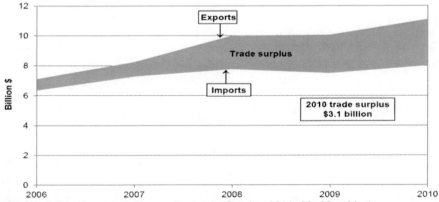

Source: USDOC, BEA, *Survey of Current Business*, October 2011, 32–33, table 1.

Figure 8.1. Telecommunication services: U.S. cross-border trade in private-sector services resulted in a U.S. trade surplus each year during 2006–10.

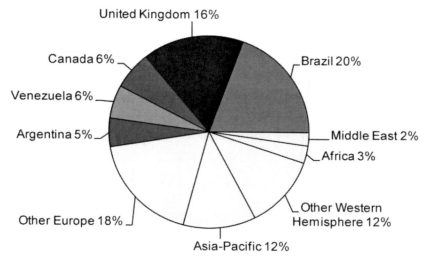

U.S. exports

United Kingdom 16%

Canada 6%

Venezuela 6%

Argentina 5%

Other Europe 18%

Asia-Pacific 12%

Brazil 20%

Middle East 2%

Africa 3%

Other Western Hemisphere 12%

Total = $11.1 billion

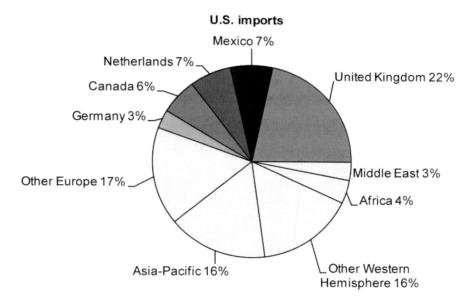

U.S. imports

Mexico 7%

Netherlands 7%

Canada 6%

Germany 3%

Other Europe 17%

Asia-Pacific 16%

United Kingdom 22%

Middle East 3%

Africa 4%

Other Western Hemisphere 16%

Total = $8.0 billion

Source: USDOC, BEA, *Survey of Current Business*, October 2011, 44–45, table 5.2.
Note: Geographic regions are shaded in yellow. Figures m ay not total 100 percent due to rounding.

Figure 8.2. Telecommunication services: Brazil and the United Kingdom were the top markets f or U.S. exports while the United Kingdom was the leading source of telecommunication services imports in 2010.

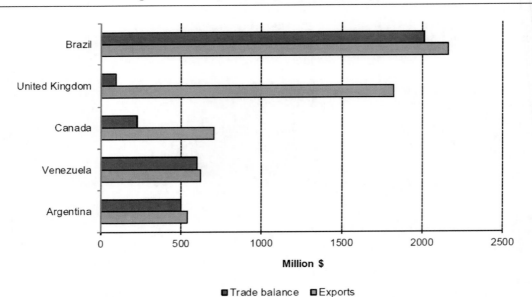

Million $

■ Trade balance   ▢ Exports

Source: USDOC, BEA, *Survey of Current Business*, table 5.2, October 2011, 44–45.

Figure 8.3. Telecommunication services: The United States showed a cross-border trade surplus with major trading partners in 2010.

Outlook

Over the next three years, the global telecommunication services industry is expected to grow at steady, if unspectacular, rates, driven by continued economic recovery and robust demand for high-bandwidth data services. Growth in industry revenues worldwide is expected to decline slightly, from 6.3 percent per annum in 2012 to 5.7 percent by the end of 2015, largely due to maturing market conditions in many countries.[391] In an effort to offset slower growth, many companies around the globe are expected to continue efforts to reduce costs and streamline operations. A growing number of carriers, for example, are expected to adopt network-sharing arrangements to reduce both up-front capital expenditure and ongoing operating costs.[392] As pressures grow to cut costs, carriers are also expected to engage in innovative partnerships and joint venture agreements. Over the next few years, a growing number of carriers are expected to cooperate under purchasing agreements wherein two or more carriers form a joint venture so they can pool their purchases of telecommunications equipment.[393] For example, in 2011, German and French incumbents Deutsche Telekom and France Télécom set up a venture specifically to purchase telecommunications equipment. France Télécom estimates that their purchasing venture will save it as much as $1.2 billion over the next three years, whereas Deutsche Telekom estimates savings of more than $500 million over the same time period. The savings will stem from both increased negotiating power with telecom equipment makers and economies of scale.[394]

Over the next few years, M&A activity is likely to increase as telecommunication companies face maturing markets and growing subscriber saturation. In developed countries, M&A activity is likely to focus on domestic consolidation, whereas M&A activity in emerging markets is likely to take the form of cross-borders acquisitions as large, multinational telecommunications companies attempt to boost revenues and subscribers by investing in fast-growing markets.[395]

SECTION 9. SERVICES ROUNDTABLE

The Commission hosted its fifth annual services roundtable on November 3, 2011, with USITC Chairman Deanna Tanner Okun presiding and USITC Vice Chairman Irving Williamson moderating. These roundtables are held to facilitate discussions among individuals from government, industry, and academia about important issues affecting services trade. This year's discussion focused on the following topics:

- The outcomes and prospects of multilateral and regional trade negotiations as well as unilateral liberalization efforts;
- The challenges and opportunities of harmonizing regulations affecting services industries; and
- Services industries' contribution to global economic activity.

Approaches to Services Trade Liberalization

Several participants stated that, while negotiations at the World Trade Organization (WTO) resulted in the landmark 1995 General Agreement on Trade in Services, the WTO has not effectively facilitated services trade liberalization in recent years. As evidence they cited the impasse in the Doha Round and the fact that many of the best offers made by WTO members fall short of actual on-the-ground levels of liberalization. One participant argued that the WTO does not adequately deal with some increasingly important services trade issues: state-owned enterprises, restrictions on data flows, forced localization of business activities, indigenous innovation, and local content requirements. The panel suggested that the slow rate of progress in the Doha Round may lower expectations for what can be achieved within the current WTO structure and motivate more countries to seek bilateral free trade agreements (FTAs) and regional trade agreements (RTAs).

The participants discussed the tradeoffs between pursuing broad multilateral negotiations and pursuing smaller "coalition-of-the-willing" negotiations. They noted that RTAs often do better at capturing de facto liberalization levels and providing more security of access with wider and deeper bindings than do "lowest common denominator" agreements among a larger number of partners. Nevertheless, one speaker pointed out that RTAs are imperfect, as they generally do not increase market access beyond policies already in place: countries often only make offers that at best ratify current market conditions, technologies, and business models, or that reflect liberalization reforms which they are already prepared to undertake unilaterally (though agreements that bind such practices are still valuable). Moreover, according to one participant, the diversity of RTAs in general, and the negative-list[396] structure of some RTAs specifically, require negotiators to learn multiple "languages" in pursuing parallel negotiating tracks at the same time. On the other hand, panelists also noted that RTA provisions are easily "multilateralizable," in that they can be extended to countries outside the agreement.

The panel also considered the merits of bilateral FTAs, which like RTAs tend to be wider and deeper than broad multilateral agreements. One speaker pointed out that in spite of the WTO's challenges, the United States is not negotiating commercially meaningful bilateral trade agreements with large important markets like India, China, or Brazil, in part because those economies are more interested in negotiating multilaterally. Many successfully negotiated U.S. FTAs are with small markets, such as the signatories to the Dominican Republic-Central America-United States Free Trade Agreement, which face challenges in enticing U.S. firms to enter their markets due to their size.

The participants also discussed unilateral liberalization undertaken by countries that simply decided such changes were in their own interest. Telecommunications was cited as a striking example of successful unilateral liberalization driven by the alignment of consumers, suppliers, and regulators. In many countries, consumers sought better telecommunications services, suppliers wished to provide them, and regulators were pushed to reform for fear of being "left behind." This sequence of events was contrasted with plurilateral negotiations that narrowly focus on requests for and offers of specific commitments, which can disregard the overall context of reforms. One participant suggested that domestic debates may be the most important forums for discussing liberalization, as they provide an opportunity to persuade consumers (and hence electorates) that gaining access to state-of-the-art infrastructure services provided by foreign firms can raise living standards and facilitate development.

The Role of Regulations

The participants discussed the role of regulations in services trade, emphasizing that some of the most vital issues in services liberalization involve the clash of regulatory systems. At the WTO, negotiations have generally taken a narrow approach to regulations by addressing them only insofar as they restrict market access. One participant explained that WTO negotiators chose to focus on services principles instead of services regulations at the onset of Uruguay Round negotiations because "principles" imply a relatively simple conversation, whereas "regulations" cover many complex conversations about hundreds of individual regulatory structures. While acknowledging the importance of harmonizing regulations, several speakers pointed out that there is often no single set of best regulatory practices, as it is difficult to determine the optimal way of addressing issues like market concentration (for example, in telecommunications) or asymmetric information (for example, the inability of consumers to judge the quality of banks). Participants noted that the financial crisis revealed flaws in developed countries' financial regulations, and suggested that ideas about what constitutes a good regulatory framework shift over time and adapt to new circumstances; furthermore, global best practices may simply not exist due to the institution-dependent nature of regulations. One speaker emphasized that the path of services liberalization in developing countries may not resemble its path in developed countries, and specifically suggested that no one set of regulatory choices can simultaneously achieve the three goals of efficiency, equity of access, and stability over time.

Another speaker noted the value of regulators talking to each other even in the absence of specific trade negotiations, pointing out that financial regulators in the United States and the EU have an ongoing dialogue about issues such as accounting standards, and that this dialogue has been a foundation for progress on recognizing regulatory equivalence.

Additionally, according to one participant, direct coordination among regulators may be the most effective means of harmonizing regulations, as it requires input and agreement from those responsible for carrying out the revised rules. As an example, the panel indicated that dialogue between financial regulators in ASEAN countries helped make it possible to create the region's integrated stock market.

The panelists indicated that it is frequently difficult to measure actual levels of openness, as many regulatory barriers to services trade are "invisible" in that they are not explicit, trade-oriented policies. (For example, retail services are affected by behind-the-border procedures for opening new stores and rules about what products can be sold in stores.) Partly for this reason, some organizations represented at the roundtable have tried to pinpoint and quantify services trade restrictiveness. In addition to the Commission, the Organization for Economic Co-operation and Development has constructed a database of services regulations, and the World Bank is developing a database of on-the-ground services policies. The participants suggested that these data can help people assess the progress of trade agreements and identify good regulatory practices.

Broader Economic Issues

The panel considered the relationship between services trade and employment. One speaker cited research showing that tradable services employ a large number of people—particularly highly educated people who are paid high wages—and that the United States could likely export significantly more services, and employ more services workers, in the absence of obstacles and restrictions. This research contrasts with what the speaker described as a prevailing stereotype that services jobs are low-paying, fueling the emphasis among politicians on creating manufacturing jobs.

The panel discussed the differences between gross services trade and embedded services trade.[397] Several participants remarked that data which include embedded services look very different from data on gross services exports, as the latter do not fully capture the ways in which services are inputs to manufacturing, or the ways in which services add value to finished manufactured goods. While India is a world leader in gross services exports, the United States exports enormous amounts of embedded services; one participant pointed out that the percentage of U.S. exports that are re-exported has grown from 1 percent to 10 percent over the past 25 years, suggesting that U.S. service providers are adding value to products manufactured overseas and making significant mark-ups. Referring to embedded services, one speaker suggested that developing countries "would be surprised at how many services they actually export." The panel considered an example of a U.S. firm sending cloth to Mexico, where workers sew it into a shirt and then send it back to the firm: this transaction could be classified as two goods transactions (an export of cloth and an import of a shirt) or as one import of tailoring services. According to the speaker, virtually everything can be thought of as a service, and adopting this perspective illustrates that "what matters is not what you make. It's what you do."

The panel noted that services trade was relatively resilient during the financial crisis and the consequent recession, perhaps because the pressure to cut costs led firms to switch from domestic to foreign sources of services. One speaker emphasized that a recession can have lasting effects on the structure of economies, both in terms of industries that emerge in good condition (insurance was cited as an example of a relatively healthy and ready-to-expand U.S. service industry) and in terms of geographic patterns of trade. The panel also noted that economic stagnation in developed countries has motivated U.S. services exporters to focus on emerging markets, with a particular emphasis on China, where middle-class growth is expected to increase demand for services.

List of external participants at the Commission's services roundtable held on November 3, 2011

Name	Title / Affiliation
Erik Autor	Vice President and International Trade Counsel National Retail Federation
Nora Dihel	Senior Trade Economist, Africa Region World Bank
Geza Feketekuty	Professor Monterey Institute of International Studies
Greg Frazier	Vice President Motion Picture Association of America
Adam Hemphill	Senior Manager of Federal Government Relations Wal-Mart
Ron Hira	Associate Professor of Public Policy Rochester Institute of Technology
J. Bradford Jensen	Associate Professor of International Business and Economics McDonough School of Business at Georgetown University
Sophia Lafargue	Chief of Staff Congressman Gregory W. Meeks
Welby Leaman	Trade Counsel House Committee on Ways and Means
David Long	Director of the Office of Services Industries U.S. Department of Commerce
Aaditya Mattoo	Research Manager, Trade and Integration World Bank
Marc Mealy	Vice President US-ASEAN Business Council
Jack Moody	Assistant Division Chief U.S. Census Bureau
Hildeguun Nordas	Senior Policy Analyst OECD
Lisa Pearlman	Counsel, Regulatory and Government Affairs Department WilmerHale
Richard Self	Trade Policy Consultant World Trade Organization
Laura Sherman	Senior Legal Advisor Transparency International USA

Name	Title / Affiliation
David Snyder	Vice President and Associate General Counsel, Public Policy
	American Insurance Association
Sherry M. Stephenson	Director of Department of Trade
	Organization of American States
J. Robert Vastine	President Coalition of Services Industries
James Wallar	Senior Vice President
	Nathan Associates

REFERENCES

Amaral, Rodrgio. "Argentina Raises Trade Barriers and Forces Insurers to Repatriate Assets." *Commercial Risk Europe*, November 4, 2011. http://www.commercialriskeurope.com/cre/1027/143/Argentina-raises-trade-barriers-and-forces-insurers-to-repatriate-assets/.

American Public Media. *Marketplace*. "Wal-Mart's Bank Ambitions in Mexico," August 6, 2010. http://www.marketplace.org/topics/world/wal-marts-bank-ambitions-mexico.

Arcentales, Luis; Arthur, Carvalho; Daniel, Volberg. "Country Commentary: 2012 Outlook." *Morgan Stanley Research: This Week in Latin America*, November 28, 2011. http://www.emta.org/keyviews.aspx.

Armstrong & Associates, Inc. "3PL Customers Report Identifies Service Trends, 3PL Market Segment Sizes and Growth Rates." Press release, 2009. http://www.3plogistics.com/PR_3PL_Customers-2009.htm.

————. "A&A's Top 50 Global Third-Party Logistics Provider (3PL) List: Largest 3PLs Ranked by 2010 Logistics Gross Revenue," n.d. http://www.3plogistics.com/Top_50_Global_3PLs.htm (accessed November 14, 2011).

————. "Global 3PL Market Size Estimates," n.d. http://www.3plogistics.com/3PLmarketGlobal.htm (accessed November 14, 2011).

————. "Global Logistics Estimates—2007," July 2007.

Armstrong, Mark A; David, Sappington. "Regulation, Competition, and Liberalization." *Journal of Economic Literature*, 44 (June 2006), 325–66.

Arnold, Jens; Boutheina, Guermazi; Aaditya, Mattoo. "Telecommunications: The Persistence of Monopoly." In *Services Trade and Development: The Experience of Zambia*, edited by Aaditya Mattoo and Lucy Payton, 89–141. New York: Palgrave Macmillan, 2007.

Arvis, Jean-François; Monica, Alina Mustra; Lauri, Ojala; Ben, Shepherd; Daniel, Saslavsky. *Connecting to Compete: Trade Logistics in the Global Economy*. Washington, DC: The World Bank, 2010. http://siteresources.worldbank.org/INTTLF/Resources/LPI2010_for_web.pdf.

Aseada, Jason. "Retailing: General." *Standard & Poor's Industry Surveys*. New York: Standard & Poor's, November 24, 2011. http://www.netadvantage.standardandpoors.com/NASApp/NetAdvantage/showIndustrySurvey.do?code=reg (registration required).

Associated Press. "Gap Plans Stores in Chile, Panama, Colombia." *Bloomberg Businessweek*, October 12, 2011. http://www.businessweek.com/ap/financialnews/D9QARAEO0.htm

Barfield, Richard; ed. *A Practitioner's Guide to Basel III and Beyond.* Pricewaterhouse Coopers LLP and Thomson Reuters, January 2011. http://www.pwc.com/en_GX/gx/financial-services/pdf/Introduction-and-chapters-final.pdf.

Ben Romdhane, Saoussen. "Liberalizing Trade in Services in Tunisia: General Equilibrium Effects." *Journal of Economics and International Finance*, 3, no. 11 (October 7, 2011), 634–45.

Bertaut, Carol. "Understanding U.S. Cross-Border Securities Data." *Federal Reserve Bulletin*, 2006. http://www.federalreserve.gov/pubs/bulletin/2006/crossbordersecurities/default.htm.

Bertaut, Carol; Laurie, Pounder. "The Financial Crisis and Cross-Border Financial Flows." *Federal Reserve Bulletin*, November 2009. http://www.treasury.gov/resource-center/data-chart- center/tic/Documents/frbulnov2009.pdf.

Betancourt, Roger R. *The Economics of Retailing and Distribution.* Cheltenham, UK: Edward Elgar, 2004.

Bhatnagar, Rohit; Viswanathan, S. "Re-engineering Global Supply Chains: Alliances between Manufacturing Firms and Global Logistics Services Providers." *International Journal of Physical Distribution & Logistics Management*, 30, no. 1, 2000.

Bhatty, Ajmal. "The Growing Importance of Takaful Insurance," September 23, 2011. http://www.oecd.org/dataoecd/23/29/46116115.pdf.

Birchall, Jonathan. "Walmart Gears Up for Global Online Push." *Financial Times,* January 29, 2010. http://www.ft.com/cms/s/0/9f944f78-0c67-11df-a941-00144feabdc0.html?nclick_check=1 (registration required).

Bloomberg. "Best Buy Shuts China Stores to Focus on More Profitable Brand," February 22, 2011. http://www.bloomberg.com/news/2011-02-22/best-buy-s-china-stores-shut-as-retailer -focuses-on- more-profitable-brand.html.

Bohme, Markus; Daniele, Chiarella; Philipp, Harle; Max, Neukirchen; Thomas, Poppensieker; Anke, Raufuss. "Day of Reckoning? New Regulation and Its Impact on Capital-Markets Businesses." McKinsey&Company, September 2011.

Bolumole, Yemisi A. "The Supply Chain Role of Third-Party Logistics Providers." *The International Journal of Logistics Management*, 12, no. 2 (2001).

Borga, Maria. "Improved Measures of U.S. International Services: The Cases of Insurance, Wholesale and Retail Trade, and Financial Services." Paper prepared for the NBER-CRIW Conference on International Services Flows, Bethesda, Maryland, April 28–29, 2006 (version dated March 2, 2008).

———. "Supplemental Estimates of Insurance, Trade Services, and Financial Services Sold through Affiliates." *Survey of Current Business*, 87, no. 10 (October 2007). http://www.bea.gov/scb/toc/1007cont.htm.

Boston Consulting Group (BCG). *The World's Next E-commerce Superpower: Navigating China's Unique Online-Shopping Ecosystem.* Boston: BCG, November 2011. http://www.bcg.com/documents/file91905.pdf.

Brainard, Lael. "What Is the Role of Insurance in Economic Development?" *Zurich Report*, January 1, 2008. http://zdownload.zurich.com/main/reports/What_is_the_role_of_economic_developement.pdf.

Brush, Silla. "Volcker Rule Will Cost Banks $1 Billion, U.S. Government Says." *Bloomberg News*, October 28, 2011. http://www.bloomberg.com/news/2011-10-28/volcker-rule-to-cost-banks-1b-u- s-government.html.

Bull, Alister. "China Agrees to Open Up Auto Insurance Market." *Insurance Journal,* February 14, 2012. http://www.insurancejournal.com/news/national/2012/02/14/235420.htm.

Bureau van Dijk. ORBIS Companies Database (accessed March 1, 2012).

Business Today. "A Happy Marriage: Partnership with UPS Enabled Toshiba to Speed Up Laptop Repair Service," December 11, 2011. http://businesstoday.intoday.in/story/innovation-toshiba- ups/1/20185.html.

Butcher, David. "The State of Logistics." *ThomasNet News,* June 23, 2011. http://news.thomasnet.com/IMT/2011/06/23/2011-state-of-logistics-cscmp-report-findings/.

Campbell, Matthew; Cornelius, Rahn. "Deutsche Telekom, France Telecom Set Up Purchasing Venture." *Bloomberg,* April 18, 2011. http://www.bloomberg.com/news/2011-04-18/deutsche- telekom-france-telecom-agree-on-procurement-venture.html.

Canada MSN Money. "Will Wal-Mart's Banking Push into Canada Succeed?" June 6, 2010. http://www.everydaymoney.ca/2010/06/walmart-makes-banking-push-into-canada.html.

Capacity Magazine. "Analysis: Boom in International Bandwidth," May 9, 2011.

CarInsuranceList.com. "Save Money with Driver Monitoring Programs," January 12, 2011. http://www.carinsurancelist.com/save-money-with-driver-monitoring-programs.htm.

Chevalier, Judith; Austan Goolsbee. "Measuring Prices and Price Competition Online: Amazon.com and BarnesandNoble.com." *Quantitative Marketing and Economics,* 1 (2003): 203–22.

China Banking Regulatory Commission. *Annual Report 2010,* n.d. (accessed February 29, 2012). http://www.cbrc.gov.cn/EngdocView.do?docID=20110419222D1DDDE39BE80AFFEB3FF789309200.

City of London. "Research and Statistics FAQ," n.d. http://www.cityoflondon.gov.uk/Corporation/LGNL_Services/Business/Business_support_and_advice/Economic_information_and_analysis/Research+and+statistics+FAQ.htm#internationalbanking (accessed March 20, 2012).

Clifford, Stephanie. "Wal-Mart Gains in Its Wooing of Chicago." *New York Times,* June 24, 2010. http://www.nytimes.com/2010/06/25/business/25walmart.html.

———. "In These Lean Times, Even Stores Shrink." *New York Times,* November 23, 2010. http://www.nytimes.com/2010/11/10/business/10small.html?pagewanted=.

CNNMoney.com. "Fortune 500 2010," n.d. http://money.cnn.com/magazines/fortune/fortune500/2010/snapshots/2358.html (accessed January 30, 2012).

Comité Européen des Assurances (CEA). "Insurers Highlight Danger of Brazilian Protectionism." Press release, January 1, 2012. http://www.insuranceeurope.eu/uploads/Modules/Newsroom/120113- insurers_highlight_danger_of_brazilian_protectionism.pdf.

Commercial Risk Europe. "Global Programmes 2011: In Search of Nirvana," n.d. http://www.commercialriskeurope.com/uploads/files/special-reports/Global-Programmes-2011.pdf (accessed February 17, 2012).

Conference Board. "Consumer Confidence Survey: The Conference Board Consumer Confidence Index Declines." News release, October 25, 2011. http://www.conference-board.org/data/consumerconfidence.cfm (link now leads to a more recent news release).

Copeland, Brian; Aaditya, Mattoo. "The Basic Economics of Services Trade." In *A Handbook of International Trade in Services,* edited by Aaditya Mattoo, Robert M. Stern, and Gianni Zanini, 84–129. Oxford: Oxford University Press, 2008.

Cowhey, Peter F; Jonathan, D Aronson. "Trade in Services Communications." In *A Handbook of International Trade in Services*, edited by Aaditya Mattoo, Robert M. Stern, and Gianni Zanini, 389–436 Oxford: Oxford University Press, 2008.

Cummins, J David. "The Bermuda Insurance Market: An Economic Analysis." www.bermuda-insurance.org, May 6, 2008. http://www.bermuda-insurance.org/pdf-downloads/ CumminsReport08.pdf.

Cuthbert, Jon. "Saudi Arabia—The Land of Logistics Opportunity." *arabian SupplyChain.com*, November 27, 2011. http://www.arabiansupplychain.com/ article-6787-saudi-arabia--the-land-of-logistics- opportunity/1/print/.

D'Innocenzio, Anne. "Gap Closing about Fifth of U.S. Stores, Expanding in China." *USA Today*, October 13, 2011. http://www.usatoday.com/money/industries/retail/story/2011-10-13/gap- closings-china-expansion/50764116/1.

Datamonitor. "Insurance in Russia," September 2011.

———. "Non-Life Insurance in Russia," September 2011.

De Sousa, Dareil; Christopher, Findlay. "Relationship between Liberalization in the Logistics Sector and Trade Facilitation." In *Trade Facilitation beyond the Multilateral Trade Negotiations: Regional Practices, Customs Valuation and Other Emerging Issues*, 245–80. United Nations Economic and Social Commission for Asia and the Pacific, 2008.

Debari, Tomoki; Daniel, Tan. "Foreign Insurance Companies in Japan—Possible Reforms?" Corporate LiveWire, June 13, 2011. http://www.corporatelivewire.com/top-story.html?id=35.

Dedrick, Jason; Kenneth, Kraemer; Greg, Linden. "Who Profits from Innovation in Global Supply Chains? A Study of the iPod and Notebook PCs." Industry Studies Association Working Papers Series, 2008. http://web.mit.edu/is08/pdf/Dedrick_Kraemer_Linden.pdf.

Deemer, Paul C. "China Amend Foreign Investment Policy: New Foreign Investment Industry Guidance Catalogue." Vinson & Elkins LLP, January 18, 2012. http://www.velaw.com/resources/pub_detail.aspx?id=20405 (accessed January 26, 2012).

Deloitte & Touche. "Unlocking the Value of Globalisation," 2005. http://www.deloitte.com/assets/Dcom- Canada/Local%20Assets/Documents/Unlock.pdf.

Deloitte and STORES Media. "Global Powers of Retailing Top 250." *Stores*, January 2012. http://www.stores.org/STORES%20Magazine%20January%202012/global-powers-retailing-top-250 (accessed June 25, 2012).

Deloitte Research. "Mastering Complexity in Global Manufacturing," 2003. http://www.deloitte.com/view/en_GX/global/insights/deloitte-research/2d61c5275d0fb110Vgn VCM100000ba42f00aRCRD.htm.

Deloitte. "2012 Global Insurance Outlook: Generating Growth in a Challenging Economy Takes Operational Excellence and Innovation," n.d. http://www.deloitte.com/assets/Dcom-UnitedStates/Local%20Assets/Documents/FSI/US_FSI_Global%20Insurance%20Outlook%202012_011312.pdf (accessed January 25, 2012).

Deloitte. Financial Services Group. "United Kingdom: MiFID II: The Deloitte Perspective," December 1, 2011. http://www.deloitte.com/view/en_GB/uk/industries/financial-services/94997ca784fc3310VgnVCM1000001a56f00aRCRD.htm (accessed January 31, 2012).

Deloitte. *Leaving Home: Global Powers of Retailing 2011*. London: Deloitte, January 2011. https://www.deloitte.com/assets/Dcom-Global/Local%20Assets/Documents/Consumer%20Business/GlobPowDELOITTE_14%20Jan.pdf.

Deutsche Post DHL. *Annual Report 2010*, 2010. http://www.dp- dhl.com/content/ dam/Investors/Publications/DPDHL_Annual_Report_2010.pdf.

Dickinson, Gerry. "Encouraging a Dynamic Life Insurance Industry: Economic Benefits and Policy Issues." OCED Directorate for Financial and Enterprise Affairs, n.d. http://www.oecd.org/dataoecd/40/11/1857811.pdf (accessed January 26, 2010).

Dobberstein, Nikolai, Carl-Stefan Neumann, and Markus Zils. "Logistics in Emerging Markets." *McKinsey Research in Brief*, no. 1 (2005).

Dublin International Insurance & Management Association Ltd. (DIMA). "Ireland's International Re/Insurance Market Factsheet 2010." Fact sheet, 2010. http://www. captive.com/assoc/dima/DIMA%20market%20factsheet%20November%202010%20(2). pdf.

Economist Intelligence Unit (EIU). *Country Commerce: Russia*. New York: Economist Intelligence Unit, November 2011.

———. "Malaysia Insurers: Mitsui Sumitomo Acquires 35% Stake in Hong Leong Takaful Unit." *Financial Services Briefing & Forecasts*, April 18, 2011. http://www.eiu.com/ index.asp?layout=ib3Article&article_id=578010642&country_id=1600000160&pubtypei d=1132462498&industry_id=710001071&category_id=.

Economist Intelligence Unit (EIU). *Country Finance: China*. New York: Economist Intelligence Unit, August 2011.

———. *Country Finance: United States of America*. New York: Economist Intelligence Unit, November 2011.

———. "World Banks: A Historic Divide." New York: Economist Intelligence Unit, October 15, 2011. Federal Deposit Insurance Corporation. "Bank Failures in Brief," 2010. http://www.fdic.gov/bank/historical/bank/2011/index.html.

———. 2011. http://www.fdic.gov/bank/historical/bank/2010/index.html.

Economist Intelligence Unit (EIU). *Industries in 2012*. New York: Economist Intelligence Unit, 2011. http://www.eiu.com/public/topical_report.aspx?campaignid=Industries2012 (registration required).

Economist Intelligence Unit (EIU). *Industries in 2012*. New York: Economist Intelligence Unit, 2011. http://www.eiu.com/public/topical_report.aspx?campaignid=Industries2012 (subscription required).

Economist. "Global Investment Banking Fees," October 8, 2011. http://www.economist. com/node/21531506.

Economist. "Sharing the Load," March 26, 2009. http://www.economist.com/node/13381538 (subscription required).

Ellison, Glenn; Sarah Fisher Ellison. "Search, Obfuscation, and Price Elasticities on the Internet." Massachusetts Institute of Technology faculty working paper, October 2007. http://econ- devel.mit.edu/files/3199.

Enright, Allison. "Shrinking to Survive." *Internet Retailer*, September 30, 2011. http://www.internetretailer.com/2011/09/30/shrinking-survive?p=1.

Environmental Protection Agency (EPA). "Green Building: Basic Information," December 22, 2010. http://www.epa.gov/greenbuilding/pubs/about.htm.

Ernst & Young. "U.S. Life Insurance Industry Outlook," December 2011.

———. "U.S. Life Insurance Outlook: Driving Growth in a Year of Uncertainty," January 2011.

———. "U.S. Property/Casualty Insurance Industry," January 2011.

————. "U.S. Property-Casualty Insurance Outlook," December 2011.

Eschenbach, Felix; Francois, Joseph. "Financial Sector Competition, Services Trade, and Growth." CEPR Discussion Paper 3573, October 2002. http://www.cepr.org/pubs/dps/DP3573.asp.

Europa. "'Solvency II': Frequently Asked Questions (FAQs)." Press release, July 10, 2007. http://europa.eu/rapid/pressReleasesAction.do?reference=MEMO/07/286&format=HTM L&aged=0&language=EN&guiLanguage=en.

Ewing, Jack; Andrea, Zammert; Wendy, Zellner; Rachel, Tiplady; Ellen, Groves; Michael Eidam. "The Next Wal-Mart?" *BusinessWeek*, April 26, 2004. http://www.businessweek.com/magazine/content/04_17/b3880010.htm.

FashionNetAsia.com. "China: The Country to Become the World's Largest Luxury Goods Market by 2012," June 14, 2011. http://www.fashionnetasia.com/en/IndustryNews/DailyHeadline/Detail.html?id=2849.

Federal Express. "Fact Sheet, FedEx Express: International," n.d. http://news.van.fedex.com/files/1109%20FedEx%20Express%20Worldwide%20Fact%20Sheet.p   df   (accessed January 18, 2012).

————. "FedEx Supply Chain Customer Success Story: Medical Device Hearing Solutions," n.d.   http://images.fedex.com/us/healthcare/pdf/FedExSupplyChainMedDeviceSuccess.pdf (accessed January 17, 2011).

Federal Reserve Bank of Philadelphia. "The Proposed Implementation of the Volcker Rule." *Banking Legislation and Policy* 30, no. 3 (Third Quarter 2011). http://www.phil.frb.org/research-and- data/publications/banking-legislation-and-policy/2011/blpq311.pdf.

Felsted, Andrea. "Retailers: Trust the Stores to Get Into Banking." *Financial Times*, April 28, 2010.   http://www.ft.com/intl/cms/s/0/27e33e38-50ca-11df-bc86-00144feab49a.html#axzz1pla8w1f1.

FiercePharma Manufacturing. "BMS Offloads U.S. Distribution to Exel," March 29, 2011. http://www.fiercepharmamanufacturing.com/story/bms-offloads-us-distribution-exel/2011-03-29.

Fink, Carsten; Aaditya, Mattoo; Randeep, Rathindran. "An Assessment of Telecommunications Reform in Developing Countries." World Bank Policy Research Working Paper 2909, October 2002. http://elibrary.worldbank.org/content/ workingpaper/10.1596/1813-9450-2909.

Francois, Joseph F; Bernard, Hoekman. "Services Trade and Policy." CEPR Discussion Paper DP7616, December 2009. http://ssrn.com/abstract=1533220.

Freeman & Co. LLC. "Securities Industry Focus," Issue 12, October 2011. http://www.freeman-co.com.

Freeman Consulting Services and Thomson Reuters. "2012 Outlook for Investment Banking Services." *Third Annual Survey of Corporate Decision-Makers*, September 30, 2011. http://www.freeman-consultingservices.com/images/uploads/publications/2012_Outlook_for_IB_Services.pdf.

Freemantle, Thomas. "The Insurance Industry: Mergers and Acquisitions 2010." International Insurance News, December 22, 2010. http://www.globalsurance.com/blog/the-insurance-industry-mergers-and-acquisitions-2010-273920.html.

Fung, Victor K; William, K Fung; Yoram, (Jerry) Wind. *Competing in a Flat World: Building Enterprises for a Borderless World*. Upper Saddle River, NJ: Wharton School Publishing, 2009.

Future of US China Trade.Com. "U.S.-China Strategic & Economic Dialogue: Joint U.S.-China Commitments," n.d. http://www.futureofuschinatrade.com/article/us-china-strategic-economic- dialogue-joint-fact-sheet (accessed January 27, 2012).

Gap Inc. "Gap Inc. Expands E-Commerce Reach from One to Sixty-Five Countries by Year End." News release, August 12, 2010. http://www.gapinc.com/content/gapinc/html/media/pressrelease/2010/med_pr_GIDinternational08122010.html.

Gaudin, Sharon. "Online and Offline Commerce on Cusp of a Convergence." *Computerworld,* October 19, 2011. http://www.computerworld.com/s/article/9220986/Online_and_offline_commerce_on_cusp_of_a_ convergence.

GCCapitalIdeas.com. "Global Reinsurance Outlook: Points of Inflection, Positioning for Change in a Challenging Market; Executive Summary," December 30, 2010. http://www.gccapitalideas.com/2010/12/30/global-reinsurance-outlook-points-of-inflection- positioning-for-change-in-a-challenging-market-executive-summary/.

Global Express Association (GEA). "Position Paper on the Current WTO Draft Consolidated Negotiating Text on Trade Facilitation." TN/TF/W/165/rev. 10, August 2011.

Global Facilitation Partnership for Transportation and Trade. "WTO Trade Facilitation Negotiations," December 26, 2011. http://www.gfptt.org/entities/TopicProfile.aspx?tid=38355869-d2ba-427a- bfe8-1c29cefbd97f (accessed January 23, 2012).

Ha, Young. "Federal Insurance Office Says Overdue Regulation Report Still Weeks Away." *Insurance Journal*, February 2, 2012. http://www.insurancejournal.com/news/national/2012/02/02/233870.htm.

Hamm, Steve; Nandini, Lakshman. "The Trouble with India." *Business Week*, March 19, 2007. http://www.businessweek.com/print/magazine/content/07_12/b4026001.htm?chan=gl.

Hart, Joanne. "Working Out a Competitive Edge in the Chinese Onshore Bond Market." *The Banker*, January 3, 2012. http://www.thebanker.com/World/Asia-Pacific/China/Working-out-a- competitive-edge-in-the-Chinese-onshore-bond-market.

Hawthorne, Robert. "Demand for Credit Insurance Product Grows As Fears about Economy Linger." *MyNewMarkets.com*, July 5, 2011. http://www.mynewmarkets.com/articles/180940/demand-for- credit-insurance-product-grows-as-fears-about-economy-linger.

Hines, Alice. "Internet Sales Tax: Democrats, Republicans Support Closing Loophole." *Huffington Post*, December 1, 2011. http://www.huffingtonpost.com/2011/12/01/internet-sales-tax- bill_n_1123024.html.

Hoekman, Bernard; Aaditya, Mattoo. "Services Trade and Growth." World Bank Policy Research Working Paper 4461, January 1, 2008. http://www- wds.worldbank.org/servlet/WDSContentServer/WDSP/IB/2008/01/02/000158349_20080102162022/Rendered/PDF/wps4461.pdf.

Hoffmann, Bert. "Why Reform Fails: The 'Politics of Policies' in Costa Rican Telecommunications Liberalization." *European Review of Latin American and Caribbean Studies*, 84 (April 2008), 3–19.

Hot Telecom and Total Telecom. *Global Telecom Market Status and Forecast Report 2010–2015*, July 2011.

IBISWorld. "General Insurance in the UK." *IBISWorld Industry Report*, March 2011.

———. "Life Insurance & Annuities in the US." *IBISWorld Industry Report*, July 2011.

———. "Property, Casualty, and Direct Insurance in the US." *IBISWorld Industry Report*, August 2011. Insurance Information Institute (III). "Accounting: International Standards and Solvency II," n.d. http://www.iii.org/issue_updates/proposed-international-standards.html (accessed February 6, 2012).

———. "Catastrophes: Global," n.d. http://www.iii.org/facts_statistics/catastrophes-global.html (accessed January 26, 2012, and April 12, 2012).

———. "Catastrophes: Insurance Issues," February 2012. http://www.iii.org/issues_updates/catastrophes- insurance-issues.html.

———. "Climate Change: Insurance Issues," October 2011. http://www.iii.org/issues_updates/climate-change-insurance-issues.html.

———. *International Insurance Fact Book 2012*, n.d. http://www2.iii.org/international-insurance-fact-book/web-extras/download-by-chapter.cfm (accessed January 17, 2012).

———. "Long-Term Care Insurance," n.d. http://www.iii.org/facts_statistics/long-term-care-insurance.html (accessed January 25, 2012).

———. "What Are the Different Types of Permanent Policies?" n.d. http://www.iii.org/articles/what-are- different-types-permanent-policies.html (accessed February 28, 2012).

———. "What is an Annuity?" n.d. http://www.iii.org/articles/what-is-an-annuity.html (accessed February 28, 2012).

———. *The Insurance Fact Book 2012*. New York: Insurance Information Institute, 2012.

———. *The Insurance Fact Book 2011*. New York: Insurance Information Institute, 2011.

———. *The Insurance Fact Book 2010*. New York: Insurance Information Institute, 2010.

———. *The Insurance Fact Book 2009*. New York: Insurance Information Institute, 2009.

———. *The Insurance Fact Book 2008*. New York: Insurance Information Institute, 2008.

———. *The Insurance Fact Book 2007*. New York: Insurance Information Institute, 2007.

IBISWorld. "Global Commercial Banks." *IBISWorld Industry Report*, May 16, 2011.

IBISWorld. "Global Investment Banking and Brokerage: J5521-GL." *IBISWorld Industry Report*, June 22, 2011.

———. "Investment Banking and Securities Dealing in the U.S." *IBISWorld Industry Report 52311*, September 2011.

IBISWorld. "Global Wireless Telecommunications Carriers: I5111-GL." *IBISWorld Industry Reports*, October 14, 2011.

———. "Global Internet Service Providers: I5121-GL." *IBISWorld Industry Reports*, May 31, 2011. International Telecommunications Union (ITU). ICT Eye database (accessed June 28, 2012).

Insurance Information Institute (III). *2012 Financial Services Fact Book*. New York: Insurance Information Institute, 2012.

International Monetary Fund (IMF). *World Economic Outlook*, April 2011. http://www.imf.org/external/pubs/ft/weo/2011/01/pdf/text.pdf.

International Monetary Fund (IMF). *World Economic Outlook: Slowing Growth, Rising Risks*. Washington: IMF, September 2011. http://www.imf.org/external/pubs/ft/weo/2011/02/index.htm.

Investment Company Institute. *2011 Investment Company Factbook*. 51st ed. Investment Company Institute, 2011. http://www.icifactbook.org.

Investopedia. "Takaful." http://www.investopedia.com/terms/t/takaful.asp (accessed April 11, 2012).

Irandu, Evaristus M. "Opening African Skies: The Case of Airline Industry Liberalization in East Africa," *Journal of the Transportation Research Forum*, 47, no. 1 (Spring 2008), 73–88. http://www.trforum.org/journal.

Jacob, Rahul. "Chinese Head to Wealth Managers." *Financial Times*, September 5, 2011. http://blogs.ft.com/beyond-brics/2011/09/05/wealth-management-services-seduce-chinese-savers/.

Jenkins, Patrick; Brooke, Masters; Alex, Barker. "EU Banks Could Shrink to Hit Capital Rules." *Financial Times*, October 12, 2011. http://www.ft.com/intl/cms/s/0/f2e62f82-f4f2-11e0-9023-00144feab49a.html (fee required).

Jenkins, Patrick; Brooke, Masters; Tom, Braithwaite. "The Hunt for a Common Front." *The FT's Year in Finance*. Financial Times Special Report, December 13, 2011. http://www.ft.com/intl/cms/s/0/90e77ab6-2030-11e1-9878-00144feabdc0.html#axzz1pfx9qApu (fee required).

Jenkins, Patrick; Martin Stabe. "EU Banks Slash Sovereign Holdings." *Financial Times*, December 9, 2011. http://www.ft.com/intl/cms/s/0/a6d2fd4e-228f-11e1-acdc-00144 feabdc0.html (fee required).

Jenkins, Patrick; Simon, Rabinovitch; Joe, Leahy. "Ambitions Thwarted by Red Tape and Competition." *Financial Times*, September 13, 2011. http://www.ft.com/intl/cms/s/0/7521ecd4-de0a-11e0-a115-00144feabdc0.html#axzz1fJz4nP3b (fee required).

Jensen, J Bradford; Lori, G Kletzer. "Tradable Services: Understanding the Scope and Impact of Services Offshoring." Institute for International Economics Working Paper Series WP 05–9, September 2005. http://www.piie.com/publications/wp/wp05-9.pdf.

Johnson, Eric. "Vietnam on the Verge." *American Shipper*, December 2007. http://www.business-in- asia.com/news/jan2009_news.html.

Kearney, AT. "Retail Global Expansion: A Portfolio of Opportunities; The 2011 A.T. Kearney Global Retail Development Index." A.T. Kearney, 2011. http://www.atkearney.com/index.php/Publications/retail-global-expansion-a-portfolio-of- opportunities2011-global-retail-development-index.html.

King, Mike. "Supply Chain under Water." *Journal of Commerce*, November 21, 2011.

Kiplinger. "Economic Outlook," December 14, 2011. http://www.kiplinger.com/businessresource/economic_outlook (accessed January 2012).

Kleindorfer, Paul R; Yoram, (Jerry) Wind; Gunther, Robert E. "Network Orchestration: Creating and Managing Global Supply Chains without Owning Them." Chap. 17 in *The Network Challenge: Strategy, Profit, and Risk in an Interlinked World*. Upper Saddle River, NJ: Wharton School Publishing, 2009.

Koncz-Bruner, Jennifer; Anne, Flatness. "U.S. International Services: Cross-Border Trade in 2010 and Services Supplied Through Affiliates in 2009." *Survey of Current Business*, 91, no. 10 (October 2011). http://www.bea.gov/scb/pdf/2011/10%20October/1011_services%20text.pdf.

Koshik, Paul. "Russian Insurance Market—Decay or Good Prospects?" Insurance Insight, December 2, 2011. http://www.insuranceinsight.eu/insurance-insight/feature/2129731/russian -insurance- market-decay-prospects.

KPMG. "Logistics in China," 2008. http://www.kpmg.com.cn/en/virtual_library/ Property_Infrastructure/LogisticsChina.pdf.

KPMG. "Solvency II: Issues for the U.S. Insurance Market," July 2011. http://www.kpmg.com/US/en/IssuesAndInsights/ArticlesPublications/insurance-briefing/Documents/KPMG_Insurance%20Briefing_Solvency%20II.pdf.

KPMG. "Telecoms Operators Are Learning to Cooperate, Finds KPMG." Press release, September 20, 2011. http://www.kpmg.com/africa/en/issuesandinsights/articles-publications/ press- releases/pages/telecoms-learning-to-cooperate.aspx.

Ladbury, Adrian. "New Approach Needed to Cope with the Global Economy—Van Santen." *Commercial Risk Europe*, February 13, 2012. http://www.commercialriskeurope.com/ cre/1206/56/New- approach-needed-to-cope-with-the-global-economy-Van-Santen/.

Lal, Akash; Naveen, Tahilyani. "Wholesale Banking in India: The Next Frontier." *McKinsey Quarterly*, March 2011. https://www.mckinseyquarterly.com/Financial_Services/ Wholesale_banking_in_India_The_next_ frontier_2762#footnote2.

Lambe, Geraldine, "2011: Goodbye and Good Riddance?" *The Banker*, December 1, 2011. http://www.thebanker.com.

Lennighan, Mary. "Irish Mobile Operators in Network Sharing Deal." *Total Telecom*, April 6, 2011 http://www.totaltele.com/view.aspx?ID=463901 (subscription required).

Lloyd's. "Solvency II Explained," August 7, 2009. http://www.lloyds.com/News_Centre/ Features_from_Lloyds/News_and_features_2009/Market_news/Solvency_II_explained.htm.

Logistics Provider (3PL) as an Orchestrator." *Journal of Business Logistics*, 32, no. 1 (2011).

Logistics Week. "DHL Breaks Down Barriers to Emerging Market Growth," October 13, 2010. http://logisticsweek.com/news/2010/10/dhl-breaks-down-barriers-to-emerging-market-growth/.

Ludolph, Charles M. "U.S.-Bermuda Economic Relations: Economic Impact Study, 2010." Prepared for Business Bermuda by Albright Stonebridge Group, Washington, DC, September 2011. http://www.mondovisione.com/_assets/files/2011-Business-Bermuda-Economic-Impact-Study.pdf.

Luhby, Tami. "Fed in AIG Rescue: $85B Loan." CNNMoney.com, September 17, 2008. http://money.cnn.com/2008/09/16/news/companies/AIG/.

MacAskill, Andrew; Kartik Goyal. "Singh's Retail Retreat Marks 'Nail in the Coffin' for India Market Opening." *Bloomberg*, December 8, 2011. http://mobile.bloomberg.com/ news/2011-12-07/singh-s-retail-retreat-a-nail-in-the-coffin-for-india-opening.

Mahoney, John. "The Role of Insurance in Global Financial Stability—A Supervisor's Perspective." Swiss Re Centre for Global Dialogue, September 20, 2010. http://cgd. swissre.com/global_dialogue/topics/regulating_systemic_risk/The_role_of_insurance_in_ global_financial_stability A_supervisors_perspective.html (accessed February 22, 2012).

Manatayev, Yerlan Yergalievich. "Commoditization of the Third-Party Logistics Industry." M.A. thesis, Massachusetts Institute of Technology (MIT), 2003.

Marchetti, Juan A; Martin, Roy. "Services Liberalization in the WTO and PTAs." In *Opening Markets for Trade in Services: Countries and Sectors in Bilateral and WTO Negotiations*, edited by Juan A. Marchetti and Martin Roy, 61–112. Cambridge: Cambridge University Press, 2008.

Matlack, Carol; Rachel, Tiplady. "The Big Brands Go Begging in Europe." *BusinessWeek*, March 21, 2005. http://www.businessweek.com/magazine/content/05_12/b3925071 _mz054.htm.

Mattoo, Aaditya, Randeep Rathindran; Arvind, Subramanian. "Measuring Services Trade Liberalization and Its Impact on Economic Growth: An Illustration." World Bank Policy Research Working Paper 2655, August 2001.

Mattoo, Aaditya; Robert, M Stern. "Overview." In *A Handbook of International Trade in Services*, edited by Aaditya Mattoo, Robert M. Stern, and Gianni Zanini, 3–47. Oxford: Oxford University Press, 2008.

Meier, Fred. "Let State Farm Spy on Your Driving, Get Cheaper Insurance." *USA Today*, August 7, 2011. http://content.usatoday.com/communities/driveon/post/2011/08/let-state-farm-spy-on-your-driving-get-cheaper-insurance/1 (accessed January 25, 2012).

Menon, Rekha. "Money Matters: The Financing of India's Infrastructure Boom." *fDi Magazine*, February 14, 2012. http://www.fdiintelligence.com/Locations/Money-matters-the-financing-of-India-s- infrastructure-boom.

Mergent. *North America: Banking Sectors*, April 2011.

MetLife. "MetLife Announces Fourth Quarter and Full Year 2009 Results." Press release, February 2, 2010. http://investor.metlife.com/phoenix.zhtml?c=121171&p=irol- news Article&ID=1382029&highlight=.

———. "MetLife Announces Fourth Quarter and Full Year 2010 Results." Press release, February 9, 2011. http://www.metlife.com/assets/cao/pr/MetLife4Q2010Rls2-9.pdf.

Meyer, Henry. "Russia Repels Retailers as Ikea Halt Curtails Medvedev Goal." *Bloomberg*, March 2, 2011. http://www.bloomberg.com/news/2011-03-01/russia-repels-retailers-as-ikea-halt-curtails- medvedev-bric-goal.html.

Middleton, James. "Share and Share Alike." *Telecoms.com*, December 16, 2009. http://www.telecoms.com/ 17067/share-and-share-alike.

Ministère de l'Économie, de l'Industrie et de l'Emploi. [Ministry of the economy, industry, and employment of France.] "La Loi de Modernisation de l'Economie" [The law on modernization of the economy], 2008. http://www.minefe.gouv.fr/lois/lme.html.

Moody, Andrew. "B&Q, Home Depot Find the Going Tough." *China Daily*, April 6, 2009. http://www.chinadaily.com.cn/business/2009-04-06/content_7651845.htm.

Mukherjee, Arpita. "Services Liberalization in PTAs and the WTO: The Experiences of India and Singapore." In *Opening Markets for Trade in Services: Countries and Sectors in Bilateral and WTO Negotiations*, edited by Juan A. Marchetti and Martin Roy, 600–32. Cambridge: Cambridge University Press, 2008.

Mukherjee, Arpita; Smita, Miglani. "Non-Tariff Barriers in the Transport and Logistics Sectors: India." European Business and Technology Centre, August 2010. http://ebtc.eu/pdf/Tariff_Barriers_in_the_Transport_and_Logistics_Sector_India.pdf.

Murray, Justin; Marc Labonte. "Foreign Holdings of Federal Debt." Congressional Research Service Report RS22331, March 25, 2011.

Nachtmann, Heather; Edward, A Pohl. "The State of Healthcare Logistics: Cost and Quality Improvement Opportunities." Center for Innovation in Healthcare Logistics, July 2009, 5.

Nasdaq, "American International Group, Inc. (AIG) Revenue & Earnings Per Share (EPS)," n.d. http://www.nasdaq.com/symbol/aig/revenue-eps (accessed April 19, 2012).

National Retail Federation. "National Retail Federation Upgrades Holiday Forecast, Expects Sales to Rise 3.8 Percent to $469.1 Billion." News release, December 15, 2011. http://www.nrf.com/ modules.php?name=News&op=viewlive&sp_id=1278.

New York Times. "Amazon v. the States," March 17, 2011. http://www.nytimes.com/ 2011/03/18/opinion/18fri3.html.

Nikishenkov, Oleg. "Insuring Russia." *Moscow News*, February 6, 2012. http://themoscownews.com/business/20120206/189433257.html.

NKSJ Holdings. "Acquisition of Shares in Turkish Non-Life Insurance Company," June 15, 2010. http://www.nksj-hd.com/doc/pdf/e_news2010/e_20100615_1.pdf.

O'Donnell, Jayne. "Higher Holiday Sales Come with Caveat." *USA Today,* December 27, 2011. http://www.usatoday.com/money/industries/retail/story/2011-12-23/retail-holiday-sales/52196132/1.

O'Neill, Jim. "Building Better Global Economic BRICs." Goldman Sachs Global Economics Papers 66, November 2001. http://www2.goldmansachs.com/our-thinking/brics/brics-reports-pdfs/build- better-brics.pdf.

OANDA. Currency Converter database. http://www.oanda.com/currency/converter/ (accessed January 10, 2012).

———. Historical Exchange Rates database. http://www.oanda.com/currency/historical-rates/ (accessed December 2, 2011).

Office of the U.S. Trade Representative (USTR). *2011 National Trade Estimate on Foreign Trade Barriers.* Washington, DC: Office of the United States Trade Representative, 2011. http://www.ustr.gov/about-us/press-office/reports-and-publications/2012-1.

Office of the U.S. Trade Representative (USTR). *2011 National Trade Estimate on Foreign Trade Barriers.* Washington, DC: Office of the United States Trade Representative, 2011. http://www.ustr.gov/about-us/press-office/reports-and-publications/2012-1.

———. *2012 National Trade Estimate on Foreign Trade Barriers.* Washington, DC: Office of the United States Trade Representative, 2012. http://www.ustr.gov/sites/default/files/NTE%20Final%20Printed_0.pdf.

Office of the United States Trade Representative (USTR). *2011 Section 1377 Review on Compliance with Telecommunications Trade Agreements.* http://www.ustr.gov/webfm_send/2788.

Office of the United States Trade Representative (USTR). *2012 National Trade Estimate Report on Foreign Trade Barriers.* http://www.ustr.gov/sites/default/files/Vietnam.pdf.

Organisation for Economic Co-operation and Development (OECD). "The Future of the Internet Economy: A Statistical Profile; June 2011 Update." Prepared for the OECD high-level meeting on "The Internet Economy: Generating Innovation and Growth," Paris, June 28-29, 2011. http://www.oecd.org/document/28/0,3746,en_21571361_47081080_47122524_1_1_1_1,00.html.

Orzag, Peter. Congressional Budget Office (CBO). "Foreign Holdings of U.S. Government Securities and the U.S. Current Account." CBO Statement to the U.S. House of Representatives, the Committee on the Budget, June 26, 2007. http://www.cbo.gov/doc.cfm?index=8264&type=0.

Pasquarelli, Adrianne. "Private Labels Are Back in Fashion." *Crain's New York Business,* May 29, 2011. http://www.crainsnewyork.com/article/20110529/SMALLBIZ/305299979.

Pharmaceutical Commerce. "Exel Wins Bristol-Myers Squibb's 3PL Services Contract," April 8, 2011. http://www.pharmaceuticalcommerce.com/frontEnd/main.php?id Section=1628.

Planet Retail. Planet Retail Database. www.planetretail.net (accessed various dates) (subscription required).

Poggi, Jeanine. "The Great Retail Shrinkage: Will Smaller Stores = Higher Profits?" *The Street,* June 23, 2011. http://www.thestreet.com/story/11133719/3/the-great-retail-shrinkage-will-smaller-stores- equal-higher-profits.html.

PricewaterhouseCoopers LLP. "A Closer Look: The Dodd-Frank Wall Street Reform and Consumer Protection Act—Implications of Derivatives Regulation and Changing Market Infrastructure for Nonfinancial Companies," July 2011. http://www.pwcregulatory.com.

PricewaterhouseCoopers. *Transportation & Logistics 2030* Volume 3, *Emerging Markets— New Hubs, New Spokes, New Industry Leaders?* 2010. http://www.pwc.com/gx/en/ transportation- logistics/tl2030/emerging-markets/new-hubs_new-spokes_new-industry-leaders.jhtml.

Private Label Manufacturers Association (PLMA). "PLMA's 2011 Private Label Yearbook: Private Label Sales Keeps Climbing, Posts Market Share Gains in 18 Countries" (sic). News release, n.d. http://www.plmainternational.com/pressupdate/pressupdate_new02. asp?language=en (accessed November 10, 2011).

———. "What Are Store Brands?" n.d. http://plma.com/storeBrands/facts11.html (accessed November 10, 2011).

Pruzin, Daniel. "U.S. in Initial Talks on Launching Services Plurilaterals outside of Doha." *International Trade Daily*, January 19, 2012.

Pyramid Research. *Pyramid Perspective 2012: Top Trends in the Global Telecommunications Industry (excerpt)*, October 2011.

Reda, Susan. "Predictions 2012."*Stores,* December 2011. http://www.stores.org/ STORES%20Magazine%20December%202011/predictions-2012.

Reserve Bank of India. "Branch Banking Statistics." March 2009 (accessed April 12, 2012). http://www.rbi.org.in/scripts/AnnualPublications.aspx?head=Branch%20Banking%20Sta tistics.

Reuters. "TPSA, TPA Sign Infrastructure Deal," December 17, 2010. http://www.reuters. com/article/2010/12/17/tpsa-idUSLDE6BG1PI20101217.

Robert, Maryse; Sherry, Stephenson. "Opening Services Markets at the Regional Level under the CAFTA-DR: The Cases of Costa Rica and the Dominican Republic." In *Opening Markets for Trade in Services: Countries and Sectors in Bilateral and WTO Negotiations*, edited by Juan A. Marchetti and Martin Roy, 537–72. Cambridge: Cambridge University Press, 2008.

Robinson, Keith; Karl, Egbert; Henry, Wang. "China: Developments in Chinese Securities Regulation." *Dechert LLP Financial Services Quarterly Report—Asia*, July 6, 2011. http://www.mondaq.com/x/137802/Financial+Services/Developments+In+Chinese+Secu rities+Regulation.

RT. "Ikea Ufa Opens Up after the Long Wait," August 25, 2011. http://rt.com/ business/news/ikea-ufa- mega-store-133/.

Rubenstein, Roy. "Technology Trends: Mobile Network Sharing: Share Issues." *Total Telecom*, July 25, 2009. http://www.totaltele.com/view.aspx?ID=446761 (subscription required).

Russia Briefing. "Foreign Capital Raises Its Share in Russian Insurance Market," February 18, 2011. http://russia-briefing.com/news/foreign-capital-raises-its-share-in-russian-insurance-market.html/.

Ryan, Daniel. "Financial Services Regulatory Highlights: Financial Regulatory Reform—The New Architecture—Will It Be a Global Footprint?" PricewaterhouseCoopers LLP, 2010. http://www.pwcregulatory.com.

Saudi Airlines Cargo News. "Saudi Airlines Cargo Hikes Investments in Domestic Hubs to SR67.6M," April 2011. http://saudiacargo.com/april-2011_news.php.

Securities Industry and Markets Association (SIFMA). *Fact Book 2010*. New York: SIFMA, 2010.

————. *Fact Book 2011*. New York: SIFMA, 2011.

————. "Global Competitiveness: Overview," n.d. http://www.sifma.org/issues/cross-border-trade-and- policy/global-competitiveness/overview/ (accessed November 22, 2011).

————. "Reform in China: Overview," n.d. http://www.sifma.org/issues/cross-border-trade-and- policy/reform-in-china/overview/ (accessed November 22, 2011).

Shirley, Mary; Tusubira, FF; Frew Gebreab; Luke, Haggarty. "Telecommunications Reform in Uganda." World Bank Policy Research Working Paper 2864, June 2002. http://www-wds.worldbank.org/external/default/WDSContentServer/IW3P/IB/2002/10/12/00009494 6_02080604013933/additional/118518322_20041117181544.pdf.

Simonian, Haig. "Swiss Banks Turn Focus to Wealth Management." *Financial Times*, November 23, 2011. http://www.ft.com/intl/cms/s/0/9a61e5a0-15df-11e1-a691-00144feabdc0.html#axzz11AmfyJwV (accessed January 31, 2012; fee required).

Simonian, Haig. "Swiss Lawmakers Put Banks in Spotlight." *Financial Times*, June 7, 2011. http://www.ft.com/intl/cms/s/0/1c01358a-911e-11e0-9668-00144feab49a.html#axzz1 lAmfyJwV (accessed January 31, 2012; fee required).

Sojung, Carol Park; Jean, Lemaire. "The Impact of Culture on the Demand for Non-Life Insurance." Working paper, The Wharton School, University of Pennsylvania, 2011. http://statistics.wharton.upenn.edu/documents/research/WP2011-02-Lemaire.pdf.

Standard & Poor's. *Industry Surveys: Banking*, June 23, 2011.

Standard & Poor's. *Industry Surveys: Insurance: Life & Health*, April 14, 2011.

————. *Insurance: Property-Casualty*, September 22, 2011.

————. *U.S. Property/Casualty Insurance 2012 Outlook: Still Stable for Personal Lines and Negative for Commercial Lines*, December 1, 2011. http://www.standardandpoors. com/ratings/articles/en/us/?articleType=HTML&assetID=1245325866103.

Standard and Poor's. *Industry Surveys: Investment Services*. October 27, 2011.

Stefansson, Gunnar. "Collaborative Logistics Management and the Role of Third-Party Service Providers." *International Journal of Physical Distribution & Logistics Management*, 36, no. 2 (2006).

Store Brands Decisions. "Sainsbury's Launches Private Label Mexican Food Line," September 13, 2011. http://www.storebrandsdecisions.com/news/2011/09/13/sainsburys-launches-private-label- mexican-food-line.

Swiss Life. *Russia*. Employee Benefits Reference Manual. 2012. http://www.swisslife.com/ content/dam/id_corporateclients/downloads/ebrm/Russia.pdf, (accessed June 25, 2012).

Swiss Re. "Natural Catastrophes and Man-Made Disasters in 2010: A Year of Devastating and Costly Events." *Sigma*, No. 1/2011. Zurich: Swiss Reinsurance Company Ltd., 2011.

————. "The Role of Insurance in Global Financial Stability," July 15, 2010. http://cgd. swissre.com/global_dialogue/news/The_Role_of_Insurance_in_Global_Financial_Stabili ty_news.html.

Taaffe, Joanne. "Subsea Cable Networks: Well Connected." *Total TelecomPlus*, February 2011. http://www.totaltele.com/view.aspx?ID=462239.

Target. "Target Corporation to Acquire Interest in Canadian Real Estate from Zellers Inc., a Subsidiary of Hudson's Bay Company, for C$1.825 Billion." News release, January 13, 2011. http://investors.target.com/phoenix.zhtml?c=65828&p=irol- newsArticle&ID= 1515822&highlight=.

Telecommunications Industry Association (TIA). *TIA's 2011 ICT Market Review and Forecast*. Arlington, VA: Telecommunications Industry Association, 2011.

TeleGeography. "New Cables and Falling Prices to Disrupt Intra-Asian Submarine Cable Market." Press release, February 29, 2012. http://www.telegeography.com/press/press-releases/2012/02/29/new-cables-and-falling-prices-to-disrupt-intra-asian-submarine-cable-market/index.html.

————. "World Telecoms M&A Timeline." GlobalComms Database, 2012.

Thau, Barbara. "Can Uniqlo's Clever Clothes Refashion the U.S. Retail Market?" *DailyFinance*, October 29, 2011. http://www.dailyfinance.com/2011/10/29/can-uniqlos-clever-clothes-refashion-the-u-s- retail-market/.

The Banker. "Top 1000 World Banks 2011," June 30, 2011.

The Banker. "Top 25 Banks in 2011: Top 1000 World Ranking," January 25, 2012.

The World Bank. "China Financial Sector Assessment." *Financial Sector Assessment Program, a Joint Initiative of the World Bank and the IMF*. SecM2011-0492, November 2011. http://www.worldbank.org/content/dam/Worldbank/document/WB-Chinas-Financial- Sector- Assessment-Report.pdf (accessed January 29, 2012).

TheCityUK. "Financial Services in Emerging Economies." *Economic Trend Series*, June 2011. http://www.thecityuk.com (accessed November 23, 2011).

Thomson Reuters. "Global Investment Banking Review: First Nine Months 2011." 2011. http://dmi.thomsonreuters.com/Content/Files/3Q11_Global_IB_Review.pdf (accessed November 30, 2011).

————. "Global Investment Banking Review: Full Year 2011," 2011. http://dmi. thomsonreuters.com/Content/Files/Global_IB_Review_Full%20Year_2011.pdf (accessed February 22, 2012).

Total Telecom. Global 100, October 2011. http://www.totaltele.com/download.aspx? ID=468485 (subscription required).

Transport Intelligence. "Agility Emerging Markets Logistics Index 2011," January 2011. http://www.agilitylogistics.com/EN/Documents/Agility_Downloads/2011_Emerging_Ma rkets_L ogistics_Index.pdf.

————. *Vietnam Logistics 2009*, February 2009.

U.S. Census Bureau. "Quarterly Retail E-Commerce Sales, 4th Quarter 2011." February 16, 2012. http://www.census.gov/retail/mrts/www/data/pdf/ec_current.pdf.

————. "2007 NAICS Definition: Sector 44–45; Retail Trade." http://www.census.gov/cgi-bin/sssd/naics/naicsrch?code=44&search=2007%20NAICS%20Search (accessed November 8, 2011).

U.S. Department of Commerce (USDOC). Bureau of Economic Analysis (BEA). "Full-Time Equivalent Employees by Industry." Interactive tables: Gross Domestic Product by Industry Accounts, December 13, 2011. http://www.bea.gov/iTable/iTable.cfm?ReqID =5&step=1.

————. "Real Value Added by Industry." Interactive tables: Gross Domestic Product by Industry Accounts, December 13, 2011. http://www.bea.gov/iTable/iTable.cfm?ReqID= 5&step=1.

————. *Survey of Current Business*, 86, no. 10 (October 2006).

————. *Survey of Current Business*, 88, no. 10 (October 2007).

————. *Survey of Current Business*, 88, no. 10 (October 2008).

————. *Survey of Current Business*, 89, no. 10 (October 2009).

————. *Survey of Current Business*, 90, no. 10 (October 2010).

————. *Survey of Current Business*, 88, no. 10 (October 2011).

————. "Table 3a. Private Services Transactions." U.S. International Transactions Accounts Data, March 14, 2012. http://www.bea.gov/international/bp_web/list.cfm?anon=71&registered=0.

————. Bureau of Economic Analysis (BEA). "Table 6.6D: Wage and Salary Accruals Per Full-Time Equivalent Employee by Industry." Interactive tables: National Income and Product Accounts, August 8, 2011. http://www.bea.gov/national/nipaweb/TableView. asp?SelectedTable=201&ViewSeries=NO&Java=no&Request3Place=N&3Place=N&FromView=YES&Freq=Year&FirstYear=2005&LastYear=2010&3Place=N&Update=Update&JavaBox=no.

U.S. Department of Commerce (USDOC). Bureau of Economic Analysis (BEA). "Full-Time Equivalent Employees by Industry." Interactive tables: Gross-Domestic-Product-by-Industry Accounts, December 13, 2011. http://www.bea.gov/iTable/iTable.cfm?ReqID=5&step=1.

————. "Real Value Added by Industry." Interactive tables: Gross Domestic Product by Industry Accounts, December 13, 2011. http://www.bea.gov/iTable/iTable.cfm?ReqID=5&step=1.

————. *Survey of Current Business*, 91, no. 10 (October 2011).

————. "Table 6.3D: Wage and Salary Accruals by Industry." Interactive tables: National Income and Product Accounts Table, August 8, 2011. http://www.bea.gov/iTable/iTable.cfm?ReqID=9&step=1.

————. "Table 6.6D: Wage and Salary Accruals per Full-Time Equivalent Employee by Industry." Interactive tables: National Income and Product Accounts Table, August 8, 2011. http://www.bea.gov/iTable/iTable.cfm?ReqID=9&step=1.

————. "Table 9: Other Private Services." In U.S. International Services, 2006–2010. http://www.bea.gov/international/international_services.htm.

U.S. Department of Commerce (USDOC). Bureau of Economic Analysis (BEA). *Survey of Current Business*, October 2011. http://www.bea.gov/scb/pdf/2011/10%20October/1011_services%20text.pdf.

————. October 2010. http://www.bea.gov/scb/pdf/2010/10%20October/1010_services.pdf.

————. October 2009. http://www.bea.gov/scb/pdf/2009/10%20October/1009_services_text.pdf.

U.S. Department of Commerce (USDOC). Bureau of Economic Analysis (BEA). "Catalog of Major Revisions to the U.S. International Accounts," June 3, 2009.

————. *Survey of Current Business*, 91, no. 10 (October 2011).

————. *Survey of Current Business*, 88, no. 10 (October 2008).

————. *Survey of Current Business*, 87, no. 10 (October 2007).

U.S. Department of Commerce (USDOC). Bureau of Economic Analysis (BEA). Operations of Multinational Companies Database (accessed various dates) (later renamed the Direct Investment & Multinational Companies database, http://www.bea.gov/iTable/index_MNC.cfm).

————. "Supplemental Detail: Table 9. Services Supplied to Foreign Persons by U.S. MNCs through Their MOFAs, 2004–05." U.S. International Services database. http://www.bea.gov/international/xls/tab9_supp.xls (accessed April 20, 2012).

————. "Supplemental Detail: Table 10. Services Supplied to U.S. Persons by Foreign MNCs through Their MOUSAs, 2002–05." U.S. International Services database. http://www. bea.gov/international/xls/tab10_supp.xls (accessed April 20, 2012).

————. "Table 9. Services Supplied to Foreign Persons by U.S. MNCs through Their MOFAs, 2006–09." U.S. International Services database. http://www.bea.gov/ international/xls/tab9_a.xls (accessed April 20, 2012).

————. "Table 10. Services Supplied to U.S. Persons by Foreign MNCs through Their MOUSAs, 2006–09." U.S. International Services database. http://www.bea.gov/ international/xls/tab10_a.xls (accessed April 20, 2012).

————. "Value Added by Industry, Gross Output by Industry, Intermediate Inputs by Industry, the Components of Value Added by Industry, and Employment by Industry." http://www.bea.gov/industry/gdpbyind_data.htm (accessed March 13, 2012).

U.S. Department of Commerce (USDOC). Bureau of Economic Analysis (BEA). International Services. "Additional Detail on Financial Services Transactions, 2006–2010," n.d. http://www.bea.gov/international/international_services.htm# detailedstatisticsfor (accessed February 23, 2012).

————. International Services. "Additional Detail on Financial Services Transactions, 1994–2005," n.d. http://www.bea.gov/international/international_services.htm#detailedstatistics for (accessed February 23, 2012).

————. *Survey of Current Business*, 91, no. 10 (October 2011). "U.S. International Services: Cross- Border Trade in 2010 and Services Supplied through Affiliates in 2009. Table G: Other Private Services Receipts." http://www.bea.gov/scb/pdf/2011/10%20October/ 1011_services%20text.pdf.

————. *Survey of Current Business*, 89, no. 10 (October 2009). "U.S. International Services: Cross- Border Trade in 2010 and Services Supplied Through Affiliates in 2007. Table G: Other Private Services Receipts." http://www.bea.gov/scb/pdf/2009/10%20October/ 1009_services_text.pdf#page=16.

U.S. Department of Commerce (USDOC). Bureau of Economic Analysis (BEA). *Survey of Current Business* 89, no. 10 (October 2009).

U.S. Department of Commerce. Bureau of Economic Analysis (BEA). "Detailed Statistics for Cross- border Trade: Travel, Passenger Fares, and Other Transportation," U.S. International Services, http://www.bea.gov/international/international_services.htm (accessed January 25, 2012).

————. *Survey of Current Business*, 86, no. 10 (October 2006).

————. *Survey of Current Business*, 87, no. 10, October 2007.

————. *Survey of Current Business*, 89, no. 10, October 2009.

————. *Survey of Current Business*, 91, no. 10, October 2011.

U.S. Department of Commerce. U.S. Bureau of the Census. "Trade in Goods with Thailand." n.d. http://www.census.gov/foreign-trade/balance/c5490.html (accessed February 10, 2012).

————. "U.S. Imports from Thailand by 5-digit End-Use Code, 2002–2011," n.d. http://www.census.gov/foreign-trade/statistics/product/enduse/imports/c5490.html (accessed February 10, 2012).

U.S. Department of Labor (USDOL). Bureau of Labor Statistics (BLS). Employment, Hours, and Earnings—National database (accessed April 12, 2012). http://www.bls.gov/ ces/#data.

U.S. Department of the Treasury (U.S. Treasury). "FAQs: Questions on Country Classification in TIC Data," n.d. http://www.treasury.gov/resource-center/data-chart-center/tic/Pages/ticfaq2.aspx#q10 (accessed January 23, 2012).

———. "Major Foreign Holders for Treasury Securities," n.d. http://www.treasury.gov/resource- center/data-chart-center/tic/Documents/mfh.txt (accessed January 23, 2012).

———. "Securities (a), U.S. Transactions with Foreigners in Long-Term Securities by Type and Country," global(set of all countries).xls, n.d. http://www.treasury.gov/resource-center/data-chart- center/tic/Pages/ticsec.aspx (accessed January 19, 2011, and February 28, 2012).

———. "The 2011 U.S.-China Strategic and Economic Dialogue U.S. Fact Sheet—Economic Track," May 10, 2011. http://www.treasury.gov/press-center/press-releases/Pages/TG1172.aspx.

———. "U.S. Fact Sheet–Economic Track of the Fourth Meeting of the U.S.-China Strategic and Economic Dialog (S&ED)," May 4, 2012. http://www.treasury.gov/press-center/press- releases/Pages/tg1568.aspx.

———. Federal Reserve Bank of New York, Board of Governors of the Federal Reserve System. *Report on Foreign Portfolio Holdings of U.S. Securities as of June 2010*, April 2011. http://www.treasury.gov/resource-center/data-chart-center/tic/Documents/shla 2010r.pdf.

———. Office of the Comptroller of the Currency (OCC). "Quarterly Report on Bank Trading and Derivatives Activities, Third Quarter 2011." http://www.occ.treas.gov/topics/capital-markets/financial-markets/trading/derivatives/dq311.pdf (accessed February 2, 2012).

———. Office of Financial Stability. "Troubled Asset Relief Program: Three Year Anniversary Report," October 2011. http://www.treasury.gov/initiatives/financial-stability/briefing- room/reports/agency_reports/Documents/TARP%20Three%20Year%20Anniversary%20Report.p df (accessed June 27, 2012).

U.S. Department of the Treasury, Web site, n.d. http://www.treasury.gov/about/organizational- structure/offices/Pages/federal-Insurance.aspx (accessed March 1, 2012).

U.S. Department of Transportation (USDOT), Office of the Assistant Secretary for Aviation and International Affairs. "International Issues," n.d. http://ostpxweb.dot.gov/aviation/intlaffairs.htm#bilateral (accessed January 20, 2012).

U.S. International Trade Commission (USITC), *Logistic Services: An Overview of the Global Market and Potential Effects of Removing Trade Impediments*, USITC Publication 3770. Washington, DC: USITC, 2005.

———. *Shifts in U.S. Merchandise Trade*, USITC Publication 4245. Washington, DC: USITC, 2011. USTR, *see* Office of the U.S. Trade Representative.

U.S. International Trade Commission (USITC). *Property and Casualty Insurance Services: Competitive Conditions in Foreign Markets*. USITC Publication 4068. Washington, DC: USITC, March 2009.

U.S. International Trade Commission Services Roundtable, Washington DC, November 3, 2011.

UK Financial Services Authority. *Prudential Risk Outlook 2011*. London: Financial Services Authority, 2011. http://www.fsa.gov.uk/pubs/other/pro.pdf (accessed February 23, 2012).

United Nations Conference on Trade and Development (UNCTAD). "Negotiations on Transport and Logistics Services: Issues to Consider." UNCTAD/SDTE/TLB/2005/3, 2006.

United Nations Conference on Trade and Development (UNCTAD). "Trade and Development Aspects of Insurance Services and Regulatory Frameworks," November 21, 2005. http://www.unctad.org/en/docs/ditctncd200515_en.pdf.

UPS Supply Chain Solutions. "Hitachi GST Streamlines Global Distribution Network," 2004. http://www.ups-scs.com/solutions/case_studies/cs_hitachi.pdf.

UPS. "Pharmaceuticals and Biotech," n.d. http://www.ups.com/content/us/en/ bussol/browse/ industries/pharma-biotech-store.html. (accessed January 24, 2012).

————. "Supply Chain Solutions for Healthcare Providers: Part 2—Supply Chain Improvement Opportunities," UPS Supply Chain White Paper, 2005.

————. *UPS 2010 Annual Report*, 2010. http://www.investors.ups.com/phoenix.zhtml? c=62900&p=irol- reportsannual.

————. "UPS and Merck Expand Their Distribution and Logistics Agreement." Press release, June 28, 2011. http://www.ups.com/content/cn/en/about/news/20110630.html.

————. "UPS to Acquire Italian Pharma Logistics Company Pieffe." Press release, December 1, 2011. http://pressroom.ups.com/Press+Releases/Archive/2011/Q4/UPS+to +Acquire+Italian+Pharma+L ogistics+Company+Pieffe.

USDOC. BEA. *Survey of Current Business* 91, no. 10 (October 2011).

————. Form BE-125 (1-2010). "Quarterly Survey of Transactions in Selected Services and Intangible Assets with Foreigners," (accessed February 29, 2012). USTR, *see* Office of the U.S. Trade Representative.

USTR, *see* Office of the U.S. Trade Representative.

USTR, *see* Office of the U.S. Trade Representative.

Wallace, Paul. "Vickers Report Leaves Investment Banking Shrouded in Uncertainty." *The Banker*, December 1, 2011. http://www.thebanker.com/World/Western-Europe/UK/ Vickers-report-leaves- investment-banking-shrouded-in-uncertainty?ct=true.

Wal-Mart. "Banco Walmart Opens Its 1 Millionth Account." Press release, March 15, 2011. http://walmartstores.com/pressroom/news/10569.aspx.

Walmart. "The South African Competition Tribunal Approves Merger and Accepts Conditions Proposed by Walmart and Massmart." News release, May 31, 2011. http://walmartstores.com/pressroom/news/10609.aspx.

————. "Walmart Announces New Stores at Skyland & Fort Totten Square." News release, November 15, 2011. http://www.walmartwashingtondc.com/walmart-announces-new- stores-at-skyland-fort- totten-square/.

————. "Wal-Mart Stores, Inc. Data Sheet—Worldwide Unit Details, September 2011," October 19, 2011. http://walmartstores.com/pressroom/news/10731.aspx.

————. "Wal-Mart Stores, Inc. Data Sheet—Worldwide Unit Details, December 2011," January 16, 2012. http://walmartstores.com/pressroom/news/10798.aspx.

Walsh, John. Office of the Comptroller of the Currency (OCC), U.S. Treasury. "Remarks before the Centre for the Study of Financial Innovation, London," June 21, 2011. http://www.occ.gov/news-issuances/speeches/2011/pub-speech-2011-78.pdf (accessed February 2, 2012).

————. "REMARKS BEFORE THe Special Seminar on International Finance, Tokyo, Japan." November 16, 2011. http://www.occ.gov/news-issuances/speeches/2011/pub-speech-2011-135.pdf (accessed February 2, 2012).

Wang, Kelly. "Foreign Investment in Securities in China." MMLC Group—MMLC Murphy Wang, June 19, 2009. http://www.hg.org/article.asp?id=6551.

Wang, Yi, Jun Xu, and Anna Yip. "China's Changing Wholesale Landscape." *McKinsey Quarterly*, March 2011. https://www.mckinseyquarterly.com/Financial_Services/Chinas_changing_wholesale_landscape_2744.

Webel, Baird. "The Dodd-Frank Wall Street Reform and Consumer Protection Act: Issues and Summary." CRS Report for Congress R41350, July 29, 2010. http://www.llsdc.org/attachments/files/232/CRS-R41350.pdf.

William Fry. "Reinsurance: Ireland." Fact sheet, 2010. http://www.williamfry.ie/Libraries/test/Reinsurance-Ireland-2.sflb.ashx.

Wohl, Jessica. "U.S. Stores Shrink, Get Make-overs to Boost Sales." Reuters, October 27, 2011. http://www.reuters.com/assets/print?aid=USN1E79O0A520111027.

World Bank. Investing Across Borders database. http://iab.worldbank.org/ (accessed December 27, 2011).

————. World Development Indicators database. http://databank.worldbank.org/ddp/home.do (accessed November 4, 2011).

World Trade Organization (WTO). "Chapter 1: Basic Purpose and Concepts." General Agreement on Trade in Services Training Module, n.d. http://www. wto.org/english/tratop_e/serv_e/cbt_course_e/c1s1p1_e.htm (accessed April 7, 2009).

————. *International Trade Statistics 2011*. Geneva: WTO Secretariat, 2011.

World Trade Organization (WTO). "Coverage of Basics Telecommunications and Value-Added Services," n.d. http://www.wto.org/english/tratop_e/serv_e/telecom_e/telecom_coverage_e.htm (accessed February 29, 2012).

World Trade Organization (WTO). "Guide to Reading the GATS Schedules of Specific Commitments and the List of Article II (MFN) Exemptions." http://www.wto.org/english/tratop_e/serv_e/guide1_e.htm (accessed April 13, 2012).

————. "Schedules of Commitments and Lists of Article II Exemptions." http://www.wto.org/english/tratop_e/serv_e/serv_commitments_e.htm (accessed January 2012).

————. "Services Database." http://tsdb.wto.org/ (accessed April 13, 2012).

————. "Working Party Seals the Deal on Russia's Membership Negotiations." News release, November 10, 2011. http://www.wto.org/english/news_e/news11_e/acc_rus_10nov11_e.htm.

World Trade Organization (WTO). "The People's Republic of China: Schedule of Specific Commitments." GATS/SC/135, February 14, 2002.

———— ."Trade Growth to Ease in 2011 but Despite 2010 Record Surge, Crisis Hangover Persists." Press release, April 7, 2011. http://www.wto.org/english/news_e/pres11_e/pr628_e.htm.

World Trade Organization (WTO). Trade Policy Review Board (TPRB). *WTO Trade Policy Review: Report by the Secretariat; European Communities*. WT/TPR/S/214/Rev.1, June 8, 2009.

Wrigley, Neil; Michelle, Lowe. "The Globalization of Trade in Retail Services." Report commissioned by the OECD Trade Policy Linkages and Services Division for the OECD

Experts Meeting on Distribution Services, Paris, November 17, 2010. http://www.oecd.org/document/33/0,3746,en_2649_36344374_46259617_1_1_1_1,00.html.

Xinhua News Agency. "More Participation Allowed in Securities Firms," December 29, 2007. http://www.china.org.cn/english/business/237495.htm.

Zacharia, Zach G; Nada, R Sanders; Nancy, W Nix. "The Emerging Role of the Third-Party

Zenith. "Fairfax Receives Regulatory Approval for Acquisition of Zenith." Press release, May 19, 2010. http://www.thezenith.com/contact/financial/pressreleases/presspdfs/2010_05 _19_fairfax_approval.pdf.

Zimmerman, Ann; Karen, Talley. "Target Is Going Abroad—to Canada." *Wall Street Journal*, January 14, 2011. http://online.wsj.com/article/SB100014240527487035834045760796904179701136.html.

End Notes

[1] This report uses timeframes based on data availability. For example, BEA data on cross-border trade are available through 2010, while data on affiliate transactions are available through 2009. More recent timeframes are used where possible.

[2] Beginning in 2008, the *Recent Trends* report has discussed the professional and infrastructure service subsectors in alternate years, to allow more detailed analysis of individual services industries. Professional services, such as education, healthcare, and legal services, are labor-intensive industries employing highly skilled individuals, and frequently require specialized licenses or training. Infrastructure services, such as banking, insurance, and logistics services, are capital-intensive industries providing critical inputs to industrial activity and economic growth, and are used by every firm regardless of economic sector.

[3] Beginning in 2008, the *Recent Trends* report has examined the professional and infrastructure service subsectors in alternate years. This division allows more detailed analysis of individual industries. Professional services, such as education, healthcare, and legal services, are labor-intensive industries employing highly skilled individuals, and frequently require specialized licenses or training. Infrastructure services, such as banking, insurance, and logistics services, are capital-intensive industries providing critical inputs to industrial activity and economic growth, and are used by every firm regardless of economic sector.

[4] BEA data are compiled from surveys. For more information, see USDOC, BEA, *Survey of Current Business*, October 2011.

[5] Data on affiliate transactions lag those on cross-border services trade by one year. Thus, while analyses of cross-border trade data compare performance in 2010 (the most recent year for which data are available) to trends from 2005 through 2009, analyses of affiliate transactions compare performance in 2009 to trends from 2006 through 2008. Note also that in 2009, BEA changed its method of reporting affiliate trade data. New affiliate data report "services supplied," a measure that better reflects services output than the prior measure, "sales of services." The change is retroactive for data from years 2005–08. For more information, see USDOC, BEA, *Survey of Current Business*, October 2009, 34–36.

[6] USDOC, BEA, "Real Value Added by Industry," December 13, 2011; USDOC, BEA, "Full-Time Equivalent Employees by Industry," December 13, 2011; USDOC, BEA, "Table 6.6D," August 8, 2011. Value added is a measure of an industry's contribution to GDP; it is the difference between the value of an industry's gross output and the cost of its intermediate inputs.

[7] This discussion draws on WTO trade data to help compare U.S. trends with those of other countries. Elsewhere, the report uses BEA data. The term "commercial services," used by the WTO, is roughly equivalent to "private services" used by the BEA: both refer to services offered by the private, rather than the public, sector. However, there are differences between the two values. These differences are the result of a lagged time period used for the WTO estimate and small differences in the activities captured by the two measures. USDOC, BEA representative, telephone interview by USITC staff, February 23, 2012.

[8] WTO, *International Trade Statistics 2011*, 2011, table A8.

[9] WTO, *International Trade Statistics 2011*, 2011, table A9.

[10] The $162.2 billion trade surplus estimated by the BEA differs from the $160.3 billion WTO estimate presented above in the "Global Services Trade" section. See footnote 5.

[11] For the purposes of this report, infrastructure services include banking, insurance, securities, transportation, telecommunication, electric power, retail, and wholesale trade services.

[12] Values are reported before deductions for expenses and taxes, as gross values are most directly comparable across countries, industries, and firms.

[13] USDOC, BEA, *Survey of Current Business*, October 2011, 32.

[14] USDOC, BEA, *Survey of Current Business*, October 2011, 32. Travel services are measured through the purchase of goods and services while traveling abroad. Such items include, for example, food, lodging, recreation, local transportation, and entertainment.

[15] Cross-border services trade, as reported in the current account, includes both private and public sector transactions. The latter principally reflect operations of the U.S. military and embassies abroad. However, because public sector transactions are not considered to reflect U.S. service industries' competitiveness and may introduce anomalies resulting from events such as international peacekeeping missions, this report will focus solely on private sector transactions, except when noted.

[16] According to the BEA, "trade-related services" consist of auction services, Internet or online sales services, and services provided by independent sales agents. USDOC, BEA, *Survey of Current Business*, October 2011, 33.

[17] This encompasses freight transportation and port services, but does not include air passenger transport services (i.e., passenger fares).

[18] USDOC, BEA, *Survey of Current Business*, October 2010, 50–51.

[19] USDOC, BEA, *Survey of Current Business*, October 2011, 34–35.

[20] U.S.-owned foreign affiliates are affiliates owned by a U.S. parent company and located abroad; conversely, foreign-owned U.S. affiliates are affiliates located in the United States and owned by foreign parent companies.

[21] The main source for this section is the USDOC, BEA, *Survey of Current Business*, October 2007– October 2011.

[22] Data for infrastructure services are underreported due to the suppression of data by BEA to avoid disclosure of confidential firm information.

[23] USDOC, BEA, *Survey of Current Business*, October 2011, tables 8–10.2.

[24] See section 2 for a discussion of infrastructure services.

[25] Hoekman and Mattoo, "Services Trade and Growth." January 2008, 1.

[26] Mattoo and Stern, "Overview," 2008, 9–13.

[27] Francois and Hoekman, "Services Trade and Policy," 2009, 10.

[28] Francois and Hoekman, "Services Trade and Policy," 2009, 10; Hoekman and Mattoo, "Services Trade and Growth," January 2008, 27. Retail services do not necessarily require large capital investments, but still may face regulations on store size, operating hours, foreign investment, and other aspects of the industry; see section 6 for a discussion of the retail sector.

[29] De Sousa and Findlay, "Relationship between Liberalization in the Logistics Sector," 252. In air transport, the introduction of competition for intracountry and intraregional air transport routes in East Africa resulted in increased service quality, decreased time and costs of air passenger and freight transport, and increased trade and tourism in the region. Irandu, "Opening African Skies," 2008.

[30] Mattoo and Stern, "Overview," 2008, 13–15. The new entity was granted a five-year monopoly, which may have contributed to the outcome.

[31] Members of the public noted that liberalization in other Latin American countries often resulted in rate increases. Hoffmann, "Why Reform Fails," April 2008. Subsequently, Costa Rica liberalized some telecommunication services as part of the Dominican Republic-Central America-United States Free Trade Agreement.

[32] For financial services, see Eschenbach and Francois, "Financial Sector Competition, Services Trade, and Growth," 2002.

[33] Mattoo and Stern, "Overview," 2008, 15, 17–18.

[34] Mattoo and Stern, "Overview," 2008, 15–16.

[35] Hoekman and Mattoo, "Services Trade and Growth," January 2008, 28. Information asymmetries arise when certain parties to a transaction have better or more complete information than others. "When such information is costly to obtain and disseminate and consumers have similar preferences about the relevant attributes of the service supplier, the regulation of entry and operations in a sector can increase welfare." Francois and Hoekman, "Services Trade and Policy," 2009, 10.

[36] Mattoo and Stern, "Overview," 2008, 13–14.

[37] Hoekman and Mattoo, "Services Trade and Growth," January 2008, 11; Copeland and Mattoo, "The Basic Economics of Services Trade," 86. Substantial gains are realized from liberalizing FDI. Romdhane, "Liberalizing Trade in Services in Tunisia," 2011.

[38] Copeland and Matoo, "The Basic Economics of Services Trade," 84.

[39] Francois and Hoekman, "Services Trade and Policy," 11. Regulations can be nontransparent if produced without industry input, applied unevenly, difficult to understand or comply with, or difficult to find.

[40] USDOC, BEA, "Full-Time Equivalent Employees by Industry," 2011; USDOC, BEA, "Real Value Added by Industry," 2011.

[41] USDOC, BEA, "Full-Time Equivalent Employees by Industry," August 5, 2011; USDOC, BEA, "Real Value Added by Industry," 2011.

[42] USDOC, BEA, *Survey of Current Business*, October 2011, table 1. For the purposes of the cross- border trade discussion, data on infrastructure services include passenger fares and other transportation services, industrial

services, financial and insurance services, telecommunications, database and other information services, operational leasing, and trade-related services.

[43] USDOC, BEA, *Survey of Current Business*, October 2011, table 9.2. Affiliate transactions data for infrastructure services cover wholesale, retail, publishing, telecommunications, broadcasting, Internet service providers, finance and insurance, utilities, and transportation and warehousing.

[44] IBISWorld, "Global Commercial Banks," May 16, 2011, 7.

[45] IBISWorld, "Global Commercial Banks," May 16, 2011, 9.

[46] IBISWorld, "Global Commercial Banks," May 16, 2011, 4.

[47] USITC calculations based on IBISWorld data.

[48] IBISWorld, "Global Commercial Banks," May 16, 2011, 4.

[49] IBISWorld, "Global Commercial Banks," May 16, 2011, 11–12.

[50] *The Banker*, "Top 1000 World Banks 2011," June 30, 2011.

[51] Federal Deposit Insurance Corporation, "Bank Failures in Brief," 2010 and 2011.

[52] EIU, *Country Finance: United States of America*, November 2011, 11.

[53] EIU, *Country Finance: United States of America*, November 2011, 15.

[54] Public Law 111-203, 124 Stat. 1375, approved July 21, 2010.

[55] Mergent, *North America: Banking Sectors*, April 2011, 13.

[56] IBISWorld, "Global Commercial Banks," May 16, 2011, 4.

[57] IMF, *World Economic Outlook*, April 2011, xv.

[58] Includes Australia, New Zealand, and neighboring South Pacific islands.

[59] EIU, "World Banks: A Historic Divide," October 15, 2011.

[60] Ibid.

[61] EIU, *Country Finance: China 2011*, August 2011, 13.

[62] China Banking Regulatory Commission, *Annual Report 2010*, 38 and 152.

[63] Brush, "Volcker Rule Will Cost Banks $1 Billion," October 28, 2011.

[64] Standard & Poor's, *Industry Surveys: Banking*, June 23, 2011, 6.

[65] Data on cross-border trade in banking services include credit card and other credit-related services and other financial services (which includes securities lending, electronic funds transfer, and other financial services). Data on affiliate transactions are aggregated with securities services as "financial services excluding insurance," and are examined in section 7.

[66] USDOC, BEA, *Survey of Current Business*, October 2011, 20.

[67] USDOC, BEA, *Survey of Current Business*, October 2011, 21.

[68] USDOC, BEA, *Survey of Current Business*, October 2011, 20-21.

[69] Data for cross-border trade in financial services by country are not broken out by industry segment in the same way as the aggregate data. These figures therefore include securities-related services, which are discussed in section 7.

[70] USDOC, BEA, *Survey of Current Business*, October 2011, 42, 44.

[71] The United Kingdom's GDP grew by 1.3 percent in 2010, lagging behind the GDP growth of Australia, Canada, and Japan at 2.7 percent, 3.2 percent, and 4 percent, respectively. While France's GDP growth mirrored that of the United Kingdom at 1.4 percent, its banking industry likely did not have the same scale of exposure to the financial crisis as that of the United Kingdom. USDOC, BEA, *Survey of Current Business*, October 2011, 42, 44.

[72] USTR, *National Trade Estimate Report on Foreign Trade Barriers*, 2011. There were 82,485 bank branches total in India as of March 2009; Reserve Bank of India, *Branch Banking Statistics*, March 2009.

[73] USTR, *National Trade Estimate Report on Foreign Trade Barriers*, 2011.

[74] Mergent, *North America: Banking Sectors*, April 2011, 13.

[75] For more information on the relationship between insurance services and development see, for example, UNCTAD, "Trade and Development Aspects of Insurance Services," November 21, 2005. See also USITC, *Property and Casualty Insurance Services*, March 2009.

[76] Brainard, "What Is the Role of Insurance?" January 1, 2008.

[77] Dickinson, "Encouraging a Dynamic Life Insurance Industry," n.d. (accessed January 26, 2010).

[78] USITC staff calculations, based on data published by the Insurance Information Institute (III).

[79] Ibid.

[80] AIG, Allianz, Assicurazioni Generali, AXA, Berkshire Hathaway, Munich Re, and Prudential ranked among the world's top 10 insurance firms in at least four of the six years from 2005 through 2010, and four of these firms (Allianz, Assicurazioni Generali, AXA, and Berkshire Hathaway) were among the top 10 in each of these years.

[81] Luhby, "Fed in AIG Rescue: $85B Loan," September 17, 2008; Nasdaq, "American International Group, Inc. (AIG) Revenue & Earnings Per Share (EPS)," n.d. (accessed April 19, 2012).

[82] CNNMoney.com, "Fortune 500 2010," n.d. (accessed January 30, 2012). The decrease in MetLife's 2009 overall revenues was largely due to a $5.1 billion loss in investment revenue, which, in turn, was principally a product of a $3.2 billion loss in derivatives, which the firm used to mitigate risks such as currency and interest rate

fluctuations. MetLife's revenues recovered in 2010 due, in part, to the firm's acquisition of American Life Insurance Company (Alico) from AIG in 2010, which expanded MetLife's global presence, particularly in Japan. MetLife, "MetLife Announces Fourth Quarter and Full Year 2009 Results," February 2, 2010; MetLife, "MetLife Announces Fourth Quarter and Full Year 2010 Results," February 9, 2011, 4.

[83] These include MetLife's acquisition of Alico (valued at $16.2 billion), Australian-firm AMP Ltd.'s acquisition of Australia-based AXA Asia Pacific Holdings Ltd. ($12.8 billion), U.S.-firm Aon Corp.'s acquisition of U.S. firm Hewitt Associates, Inc. ($4.9 billion), and U.S.-firm Prudential Financial, Inc.'s acquisitions of Japan-based AIG Star Life Insurance Co. Ltd. and AIG Edison Life Insurance Co. ($4.8 billion), among others. III, *The Insurance Fact Book 2012*, 2012, 20.

[84] Freemantle, "The Insurance Industry," December 22, 2010.

[85] Takaful insurance products are designed to comply with sharia law by employing a pooling system in which risks are shared among customers. By contrast, traditional insurance products enable customers to transfer risk to an insurance firm, and as such may conflict with sharia prohibitions against gambling and interest earnings. Investopedia, "Takaful" (accessed April 11, 2012); Bhatty, "The Growing Importance of Takaful Insurance," September 23, 2011, 2.

[86] Bureau van Dijk, ORBIS Companies database; EIU, "Malaysia Insurers," April 18, 2011; NKSJ Holdings, "Acquisition of Shares in Turkish Non-Life Insurance Company," June 15, 2010.

[87] III, *The Insurance Fact Book 2012*, 2012, 20.

[88] IBISWorld, "Life Insurance & Annuities in the US," July 2011, 25.

[89] IBISWorld, "Life Insurance & Annuities in the US," July 2011, 18. For example, permanent life insurance policies—such as whole life and variable life policies—include an account on which policyholders may earn interest or dividends, and annuities, which earn interest and provide customers with a guaranteed income. III Web site, http://www.iii.org/articles/what-are-differenttypes-permanent-policies.html (accessed February 28, 2012); III Web site. http://www.iii.org/articles/what-is-an-annuity.html (accessed February 28, 2012).

[90] Sojung and Lemaire, "The Impact of Culture on the Demand for Non-Life Insurance," 2011.

[91] IBISWorld, "Property, Casualty, and Direct Insurance in the US," August 2011, 17–18.

[92] Deloitte, "2012 Global Insurance Outlook," n.d., 12 (accessed January 25, 2012); Standard & Poor's, *Industry Surveys: Insurance: Life & Health*, April 14, 2011, 10–12; IBISWorld, "Life Insurance & Annuities in the US," July 2011, 18; IBISWorld, "Property, Casualty, and Direct Insurance in the US," August 2011, 18.

[93] "Face value" refers to the amount of coverage that an insurance policy provides, while "cash surrender value" is the amount that an insured will receive upon surrendering or canceling the policy. IRMI Web site, http://www.irmi.com/online/insurance-glossary/default.aspx (accessed March 1, 2012).

[94] Standard & Poor's, *Industry Surveys: Insurance: Life & Health*, April 14, 2011, 10–12.

[95] IBISWorld, "Life Insurance & Annuities in the US," July 2011, 18.

[96] Hawthorne, "Demand for Credit Insurance Product Grows," July 5, 2011.

[97] IBISWorld, "Life Insurance & Annuities in the US," July 2011, 18.

[98] Ernst & Young, "U.S. Life Insurance Outlook," January 2011, 4.

[99] Ernst & Young, "U.S. Life Insurance Outlook," January 2011, 4.

[100] IBISWorld, "Life Insurance & Annuities in the US," July 2011, 18.

[101] Ernst & Young, "U.S. Life Insurance Outlook," January 2011, 4.

[102] IBISWorld, "Property, Casualty, and Direct Insurance in the US," August 2011, 18.

[103] III, "Long-Term Care Insurance," n.d. (accessed January 25, 2012).

[104] Deloitte, "2012 Global Insurance Outlook," n.d., 12 (accessed January 25, 2012).

[105] Ernst & Young, "U.S. Property/Casualty Insurance Industry," January 2011, 2; Standard & Poor's, *Industry Surveys: Insurance: Property-Casualty*, September 22, 2011, 8–9.

[106] Standard & Poor's, *Industry Surveys: Insurance: Life & Health*, April 14, 2011, 19–20.

[107] Variable annuities offer policyholders a guaranteed minimum return regardless of market performance. Since the 2008 market downturn, many insurance firms have raised variable annuity prices, lowered benefits, or stopped providing such products. Standard & Poor's, *Industry Surveys: Insurance: Life & Health*, April 14, 2011, 20.

[108] Standard & Poor's, *Industry Surveys: Insurance: Life & Health*, April 14, 2011, 20; industry representative, telephone interview by USITC staff, March 1, 2012.

[109] For example, investment income accounts for approximately 28 percent of life insurers' revenues. IBISWorld, "Life Insurance & Annuities in the US," July 2011, 7.

[110] Ernst & Young, "U.S. Life Insurance Outlook," January 2011, 2.

[111] Public Law 111-203, 124 Stat. 1375, approved July 21, 2010.

[112] The possible implications of the Dodd-Frank Act are discussed in more detail in the "Outlook" section of this section, and additional details of the Act are provided in box 7.1.

[113] These regulatory guidelines are described in the "Outlook" section of this section.

[114] Swiss Re, "Natural Catastrophes and Man-Made Disasters in 2010," 2011, 1; III, "Catastrophes: Global," n.d. (accessed January 26, 2012).

[115] IBISWorld, "Property, Casualty, and Direct Insurance in the US," August 2011, 12.

[116] In 2010, about 30 percent of catastrophe-related insurance losses were the result of earthquakes. Swiss Re, "Natural Catastrophes and Man-Made Disasters in 2010," 2011, 1, 14.

[117] Swiss Re, "Natural Catastrophes and Man-Made Disasters in 2010," 2011, 1.

[118] Ladbury, "New Approach Needed to Cope with the Global Economy," February 13, 2012.

[119] IBISWorld, "Property, Casualty, and Direct Insurance in the US," August 2011, 12.

[120] Financial services firms outside of the insurance industry have been permitted to supply insurance since the Glass-Steagall Act was revoked in 1999. Standard & Poor's, *Industry Surveys: Insurance: Life & Health*, April 14, 2011, 17.

[121] Standard & Poor's, *Industry Surveys: Insurance: Life & Health*, April 14, 2011, 17.

[122] This program's compliance with insurance regulations has been questioned. Deloitte, "2012 Global Insurance Outlook," n.d., 12 (accessed January 25, 2012).

[123] Ernst & Young, "U.S. Life Insurance Outlook," January 2011, 3.

[124] "Green building" means carrying out activities integral to a structure's life cycle (including construction, deconstruction, maintenance, and design, among others) in an environmentally friendly and resource-conscious way. EPA, "Green Building: Basic Information," December 22, 2010 (accessed April 13, 2012). Standard building insurance does not always cover risks specifically associated with green building. For example, green building insurance may cover the cost of renovating a building to meet changing green certification standards (which can determine eligibility for tax incentives or reduced loan rates).

[125] Deloitte, "2012 Global Insurance Outlook," n.d., 12 (accessed January 25, 2012).

[126] CarInsuranceList.com, "Save Money with Driver Monitoring Programs," January 12, 2011.

[127] The Drive Safe & Save program, which was originally based on mileage, has begun to monitor and base discounts on additional behaviors such as braking, speed, and acceleration, among others. As of January 2012, the expanded program was available only in Illinois. State Farm Web site, http://www.statefarm.com/insurance/auto_insurance/drive-safe-save/drive-safe-save.asp (accessed January 25, 2012); Meier, "Let State Farm Spy on Your Driving," August 7, 2011.

[128] GCCapitalIdeas.com, "Global Reinsurance Outlook," December 30, 2010.

[129] A large volume of insurance business is conducted in Bermuda due to that country's accommodating regulatory structure, lack of income tax, stable monetary and political environments, well-developed infrastructure, and educated labor force, among other factors. Cummins, "The Bermuda Insurance Market," May 6, 2008, 1.

[130] Ludolph, "U.S.-Bermuda Economic Relations: Economic Impact Study, 2010," September 2011, 8.

[131] William Fry, "Reinsurance: Ireland," 2010; DIMA, "Ireland's International Re/Insurance Market Factsheet," 2010.

[132] Debari and Tan, "Foreign Insurance Companies in Japan?" June 13, 2011.

[133] IBISWorld, "General Insurance in the UK," March 2011, 19.

[134] Data for certain key markets were suppressed in order to avoid disclosure of information for specific firms. Most notably, BEA did not publish 2008 or 2009 data for France (which is home to AXA, the world's second-largest life insurance firm in 2010), or the Netherlands (which is home to Aegon, the world's seventh- largest life insurance firm). III, *The Insurance Fact Book 2012*, 2012, 5.

[135] III, *The Insurance Fact Book 2012*, 2012, 20; Zenith, "Fairfax Receives Regulatory Approval for Acquisition of Zenith," May 19, 2010.

[136] *Commercial Risk Europe*, "Global Programmes 2011," n.d. (accessed February 17, 2012); industry representative, telephone interview with USITC staff, February 16, 2012.

[137] Industry representative, telephone interview by USITC staff, February 16, 2012; industry representative, telephone interview by USITC staff, March 1, 2012.

[138] USTR, *2011 National Trade Estimate on Foreign Trade Barriers*, 2011, 73; industry representative, telephone interview by USITC staff, March 1, 2012.

[139] Industry representative, telephone interview by USITC staff, March 1, 2012.

[140] Industry representatives, telephone interview by USITC staff, February 13, 2012; industry representative, telephone interview by USITC staff, February 16, 2012; industry representative, telephone interview by USITC staff, March 1, 2012; USTR, *2011 National Trade Estimate on Foreign Trade Barriers*, 2011.

[141] Bull, "China Agrees to Open Up Auto Insurance Market," February 14, 2012.

[142] Industry representative, telephone interview by USITC staff, March 1, 2012; and USTR, *2012 National Trade Estimate*, 114.

[143] Comité Européen des Assurances (CEA), "Insurers Highlight Danger of Brazilian Protectionism," January 1, 2012; Amaral, "Argentina Raises Trade Barriers and Forces Insurers to Repatriate Assets," November 4, 2011; Industry representatives, telephone interview by USITC staff, February 13, 2012; Industry representative, telephone interview by USITC staff, February 16, 2012; Industry representative, telephone interview by USITC staff, March 1, 2012.

[144] Ernst & Young, "U.S. Life Insurance Industry Outlook," December 2011, 1; Ernst & Young, "U.S. Property-Casualty Insurance Outlook," December 2011, 1.

[145] IBISWorld, "Life Insurance & Annuities in the US," July 2011, 10; IBISWorld, "Property, Casualty, and Direct Insurance in the US," August 2011, 10.

[146] Ernst & Young, "U.S. Life Insurance Outlook," January 2011, 3.

[147] Dodd–Frank Wall Street Reform and Consumer Protection Act, Public Law 111-203 (July 21, 2010); Standard & Poor's, *Industry Surveys: Insurance: Life & Health*, April 14, 2011, 4–5; Ernst & Young, "U.S. Life Insurance Outlook," January 2011, 3.

[148] Ernst & Young, "U.S. Property-Casualty Insurance Outlook," December 2011, 2.

[149] At the time of writing, this report had not yet been released. U.S. Department of the Treasury, Web site, n.d. (accessed March 1, 2012); Ha, "Federal Insurance Office Says Overdue Regulation Report Still Weeks Away," February 2, 2012; industry representative, telephone interview by USITC staff, February 13, 2012.

[150] Standard & Poor's, *Industry Surveys: Insurance: Life & Health*, April 14, 2011, 4–5; Standard & Poor's, *Industry Surveys: Insurance: Property-Casualty*, September 22, 2011, 14.

[151] Solvency II includes provisions for determining the equivalence of third-country regulatory regimes, thus harmonizing the treatment of insurers from particular countries across all EU member states. Lloyd's, "Solvency II Explained," August 7, 2009, Web page, n.d. (accessed January 20, 2010); and Europa, "'Solvency II:' Frequently Asked Questions (FAQs)," press release, July 10, 2007, (accessed January 21, 2010).

[152] KPMG, "Solvency II," July 2011, 1-2; Ernst & Young, "U.S. Life Insurance Outlook," January 2011, 3.

[153] Ernst & Young, "U.S. Life Insurance Industry Outlook," December 2011, 1; Ernst & Young, "U.S. Life Insurance Outlook," January 2011, 3.

[154] III, "Accounting: International Standards and Solvency II," n.d. (accessed February 6, 2012); Ernst & Young, "U.S. Life Insurance Outlook," January 2011, 3.

[155] The earthquake and subsequent tsunami that struck Japan in March 2011 accounted for $210 billion, or about 55 percent, of overall global losses from natural and man-made losses in 2010. III, "Catastrophes: Global," n.d. (accessed April 12, 2012).

[156] III, "Catastrophes: Global," n.d. (accessed January 26, 2012).

[157] III, "Catastrophes: Insurance Issues," February 2012.

[158] III, "Climate Change: Insurance Issues," October 2011.

[159] III, "Catastrophes: Insurance Issues," February 2012; Swiss Re, "Natural Catastrophes and Man-Made Disasters in 2010," 2011, 1.

[160] IBISWorld, "Life Insurance & Annuities in the US," July 2011, 12; industry representative, e-mail message to USITC staff, February 17, 2012.

[161] Standard & Poor's, *U.S. Property/Casualty Insurance 2012 Outlook*, December 1, 2011; Deloitte, *2012 Global Insurance Outlook*, 2012, 6.

[162] Industry representative, e-mail message to USITC staff, February 17, 2012.

[163] IBISWorld, "Life Insurance & Annuities in the US," July 2011, 12; IBISWorld, "Property, Casualty, and Direct Insurance in the US," August 2011, 28.

[164] USITC, *Logistic Services*, 2005, 2-1. Certain services may be transported by logistics firms as well, including architectural plans, legal briefs, and franchising materials.

[165] "Supply chain management" refers to the design and management of transportation and distribution networks, and may include software implementation and inventory management.

[166] Bolumole, "The Supply Chain Role of Third-Party Logistics Providers," 2001, 90.

[167] Zacharia, Sanders, and Nix, "The Emerging Role of the Third-Party Logistics Provider," 2011, 41. In its annual report, UPS characterizes its customers' decision to outsource supply chain functions as part of an effort "to streamline and gain efficiencies [in their operations], to improve service, to support new business models and to strengthen their balance sheets." UPS, *UPS 2010 Annual Report*, 2010, 4.

[168] Bhatnagar and Viswanathan, "Re-engineering Global Supply Chains," 2000, 13–34.

[169] Armstrong & Associates, Inc., "3PL Customers Report Identifies Service Trends," 2009; Zacharia, Sanders, and Nix, "The Emerging Role of the Third-Party Logistics Provider," 2011, 42.

[170] Zacharia, Sanders, and Nix, "The Emerging Role of the Third-Party Logistics Provider," 2011, 40.

[171] Kleindorfer, Wind, and Gunther, "Network Orchestration," 2009, 300–302. Michael Porter recognized that supply chains "deliver not only products but value," thus giving rise to the term "value chain."

[172] Zacharia, Sanders, and Nix, "The Emerging Role of the Third-Party Logistics Provider (3PL) as an Orchestrator," 2011, 40. The authors discuss a company's "need to coordinate, communicate, and collaborate" with other members of the supply chain to remain competitive. They also discuss the role of 3PL firms as serving as an "orchestrator" to carry out these activities.

[173] While transportation infrastructure serves as the backbone of a 3PL's services network, the seamless operation of that network is enabled by sophisticated IT systems that permit a 3PL to monitor and control the movement of goods throughout the supply chain. In addition, a successful 3PL has the ability to "plug into" the network of another transport provider (e.g., a commercial airline or maritime shipping firm) when its own transportation network does not have sufficient reach. Stefansson, "Collaborative Logistics Management and the Role of Third-Party Service Providers," 2006, 70.

[174] Manatayev, "Commoditization of the Third-Party Logistics Industry," 2003, 45.

[175] Armstrong & Associates, Inc. "Global Logistics Estimates—2007," July 2007; Armstrong & Associates, "Global 3PL Market Size Estimates," n.d.

[176] Butcher, "The State of Logistics," June 23, 2011.

[177] Armstrong & Associates, "Global Logistics Estimates—2007," July 2007; Armstrong & Associates, "Global 3PL Market Size Estimates," n.d. (accessed November 14, 2011).

[178] PricewaterhouseCoopers, *Transportation & Logistics 2030*, 2010, 31.

[179] Hyundai GLOVIS Company website. http://www.glovis.net/Eng/about/company_idea.asp (accessed December 9, 2011).

[180] Panalpina Company Web site, http://www.panalpina.com/content/www/global/en/home.html (accessed December 12, 2011).

[181] Kuenhne + Nagel Company Web site, http://www.kn-portal.com/industry/ (accessed December 12, 2011).

[182] UPS Company Web site, http://www.ups-scs.com/consulting/demand.html (accessed December 12, 2011).

[183] WTO, "Trade Growth to Ease in 2011," April 7, 2011. For instance, in 2010, exports of automotive parts and components accounted for nearly 40 percent of total exports of automotive products (including vehicle exports) by countries in Asia, and roughly 35 percent of such exports from Europe.

[184] Fung, Fung, and Wind, *Competing in a Flat World*, 2009, 4–8.

[185] Deloitte Research, "Mastering Complexity in Global Manufacturing," 2003, 26–27.

[186] Deloitte & Touche, "Unlocking the Value of Globalisation," 2005, 17; Con-way, Inc., company Web site. http://www.con-way.com/en/about_con_way/history/ (accessed December 13, 2011). CNF was renamed Con-Way, Inc. in 2006. Con-way, Inc. is the parent company of global 3PL firm Menlo Worldwide Logistics.

[187] UPS Supply Chain Solutions, "Hitachi GST Streamlines Global Distribution Network," 2004. UPS also consolidated Hitachi's 72 distribution facilities for its hard disk drives (some of which were acquired from IBM) into 52 facilities.

[188] Armstrong & Associates, "Global Logistics Estimates—2007," July 2007, 2; Armstrong & Associates, "Global 3PL Market Size Estimates," n.d. (accessed November 14, 2011). For example, between 2006 and 2010, logistics revenues in Brazil rose 61 percent; in China 100 percent; in India 44 percent; and in Mexico 31 percent.

[189] *Logistics Week*, "DHL Breaks Down Barriers to Emerging Market Growth," October 13, 2010.

[190] PricewaterhouseCoopers, *Transportation & Logistics 2030*, 2010, 36.

[191] In 2002, the value of U.S. imports from Thailand was roughly $15 billion; by 2011, it was nearly $25 billion, with computer accessories, peripherals, and parts accounting for 13 percent of such imports. USDOC, U.S. Census Bureau, "Trade in Goods with Thailand," n.d. (accessed February 10, 2012); USDOC, U.S. Census Bureau, "U.S. Imports from Thailand," n.d. (accessed February 10, 2012).

[192] King, "Supply Chain Under Water," 2011, 12–14.

[193] Transport Intelligence, *Vietnam Logistics 2009*, 2009, 6; Johnson, "Vietnam on the Verge," *American Shipper*, December 2007.

[194] Dobberstein, Neumann, and Zils, "Logistics in Emerging Markets," 2005, 16.

[195] Panalpina Company Web site, http://www.panalpina.com/content/www/global/en/home.html (accessed January 10, 2012).

[196] UPS Company Web site, http://ups-scs.com/solutions (accessed January 10, 2012).

[197] *Business Today*, "A Happy Marriage," December 11, 2011.

[198] UPS Web site, http://www.pressroom.ups.com/Fact+Sheets/UPS+Fact+Sheet (accessed January 18, 2012).

[199] FedEx Express, "Fact Sheet," September 2011.

[200] Transport Intelligence, "Agility Emerging Markets Logistics Index 2011," January 2011, 17–18.

[201] Transport Intelligence, "Agility Emerging Markets Logistics Index 2011," January 2011, 18; *Saudi Airlines Cargo News*, "Saudi Airlines Cargo Hikes Investments in Domestic Hubs," 2010, April 3, 2011.

[202] Deutsche Post DHL, *Annual Report 2010*, 2010, 218–21; Cuthbert, "Saudi Arabia—The Land of Logistics Opportunity," November 27, 2011.

[203] WTO, "Trade Growth to Ease in 2011," April 7, 2011.

[204] Ibid.

[205] USITC, *Shifts in U.S. Merchandise Trade 2010*, 2011, US.9. See "TABLE US.3 All merchandise sectors: U.S. exports of domestic merchandise, imports for consumption, and merchandise trade balance, by selected countries and country groups, 2006–10."

[206] Foreign affiliates are U.S. parent firms' majority-owned nonbank affiliates in foreign markets, whereas U.S. affiliates are foreign parent firms' majority-owned nonbank affiliates in the U.S. market.

[207] BEA, *Survey of Current Business*, October 2011, 54; *Survey of Current Business*, October 2009, 61. These data include countries within Europe, Latin America, and the Asia Pacific region, but do not include Canada, for which information on foreign affiliate sales to U.S. entities is unavailable. The latest year for which Canadian affiliate sales are available is 2006. In that year, such sales equaled $4.7 billion, or nearly 13 percent of total sales by foreign transportation and warehousing affiliates.

[208] BEA, *Survey of Current Business*, October 2011, 55–56. Data on foreign affiliate sales in Switzerland for 2008 are unavailable.

[209] BEA, *Survey of Current Business*, October 2011, 55–56; BEA, *Survey of Current Business*, October 2006, 72.

[210] As of August 1, 2011, the United States had concluded bilateral air transport agreements with 130 countries.

[211] USDOT, "International Issues," n.d. (accessed January 20, 2012). Open skies agreements enable airlines to serve the other party to the agreement without restrictions found in Bermuda I and Bermuda II bilateral air transport agreements. The latter agreements restrict the frequency with which airlines can fly to and from destinations located in the signatory countries, the type of aircraft they may deploy, and the cities they may serve.

[212] WTO, "The People's Republic of China," February 14, 2002.

[213] KPMG, "Logistics in China," 2008.

[214] USTR, "2012 National Trade Estimate Report on Foreign Trade Barriers," 404, (accessed April 11, 2012).

[215] "Mexico Foreign Investment Law," http://www.mexicolaw.com/LawInfo26.htm (accessed June 26, 2012).

[216] Hamm and Lakshman, "The Trouble with India," March 19, 2007.

[217] Dobberstein, Neumann, and Zils, "Logistics in Emerging Markets," 2005, 16; Arvis et. al., *Connecting to Compete*, 2010, 8. The World Bank's logistics performance index (LPI) indicates that, in 2010, India ranked 47th out of 155 countries in terms of the efficiency of its logistics sector, far below developed economies but still within the top third of all countries included in the index.

[218] PricewaterhouseCoopers, *Transportation & Logistics 2030*, 2010, 36; Armstrong & Associates, "Global 3PL Market Size Estimates," n.d. (accessed November 14, 2011). In 2010, India spent 13.0 percent of its GDP on logistics-related costs. This number was higher than the average logistics expenditure ratio among all countries in 2010, 11.1 percent.

[219] UNCTAD, "Negotiations on Transport and Logistics Services," 2006. Core logistics services identified in the checklist include "services auxiliary to all modes of transport," such as "cargo handling services" (CPC 7411); "storage and warehousing services" (CPC 742); and "transport agency services" (CPC 748). In addition, freight transport services and wholesale and retail distribution services, among others, were identified in the checklist as related but non-core logistics services.

[220] Global Express Association (GEA), "Position Paper," August 2011; Global Facilitation Partnership for Transportation and Trade, "WTO Trade Facilitation Negotiations," December 26, 2011. GATT Article V pertains to "Freedom of Transit [of goods]"; Article VIII, to "Fees and Formalities Connected with Importation and Exportation"; and Article X, to "Publication and Administration of Trade Regulations."

[221] Pruzin, "U.S. in Initial Talks," January 19, 2012.

[222] WTO, "Trade Growth to Ease in 2011," April 7, 2011.

[223] UPS, *UPS 2010 Annual Report*, 3–7, 12.

[224] *Logistics Week*, "DHL Breaks Down Barriers to Emerging Market Growth," October 13, 2010.

[225] Pruzin, "U.S. in Initial Talks," January 19, 2012; Mukherjee and Miglani, "Non-Tariff Barriers in the Transport and Logistics Sectors," August 2010, 12–20. See section 9 for a discussion of plurilateral, bilateral, and unilateral liberalization.

[226] U.S. Census Bureau, "2007 NAICS Definition: Sector 44–45; Retail Trade" (accessed November 8, 2011).

[227] Betancourt, *The Economics of Retailing and Distribution*, 2004, 19–23.

[228] Retailing accounted for 12.9 percent of employment in service industries. USDOL, BLS, Employment, Hours, and Earnings—National Database. Seasonally adjusted statistics; figures quoted are for December 2011.

[229] USDOC, BEA, "Value Added by Industry" (accessed November 8, 2011, and December 2, 2011).

[230] Planet Retail database (accessed August 22, 2011).

[231] In 2005, Russia was the 11th largest retail market, accounting for 2.3 percent of global sales.

[232] The term "BRIC" originated in O'Neill, "Building Better Global Economic BRICs," November 2001.

[233] Canada, France, Germany, Italy, Japan, the United Kingdom, and the United States.

[234] Planet Retail database (accessed August 22, 2011).

[235] World Bank, World Development Indicators database. Calculated using constant local currencies. The "developed" group includes the countries classified by the World Bank as "High Income: OECD," (i.e., high-income members of the Organisation for Economic Co-operation and Development), while "developing" includes those countries classified as "Low and Middle Income."

[236] U.S. Census Bureau, "Quarterly Retail E-Commerce Sales, 4th Quarter 2011," February 16, 2012. The figure quoted in the text is a seasonally adjusted preliminary estimate.

[237] The United States Supreme Court's *Quill Corp. v. North Dakota* decision (1992) prevents states from forcing firms without a "nexus" (physical presence) in a state to collect state sales taxes. However, states such as New York have sought to increase tax collections from online retailers via more expansive definitions of "nexus." Such efforts have led to legal disputes between the states and online retailers. At the time of the writing of this report, the U.S. Congress was considering a bill that would require online retailers across the United States to collect state sales taxes (Hines, "Internet Sales Tax," December 1, 2011; *New York Times,* "Amazon v. the States," March 17, 2011).

[238] Boston Consulting Group (BCG), *The World's Next E-commerce Superpower*, November 2011, 5–7.

[239] John Donahoe, President and Chief Executive Officer of eBay, quoted in Gaudin, "Online and Offline Commerce on Cusp," October 19, 2011.

[240] A growing literature examines the effects of online retailing on prices. While studies find that consumers are highly sensitive to prices online (i.e., the price elasticity of demand for products sold online is high), demand on some retail sites may be more elastic than others (Chevalier and Goolsbee, "Measuring Prices and Price Competition Online," 2003, 220). In addition, some online retailers use "obfuscation" strategies to increase sales of higher-priced items, such as advertising low-quality merchandise at very low prices, but drawing consumers' attention to higher-priced merchandise once they enter the retailers' Web sites (Ellison and Ellison, "Search, Obfuscation, and Price Elasticities on the Internet," October 2007, 8–9).

[241] JCPenney Company Web site, http://www.jcpenney.com/jcp/default.aspx (accessed November 2, 2011).

[242] Enright, "Shrinking to Survive," September 30, 2011.

[243] Planet Retail database (accessed August 22, 2011).

[244] Conference Board, "Consumer Confidence Survey," October 25, 2011.

[245] National Retail Federation, "National Retail Federation Upgrades Holiday Forecast," December 15, 2011; O'Donnell, "Higher Holiday Sales Come with Caveat," December 27, 2011.

[246] Poggi, "The Great Retail Shrinkage," June 23, 2011.

[247] Clifford, "In These Lean Times, Even Stores Shrink," November 9, 2010.

[248] Wohl, "U.S. Stores Shrink," October 27, 2011.

[249] Walmart, "Walmart Announces New Stores," November 15, 2011.

[250] Clifford, "Wal-Mart Gains in Its Wooing of Chicago," June 24, 2010.

[251] Matlack and Tiplady, "The Big Brands Go Begging," March 21, 2005.

[252] Private Label Manufacturers Association (PLMA), "PLMA's 2011 Private Label Yearbook," n.d. (accessed November 10, 2011).

[253] Retailers either produce store-brand merchandise in-house or contract with firms that specialize in producing such goods. Merchandise produced through these methods is typically cheaper for retailers than comparable merchandise produced by brand-name manufacturers. PLMA, "What Are Store Brands?" n.d. (accessed November 10, 2011).

[254] The term hard discounter connotes that a retailer competes especially aggressively on price across merchandise categories. One source defines a hard discounter as "a retailer that pushes prices even lower than traditional discounters." Ewing et al., "The Next Wal-Mart?" April 26, 2004.

[255] Store Brands Decisions, "Sainsbury's Launches Private Label," September 13, 2011.

[256] Pasquarelli, "Private Labels Are Back in Fashion," May 29, 2011; Material Girl Collection Web site, http://materialgirlcollection.com/feb_2011/spring_2012/ (accessed April 13, 2012).

[257] Deloitte, "Leaving Home," January 2011, G8; A.T. Kearney, "Retail Global Expansion," 2011.

[258] Planet Retail database (accessed August 22, 2011).

[259] D'Innocenzio, "Gap Closing about Fifth of U.S. Stores," October 13, 2011; Associated Press, "Gap Plans Stores in Chile, Panama, Colombia," October 12, 2011.

[260] Walmart, "Wal-Mart Stores, Inc. Data Sheet," October 19, 2011; Walmart, "The South African Competition Tribunal Approves Merger," May 31, 2011.

[261] Bloomberg, "Best Buy Shuts China Stores," February 22, 2011. However, Best Buy did continue to operate its Five Star chain of stores, which it purchased in 2006.

[262] Meyer, "Russia Repels Retailers," March 2, 2011; RT, "Ikea Ufa Opens Up," August 25, 2011.

[263] Target, "Target Corporation to Acquire Interest in Canadian Real Estate," January 13, 2011.

[264] Zimmerman and Talley, "Target Is Going Abroad," January 14, 2011.

[265] Thau, "Can Uniqlo's Clever Clothes Refashion the U.S. Retail Market?" October 29, 2011.

[266] Growth in 2008 was similar to that in 2007 (9.6 percent) and 2006 (8.4 percent). However, in 2005— the first year for which year-on-year comparison data are available—growth totaled 36.2 percent. The reason for the large jump in 2005 is unclear, but it may have been due in part to Walmart's entry into five Central American countries in September of that year. USDOC, BEA, "Supplemental Detail: Table 9" and "Table 9"; Walmart, "Wal-Mart Stores Inc. Data Sheet," January 16, 2012.

[267] BEA publishes data for only eight individual countries. Several important markets (e.g., Brazil and China) are not broken out separately.

[268] Deloitte and STORES Media. "Global Powers of Retailing," January 2012.

[269] USDOC, BEA, Operations of Multinational Companies Database (accessed January 30, 2012).

[270] Amazon Web site, http://www.amazon.com/Locations-Careers/b?ie=UTF8&node=239366011 (accessed January 30, 2012).

[271] USDOC, BEA, Operations of Multinational Companies database (accessed December 21, 2011).

[272] Seven & i Holdings Company Web site, http://www.7andi.com/en/company/group.html (accessed June 25, 2012).

[273] However, foreign direct investment is permitted in wholesaling, and both Walmart and Carrefour have opened wholesale "cash & carry" stores in India that are open to business and institutional customers. The Indian government announced a plan to open multibrand retailing to foreign investment in November 2011, only to suspend these plans due to intense opposition from small shopkeepers and their allies in parliament. MacAskill and Goyal, "Singh's Retail Retreat," December 8, 2011.

[274] World Bank, Investing Across Borders Database. Currency conversion using OANDA, Currency Converter database.

[275] The relevant regulation states that "The establishment of retail sales outlets in addition to the first retail sales outlet... shall depend on the number of retail sales outlets, market stability, population density in the province or city where the retail sales outlet is to be set up, and consistency of the investment project with the master plan of such province or city." Yet the regulation does not describe how regulators will determine whether the criteria are satisfied. Socialist Republic of Vietnam, Ministry of Trade, Circular No. 09-2007-TT- BTM, July 17, 2007, http://www.itpc.gov.vn/investors/how_to_invest/law/2008-09-25.304363/mldocument_view/?set_language=en (accessed April 19, 2012).

[276] Ministère de l'Économie, de l'Industrie et de l'Emploi, [Ministry of the Economy, Industry, and Employment of France,] "La Loi de Modernisation," 2008.

[277] By comparison, 133 members had made commitments for hotels and restaurants and 104 had done so for banking (note: the figures quoted here count as one member the 12 European countries that were party to the original "European Communities" GATS schedule). WTO, Services Database (the database has not been updated since 2008).

[278] A limitation on national treatment reserves the member's ability to treat foreign services and service suppliers less favorably than domestic services and service providers. WTO, "Guide to Reading the GATS."

[279] WTO Secretariat representative, e-mail to USITC staff, January 7, 2012; WTO, "Schedules of Commitments" (accessed January 2012).

[280] United States-Panama Trade Promotion Agreement, Side Letter on Retail Sales. The agreement had not yet entered into force as of June 2012.

[281] EIU, *Industries in 2012*, 2011, 9.

[282] IMF, "World Economic Outlook," September 2011, 78.

[283] IMF, "World Economic Outlook," September 2011, 75; *Kiplinger*, "Economic Outlook," December 14, 2011; EIU, *Industries in 2012*, 2011, 9.

[284] Aseada, "Retailing: General," November 24, 2011, 9.

[285] *FashionNetAsia.com*, "China," June 14, 2011.

[286] Arcentales, Carvalho, and Volberg, "Country Commentary," November 28, 2011.

[287] Reda, "Predictions 2012," December 2011; EIU, "Industries in 2012," 9.

[288] EIU, "Industries in 2012," 9.

[289] Thomson Reuters, "Global Investment Banking Review," 2011, 5.

[290] Standard & Poor's, *Industry Surveys: Investment Services*, October 27, 2011, 3.

[291] Thomson Reuters, "Global Investment Banking Review," 2011, 3–5.

[292] Lambe, "2011: Goodbye and Good Riddance?" December 1, 2011.

[293] IBISWorld,"Global Investment Banking and Brokerage," June 22, 2011, 9.

[294] Investment banking fees earned in Japan during the period represented 5 percent of the total while fees earned in Oceania represented 3 percent. IBISWorld, "Global Investment Banking and Brokerage," June 22, 2011, 10; Thomson Reuters, "Global Investment Banking Review," 2011, 3–4.

[295] Investment Company Institute, *2011 Investment Company Factbook*, 2011, 23.

[296] SIFMA, *Fact Book 2011*, 2011, 97.

[297] Walsh, "Remarks before the Special Seminar on International Finance," November 16, 2011, 2.

[298] A derivative is a financial instrument whose value is tied to the price of an underlying security (for example, a U.S. Treasury bond) or to another financial price (such as a foreign-exchange rate). Mortgage- backed securities are asset-backed securities created by grouping pools of mortgage loans to make the financial commitments between home buyers and mortgage lenders into tradable instruments. Derivatives are further discussed in the "Demand and Supply Factors" section.

[299] IBISWorld, "Investment Banking and Securities Dealing in the U.S.," September 2011, 4.

[300] The U.S. Treasury invested $245 billion to support U.S. banks during the crisis, part of the $475 billion total authorized Troubled Asset Relief Program spending. As of August 31, 2011, the government had recovered $256 billion through repayments, dividends, interest, warrant sales, and other income, exceeding the original investment by $11 billion. U.S. Treasury, OFS, "TARP: Three Year Anniversary Report," October 2011, 3–4.

[301] IBISWorld, "Investment Banking and Securities Dealing in the U.S.," September 2011, 24–26.

[302] IBISWorld, "Global Investment Banking and Brokerage," June 22, 2011, 9, 35–37.

[303] Return on equity, calculated as net income divided by average shareholders' equity, is a common measure of profitability for financial institutions. A bank's tier 1 equity capital consists of its common stock outstanding plus retained earnings and may also include any nonredeemable preferred stock that is outstanding. A bank's "leverage" refers to the ratio of total assets to tier 1 equity capital, indicating the degree to which investments are financed with equity rather than debt. IBISWorld, "Investment Banking and Securities Dealing in the U.S.," September 2011, 20.

[304] Jenkins, Masters, and Braithwaite, "The Hunt for a Common Front," December 13, 2011, 2; Bohme et al., "Day of Reckoning?" September 2011, 21.

[305] IBISWorld, "Global Investment Banking and Brokerage," June 22, 2011, 11; Thomson Reuters, "Global Investment Banking Review, 2011," 3; *Economist*, "Global Investment Banking Fees," October 8, 2011.

[306] This includes the United States (81 percent of the regional total) and Canada (12 percent of the regional total), as well as markets in the Caribbean and in Central and South America. Thomson Reuters, "Global Investment Banking Review," 2011, 4.

[307] Thomson Reuters, "Global Investment Banking Review," 2011, 9.

[308] IBISWorld, "Investment Banking and Securities Dealing in the U.S.," September 2011, 20.

[309] European market rankings include investment banking activities in Europe, Middle East, and Africa. Thomson Reuters, "Global Investment Banking Review: Full Year 2011," 9.

[310] IBISWorld, "Investment Banking and Securities Dealing in the U.S.," September 2011, 11.

[311] *TheCityUK*, "Financial Services in Emerging Economies," June 2011.

[312] Freeman Consulting, "2012 Outlook for Investment Banking Services," September 30, 2011, 15–18.

[313] Menon, "Money Matters," February 14, 2012.

[314] Wang, Xu, and Yip, "China's Changing Wholesale Landscape," March 2011.

[315] Jenkins, Rabinovitch, and Leahy, "Ambitions Thwarted by Red Tape and Competition," September 13, 2011; SIFMA, "Reform in China: Overview," n.d. (accessed November 22, 2011).

[316] Jacob, Rahul, "Chinese Head to Wealth Managers," September 5, 2011.

[317] Lal and Tahilyani, "Wholesale Banking in India," March 2011, 6.

[318] Hart, "Working Out a Competitive Edge," January 3, 2012; Menon, "Money Matters," February 14, 2012; TheCityUK, "Financial Services in Emerging Economies," June 2011, 4–5.

[319] Freeman & Co. LLC, "Securities Industry Focus," October 2011, 7.

[320] IBISWorld, "Investment Banking and Securities Dealing in the U.S.," September 2011, 13.

[321] Simonian, "Swiss Banks Turn Focus to Wealth Management," November 23, 2011.

[322] IBISWorld, "Investment Banking and Securities Dealing in the U.S.," September 2011, 4–11.

[323] USDOC, BEA, "U.S. International Services," October 2011, 20.

[324] Standard and Poor's, *Industry Surveys: Investment Services,* October 27, 2011, 4–5; UK Financial Services Authority, *Prudential Risk Outlook 2011,* 2011, 62–66.

[325] Lambe, "2011: Goodbye and Good Riddance?" December 1, 2011; Jenkins and Stabe, "EU Banks Slash Sovereign Holdings," December 9, 2011; Jenkins, Masters, and Barker, "EU Banks Could Shrink to Hit Capital Rules," October 12, 2011.

[326] Bohme et al., "Day of Reckoning?" September 2011, 1.

[327] Public Law 111-203, 124 Stat. 1375, approved July 21, 2010.

[328] Ryan, "Financial Services Regulatory Highlights," 2010, 1–5.

[329] Barfield, *A Practitioner's Guide to Basel III and Beyond*, January 2011, chapter 1, 1–4; Walsh, OCC, "Remarks before the Special Seminar on International Finance," November 16, 2011, 4.

[330] Standard and Poor's, *Industry Surveys: Investment Services,* October 27, 2011, 9.

[331] Bohme et al., "Day of Reckoning?" September 2011, 1.

[332] Lambe, "2011: Goodbye and Good Riddance?" December 1, 2011; Freeman & Co. LLC, "Securities Industry Focus," October 2011, 10.

[333] U.S. Treasury, OCC, "Quarterly Report on Bank Trading and Derivatives Activities," 2011, 1. (accessed February 2, 2012). Derivative transactions are typically structured as a "swap" (an agreement to exchange one series of cashflows for another over the life of the transaction), an "option" (a right but not an obligation to trade an underlying security at a future date at a prearranged price), or some combination of the two. The majority of derivatives traded are interest-rate related products; these comprised 82 percent of total derivatives traded in the third quarter of 2011 by U.S. banks, while credit derivatives comprised 6.3 percent.

[334] Walsh, OCC, "Remarks before the Center for the Study of Financial Innovation," June 21, 2011, 3.

[335] OTC trading between individual broker-dealers is a market in which London in particular has achieved global dominance. Deloitte, "MiFID II: The Deloitte Perspective," December 1, 2011.

[336] Bohme et al., "Day of Reckoning," September 2011, 1.

[337] City of London, "Research and Statistics FAQ," n.d. (accessed March 20, 2012).

[338] Walsh, OCC, "Remarks before the Special Seminar on International Finance," November 16, 2011, 5; Walsh, OCC, "Remarks before the Centre for the Study of Financial Innovation," June 7, 2011, 5.

[339] Wallace, "Vickers Report Leaves Investment Banking Shrouded in Uncertainty," December 1, 2011.

[340] Walsh, OCC, "Remarks before the Special Seminar on International Finance," November 16, 2011, 6.

[341] Simonian, "Swiss Lawmakers Put Banks in Spotlight," June 7, 2011; Simonian, "Swiss Banks Turn Focus to Wealth Management," November 23, 2011.

[342] USDOC, BEA, "Additional Detail on Financial Services Transactions, 2006–2010," n.d.; USDOC, BEA, "Additional Detail on Financial Services Transactions, 1994–2005," n.d. (accessed February 23, 2012).

[343] Country market breakdowns specifically for securities services trade flows are not available, except at the aggregated "financial services" level (see section 3). USDOC, BEA, "U.S. International Services," October 2011, 20–21.

[344] Securities with maturities of greater than 12 months, such as Treasury bonds and other government bonds.

[345] U.S. Treasury, "U.S. Transactions with Foreigners in Long-Term Securities," n.d. (accessed February 28, 2012).

[346] For example, an investment bank in the United Kingdom would purchase a U.S. Treasury bond for deposit in a customer's UK securities account, although the customer is located in a third country. This "custodial bias" contributes to the large recorded foreign holdings of U.S. securities in major financial centers, such as Belgium, the Caribbean banking centers, Luxembourg, Switzerland, and the United Kingdom. U.S. Treasury, "FAQs: Questions on Country Classification in TIC Data," n.d. (accessed January 23, 2012).

[347] In 2010, only 2 of the top 10 global insurance brokers by revenues were based outside the United States, and both of these were based in the United Kingdom. A similar pattern is seen for reinsurance brokers, where 3 of the top 10 were based in the United States and 7 were based in the United Kingdom. III, *2012 Financial Services Fact Book*, 198–99.

[348] SIFMA, *Factbook 2011*, 2011, 99–101.

[349] Ibid.

[350] In 2010, 2 of the top 10 global reinsurance firms by revenues were based in Bermuda. III, *2012 Financial Services Fact Book*, 2012, 198; Bertaut, "Understanding Cross-Border Securities Data," 2006, A66.

[351] WTO, Trade Policy Review Board (TPRB), *WTO Trade Policy Review*, June 8, 2009, 139.

[352] Wang, "Foreign Investment in Securities in China," June 19, 2009.

[353] Robinson, Egbert, and Wang, "China: Developments in Chinese Securities Regulation," July 6, 2011.

[354] *Future of US China Trade.Com*, "U.S.-China Strategic & Economic Dialogue," n.d. (accessed January 27, 2012); U.S. Treasury, "The 2011 U.S.-China Strategic and Economic Dialogue," May 10, 2011.

[355] In 2010, there were 130 foreign commercial banks operating in China through local branches or locally incorporated foreign subsidiaries. Their combined assets totaled RMB1.742 trillion, equivalent to 1.6 percent of total bank assets in China. The World Bank, "China Financial Sector Assessment," November 2011, 25, table 4.

[356] Deemer, "China Amends Foreign Investment Policy," January 18, 2012.

[357] U.S. Treasury, "U.S. Fact Sheet–Economic Track of the Fourth Meeting of the U.S.-China Strategic and Economic Dialogue," May 4, 2012.

[358] SIFMA, "Global Competitiveness: Overview," (accessed November 22, 2011); Wallace, "Vickers Report Leaves Investment Banking Shrouded in Uncertainty," December 1, 2011.

[359] Walsh, OCC, "Remarks before the Special Seminar on International Finance," November 16, 2011, 4–7.

[360] Wallace, "Vickers Report Leaves Investment Banking Shrouded in Uncertainty," December 1, 2011. For example, UBS has reportedly threatened to move its investment banking operations out of Zurich if certain regulatory initiatives on the quality of capital are enacted by the Swiss parliament. Simonian, "Swiss Lawmakers Put Banks in Spotlight," June 7, 2011.

[361] Walsh, OCC, "Remarks before the Special Seminar on International Finance," November 16, 2011, 8.

[362] These include frame relay, asynchronous transfer mode, virtual private network, and private leased-line services, all of which support voice or data transmission within firms.

[363] WTO, "Coverage of Basic Telecommunication and Value-Added Services," n.d. (accessed December 14, 2011).

[364] Internet services include both dial-up and broadband Internet services.

[365] Market- and country-level revenue statistics used in this section were calculated by Commission staff using data reported by the Telecommunications Industry Association (TIA). TIA, *TIA's 2011 Market Review and Forecast*, 2011.

[366] Hot Telecom, *Global Telecom Market Status and Forecast Report 2010–2015*, July 2011, 6.

[367] TIA, *TIA's 2011 Market Review and Forecast*, 2011.

[368] Ibid.

[369] Ibid.

[370] IBISWorld, "Global Wireless Telecommunication Carriers," October 14, 2011, 15; IBISWorld, "Global Internet Service Providers," May 31, 2011, 14.

[371] IBISWorld, "Global Wireless Telecommunication Carriers," October 14, 2011, 15.

[372] IBISWorld, "Global Internet Service Providers," May 31, 2011, 14; IBISWorld, "Global Wireless Telecommunication Carriers," October 14, 2011, 15.

[373] IBISWorld, "Global Internet Service Providers," May 31, 2011, 15; IBISWorld, "Global Wireless Telecommunication Carriers," October 14, 2011, 15–16.

[374] EIU, *Industries 2012*, 2011, 16.

[375] Pyramid Research, *Top Trends in the Global Communications Industry*, October 2011, 8; TIA, *TIA's 2011 Market Review and Forecast*, 2011, 1-50 to 1-58.

[376] Hot Telecom, *Global Telecom Market Status and Forecast Report 2010–2015*, 2011, 15–17.

[377] TeleGeography, *World Telecoms M&A Timeline*, GlobalComms Database, 2012.

[378] Middleton, "Share and Share Alike," December 16, 2009; Rubenstein, "Technology Trends: Mobile Network Sharing," July 25, 2009; *Economist*, "Sharing the Load," March 26, 2009.

[379] KPMG, "Tower Operators Are Learning to Compete," September 20, 2011.

[380] Reuters, "TPSA, TPA Sign Infrastructure Deal," December 17, 2010.

[381] Lennighan, "Irish Mobile Operators in Network Sharing Deal," *Total Telecom*, April 6, 2011.

[382] USDOC, BEA, *Survey of Current Business*, October 2011, 20–21, Table G and Table H.

[383] USDOC, BEA, *Survey of Current Business*, October 2011, 20, Table G.

[384] USDOC, BEA, *Survey of Current Business*, October 2011, 20.

[385] USDOC, BEA, *Survey of Current Business*, October 2011, 21, Table H.

[386] USTR, *2011 Section 1377 Review*.

[387] Foreign affiliates are U.S. parents companies' majority-owned nonbank affiliates in foreign markets, whereas U.S. affiliates are foreign parent companies' majority-owned nonbank affiliates in the U.S. market.

[388] USDOC, BEA, *Survey of Current Business*, October 2011, 54, table 9.2. The BEA suppressed sales data related to U.S. foreign affiliates in 2007 and 2008 to avoid disclosure of data of individual companies.

[389] The BEA suppressed sales data related to the U.S. affiliates of foreign telecommunication companies in 2004 and 2005 to avoid disclosure of data of individual companies.

[390] ITU, ICT Eye database.

[391] TIA, *TIA's 2011 Market Review and Forecast*, 2011, 1–3.

[392] Hot Telecom, *Global Telecom Market Status and Forecast Report 2010–2015*, 2011, 29.

[393] Pyramid Research, "Pyramid Perspective 2012," October 2011, 23.

[394] Campbell and Rahn, "Deutsche Telekom, France Telecom Set Up Purchasing Venture," *Bloomberg*, April 18, 2011.

[395] Hot Telecom, *Global Telecom Market Status and Forecast Report 2010–2015*, 2011, 29.

[396] In a negative-list approach, liberalization provisions apply to all industries except for those industries, or those discriminatory measures, that are explicitly excluded. The WTO employs a positive-list approach, in which liberalization provisions apply only to industries or measures that are specifically identified by members.

[397] Embedded services refer to services that are integrated or bundled with goods. For example, software design services and marketing services are embedded in mobile phones.

INDEX

C

D

F

G

N

O

Q

R

S